Reconciliation
in Divided Societies

Pennsylvania Studies in Human Rights

Bert B. Lockwood, Jr., Series Editor

A complete list of books in the series is available from the publisher.

Reconciliation in Divided Societies

Finding Common Ground

Erin Daly and Jeremy Sarkin

PENN

University of Pennsylvania Press

Philadelphia

Copyright © 2007 University of Pennsylvania Press
All rights reserved
Printed in the United States of America on acid-free paper

10 9 8 7 6 5 4 3 2 1

Published by
University of Pennsylvania Press
Philadelphia, Pennsylvania 19104-4112

Library of Congress Cataloging-in-Publication Data

Daly, Erin.
   Reconciliation in divided societies: finding common ground / Erin Daly and
Jeremy Sarkin.
       p.   cm. — (Pennsylvania studies in human rights)
   ISBN-13: 978-0-8122-3976-8 (cloth : alk. paper)
   ISBN-10: 0-8122-3976-8 (cloth : alk. paper)
   (Contents: Finding common ground — Reconciliation in layers — Reconciliation's
internal logic — Reconciliation reconstructed.)
   Includes bibliographical references and index.
   1. Reconciliation—Political aspects. 2. Social change—Political aspects. I. Title.
II. Sarkin-Hughes, Jeremy. III. Series
JC571 .D332   2007
303.6'6—dc22   2006044659

This book is dedicated to our families—
David Williamson, and Jasper and Alex
Rosanne Sarkin, and Eryn and Hannah

Contents

Part IV: Reconciliation Reconstructed

Foreword
Archbishop Emeritus Desmond Mpilo Tutu

A reconciliation movement is taking place throughout the world. People are beginning to see that there is a way out of the bloodshed and fighting and violence. They are beginning to see that if they try to understand one another, try to see the humanity in every person, then they can learn to get along, or at least live in peace with one another.

This reconciliation movement did not start in South Africa; people have been trying to reconcile for centuries. But in South Africa, it became a centerpiece of our transition to democracy. And it did not start with an announcement by President Mandela that a commission would be named. It started in the hearts of millions of people who wanted to build the new South Africa on pillars of love and understanding and redemption. At the end of apartheid, as in the aftermath of all kinds of oppression throughout the world, many people didn't want to be vengeful. They didn't want to commit crimes against those who had committed crimes against them. They didn't want people to languish in horrible jails just because that is what had been done to them. But they also knew that they could not just ignore the past. They couldn't pretend that the pass laws, the banning, the arbitrary arrests, the daily degradations had never happened. Because they did happen, and they left indelible marks on every person who suffered under apartheid. But the people who inherited the new South Africa did not want to perpetuate the anger and hatred that had been directed against them. They wanted another way out. They needed to deal with the pain in their hearts, but they wanted to transcend it. They wanted nurturing for themselves not punishment for others.

Reconciliation was the way out. It is a way to transform individuals, and the whole of society. It is a way to look at perpetrators of human rights abuses and see brothers and sisters. A way to look at the victim in oneself

and see a survivor. Through reconciliation, we can see the fluidity of everything in the universe: how the past influences the present and the future;
how punishment is just the flip side of redemption, how the religious
and the political are inseparable, how we are all victims, perpetrators, bystanders, everyone part of the same family of humanity. Reconciliation
embodies the idea of the oneness of everything.

But reconciliation is not just a spiritual idea, though it is that. Reconciliation is a mass movement. Everyone can get involved in it. Everyone
can do his or her part to help move things along the path of peace and
non-violence. Reconciliation can not be imposed by law, or ordained by
the government. The government can help it along, but for it to be truly
successful people have to believe in the capacity to transform. They have
to believe that it is possible for someone who did horrible things under
horrible circumstances to do good. They have to believe, as the Quakers
say, that there is that of God in everyone. Reconciliation is not about closure. It is about new beginnings.

In many different countries, people have taken up the call to reconciliation. Some countries have established commissions, similar to ours in
South Africa. In many other countries, individuals have come together in
small groups, and sometimes in larger groups, to help people reconcile.

In one way, reconciliation is a very simple idea. It is what a married couple does instinctively after an argument: they talk about what happened,
one or both spouses apologize, they recommit their love for each other.
They don't have a commission to organize it; they know in their hearts
how to reconcile. Reconciliation is the most natural thing in the world.
But it is also a complicated thing. And it gets more complicated when we
are talking not about a husband and wife, but about a nation, with a long
history of oppression and abuse and violence. How can we expect victims
to forgive their torturers? How much truth is enough? How much is too
much? As each country goes through its own transition, each must develop
its own way of helping people to reconcile with one another.

Erin Daly and Jeremy Sarkin survey the landscape of the reconciliation
movement. They reveal reconciliation in its multiple dimensions be it as
a spiritual idea, as a psychological need, as a social movement, and a political imperative. They take us on a voyage around the world, to the many
countries that are taking the chance that reconciliation is the best way to
avoid continued violence. They take us into the minds of men and women
who have worked their whole lives to make reconciliation happen in
their country, as well as in the minds of people who resist the call to
reconciliation.

Even though people around the world are getting involved in reconciliation programs, there has been no comprehensive effort, until now, to
ask the difficult questions and to develop a full idea of what reconciliation

actually means. It is very easy to restate the clichés: you can't have reconciliation without truth, or justice; if you don't face the past, you are condemned to repeat it, and so on. But it is quite another to try, as the authors do, to dig beneath the surface and to explain what truth, justice, and reconciliation really mean in societies that are emerging from war, genocide, dictatorships and other kinds of oppression.

Erin Daly and Jeremy Sarkin effectively disentangle all the various strands of reconciliation and then weave them back into a holistic tapestry. They rightly focus our attention on the future as much as on the past. Reconciliation, they argue, is best thought of as a tool for transformation. It is the engine that helps people transform themselves from victims full of hatred into survivors who have moved beyond their pain and trauma. It helps whole societies transform themselves from violent and chaotic places into communities where people work together to raise children and live productive and hopeful lives. The book shows us how this transformation happens so that we can all gain a better understanding of how, and why, reconciliation really works. It is an almost indispensable tool for those who want to engage in reconciliation.

Preface

In the last ten or twenty years, scores of countries around the world have turned to reconciliation as a salve in times of transition. Curiously, notwithstanding the consensus that reconciliation is necessary in divided societies, there is no consensus as to what reconciliation actually entails, either across cultures or even within a single society. Does reconciliation in Iraq require debaathification, or does it entail the politics of inclusion? Does reconciliation in Bosnia require separate statelets for the Croatian and Bosnian populations, or will it grow only from (forced) integration? Does reconciliation in South Africa mean peace and stability without vengeance, or does it mean blacks and whites working and playing together and sharing meals? Is reconciliation compelled political correctness, a spiritually-imbued act of forgiveness, or a pragmatic decision to move on?

The widespread commitment to the politics of reconciliation coupled with the lack of any agreement whatsoever as to what reconciliation means presents both conceptual and pragmatic challenges. People do not know what to expect from governmental programs promising reconciliation. Governments do not know what promises are reasonable to make, nor what steps are necessary to meet those promises. Social scientists do not know how to measure whether programs have worked. Donors do not know how long reconciliation will take. And no one knows how to determine whether reconciliation has been accomplished.

We believe that reconciliation has enormous potential to help nascent and divided nations maneuver through the rocky shoals of political transition, but only if it is properly understood within the relevant society: its meaning must be clearly articulated within a specific political and historical context if it is to have any relevance at all.

This book has two basic goals. The first goal is to deconstruct the current understanding of reconciliation by analyzing its various strands. In the first half of the book, we analyze what people mean when they talk about reconciliation. As a political matter, people use this single term to describe different levels of recovery—from personal healing, to interpersonal relationships, to community rebuilding, to national stability and international peace. Each of these levels is analyzed in turn. At a conceptual level, people associate reconciliation with justice, with truth, and with forgiveness and in the subsequent chapter, we examine the work that "reconciliation" does in these varied contexts. By the end of this first section, we come to the conclusion that the conventional understandings of reconciliation—which tend to be backward looking and to stress interpersonal relationships—are not really much help at all in explaining what reconciliation can contribute to the process of political transition.

The second goal of the book, then, is to reconceptualize reconciliation in a way that is relevant for nations in transition. Here, we argue that a more structural understanding of reconciliation will be more useful to divided nations: rather than focusing on "looking the beast in the eye" and "forgiveness," transitional governments are advised to spend their limited capital creating political and economic structures that are rooted in the needs of the particular society at that time, but that are inclusive enough that all the people within the polity are able to participate in public life on an equal footing. We argue that this structural understanding of reconciliation is likely, in the long run, to be more effective at securing peace and ensuring long-term stability within formerly divided societies. In the second half of the book, we offer first a conceptual justification for this new structural approach, and then a practical assessment of how this approach might be implemented.

We are grateful to the Widener University School of Law and the University of the Western Cape for their generosity, as well as to Shauna, Eudice and Les Daly, David Williamson, and Rosanne Sarkin for their love and support.

Part I
Finding Common Ground

Chapter 1
The Lay of the Land

Peace is very much more complicated than war.

A flood of political transitions has marked the turn of the twenty-first century. Countries throughout the world are transforming themselves, sloughing off the shackles of colonialism, communism, military dictatorship, racism, or some combination of these, and marching, tentatively or not, toward some version of democratic liberalism. Throughout Latin America, Eastern Europe, Africa, Asia, and the Middle East, many countries are engaged in transitions that have nothing in common, save one thing: the incipient governments in many of these countries are touting reconciliation as a panacea for their countries' unique ills.

Reconciliation was Nelson Mandela's mantra as he directed South Africa's "miraculous" transition from apartheid to democracy. And since the mid-1990s, there has been a dramatic increase in reconciliation-speak throughout the world. Countries as diverse as Algeria, Canada, El Salvador, Namibia, Nicaragua, and South Africa have enacted laws to promote reconciliation to heal divided nations.[1] Dozens of other nations have inaugurated prominent reconciliation commissions in recent years, including Chile, Sierra Leone, Timor Leste, and Morocco, to name just a few.[2] Still other countries have permanent reconciliation ministries.[3] And, increasingly, international peace agreements are including provisions to mandate them. The first postwar government in Angola has promoted a formal and comprehensive framework of national reconciliation, while the Liberian opposition movement (the Liberian Unity and Reconciliation Defense) at least claims to promote reconciliation, as does the new government of Ellen Johnson-Sirleaf. Even North and South Korea may be showing tentative signs of moving toward reconciliation, while Japan and China are beginning to mend the fences that were broken during World War II.

Throughout Eastern Europe, in countries such as the Czech Republic, Bulgaria, Romania, Poland, and Albania, the fall of communism prompted the call for reconciliation between former communists and resisters.[4] It is possible that many countries that have not yet embarked on a reconciliation program may move in that direction, including, for instance, Afghanistan, Brazil, Zimbabwe, and Israel and Palestine.[5]

The prevalence of reconciliation programs throughout the world has produced an unlikely problem. Reconciliation is so easily invoked, so commonly promoted, and so immediately appealing that few policy-makers are stopping to consider the scores of serious questions that reconciliation programs raise. Scant attention is being paid to the specifics of advancing reconciliation, or to the complex ways in which reconciliation touches other problems of transitional politics, such as the possibility of justice after "radical evil," the redistribution of wealth, the creation of civil society, and the relevance of the past to the present and the future, among numerous others.

Understanding reconciliation in times of political transition raises fundamental and ultimately unanswerable questions about the human condition. Talk of reconciliation invariably comes after there has been some gross violation of norms: "disappearances," killings, torture, kidnaping, rape, widespread abuse of children. Reconciliation necessarily conjures up its antecedents, and forces us to ask how people can visit such horrors upon one another. When we look at the face of evil, are we in fact seeing ourselves, as many people contend? Or, on the contrary, are some people capable of evil in a way that others could never approach?

Reconciliation is deeply compelling precisely because it implicates not only the worst that human beings are capable of, but the best as well. Reconciliation embodies the possibility of transforming war into peace, trauma into survival, hatred into forgiveness; it is the way human beings connect with one another, against all odds. It exemplifies the potential for virtually limitless strength and generosity of spirit that is also immanent in human nature.

This book explores the many facets of reconciliation: what does reconciliation mean in all these vastly disparate situations? And what is the relationship between reconciliation and the many other values of so many transitional societies, including the need for justice, the creation of civil society, instilling democratic political values, and the need to remedy maldistribution of resources and wealth? It was prompted by the observation that, despite the enormous amounts of political and economic capital being spent in transitional nations on reconciliation-promoting projects, there is almost a complete failure to understand reconciliation and to confront its multitudinous and sometimes contradictory relationships. In too many cases, these failures defeat the best intentions of the reconciliation-promoters, because their programs are based on unquestioned platitudes, and not on realistic assessments of the attitudes and capacities of the people whom they are meant to benefit.

Generally speaking, reconciliation describes coming together; it is the antithesis of falling or growing apart. Reconciliation has a normative—almost a moral—aspect as well. It is the coming together (or re-coming together) of things that *should* be together. Unlike its less common relative, conciliation, reconciliation connotes the coming together of things that once were united but have been torn asunder—a return to or recreation of the status quo ante, whether real or imagined. For many, it is encompassed in the question as to how a society ravaged by war returns to some kind of normality when neighbors living side by side have endured and perpetrated against one another crimes of unimaginable horror. Perhaps because of its promise of a return to normalcy, reconciliation is broadly appealing to nations in transition, and the danger of not achieving it is tantamount to ongoing and future conflict and violence.[6]

But what does "reconciliation" mean in these different countries? Is it national unity? Is it peace? Is it healing? Is it empathy? Is it stability? Is it harmony? Is it developing a democracy that ensures the fullest sense of inclusivity and opportunity, as well as access to resources for those who reside in the country? Is it all of these? Or none? Is it just moving on?

The answer turns out to be different in each country. In Angola, for example, national reconciliation has been seen as "the coming together once again of Angolans to live together peacefully in the same Fatherland and in a spirit of cooperation, in the pursuit of the common good."[7] In Fiji, the goal of reconciliation is "to promote racial harmony and social cohesion through social, cultural, educational, and other activities at all levels within the indigenous Fijian community and between various racial groups."[8]

But one does not have to scratch too deeply beneath the surface platitudes to glimpse the difficulty of applying these glossy definitions to real-life, postconflict situations. Implementing reconciliation policies requires the development of clear answers to very complex questions: How much focus should there be on the past? Is reconciliation compatible with justice and respect for human rights? Does reconciliation require that erstwhile enemies forgive and embrace one another? And so on. Each one of these questions raises its own multiplicity of questions, like the heads of the Hydra.

For instance, the relationship between truth and reconciliation is an extremely complicated one.[9] It is commonly stated that truth leads to reconciliation. The South African Truth and Reconciliation Commission, with its slogan "Truth: The Road to Reconciliation," insists on the indispensability of truth because it disinfects the wounds, has a cathartic effect, and helps people to heal.[10] Even accepting the desirability or necessity of establishing truth as a precondition to reconciliation, it remains to be determined what constitutes the "truth." Is it just the facts that happened and can be proven forensically, or does truth entail a more complex and multifaceted narrative? Alternatively, it could be argued that the truth actually impedes reconciliation, because the truth can be so terrible that attitudes harden and forgiveness and empathy are all but impossible. Or does striving for reconciliation simply avoid the truth because it attempts to get people to forget the past? Or perhaps the relationship works in the opposite direction: reconciliation leads to truth by creating the conditions in which the truth can emerge.[11]

No less complex is the relationship between reconciliation and justice. This issue will be discussed in greater detail below, but it is worth noting at the outset that even the most basic aspects of this relationship are extremely difficult to resolve at all satisfactorily. The link between justice and reconciliation becomes critical in times of transition, particularly in societies where the past has been characterized by strife, violence, polarization, and caste. Reconciliation often comes up in the context of the question of what to do about the perpetrators—a broad term meant to embrace everyone from the architects of the offenses of the past, to the foot soldiers. The current dominant ideology is that reconciliation and justice are incompatible, and justice is to be favored at the expense of reconciliation at every juncture. Where reconciliation is accepted, it is at most a byproduct of the criminal justice system. In this view of reconciliation, the process rejects prosecution and therefore could potentially thwart, rather than advance, the cause of justice. In other views, however, reconciliation can be seen as promoting justice, insofar as both aim to restore and heal troubled communities, and to redress the imbalance of the past trauma. At the very least, reconciliation can be indifferent to justice.

In reality, the choice between justice and reconciliation may be a luxury that many countries recovering from traumatic political transitions cannot afford. In too many situations around the world, justice (as commonly understood) may be illusory: the tragedies are so huge that no justice is even conceivable. In other ways, the failure of justice is a practical problem. On the one hand, punishing the perpetrators may increase tensions in the fledgling society, particularly if they retain political power, and thereby retard movement toward reconciliation; on the other hand, not punishing the perpetrators undermines the new regime's efforts to promote the democratic ethos and rule of law values, and to reinforce the "thick line" between the old, oppressive regime and the new, democratic, human-rights-respecting order. Taken to its logical extreme, failure to punish can turn the successors into collaborators.

Even if the new state has put measures in place to promote reconciliation, progress can be easily destabilized by persistent inequalities that continue to spawn renewed conflict. Economic conditions have significant implications for the prospects of reconciliation in a country.[12] A growing economy, with an increasing per capita income, must provide the most favorable circumstances for reconciliation to develop. In this regard it has been argued that, of the new democracies in Africa, only South Africa, and Seychelles are economically prepared for democracy.[13]

Additionally, reconciliation may be more usefully thought of, not as a static item that either exists or not in a society, but rather as a process that is continually evolving. If so, how does one measure the degree to which reconciliation has been reached in a society? What are the indicators? What measurements can one use? Can absolute reconciliation ever be achieved?

The questions can be dizzying. The only certainty is that the basic premises underlying the enthusiasm for reconciliation must be carefully examined and that, in fact, reconciliation's contribution to transitions must be assessed. Notwithstanding these important challenges, it is critical to avoid both overestimating and underestimating the value of reconciliation in transitional contexts; to expect too much of it—to assume that it will produce instant happiness and peace—is to court disaffection and cynicism, while expecting too little risks abandoning a potentially fruitful resource on which to found a new democracy.

The Emergence of Reconciliation as an Element of Transition

The notion of reconciliation has been a part of African systems of dispute resolution for centuries.[14] Since the traditional unit of African society was the group, not the individual, legal proceedings were community affairs in which a central aim was to reconcile the disputing parties, to restore harmonious relationships within the community, and to compensate the victims. Less important was punishment of the guilty.

Such examples are still prevalent today on the continent. In Uganda, the Acholi culture used the so-called *mato oput* ritual to achieve reconciliation between enemies. This practice sees the wrongdoer giving a full and truthful account of what he or she has done, admitting responsibility, and making some sort of restitution. The offender and the victim then share a drink made of bitter hops before witnesses to indicate and confirm that reconciliation has occurred. Thus, ritual, ceremony, and the sharing of a meal are indicators of process.[15]

Until recently, no one talked about reconciliation per se. When scholars, politicians, and practitioners spoke about the restoration of community peace, they did not use the word "reconciliation." Now, people use the word all the time, even when they are not exactly sure to what they are referring. But why has it become so fashionable lately? What accounts for the increased attention to reconciliation? Why does it have such appeal now? And does it deserve all the attention it receives?

The short answer is that South Africa's much lauded and deftly exported experiment with truth and reconciliation has made both prominent features of the post-1990s transitional landscape. The highly publicized and generally successful Truth and Reconciliation Commission (TRC) demonstrated the independent value of reconciliation in times of transition: reconciliation is a banner around which diverse groups can rally. And South Africa provided one model of how transitional governments can promote reconciliation.

But many other political and cultural developments of the last century seem also to have contributed to the growth of the reconciliation movement. Probably the single most significant factor is the flood of transitions that have taken place in the world since the end of the Second World War and especially in the last decade of the twentieth century.[16] These transitions seem to have occurred in waves, with significant transitions to democracy occurring in various parts of the world at various times. Many of these were part of broader international trends. The disintegration of colonialism created a phalanx of new countries in Africa, Asia, the Middle East, and the Caribbean, a trend that continues to this day, with the emergence of Timor Leste, and tentative moves toward democracy in Burundi, Sierra Leone, Iraq, and possibly in the longer term in Burma and the Democratic Republic of the Congo.

In many of these places, there have been subsequent waves of transitions toward democracy in the ensuing years, particularly as the first postcolonial leaders died or were forced into exile. In the 1980s, democratically elected governments replaced military dictatorships in many Latin American countries, from Guatemala to Argentina. And at the end of that decade, with the breakup of the Soviet Union, dozens of countries under its control, from East Asia to the Baltics to central Europe, moved toward democracy, resulting in the birth of many new or newly democratic nations. The trend has continued in Africa, with democratic elections in South Africa, Kenya, Tanzania, Liberia, and elsewhere. By some estimates, fully 60 percent of the constitutions in effect by the early 2000s were adopted since 1989.

In all these cases, the thorny question of what to do about the past became a prominent feature of the transitional landscape. In the most difficult cases, the transition occurs in the wake of civil wars or massive upheavals, such as in South Africa, Lebanon, Iraq, Liberia, and the nations of the former Yugoslavia. Here, especially, the people and their leaders have looked to reconciliation as a means of healing and uniting a wounded and divided people.

Shifts in the nature of military victory over the past century have also contributed to the reconciliation movement. Where the victory is complete and the losing side is totally vanquished, the victors can impose whatever terms they want without fear of retribution or reprisal. This was the case of most transitions up through the Second World War, where surrender was unconditional and Allied occupation ensured the security of Allied interests. But this model is not typical of twentieth- and twenty-first-century transitions. Most modern transitions come about through negotiation, as in South Africa or Uruguay, or evolution, as in post-communist Europe, or under the terms of a ceasefire, as has been common in Africa. As a result, the relationship between the contending sides must, to a much greater extent, be defined by accommodation and dialogue, rather than by the imposition of victor's justice.

The political imperative to recognize and deal with the leaders of the prior regime and with their adherents virtually defines these transitions. Whereas the occupying powers of postwar Europe had little need or desire to reconcile with the defeated leaders (or with their defeated people), the inheritors of power in current transitions have little choice but to promote reconciliation. In many Latin American countries, for instance, the democratic presidents who succeeded military regimes felt that their governments would not survive unless they acceded to the military's demands for amnesty, which they did—in the name of reconciliation. Viewed this way, reconciliation may be the silver lining that accompanies the morally ambiguous nature of modern transitions—the most effective way to wrest advantage from the necessity of negotiating with the enemy. Indeed, in many instances, including perhaps most recently the International Criminal Tribunal for Yugoslavia (ICTY), prosecution has faltered because of the difficulty of choosing between negotiating with or indicting suspected criminals. It is morally awkward and politically infeasible to do both. Promoting reconciliation as a first choice avoids that dilemma.

Irreversible changes in military tactics have also contributed to the call for reconciliation as a post-military strategy. Unfortunately, it is now the case that most military battles are fought not on open fields but in population centers—in Mostar, in Fallujah, in Gisyeni—and that civilians, rather than soldiers, have become the primary victims of modern warfare.[17] The pervasive participation of civilians in warfare, as both perpetrators and victims, requires postwar strategy to contend with the detritus: when the war is over, the combatants return to their homes, their schools, their churches, their lives. And they must learn how to live with one another.

In addition to developments within countries, international law has also shifted attention toward conciliatory policies. The most notable development of the twentieth century in international law is the rise of what has been referred to as the principle of humanity—the global recognition that each individual has rights simply as an incident of being born, re-gardless of age, gender, ethnicity, religion, beliefs, or any other category one might use. Although the content of these rights may vary—and it is continually growing—the basic principle that human beings are the proper subjects of protection is now well established in international law. During the twentieth century, this principle came to be justified not only as an eth-ical matter but as a practical matter as well: beginning with the League of Nations, international law has recognized that collective security is im-possible without a degree of protection for the social and economic inter-ests of all people.

This principle of humanity was manifested in two seismic shifts in inter-national law in the last century. First, international law has increasingly emphasized social and economic matters, shifting them from a position of marginal significance in the League of Nations to a central role in all facets of modern international law. Scores of treaties and the creation of the International Criminal Court, whose jurisdiction includes crimes against humanity, reveal this shift.[18] Second, international law has become increasingly comfortable interposing itself between sovereign states and their own citizens. The intersection of these new emphases suggests the emergence of the reconciliation movement.

Increased attention to the lives of individuals is also reflected in our understanding of how power works within a regime. Until recently, polit-ical acts were likely to be seen as the acts of single individuals or small cabals. Indeed, the Nuremberg trials are paradigmatic examples of this "command responsibility" view of power. But this top-down view sits un-comfortably next to the recognition that political events are not the exclu-sive province of leaders, but are intertwined with the population as whole. As Hannah Arendt so perceptively wrote, "The trouble with Eichmann was precisely that so many were like him, and that the many were neither perverted nor sadistic, that they were, and still are, terribly and terrifyingly normal. From the viewpoint of our legal institutions and of our moral standards of judgment, this normality was much more terrifying than all the atrocities put together."[19]

It is easy enough to say generally that "everyone" was involved, but quite difficult to determine exactly *how* everyone was involved—what was the nature and extent of each individual's collaboration? As a factual, legal, or even moral matter, how do we distinguish among those who harbored ill feelings, those who benefited from unjust policies, those who voted for unjust policies, those who worked for the government, those who worked in the security forces, those who actively murdered and tortured, those who did so under duress and those who enjoyed it, those who issued orders, and those, on the other side, who fought against the injustice?

To complicate matters further, it should also be recognized that even among those who had similar degrees of involvement, there may be variations in the proper allocation of responsibility.

Throughout the world, a wide range of the population has inhabited what has been called the "gray zone"[20]—that huge space between guilt and innocence, between good and evil. The problem of the gray zone has implications not only for assigning responsibility for acts committed in the pre-transition phase, but also for building up civil society after the transition. This is especially true insofar as the transition is toward a democratic regime, as it inevitably is: in most cases, the very purpose of the transition is to install a democratic government—that is, a government *by the people.* But if *the people* are so thoroughly conditioned—to discriminate against or to spy on their fellow citizens, to accept communism or violent attacks on or disappearance of their neighbors, to teach their children the mis-history that they themselves have been taught—then that conditioning, that frame of mind, is likely to persist notwithstanding a change of political regime. The crumbling of a wall doesn't automatically turn former communists into democrats. Nelson Mandela may be released and elections may have produced a new dispensation, but the apartheid-supporters of yesterday did not suddenly become egalitarians and integrationists.

Indeed, throughout Eastern Europe, citizens are electing former communists to leadership positions, not having fully committed themselves to the rejection of their communist past. The very same people, with the very same conditioning, who are at least in part responsible for the oppression of the past are now being depended on for the democratic institutions of the future. Without these people, there can be no vibrant democracy, no stable society, no lasting peace. Perhaps an unlikely source to encapsulate this idea is the late Yasser Arafat, who wrote in the *New York Times* that "Israel's peace partner is, and always has been, the Palestinian people. Peace is not a signed agreement between individuals—it is reconciliation between two peoples."[21] It is only when peoples have reconciled that war will end.

Any resolution of a political conflict must therefore incorporate the role of the people and address their relationship to one another. This, in turn, has drawn attention to the psychological needs of individuals who are recovering from trauma. If democracy requires the participation of the people, then those people must be able to function in their private lives and be able to contribute to public life. Individual healing then, is seen as having public dimension, demanding the attention of policymakers at the highest level. Increasingly, war-torn governments are recognizing the need to fund trauma centers and to provide psychological support for people as part of their reconstruction efforts. It is not all bricks and mortar.

Ultimately, this convergence of the national and international, the blurring of boundaries between the perpetrators and victims, and the interdependence of the private and public lives of individuals all contribute to the explosion of reconciliation programs at the turn of the century. The current interest in reconciliation reflects a view that transitions, and the events that lead to them, are complex matters. Crimes of state are both legal and political. Reconstruction of community has both legal and political dimensions. And both of these—transition's past and future—are profoundly influenced by the particular historical, cultural, and economic currents that flow through each transitional society.

Reconciliation initiatives are appealing because they can respond to the multifarious needs of each nation as it transitions from one dispensation to another. They can simultaneously be legal and political; they can be national and international; they can respond to both public and private needs; they can be moral and pragmatic; they can be transformative, while maintaining connection to the past. The appeal of reconciliation is broad because its promise is virtually infinite. How it can achieve its promise is the subject of the rest of the book.

Why Nations Pursue Reconciliation

To say that reconciliation ranks high on the agendas of most transitional nations is to state a truth and an untruth simultaneously. It is true that leaders, as well as opposition groups, in many transitional nations prominently assert the rhetoric of reconciliation through speeches of leaders, adoptions of charters, special commissions, governmental departments, or otherwise. Sometimes it is done by symbolic acts. But the extent to which the goal of reconciliation genuinely animates the policies and politics of the transitional government is open to question. The appeal of reconciliation, at least at the rhetorical level, is so strong that it may be subject to exploitation. How is one to tell, for instance, whether executive endorsement of an amnesty law represents an unprincipled capitulation to the perpetrators of the past or an honest effort to move the country forward toward true reconciliation and healing? Or how does one determine whether a government-sponsored reconciliation conference amounts to a genuine offer of an olive branch, or rather is "like a broken-winged bird that can not fly"?[22]

Governments say they pursue reconciliation for a variety of reasons. In some cases, reconciliation may be said to promote the cause of justice, particularly as it is understood in the context of restorative justice. Governments may also say that reconciliation promotes the value of deterrence. Deterrence is important both for its intrinsic value in having peace and for its instrumental value in promoting respect for the rule of law and drawing a bright line between the old dispensation and the new.[23] Reconciliation programs may also help to consolidate democracy. Achieving reconciliation can also have a very positive effect on the way outsiders see the country. If a country has moved from violence to reconciliation, then outside investors would be more likely to visit, do business, trade, and create factories, among other activities. Tourists, with their spending power, are also more likely to visit that country. A stable society, particularly in a heterogeneous state, is contingent on peaceful relationships between those groups. If there have been periods of strife, then for those groups to trust each other and work together, reconciliation must be a prominent issue on the agenda of any new government. Finally, governments may promote reconciliation because the people want or demand it, or because they need it. These are, after all, situations in which many people have fought tirelessly for the right to insist on peace and reconciliation. We consider each of these rationales in detail throughout the book, but we pause here to give these questions a preliminary glance.

Reconciliation and Justice

Reconciliation has a complicated relationship with justice—so complicated in fact that we explore these questions in greater detail in Chapter 6. Both terms can be elastic and elusive and their intersection is difficult to map. Perhaps the most common conclusion about the relationship between justice and reconciliation is that there is none. In Rwanda, this has meant that the government would not promote reconciliation until after the regime of prosecutions against the accused genocidaires had run its course. In this view, reconciliation is independent of and subordinate to the primary goal of retributive justice.

Another way to describe the intersection between justice and reconciliation is that the two are incompatible: reconciliation obstructs justice and, likewise, retributive justice impedes the cause of reconciliation. The experience in some Latin American countries may lend support to the view that reconciliation obstructs justice or vice versa. On one reading of the events, reconciliation was the justification for the concessions that were made to the former military leaders in the form of amnesty grants or laws. These concessions were founded in politics, not law; in power, not justice, and were viewed by most people as unjust, if not also unnecessary. But they were rationalized by the rhetoric of reconciliation.

Even when leaders are not directly disingenuous about reconciliation, it can nonetheless be argued that reconciliation and justice are simply at odds. Where justice is punitive, reconciliation is forgiving. Where justice seems principled, reconciliation seems pragmatic. For those who want vengeance or redress, reconciliation's tendency to insist on forgiveness and on moving forward may exact more than many victims are able, willing, or should be required to give. For those who believe that establishing rule of law values is a paramount obligation of transitional governments, the flexibility that characterizes reconciliation may threaten the government's ability to insist on absolute respect for law. According to this view, reconciliation is at best a face-saving, lesser-of-two-evils choice where trials are impossible for political or economic reasons; at worst, it is capitulation to and continuation of the abusive policies of the past.

On the other hand, some conceptions of reconciliation and some conceptions of justice permit the conclusion that they can be congruent, even mutually reinforcing. Reconciliation may be said to promote justice insofar as true, deep reconciliation involves redressing the balance, vindicating the victims, and restoring them to their former, pre-violation selves, as does every conception of justice, including punitive justice. Broader conceptions of both reconciliation and justice may advance both individual and societal healing. Whether or not they can in fact achieve this plethora of goals depends on how committed the nation is to achieving both justice and reconciliation and how well it balances these competing interests. The procedures the government chooses to use to promote reconciliation may also be as important as the substance of its policies. For instance, inclusive policies that entail true consultation with the widest broadest segments of the population are most likely to engender the feeling that justice has been done.

Recent years have seen a new conception of criminal justice, one that has direct parallels in the reconciliation movement. Restorative justice constitutes a paradigm shift that has been occurring over the last thirty years throughout the world.[24] It reconceptualizes crime in fundamental ways that have broad implications for the practice of criminal justice. In this understanding, crime is viewed as a violation against the victim, rather than against the inchoate state or the society in any abstract way. Given its focus on the parties most affected by crime, "A restorative justice process maximizes the input and participation of these parties—but especially primary victims as well as offenders—in the search for restoration, healing, responsibility and prevention."[25] The process is inclusive and assumes maximum participation of the victim, the perpetrator, and the affected members of the community, rather than sidelining these to the role of complainant, witness, or passive defendant. It is cooperative and intended to be transformative rather than adversarial. Notwithstanding its backward-looking name, it aims to rebuild and strengthen and not merely to "restore."

What is said of crime in the context of restorative justice may be said of political violence in the context of transitional justice. That is, the paradigm shifts from viewing the crimes of a predecessor regime as harming the present regime or the state to recognizing that those crimes harmed individuals selected for particularly harsh treatment, or individuals within the polity who were discriminated against, starved, kidnaped into military service, or otherwise abused. These wrongs are then viewed as very personal acts with very personal consequences, rather than as political acts in the abstract sense. This attention to the consequences of political crime on individual victims and survivors is beginning to influence those who promote reconciliation. Reconciliation is a mechanism for dealing with the past that is forward-looking—constructive and transformative rather than punitive or retributive. The goals are aimed at healing the victim, educating society, and helping the perpetrator to reintegrate into society. It avoids the stigmatization and alienation that often characterize penal justice. The means by which it achieves these goals tend to be inclusive of all interested parties, entailing active participation of both victim and perpetrator. In South Africa, the TRC integrated restorative justice into its conception of reconciliation.

If justice is understood broadly enough to encompass restorative justice, there is no inconsistency between justice and reconciliation.[26] But even a more conventional conception of justice does not preclude reconciliation. Here, as elsewhere, the details can be determinative: the extent to which reconciliation achieves justice and justice achieves reconciliation will inevitably depend on how it is done and how it is interpreted by supporters and skeptics alike. Trials can promote reconciliation if they are seen to be part of an unbiased process aimed not at scapegoating a few who ended up on the losing side but at dealing responsibly with gross abuses of human rights committed on all sides. In this way, those who are not guilty can distinguish themselves from their culpable counterparts and reconcile themselves with erstwhile opponents. In other instances, however, not prosecuting may be more conducive to reconciliation, as for instance where there are insufficient resources to conduct fair trials.

Ultimately, one reason why reconciliation is such a difficult concept is that it entails unusually slippery concepts. "Justice" can be restorative, retributive, or punitive; trials can sometimes impede and other times advance reconciliation, as can amnesty, as can doing nothing at all. Clearly, there are few constants in this area.

Reconciliation and Deterrence

Another reason for promoting reconciliation is for deterrence. This is evident from the rhetoric, going back to the response to the Holocaust, which promised that "never again" should such atrocities occur. This rallying cry has been imported into the transitional justice reconciliation movement, particularly in Latin America where no fewer than four commission reports have adopted the title *Nunca Más*.[27] As President Alfonsín put it, his chief aim was to prevent rather than to punish, and thus "to guarantee that never again would an Argentinean be taken from his home at night to be tortured or assassinated by agents of the state.'"[28] Likewise, the report of the Chilean Truth and Reconciliation Commission argues that "national reconciliation . . . is an utter necessity and is also the primary condition for avoiding a repetition of past events."[29] The recent report of the Peruvian truth commission says the same.[30]

The conventional wisdom in nontransitional contexts is that prosecuting (at least some) wrongdoers promotes deterrence. In transitional contexts, the new conventional wisdom is that truth commissions also have deterrent power. Indeed, the "expressed intent of most truth commissions is to lessen the likelihood of human rights atrocities reoccurring in the future."[31]

But it is not obvious how a program of reconciliation—whether through trials or truth commissions, or otherwise—would actually promote deterrence. One answer is that the publicity accorded to a commission, and to those perpetrators who appear or who are named, gives greater visibility to the acts and individuals, thus diminishing the likelihood of recurrence. In other words, publicity can be an effective agent of deterrence. Another possibility of the deterrent potential of a commission is the educative role it can play in ensuring that awareness of human rights is enhanced and promoted, thus reducing the likelihood of their abuse.

One important question for transitional governments is, who is meant to be deterred by reconciliation? Given the modern recognition of the role of the public in the commission of human rights abuses, it is no longer satisfactory to simply say that the leaders must be deterred. They are perhaps not the only wrongdoers. In fact, the allegation made by leaders often is that they knew nothing of what the foot soldiers were doing. Critically, most leaders do not sully their hands with the actual carrying out of the human rights violations. They are, however, just as culpable, and possibly even more so, even if they are often the least likely to face justice.

But even focusing for the moment just on the leaders, it is not at all clear that reconciliation deters past leaders from committing crimes again or would-be leaders from embarking on a campaign of human rights abuses. If reconciliation is a euphemism for impunity, it obviously has no deterrent powers. If it is conceived as peace or unity among the people, it does not follow that the leaders would be consequently less likely to engage in programs of violence.[32]

Even reconciliation between former adversaries—a handshake, a signed agreement, a pipe, or a bottle of rare wine—would not necessarily deter people who defied the rule of law once, from doing so again. After all, recidivism is not unknown even in transitional contexts. Moreover, a new despot may readily distinguish himself from the previous one either on the grounds that he will not get caught, or that his repression is not as bad, or that his justification is greater. But he is unlikely to be transformed by a program of reconciliation. On the other hand, there are a few examples of leaders who have been rehabilitated, leaders who once ran prison states but converted to democracy after reconciliation with their former adversaries. At most a leader, such as F. W. de Klerk in South Africa or, eventually, Eduard Shevardnadze in Georgia, moves out of the way to make room for the truly democratic-minded politicians. But reconciliation is unlikely to produce a change of heart among the leadership, whether it comes through amnesty, prosecution, or some third way such as a truth commission. Despots are largely immune from reconciliation programs because they are motivated not by a failure of understanding of their adversaries but by their own mindsets (i.e., the degree to which they are obsessed by a perceived threat to national security; the degree to which they are susceptible to groupthink; the degree to which they seek grandeur, status, and prestige; and so on).

Societies that produce despots are polarized ones in which enough members are disaffected that they are willing to turn against, or support, a regime that turns against their fellow citizens. If reconciliation is going to have a deterrent effect, it must be reconciliation among the people, not just between the leaders. Leaders may be involved in order to show a good example, as Archbishop Tutu urged them to do, but such actions by leaders will have only marginal impact. Effective reconciliation will need to be from the ground up, not the top down.

Despotism will be deterred when the people will have enough connection to one another that they will not allow a despot to divide them; when the people have enough respect for human rights that they will not tolerate abusive means even to achieve ends that they might otherwise like; when they are sufficiently invested in their communities and in their nation that they ask questions and demand accountability from their leaders. Public education and truth-producing institutions may contribute to this kind of reconciliation.[33] But the transformation of the society from one that accepted or supported human rights abuses into one that would resist them will require much more than a short-term solution like a truth commission, or a particularized response like prosecution. The question of deterrence, then, is closely linked to the consolidation of democracy.

Reconciliation and Democracy

Democracy seems to be the least common of the justifications for reconciliation, but it is probably the most persuasive. Democracy is, by definition, the very purpose of the transitions involved here: to establish stable societies founded on the premise that the governors are controlled by the governed and to consolidate that democratic ethos. To the extent that reconciliation is largely about how new regimes deal with their predecessors, it is a mistake, as Neil Kritz has suggested, "to compartmentalize, by viewing the need to 'clean up old business' as unrelated to the democratisation process."[34] And yet, the way in which the two interrelate has not been fully understood.

How a nation deals with its past also has repercussions for the present. The success of the new regime is often judged, both by locals and by the international community, by its treatment of the past—how victims and perpetrators are treated as viewed by themselves, each other, and the society in general. Although it is not necessarily the most important job of the new regime—redistributing resources or overhauling the educational, health, housing, or other welfare systems might be more important in the long run—it may be the salient litmus test. The abuses of the past are often what prompted the transition in the first place, and the public may require prompt assurance, and other confidence-building measures, that the enormous effort and cost exerted to change the regime were worth the time, sacrifice, and other trouble endured. This is also where the new government can most simply and visibly demonstrate the difference in values between the old and the new. A government that takes a firm line on the perpetrators of past abuses demonstrates how committed it is to the rule of law and to traditional notions of justice. Taking a more conciliatory, victim-oriented stance, on the other hand, models values of empathy and forgiveness. Either way, a government that puts the past on the public agenda establishes values of openness and transparency and either implicitly or explicitly eschews the secrecy and suppression that characterized the predecessor regime.

The past is also the foundation for the future. George Orwell saw years ago that whoever controls the past controls the future and whoever controls the present controls the past.[35] The present-day version of this is the quip commonly heard in transitional cultures that the future is known, it is only the past that is unpredictable.[36] There is a fluidity between past and future that withstands even the most abrupt political schisms. What a nation takes from the past will determine in part how it brings its history into the future. The critical question is the role and form that memory takes in relation to the future.

In looking to the future, it becomes apparent that the consolidation of democracy must be preeminent among a government's transitional goals. Other important values, such as respect for the rule of law and for human rights, are impossible or virtually irrelevant if they exist outside the framework of a functioning democracy. These other values or goals, including reconciliation, must therefore be in the service of the consolidation of democracy.

Because the democracy argument considers reconciliation in the context of establishing a functioning democracy, it shifts the reconciliation paradigm from one that is primarily backward-looking to one that is primarily forward-looking.[37] Reconciliation is conventionally thought of as one approach to dealing with the past. It emerged out of criminal justice discourse, presented either as a silver lining within or as an alternative to the traditional conceptions of criminal justice. But criminal justice is justified wholly by past actions—it comes into play only because of past actions—whereas democracy can take root regardless of what occurred in the past. The essence of the democratic framework is the same regardless of the existence of past atrocities, and regardless of the nature of the particular abuses. If reconciliation is reconfigured to promote values relating to democracy, the past recedes while the present and the future predominate.[38]

The link between reconciliation and democracy is not hard to identify. The deterrence argument is one part of it, but the democracy claim goes much further. The deterrence argument is that reconciliation among the people will preclude the rise of future dictators who thrive on divisions and suspicions among the people. The democracy argument is that reconciliation among the people establishes the minimally cohesive society that is necessary for democracy to function. In this view, democracy is more than simply the formal institutions that characterize a democratic dispensation: the constitutions, the courts, the fair and free elections, the public-protecting departments. Rather, it focuses on the idea that for democracy to work there needs to be some concept of a polity that is minimally cohesive—meaning that while there may be diversity and deep divisions within the polity, there is at least common agreement to participate in the democracy and to accept and respect the choices made by others. That is the essence of a functioning democracy, and it is the essence of reconciliation.

Reconciliation is the soil in which democracy takes root. Democracy can thrive only where the disparate factions in society have chosen to be governed in common. Democracy requires that the disappointed minority accede to the will of the majority—a concession that can happen only if the minority and the majority are sufficiently reconciled that they accept each other's presence in the polity and the content of each other's choices as legitimate, even if they don't agree with them. It is the will to agree to disagree. Without that commitment, the factions continue to fight, and democracy never takes root. We explore, in Chapter 8, ways in which a new government might develop democratic institutions that promote reconciliation

Reconciliation and Popular Choice

In some situations, a new government may pursue reconciliation not for any moral reasons but simply because that seems to be the course favored by a majority of the population. This can occur in several ways. Public opinion that favors reconciliation rather than vengeance is, in and of itself, noteworthy: what makes people want to reconcile? What gives people the ability to forego vengeance? Is it exhaustion? A perception of the futility of violence? An understanding of the interdependence of warring communities that defies the rhetoric of violence of the leadership? And how does the public communicate with the government to make its views known?

One possibility is that civil society simply demands inclusion in a process of reconciliation. More often, however, civil society responds only when government has asked. The government may submit the choice to the people through a popular referendum or some equivalent mechanism. This option may be favored by those who believe that reconciliation bears a moral burden of justification because it departs from the conventional approach to dealing with crimes. One aspect of that burden is that reconciliation programs must, both in word and in deed, represent the values of the new dispensation, including its commitment to the rule of law. In that case, any major initiative of a new, democratic dispensation should go through the democratic process of popular approval.

The people of a new democracy may express their will not only through referenda on specific issues, but also through regular democratic elections. In post-transition elections, reconciliation is a major campaign issue. In many former communist nations, the people's preference for reconciliation over "thick line" politics was seen in the re-election of many adherents to the previous regime. To the surprise of onlookers, particularly in the West, the voting public roundly rejected the repeated efforts of the new political elites to perpetuate a political climate of division and reprisal.

Other reasons for rejecting thick-line campaign rhetoric include the recognition that such a line is impossible to draw in the context of communism and its fall. As noted, what is true everywhere in the world was especially true in communist Europe: it was impossible to distinguish between those who were implicated and those who were not, and to assign moral responsibility in accordance with the degree of collaboration. Nearly everyone played a part; determining exactly where that thick line should be drawn, therefore, was both difficult and dangerous. Furthermore, unlike other "atrocities" from which nations transition, such as apartheid, or Nazism, or military dictatorship, the fall of communism did not bring with it a universal conviction that communism was evil. Given the ambivalence that many people felt toward communism, it was difficult for the leaders to gain political advantage from vilifying the communists.

Especially where regimes come and go with some frequency, people may see repeated efforts to deny, reconstruct, glorify, or demonize the past as part and parcel of transitions. Not even reconciliation can escape the accusation of victor's justice. At this time, people may be more interested in moving forward than in sorting out the past. Their needs are great and immediate—housing, food, education, their children's future—and their sense of the moral righteousness of any given system is minimal. They may simply prefer to look forward rather than backward, recognizing that stability, and ultimately growth, lie in the future and not in the past.

In many situations, a government may promote reconciliation not as a result of explicit popular demand but in response to an obvious need. Where people have suffered tremendously under prior regimes, as the result either of systemic oppression (communism, apartheid) or of individualized victimization (torture, death squads), people need the psychological healing that reconciliation can bring. As one observer on the situation in Sierra Leone found, people there deeply desired to live normal lives: "The priority of the people especially those living precariously in the vast areas that are not under the control of the legitimate government, is peace and freedom from fear, freedom to live their lives like normal human beings. And for this they are ready to go a long way, even to reconcile with those who were hurting them yesterday."[39]

The South African Truth and Reconciliation Commission was particularly attuned to its role as healer of souls and restorer of individual dignity. This "Kleenex Commission," as some called it, placed emphasis on processes needed by those victims of apartheid who approached the commission to heal and on its ability to contribute to that process.[40] Though the main thrust of this justification is personal, there may be a structural aspect to personal healing as well; democracy is more likely to thrive if its constituency is physically and psychologically healthy, and conversely, more precarious if people remain profoundly scarred.

None of this has been lost on the international donor community, which has, increasingly, supported reconciliation projects throughout the world.[41] Whether because reconciliation projects are inherently appealing, or because they are viewed by the donor class as the sine qua non of stability and the cornerstone of democracy, reconciliation now has a significant cash value. Transitioning nations promoting reconciliation can virtually depend on generous donations by Western nations, including the United States and the nations of northern Europe.

Reconciliation for Its Own Sake

Some nations may pursue reconciliation as an end in and of itself. It is idealistic to suggest that the deep cleavages that caused civil war and oppression will ever be truly eradicated, replaced by harmonious relations among the erstwhile enemies. What may be achieved is a move along a continuum toward better relationships at both the personal and communal level, a society that is less fractured and polarized. It is not impossible to imagine a time, in almost any transitional nation, when the matter of reconciliation—the relations among the peoples and between the people and their government—is converted into other issues, the issues that face a normal, nontransitional democracy. Reconciliation may be pursued simply because it represents a kind of peace, a resting place, a calm after the storm.

How Nations Pursue Reconciliation, or not

Reconciliation has always been, at least in part, about what to do about the past. It has much to do with dealing with the legacy of the past. In this vein it is important to find the balance between too much remembering and too much forgetting. Must we forgive? May we forgive? Must we punish? May we punish? How do we punish the wrongdoers if we don't know who they are? How do we forgive if we don't know what we are forgiving for? In Martha Minow's words: "Forgiveness is a power held by the victimized, not a right to be claimed. The ability to dispense, but also to withhold, forgiveness is an ennobling capacity and part of the dignity to be reclaimed by those who survive the wrongdoing. Even an individual survivor who chooses to forgive cannot forgive properly in the name of other victims. To expect survivors to forgive is to heap yet another burden on them."[42]

The language of reconciliation is often explicitly backward-looking: working through the past, coming to terms with the past, confronting or reckoning with the past, settling accounts. The principal vehicles for promoting reconciliation are those nations that have chosen to deal with the past. These mechanisms primarily include trials, amnesty, or what has become known as a third way, which includes special truth commissions, other commissions of inquiry, lustration programs, or something else. In some situations, reconciliation may be promoted by doing nothing about the past.

Sometimes, in the course of dealing with the past, nations pursue reconciliation directly and explicitly. South Africa and those who have followed in its wake have made reconciliation part of their "dealing with the past" program. Other governments pursue the course they would have otherwise selected but assert that reconciliation is an important byproduct of that choice. Many of the Latin American transitions of the 1980s reflect this path. Thus, amnesty or truth commissions, or in some cases trials, were pursued for largely independent reasons, but the rhetoric of reconciliation was appended to those policies with the hope of increasing their appeal to both the domestic and the international public. In still other situations, the governments pursued their policies with only the slightest nod to reconciliation. In Rwanda, as noted, the government resisted international calls for reconciliation for years, insisting that "justice" needed to be done first. Whatever the relation of the policy to the goal of reconciliation, the conventional wisdom is that reconciliation is, ultimately, about how the nation deals with its past or the legacy of the past.

Trials

Punishing agents of the prior regime is something of a birthright of the successor. It has been done for centuries, and the great innovation in the last 500 years is the expectation of a trial before the execution. Even during the French Revolution, the revolutionary tribunal was holding facsimiles of trials to satisfy the public's need for the appearance of justice.[43] After Waterloo, Napoleon put the British forces in a quandary: while Prussia (which had experienced the brunt of Napoleon's expansionist ambitions) would have had him shot on sight, the British favored banishment; but neither proposed an honest trial with due process and the possibility of acquittal; to this day, the "Napoleonic precedent" refers to punishing an enemy without the benefit of law.[44] The beginning of the twentieth century saw the germination of a preference for British- or American-style due process to accompany the punishment of a conquered enemy. At the close of World War I, neither the British nor the French ever "considered simply shooting" Kaiser Wilhelm II, and always assumed that he would be afforded some measure of due process. World War II also ended with an insistence on legalism that culminated in the Nuremberg and Tokyo trials (although this result was by no means a foregone conclusion). The most recent example is the highly publicized trial of Saddam Hussein, marking the bright line between his regime and the new regime in Iraq. The summary trials and prompt execution of Romanian leader Nicolai Ceausescu and his wife were notable exceptions to this modern trend favoring legal responses to political wrongdoing.

The prosecutorial turn has brought with it a cavalcade of difficult questions. What, exactly, are the crimes of warfare? How far does "command responsibility" extend? How much process is due? And what happens if an excess of process results in acquittal? How are suspects arrested and, if necessary, extradited? And who, in the context of international politics, is morally virtuous enough to cast the first stone? Although these questions remain unanswerable, the mere formality of trials, for many people, suffuses the legal process with sufficient legitimacy. As Frederick

Smith, the British attorney general at the end of World War I, argued, the "only advantage of judicial procedure over the other alternative—a high exercise of executive and conquering force submitting itself to the judgment of history—lies in the fact that for all time it may claim the sanction of legal forms and the protection—in favour of the prisoner—of a tribunal whose impartiality can be established in the face of any challenge."[45]

Even Smith, however, recognized that "This advantage . . . largely disappears if the fairness of the tribunal can be plausibly impeached."[46] If the legitimacy of the procedure can be impeached, then, as Chamberlain also noted about a possible trial of the Kaiser, "His defence might be our trial."[47] What was true at the beginning of the twentieth century's experiment with international war crimes tribunals is equally true at the end, as Milosevic's remonstrances against the ICTY have shown.

The modern predilection for trials derives in large part from the International Military Tribunal set up in Nuremberg and its sister trials in Tokyo.[48] These have become the model of political criminal justice. They proved that some measure of due process is not incompatible with convictions (and ultimately, executions) of even the most horrific defendants. Furthermore, they established, beyond peradventure, that crimes of war and crimes against humanity are judicially cognizable. The Nuremberg trials took place in an international context, but many countries have incorporated that precedent in dealing with their own pasts, prosecuting their own citizens under their own domestic law. Perhaps the most extreme version of this is in Rwanda, where 125,000 people have been detained for involvement in the genocide and are subject to prosecution either in the country's domestic courts or in the community courts. In Ethiopia, about 3,000 officials of the Mengistu regime were slated for trial.[49] In Greece, the number of trials was much smaller, though still significant, and on the whole the program seems to have been effective as a means of promoting reconciliation.[50] Many other nations have also pursued a regime of trials as the primary or exclusive means of effectuating a transition to democracy, though the Greek example is often given as the most successful of these.

Given the political pressures in transitional times, some countries have developed creative ways to mediate between their commitment to prosecution and political or economic demands that militate against trials.

Another approach, which maintains the traditional structure of the judicial process, was adopted in Argentina. There, the judges took the position that the amnesty laws precluded the imposition of punishment, but did not preclude the investigation of crimes that would ordinarily attend a full-scale trial.[51] The German government adopted a similar view when it empowered tribunals to "investigate and expose crimes of the GDR state and party structures" but did not give them the power to punish.[52] Predictably, this approach has also been both criticized and praised by those who say it presents the worst of both worlds (opening the old wounds but no closure), or the best (letting the truth emerge, without unnecessary retribution), respectively. Some of these alternatives merely supplement the normal run of trials, as in Rwanda and Germany (where the border guards were famously prosecuted by ordinary municipal courts), while in other instances these variations suggest creative circumventions to legal or other impediments to regular trials.

The best-known variations on traditional municipal prosecutions are the international criminal tribunals that, until now, have been established on an ad hoc basis where needed for a particular country. The process now has a permanent body in the International Criminal Court (ICC). The ICC has jurisdiction to try crimes against humanity, war crimes, and genocide committed since July 2002, if the country where the accused is a citizen or where the crime was committed ratified the 1998 Rome Statute establishing the court.[53] A case can also be referred to the court by the Security Council.[54] The ICC is likely to be a prominent feature of transitional justice in the future.

When a country has been through a period of unrest and conflict, or has experienced a transitional period in governments, there are often numerous human rights abuses. The international criminal bodies are useful in prosecuting those offences, and these prosecutions can help achieve national reconciliation. The prosecution of an individual in an international court can relieve the need for a domestic court to try the case, thereby avoiding many of the problems of domestic courts. The value of international trials may be largely symbolic, given that the experience of these tribunals shows that they cannot run numerous trials. The internationalization of criminal law can also be seen in the increasing prevalence of the principle of universal jurisdiction, which has also facilitated the trial of wrongdoers of one nation in another nation's courts.

Whichever way they are configured, trials have gained a moral authority that exerts a certain pressure on the reconciliation movement. Alexander Solzhenitsyn put it simply when he wrote: "When we neither punish nor reproach evildoers, we are not simply protecting their trivial old age, we are thereby ripping the foundations of justice from beneath new generations."[55] José Zalaquett traces the morality of trials back to Nuremberg, which, along with the policies that several European nations adopted at the time concerning war criminals, "emphasized the duty to prosecute and punish those guilty of certain crimes so as to preserve the collective memory and build up an effective deterrent. This policy, which is mandated by human conscience and several international legal norms, has guided the prosecution of war criminals for decades. As a consequence, the lessons of World War II have been further engraved in the conscience of international public opinion."[56] According to this view, trials have become not just an option, but a moral mandate.

This moral dimension of trials raises the obligation to punish to the level of a nonderogable duty. "Some advocates of prosecutions assert claims of an absolute duty, based upon fundamental conceptions of justice, to punish atrocious crimes."[57] As a result of the widespread belief in this moral obligation, using trials for the purpose of promoting reconciliation is a difficult task that few countries have successfully managed.

Several rejoinders to this duty-to-prosecute argument present themselves. One response, which is emerging in the literature but is still contrary to practice, is to reject the very premise of the moral sanctity of trials.[58] Another response is to accept the challenge and present a moral defense of reconciliation that casts it as something more than a vague "social benefit." Some of the goals of reconciliation mentioned previously, if taken seriously, could rise to the level of a moral imperative. A third response is to accept both parts of the argument—both criminal justice and social reconciliation have moral force—but reject the underlying premise that they are incompatible. Rather, one would argue, not only are the two mutually reinforcing but neither is complete without the other. Indeed, no country that has promoted genuine reconciliation as a national goal has done so to the exclusion of trials. Even in South Africa, which probably has the most developed conception of reconciliation, the TRC has been careful to emphasize the complementary value of trials.[59]

Even accepting the moral need, it cannot be taken literally. Few people would argue that every crime must be punished, and not even the most developed criminal justice systems on earth have the resources or the patience to investigate and prosecute every single crime, or even every single major crime. In transitional nations, where the lack of funds inevitably restricts a nation's choices, it is even less realistic to expect retribution for every crime of the preceding regime. Moreover, advocates of punishment recognize that their zeal must be tempered if a program of retribution leads to more and greater abuses of human rights, as can sometimes happen.[60]

Even if punishment is taken as a moral obligation, it is not obvious that trials in fact fulfill that duty. There is, to begin with, a problematic relationship between trials and punishment. If trials are fair, then the outcome is uncertain; only with show trials can one confidently predict a conviction. Trials that are contemplated as being morally required could end either in acquittal or in conviction. And yet, the moral values that are associated with trials are inevitably those associated with conviction and punishment. It turns out that the imperative is not to try, but to convict. A critical issue that must be taken into account in the process of determining whether to prosecute is whether the likelihood of success is high. An acquittal can have a devastating effect on victims and the nation in general.[61] But a conviction obtained without due process casts a shadow of illegitimacy over the entire new regime.

It is possible that there is something to be gained simply by subjecting fallen leaders to the criminal process, as when former South African President P. W. Botha was brought before a black magistrate to determine his amenability to testify before the TRC.[62] There was value in the process, even though it ultimately ended in victory for Botha. As Wole Soyinka reminds us, in Malawi, "the once President-for-Life Hastings Banda did go on trial for his life: he was acquitted, yes—largely on a technicality—but the process of reducing the once all-powerful controller of freedom and restraint, of life and death to an egalitarian uncertainty with his erstwhile victims, is a model of social restitution whose validity cannot be contested."[63] When Augusto Pinochet was charged with tax fraud, even human rights lawyers said it was a huge victory.[64]

More commonly, however, the values generally associated with trials are not in fact the values of the process, but rather of the conviction: retribution or punishment, deterrence by showing that crime does not pay, drawing the line between the good and the bad, reinforcing rule of law values by showing the new regime's commitment to punishing those who do not respect human life, vindicating victims.

None of these values are obtained when the defendant is acquitted. And yet, acquittals happen with some frequency, particularly in the high-profile cases where defendants have everything at stake and ample resources with which to defend themselves. Prominent cases of acquittals include those of Erich Honecker in Germany and most of the high-level cases in South Africa, including the apartheid defense minister, and the architect of South Africa's biological warfare program. Equating trials with punishment, then, is neither semantically correct nor realistic; accepting the distinction, however, weakens the moral pull of prosecution.

To the extent that the morality of trials lies in their deterrent effect, similar questions may be asked. Is there in fact any evidence that prosecuting leaders of fallen regimes deters them or their would-be imitators? Is it true that deterrence works with political crimes the same way it is said to work with individual crimes, which tend to be motivated by the prospect of instant gain or by an uncontrollable impulse to harm? Political crimes are rarely motivated by an individual's calculation that there is more to be gained than lost in committing the crime. Rather, at least for high-level actors, the motivation for political crimes is more likely to depend on an idiosyncratic concatenation of social, political, and economic factors that are likely to remain unaffected by the trial and punishment of last year's perpetrator. For lower-level wrongdoers, trials may very well deter some people from committing crimes—after all, it is often they who are scapegoated. Here, however, other factors, such as peer pressure, opportunities for personal advancement or remuneration, belief in the cause, or the perception of helplessness, may counteract the deterrent effect. In the end, social transformation—in the form of reconciliation— is probably more likely to deter future wrongdoing.

Trials are said to achieve more than punishment, and more than deterrence. They are said to contribute to the healing of the society by elucidating the truth of past events. Like the deterrence and rule of law arguments, the therapeutic argument also rests on the assumption that wrongdoers will be punished and that, by and large, only the innocent will go free; it is not clear how a string of acquittals of known operatives of the prior criminal regime can be therapeutic for the community. It seems only logical that acquittals can have detrimental effects both for the time at which they occur and in the future.

The argument that trials may expose the truth is not as dependent on the outcome as it is on the process of proffering evidence that produces the truth or a version of the truth. But here, the salient question is, assuming that the disclosure of truth is a moral imperative, are trials the best way to achieve that goal? Certainly the advent of truth commissions has challenged the notion that trials are the exclusive or even a preferred method of discovering the truth. Courts have the advantage of a subpoena power, to try and wrest the truth from the mouths of the reluctant, but a truth commission with the same power may do just as well. One question that needs to be asked is whether truth commissions are viewed by the general public with the same seriousness as a court and whether this view impacts on the veracity of statements made by those who appear before these bodies. Most other aspects of prosecution make it less efficacious at eliciting the truth than commissions or other tribunals. The truth that trials produce is radically limited by the focus of the trial (on a small number of defendants and a small number of acts, as opposed to the examination of a "master plan"); by the adversarial nature of litigation which limits the narrative to the perspective of two biased parties; and by the rules of evidence, which may privilege values other than truth.

Notwithstanding these legitimate arguments, the common practice, both domestically and internationally, is to prefer trials to any other means of dealing with the past. This is most explicitly articulated in the statute of the International Criminal Court, the basic premise of which is to punish the grave crimes that "threaten the peace, security and well-being of the world," as well as by the Rome Statute's insistence on the exercise by states of their national criminal jurisdiction and its rejection of other domestic means of treating perpetrators of political crimes.[65] Given the historic attachment of the international community to trials, proponents

of reconciliation might do better to emphasize the moral parity of prosecution and reconciliation and to argue that a regime of trials is not
incompatible with progress toward reconciliation. This moral parity argument recasts of the values of reconciliation to reflect more than just a
transient or subordinate social benefit. For example, one might argue that
the need to restore human dignity after severe physical or psychological
trauma is a moral imperative that is at least as fundamental to the health
of an individual as is seeing a perpetrator punished. Further, one might
argue that a culture that respects human rights and chooses civil rather
than violent means to mediate disputes among the citizens is not one
choice among several but rises to the level of an absolute necessity, particularly for a society recovering from trauma. Or one could point to the
need for a polity of sufficient cohesion to enable a democratic order to
function and thrive. Any of these could be seen as at least as important
as retribution from the perspective of morality or from any other.

The importance of reconciliation becomes even more obvious when
one considers the relations among the various values. While retribution
may promote respect for human dignity and for the rule of law, both of
these are dependent on a functioning democracy.[66] Indeed, if there is
no democratic order that fairly selects judges, allocates funds for court-
houses, and secures jails, how can there be legitimate prosecutions, convictions, or punishment? Democracy, retribution, and reconciliation are
mutually reinforcing values, and no one is complete without the others.

If reconciliation is a significant transitional value, then the question
remains whether trials assist or impede its progress. It can be argued,
for instance, that the therapeutic value of trials not only encourages the
healing of the community, but promotes a deeper understanding by the
community of the perpetrator and his or her motives, which may be a
component of reconciliation. Likewise, some have suggested that trials
vindicate the victims, by corroborating the victims' experience and by insisting on the wrongness of the perpetrator's actions—two feats that can
be accomplished whether or not the trial ultimately ends in conviction
and punishment of the defendant. If it does end that way, the trial can
also correct the inversion of justice felt by an innocent victim who was
oppressed by one who previously held power. As Sven Alkalaj has written
about the ICTY: "That is exactly why today's war crimes tribunal is so
important. Not only will it dispense justice by punishing the guilty, but it
will show what happened during the past four years and would even eventually absolve the innocent. That way, the groundwork for reconciliation
would be possible."[67]

However, it is difficult to make the case that the result of a trial or of
a truth commission inquiry can always have a particular result. The manner in which they are conducted as well as many other factors come into

play before one can determine that a particular course has produced a particular effect.

It is possible that trials do promote reconciliation, particularly insofar as they establish the moral foundations on which the newly reconciled society will rest. A highly visible trial, like that of Saddam Hussein, tells the world that the new Iraq is based on the rule of law. If the process and outcome of a trial resonate throughout the society, they may embody some of the principles and the common experiences around which the society may coalesce. It is important to note, however, that international and foreign tribunals are far less likely to promote reconciliation insofar as the trials are not of and do not speak directly to the troubled society.[68] In this sense, particularized solutions such as participatory community courts may have more relevance. On the other hand, international and even foreign trials do establish a worldwide consensus on the moral unacceptability of crimes against humanity, even if they may not directly promote healing in the society most affected.

Amnesty

Not all transitional nations prosecute the wrongs of their predecessors. Nascent governments may make the political calculation to grant amnesty in order to gain the support or acquiescence of outgoing officials. A de facto amnesty may also come about as the result of a deliberate conclusion that doing nothing is better than doing anything, and that the best way to move forward is not to look back at all. One last alternative is de facto amnesty that results from the opposite intention: a new government attempts to prosecute the crimes of the past, but lacks the political or economic resources to do the job successfully. Or, the government might simply decide that amnesty will further reconciliation, as the government of the Democratic Republic of Congo did in November 2005.

Amnesty is a broad term that encompasses a range of situations. In some cases amnesty is morally and politically defensible, while in others it is hard to view amnesty as anything other than capitulation, or even collaboration, with the criminals of the prior regime.[69] An important distinction can be drawn between impunity, which is never defensible, and amnesty, which may be. Impunity is not just the absence of punishment, but the failure to punish in a way that reflects or reinforces a cultural norm that wrongful actions are permissible. Impunity is the absence of punishment where there is no rule of law, no respect for the lives or bodies or dignity of others.[70] Impunity may take the form of a formal act of amnesty or of an omission, a deliberate absence of prosecution. Amnesty may amount to impunity if the act of amnesty confirms a lack of accountability and of responsibility—if it denies the wrongfulness of the prior regime's actions and, ultimately denies the fact of those actions. This kind of amnesty reveals its shared etymological root with amnesia in the Greek word for forgetfulness and oblivion.

Events in recent years, notably in South Africa, have revealed the affirmative potential of amnesty. Amnesty may be a valuable tool in the arsenal of transition teams. It may enable a peaceful transition in the first place. The promise of amnesty is usually required to secure the departure of leaders who, by definition, either head or have the support of the military establishment.[71] They are unlikely to give up that protection without some equivalent protection in return. In the case of Uruguay, for instance, there is no evidence that putative president Sanguinetti promised amnesty to the military junta, but it is generally assumed that he did, because the Club Naval Pact is unexplainable on any other grounds.[72] While an idealist might say that the military and its allies should give up power voluntarily and submit to the rule of law, a pragmatist might respond that, in the real world, military power is not relinquished without a fight or tough negotiation, and that amnesty is a justifiable offering in exchange for the handing over of power and establishment of peace. Once the transition has been effectuated, amnesty, if cleverly managed, might be used to extract further concessions.

The critical point is that grants of amnesty may transcend charges of impunity if they are sufficiently well structured and managed. First, amnesty should be individual, requiring each applicant to submit voluntarily to the terms of the amnesty; blanket amnesty should be disfavored. Second, amnesty should be conditional; it should not be given away for free or in exchange for a preexisting duty (such as the duty to obey the law).[73] The military should not be able to hold the country hostage by saying it will stage a coup unless it is given amnesty, although this is often the basis for initial negotiation. But as each state's circumstances and conditions are peculiar to it and are not replicated in other situations, the exact nature of those truly compelling state interests must remain contingent upon the particularities of each state at the time of transition.

These two requirements ensure that the link between amnesty and accountability is not broken. They can help avoid the perception that amnesty amounts to impunity and can increase the likelihood that amnesty will promote true reconciliation. If perpetrators must apply for amnesty individually, they are more likely to be seen as taking responsibility for their actions, which can promote reconciliation at least on an individual level. If they must do something—provide the details of their crimes, look into the eyes of their long-suffering victims, or simply apologize—they are holding themselves accountable to the community at large and to the victim in particular. It is true, as Wole Soyinka says, that nothing in the TRC process prevented an amnesty applicant from saying, "Oh yes, given the same circumstances, I would do the same thing all over again."[74] Nevertheless, the structure of the process minimized the likelihood of that happening. The mere fact of participation in the process signaled a measure of willingness to play by the new rules. Indeed, many recalcitrant perpetrators, particularly whites, refused to apply for amnesty, preferring to take the chance that they would not be prosecuted. Amnesty did not, in this scenario, produce a change of heart, but neither was it given away for free. Furthermore, remorse could have been a condition of amnesty, if that had been a primary value of the South African transition.

The condition upon which amnesty can be granted is a burden that the perpetrator chooses to carry and that the victim may have a hand in imposing. This burden may even promote rule of law values more than criminal punishment, which is imposed on a defendant whether or not he or she acknowledges the wrongfulness of the actions. It guarantees that though a crime is amnestied, it is not forgotten, nor even necessarily forgiven. It is not prosecuted, but neither is it denied.

Although it is tempting to dismiss politicians' claims that amnesty can promote reconciliation, the reality is not so simple. Indeed, it has been argued that punishment correlates negatively to democracy, while amnesty can be a positive in the transition to democracy. Referring to the claims of such men as Alfonsín, Sanguinetti, and Aylwin that the amnesties they promoted or conceded to were justified on "reconciliation grounds," Ruti Teitel argues, "While this argument appears rhetorical when used by government officials; as a historical matter, conditional amnesties, and not punishment, appear to have been precursors to the transition to democratic rule."[75] The relevant question, then, is not whether or not to grant amnesty, but how to structure an amnesty program to maximize its ability to promote as many benefits as possible, including reconciliation.

A Third Way

Increasingly, nations in transition are looking for alternative ways of promoting reconciliation. Truth commissions are perhaps the most popular of these mechanisms, but they are by no means the only option for nations that cannot afford a regime of trials but do not savor blanket amnesty. The first truth commissions were used in the 1970s, but they have enjoyed two surges in popularity: in the mid-1980s, after the apparent success of the Salvadoran commission in 1984[76]; and in the mid-1990s, following in the footsteps of the South African TRC. Nigeria, Sierra Leone, Ghana, Timor Leste, and Peru are just a few of the nations that have established truth commissions in the last few years.

This explosion in the number of truth commissions has led, predictably, to a diversification in their form. Truth commissions vary from one place to another in every important structural aspect. It has become increasingly common to require the establishment of a truth commission as part of a peace accord, although most commissions emerge from within the culture. Most are mandated by the government, although some successful truth commissions have been developed by the United Nations (El Salvador), by international NGOs (Rwanda in the early 1990s), or domestic NGOs (Brazil). Governmental commissions can be created by executive order (Chile) or by legislation (South Africa). Most are limited in duration, though some are not (Chad and Uganda).[77] Some have extensive powers, including the power to subpoena persons and things, while some depend on the participation of volunteers.[78] The jurisdiction of some truth commissions extends to the examination of a broad historical pattern of abuses occurring over a lengthy period of time (Chile), while others are limited to examining specific acts committed by specific people.[79] Some involve as wide a segment of the population as possible (Sierra Leone, Timor Leste, South Africa), while others operate in secret and at the margins (Guatemala). Some are required to "name names," others are prohibited from doing so, while others have no mandate one way or the other and sometimes do and sometimes do not.[80]

As a whole, truth commissions are generally assumed to be the most likely institutions to actually promote reconciliation, if only because they are usually designed specifically for that purpose. By contrast, trials, which are primarily designed to punish perpetrators, and amnesty laws, which are primarily designed to absolve them, both promote reconciliation, if at all, only as a byproduct of their principal aims. Nonetheless, there has been no quantitative study to assess the success of truth commissions.[81] A variety of reasons explain the absence of data. The first may be financial, as local resources and donor dollars are more likely to be allocated to the primary work of promoting reconciliation than to the secondary work of studying it. There are also numerous epistemic challenges, such as the difficulty of identifying how much of the reconciliation that was achieved is attributable to the commission and how much to other factors, including other institutions and the trials and amnesty programs with which truth commissions often coexist.

Perhaps the most fundamental impediment to a thorough study is the difficulty in determining exactly what reconciliation is, in order to quantify the extent to which a particular mechanism has promoted it. If reconciliation is conceived primarily as the working through of the past, then it stands to reason that truth commissions—whose stock in trade is the truth about the past—would promote a greater understanding of the past and increase the ability of people to deal with it. If, however, it is conceived as more forward-looking—as the foundation of the new dispensation rather than as the capstone of the previous one—then a commission of inquiry might not be ideal and a different modality might be called for, such as democracy-building institutions that either directly or indirectly promote reconciliation. These alternative models are examined in more detail in Chapter 8.

Still experimental are ministry departments devoted to reconciliation. These have the potential to advance reconciliation because they are not limited in time and tend to have larger administrative staffs and broader mandates than commissions. Rwanda's National Unity and Reconciliation Commission is ostensibly devoted to understanding and promoting reconciliation throughout the country.[82] The Fijian Department of National Reconciliation is another example. These governmental agencies are noteworthy in a few respects. First, they integrate several areas that, outside the transitional justice context, would normally be treated separately. The Fijian department, for instance, deals with economic matters (such as rehabilitation of families and economic "development disparities"), religious matters (by encouraging Christian and traditional leaders to work together), and matters of public safety (by working with the police), all the while trying to promote "patriotism and national allegiance."[83] This range of responsibilities illustrates the multifaceted (if not downright amorphous) nature of reconciliation. But it is not yet clear whether these ministerial departments are actually effective. Second, public education and information constitute a major part of the work of these organizations. The public education components have both normative and descriptive aspects in that the government is simultaneously helping people understand the issues and fostering a certain viewpoint, trying to reconcile, as it were, the past and the future. Nonetheless, these departments are much more focused on the future than alternative means of promoting reconciliation such as trials or truth commissions.

The Way Forward

If reconciliation is going to make a meaningful contribution to societies in transition, it is going to have to be understood in much better terms than is currently the case. Reconciliation may mean quite different things in different societies at different times. This means that the term can be molded to suit each transition's needs. The nature of each society at the transitional moment needs to be carefully evaluated in order to determine exactly what conception of reconciliation is appropriate at that time and in the nation's future. Questions can be broken down temporally, because reconciliation must be understood in the context of what happened before the transition, the nature of the transition, and the condition of the society in the wake of the transition.

The pre-transition stage is when the human rights violations took place. It would be useful to understand the nature of those violations: were they individuated crimes such as torture, disappearances, kidnaping, and murder with specific and identifiable targets? Or were they widespread, such as legislative oppression under communism, totalitarianism, and some aspects of apartheid? We might also investigate the extent to which the major human rights violations were committed by the government (or the opposition) against the people (as in Guatemala) or with the participation, support, collaboration, or at the urging of major portions of the population. What was the extent of foreign involvement in the conflict? Was the conflict bilateral or multilateral? Was it largely covert or was it overt? How atrocious were the atrocities? What was the basis of the oppression? Were people victimized for their political beliefs and activities or because of religious, racial, ethnic, or tribal differences? How deep are those affiliations and how long-standing the conflict? Are these conflicts that have simmered and periodically boiled over for centuries, are they conflicts that were incited by colonization, or are they of even more recent vintage? How long did the oppression last? A few months? Years? Decades? Generations? Longer than memory?

Questions about the transition itself are also relevant to the development of an understanding of reconciliation. Did the transition take place by force, or by negotiation, or by a little of both? What concessions were made to the outgoing regime and what was received by the incoming regime in exchange? How much support does the despotic regime retain in the population and in state institutions such as the judiciary and the security forces? Is it thoroughly discredited, or is it likely to reemerge as a political force either in identical form or thinly disguised? On the other hand, how much support does the incoming regime have in the population? Was it installed by foreign interests or does it represent the choice of the people in legitimate elections?

The condition of the society in the wake of the transition is also relevant to how much and what kind of reconciliation can legitimately be expected to take place. How heterogeneous is the society after the transition? Is there a common language, religion, or set of beliefs on which one can build a cohesive society? Does one need to have a homogenous society? Is it true that a heterogeneous society is richer, with all its different flavors, but in need of greater conflict and diversity management?

How much moral consensus is there on the evil of the prior regime? How much do people know about the atrocities? Will they be shocked at the truth—at the nature of the oppression, the depth or extent of its sadism? What is the relative size of the relevant groupings—the ratio of the sector of the population that holds power to the sector that is out of power? What is the ratio of victims to perpetrators? What remains of the victimized population? Was it decimated, or worse? Or is it in power? How traumatized are the children?

Is there a cultural memory of previous regimes? In some Eastern European countries, many adults remember the fall of democracy and the rise of Nazism, the fall of Nazism and the rise of communism; now the fall of communism fits into a particular kind of cultural memory. In such a situation, people's support for purges, for instance, may be tempered by their sense that the past is repeating itself.

What is the present economic condition of the country? What are the nation's economic resources and how fairly are they distributed throughout the population? What is the society's infrastructure in the wake of the oppression? This might include everything from the ability of people to get food and water, to the condition of the educational system, to the existence of governmental departments such as courts and public welfare agencies. Do any of society's building blocks remain intact, or are families and communities dysfunctional? What is the balance of power between the national government and local authorities, such as municipal governments, or tribal chiefs, or local "warlords"? Are those vertical relationships tense or generally cooperative?

Who can assist in the transition? Are there strong nongovernmental organizations like human rights groups, churches, unaffiliated groups (such as traditional or tribal leaders, Argentina's Madres de la Plaza de Mayo, or the Soviet Union's Memorial)? Does the conscience of the nation have a voice in the writers or journalists? In many countries, women's groups have come to the fore to promote reconciliation and reconstructive projects.

Perhaps the most important aspect of understanding the transitional society is to recognize the cultural particularities of each society. These cultural features may differ radically from one place to another but can stay relatively constant in a society, transcending even long periods of trauma and dislocation. One critical question is the relative significance of time, both backward and forward, in any given society. The conception of memory may differ from one place to another: in some places, memory is long and vital for the culture, while in others, what happened yesterday is relatively unimportant. Cultures may also look at the future differently: Some societies may be willing to devote generations to the promotion of reconciliation, while others may prefer to see the bulk of the work accomplished according to a fixed schedule with a clear ending date. Likewise, revenge (or, conversely, remorse) may figure prominently in some cultures but not in others. In some cultures, authority and social hierarchy are immanent, while other cultures may have a greater comfort level with social equality or fluidity. All of these may play a part in how a nation needs to understand reconciliation for itself. These features are extraordinarily difficult to identify and to calibrate, but they may have critical bearings on the success or failure of a reconciliation program, especially if it is externally designed or imposed.

In any culture, reconciliation intersects with several different transitional issues and it is critical to assess these interlaced relationships. Such issues may include economic justice, truth, the past, democracy, retribution, and religion. Once reconciliation is better understood, governments and NGOs can design institutions, programs, and policies to promote it. Achieving a modicum of reconciliation is a measure of stability that has profound psychological, social, and economic implications.

Part II
Reconciliation in Layers

Chapter 2
The Divided Self

> Men and women not only need to reconcile with each other, but also need to reconcile themselves as a people. They need to reconcile their own history as a nation. History is their mirror and, in order to reconcile themselves, they first need to recognize themselves in that mirror.
>
> —Jorge Correa Sutil

Reconciliation can happen alone or it can happen with others. It can happen when millions of people do something together, like singing a national anthem, or watching a national sporting event, or when millions of people do something individually, like casting a ballot. Reconciliation can be oral ("I'm sorry"; "I forgive you") or written (a charter or a peace accord) or symbolic (a handshake, or wearing of the other side's colors, the payment of money, the sharing of a drink, a hug). It can be the speech of a leader or the decision not to act, as in the foregoing of violence or stepping down from a position of power. It can occur anywhere that people are. It can happen on the streets, in schools, on the sports fields, in places of worship, or in Parliament. It can happen in a sitting room of a modest home. It can happen in a board room of a corporate giant. It can happen on national television, or in the privacy of one's mind. When it happens, it can be an emotional experience, a spiritual experience, an intellectual experience. It can be deep or it can be superficial.

This section surveys some of the ways in which transitional reconciliation has been manifested throughout the world in recent years. The vast majority of transitional justice literature and practice focuses on national reconciliation; indeed, several countries have given their transitional governments the moniker "national reconciliation."[1] And yet, that is by no means the only level of society at which reconciliation can or should occur. There can be reconciliation at the level of the individual who strives to reconcile himself or herself to an event. There can be interpersonal reconciliation, as between a victim and a perpetrator of political violence; here, the aim might be anything from avoidance of revenge to the emergence of true friendship. Reconciliation might also occur within or among communities that constitute civil society. At the national level, the government is likely to be the major actor. Increasingly, attention is being paid to international reconciliation. When reconciliation involves greater numbers of people, it usually involves a process—events converging over a period of time, sometimes generations. These are clearly the more complex versions of reconciliation. At these broader levels, some individuals or subgroups may be reconciled while others are not, and it is often far more difficult to discern whether or not reconciliation has actually happened.

With so many intertwined alternatives, societies embarking on reconciliation projects need to specify the level at which they aim their reconciliation efforts. Transitional societies have notoriously little capital—they lack financial resources, and their people may lack patience. Reconciliation programs must therefore be well targeted to the specific problems of the society so that the country's limited resources are not wasted. A national reconciliation commission may not promote reconciliation at the communal or individual level; conversely, funding trauma centers may not promote political or national reconciliation. In Rwanda, for instance, almost every village was scarred by the 1994 genocide because in virtually every village neighbors terrorized neighbors. Rwanda's reconstructive program therefore, must at the very least include an element of communal reconciliation. By contrast, in Latin America, most of the damage was done by governments against their people. The same can be said of South Africa, where the policy of apartheid segregated people by race into separate towns and villages. Here, the major thrust of reconciliation efforts should be at the national level, with an eye toward fortifying the bonds of national identity.

In many parts of the world, from the Horn of Africa to the Pacific Islands to the Balkans, violence is both intracommunal and intercommunal: members of one community take up arms against their neighbors in their own and then in neighboring areas. Less violent but nonetheless pernicious would be the spying that took place throughout much of the Soviet bloc, especially in East Germany. Here, bilateral and communal reconciliation may be an appropriate focus, as the main problem may be seen to be the rebuilding of modes of life that permit people to live side by side. Many countries—perhaps the worst situations—find multiple levels of abuse operating simultaneously. In the former Yugoslavia, in Rwanda, and in Iraq under Saddam Hussein, the government orchestrated mass violations of human rights, so that violence took place between friends and neighbors as well as between citizens and their government. The genocide in Rwanda in particular was not carried out by individuals in the employ of the state or working for the state in any meaningful way, but it was certainly at the behest of state officials and as part of a deliberate government policy to exterminate a large portion of the Rwandan population.[2] A twist on this was the policy of the South African government to support the Inkatha Freedom Party's violent attacks against the African National Congress, in order to promote rivalry between the two groups. This national policy resulted in the deaths of 16,000 people between 1990 and 1994 alone.[3] Reconciliation in South Africa, then, must take place at the national level, as well as within the communities that were most scarred by apartheid. These examples provide access points, or ways to get into the culture to promote change. And the question in each case is which access point or points will be most effective for promoting reconciliation.

We begin with the individual level, the smallest unit recognized in society, where, as Jorge Sutil Correa says, men and women try to reconcile themselves as people.

Political conflict engenders a wide range of personal traumas. In the aftermath of political conflict, people might be dealing with the horror of discrete events such as a rape or the loss of a loved one, or with an ongoing condition, such as imprisonment, an act or repeated acts of torture, displacement, or famine or disease caused by political upheaval, or long-term fear as when people live under totalitarianism or the authority of warlords or unregulated militias. The trauma might be inflicted on the survivor herself or on others whom she loved or whose trauma she witnessed. In these situations, feelings of guilt, helplessness, or inadequacy might be just as strong and debilitating as if the survivor had endured the physical pains herself. Most conflicts involve multiple hardships, and survivors must reconcile themselves to some or all of them.

Trauma is often experienced as a break, a rupture, a shattering. "These fragments I have shored against my ruins," wrote T. S. Eliot in *The Wasteland.* In Cambodia, evil is symbolized as *armbaeg,* shards of broken glass.[4] Pumla Gobodo-Madikizela describes one South African woman's experience of losing her eleven-year-old boy: "The pieces of that fateful day were shattered, like broken china that can not be put back together."[5] "The image," she writes, "is of a broken person trying helplessly, not altogether with success, to recover some sense of coherence in an inner world that has become broken, a world where the ever-present trauma refuses to be silenced, to be buried under the grass," to use the Xhosa phrase.[6] Sometimes this rupture is explicit. One East Timorese woman, recounting prolonged torture and sexual enslavement over a period of ten years, testified that she told herself: "Okay, I'll cut myself in half. The lower half I'll give to him, but the upper half is for my land, the land of Timor."[7] In

South Africa, a woman tells a story of torture during the apartheid years. She describes the torture, the room, the people. She says that to survive, she imagined that her soul had left her body; she placed it in a corner of the room, so that it would not be touched by the atrocities being visited upon her body. But then she left it there. Telling the story to the South African Truth Commission, she said, she never went back to get her soul. To reconcile oneself to a traumatic event is to begin to put the pieces back together, to become whole again.

Personal reconciliation is a process of making two seemingly incompatible things fit together: the survivor's knowledge of the traumatic event and her values and perceptions of the world that she held before the trauma. What makes an event traumatic is the inconsistency between these two. A person seeking to reconcile herself to an event needs "to develop a new mental schema for understanding what has happened."[8] Kader Asmal, Louise Asmal, and Ronald Suresh Roberts define reconciliation as making "inevitable and continuing conflicts and differences stand at least within a single universe of comprehensibility."[9]

In one sense, individual reconciliation is a deeply personal affair, often with no visible external effects.[10] Unlike reconciliation at other levels, individual reconciliation is less often an affirmative event than the absence of a negative event, the vitiation of the impact of the trauma. It might be something that no one else notices, realizes or understands either wholly or in part. In fact, the victim might not notice or realize what she is going through herself; she might only notice afterwards that it has happened—that at some point the nightmares have abated, the pull of the memories has weakened, the fear of recurrence has dissipated.

But individual psychological injury often has external effects as well. Abundant literature on post-traumatic stress syndrome indicates that individuals who have been traumatized by an event or by a series of events are more prone to destructive behaviors. Trauma survivors who have not healed are less likely to be positive role models for children or peers; they may be more prone to violence, antisocial behavior, or alcohol or drug abuse; they may have more difficulty discharging responsibilities or taking on new ones. In places where the trauma is widespread and the effects are ongoing, the societal effects can be devastating. One survey in Cambodia found that fully 28 percent of the population suffer from symptoms commonly associated with post-traumatic stress syndrome; it is necessary to wonder whether the traumatic stress syndrome is really "post," or whether the trauma is in some sense still ongoing.[11] In these situations, one must ask, what is the normal track that reconciliation is meant to get a person back on? What are people reconciling themselves to?

Because individuals are the fundamental elements of society, pervasive trauma throughout a population can impede the reconstruction of the nation at every other level. In other words, good national health depends on individual healing. It is incumbent on new governments, then, to foster individual reconciliation when personal trauma is widespread; failure to do so can impede national reconciliation and reconstruction.

And yet, widespread individual healing is difficult to achieve. First, it requires significant outlay of resources because of the need for highly trained personnel. Second, it requires individualized assessment because each individual responds differently to trauma and to treatment. Third, it can be significantly hampered by external factors over which the government has little or no control, including family stability and other support apparatus, employment opportunities, the physical health of the individual, and so on.

Reconciliation as Healing

The medical metaphor of healing is pervasive throughout the reconciliation literature, but most emphatic in the context of individual reconciliation.[12] Individual reconciliation is about healing the physical and psychological wounds of trauma. Victims of trauma, it is said, rarely heal on their own, or at least not as fully or as quickly as they would with professional treatment. Consequently, current trends in the literature of the psychology of trauma emphasize the importance of *some* intervention.

But intervention programs must be as varied as the individuals involved: some may need an elaborate and individualized course of treatment, while others may need little psychological assistance. In fact, some individuals may rightly believe that they would be better off with no intervention at all.[13] Governments aiming to promote individual reconciliation need not resolve this issue, but should recognize that individual response to trauma may be infinitely varied. No single program can be expected to help everyone at all or to the same extent. And no program should be coercive: survivors should be welcome to participate in a program on their own terms and at their own pace, or not at all. Mandatory programs may reinforce the feelings of helplessness and lack of free will engendered by the original trauma.

Even within the group that would benefit from some form of intervention, there exists a wide range of appropriate programs. In many of the world's industrialized nations, individual therapy is the preferred method of psychological healing.[14] According to the therapy model, most trauma survivors need to understand the past thoroughly in order to move forward. Many psychologists believe that what is said at the historical level—that those who do not remember the past are condemned to repeat it—is true at the personal level as well. This form of traditional therapy entails a sustained and carefully developed course of treatment that often helps the survivor to navigate through the minefields of the traumatic experiences. Only once that course has been pursued can the survivor feel well enough to reconnect with others and eventually contribute to society. Other forms of therapy may be more forward-looking, emphasizing present empowerment and future goals instead of past trauma. These models may entail peer support groups, skills enhancement, behavior modification, and other kinds of what the South African TRC called "capacity-building" mechanisms.

In either event, survivors of mass violence may require two related but distinct kinds of healing.[15] The simplest level may be cognitive: they need to understand what happened to them. Although they experienced a personal trauma, their experience was in the context of larger political violence which many victims don't fully comprehend. This is especially true where the victims are children or are chosen randomly or where they are used as pawns by political forces.[16] For instance, in Australia, many aboriginals did not understand that their personal experience of being taken away from their families was part of Australia's policy of purging itself of the aborigines.[17] Cognitive healing is also important where the perpetrators maintained secrecy about the fate of victims. In Latin America, a principal form of violence was to cause people to "disappear," and the fate of many *desparecidos* remains unknown to this day.[18] Hamber and Wilson describe this as an "ontological uncertainty among survivors and a psychological experience of what Freud termed the *uncanny*."[19] This phenomenon, they argue, is common among "survivors who must mourn without a corpse: The uncanny feeds on uncertainty (Is he/she alive? Is he/she dead?) Both the survivor and the dead inhabit a symbolically liminal social space. Both are part of society but removed from society."[20] Cognitive healing entails obtaining information about the political context in which the individual crimes occurred and specific details about the fate of individual victims. This can have major benefits for the healing process of the individual because it removes the haunting doubt and sense of isolation that often accompanies ongoing psychological stress. Cognitive healing alleviates the burden of feeling that one has to bear the brunt of the violation on one's own.

The more complex kind of healing is psychological. Survivors of trauma and other types of political violence suffer from a huge range of psychological maladies. These may include fears that manifest themselves in nightmares, hyperarousal, and mood swings that oscillate between controlling and withdrawal; disconnection from society at large and from formerly close friends and family in particular; feelings of worthlessness and insignificance. Often these are direct results of deliberate efforts by torturers and other perpetrators of abuse to dehumanize people, to weaken their personality, and to diminish their sense of dignity. This lack of self-esteem in the aftermath of trauma is likely to have material consequences for the survivor, who may be less able to function productively at a job or in a social setting or even in the day-to-day obligations of caring for a family. Survivors are also often confused by the conflicting desires simultaneously to forget the trauma and hold onto it. Holding on may seem counterintuitive, but many survivors need to retain the reality of the trauma, sometimes just long enough to make sense of it, but sometimes longer, because it has become a part of their self-identity.

The themes of cognitive and psychological healing permeate the psychological literature of trauma studies, although relatively little attention has been paid to the overlap between personal healing and political reconciliation. Maria Ericson has identified a number of psychological issues that arise in conflict situations, such as the destruction of the victim's fundamental assumptions about the safety of the world, the positive value of the self, deep animosity and distrust of others, as well as experiences of separation and inequality, which deepen as parties to the conflict compete for political or economic dominance. In order to address all these, she proposes various interventions, including

- The establishment of safety, including bodily integrity, basic health needs, safe living conditions, financial security, mobility, a plan for self-protection, safe and reliable relationships, and social support.
- Remembrance and mourning, telling the story of one's trauma.
- Reconnection with ordinary life. This includes taking steps toward empowerment to protect oneself against future danger, as well as engagement with particular individuals and pursuing justice in the form of holding perpetrators accountable. It also includes recognizing the gender dimension of the process of mourning.[21]

While these interventions are designed to help individuals heal, they also help to promote social reconciliation, which Ericson defines as "the establishment of a positive and sustainable peace between people involved in armed conflict."[22]

Psychologist Judith Herman has likewise focused on the same three stages of safety, remembrance and mourning, and reconnection, although her work focuses on trauma outside the political context.[23] The confluence of the psychological and the political is clear: aspects of political reconciliation virtually permeate all three stages of psychological healing. It may be useful, then, to understand individual reconciliation in terms of these stages, laid across a political landscape.

The three stages of recovery marked by both Herman and Ericson provide some clues as to how government can assist in the recovery and healing of individuals. One important caveat is that the three stages may occur at different times or at varying degrees in different individuals. A therapist with a single patient recovering from a particular trauma can calibrate the stages to correspond to the needs of her individual patient; a national government cannot calibrate its response to correspond to individual needs and must therefore design its program to permit each individual to move through the stages according to his or her own time frame.

Safety. The first stage has two basic components. First, there must be actual physical safety enhanced by the *feeling* of physical safety: the survivor must feel that there is no reasonable likelihood of the trauma recurring. This feeling of safety not only serves to ameliorate the most extreme symptoms of stress, including hypersensitivity and fear, but also provides a safe space in which the survivor can heal. Safety thus has physical as well as psychological aspects. Second, the safe space helps the survivor shift from vulnerability to control. She must begin to feel that she is more in control of her own body, and of her life. This is a necessary precondition to the process of healing.

In indigenous cultures, reintegration ceremonies can signify the safety of the community, but national governments can also help establish and promote safety in a number of ways. One is to publicly allay fears through public announcements and formal campaigns that deter would-be violators. Obviously, public statements need to be backed up by concrete action. A ceasefire ending hostilities that is *in fact* adhered to can restore calm and allay fears to some extent. Deploying law enforcement officials—whether local police, military, or UN peacekeepers—can make real the promise of a ceasefire. Arrests and detention of those suspected of committing crimes and successful prosecution of wrongdoers can promote the twin aims of actually separating the perpetrators from the rest of society, and of communicating the message that human rights abuses will no longer be tolerated. These strategies are necessary to reinforce the feeling of safety that survivors need.

To attain these goals, law enforcement officials must avoid committing human rights abuses of their own and must be committed to the promotion of safety. If the policy or its implementation is perceived to be only partially available, the process of reconciliation will suffer severely. It is the job of government to prevent that from happening. In states recovering from war and political trauma, that job is nonderogable, since the health of the population, and ultimately of the nation, depends on it. The national government should ensure that local law enforcement officials are capable of adhering to these standards and should call in international peacekeepers where the local police do not have this capability.

Achieving these goals can have a significant impact of the level of human rights within a society. As Hamber and van der Merwe explain, "reconciliation is seen as a process which can only be achieved by regulating social interaction through the rule of law and preventing certain forms of violations of rights from happening again."[24] Indeed, transitions are most likely to be successful where the feeling exists that turning back is impossible. This occurred in South Africa when apartheid was being dismantled and in many European countries in the late 1980s and early 1990s when Soviet control was crumbling. South Africa, after the election of Nelson Mandela, enjoyed a decline in political violence in most areas of the country, in large part because continuing to fight to maintain the status quo ante clearly seemed futile.[25] Critically, victims who were inclined to speak out against the former regime could do so without fear of reprisal from the white establishment, and those who had suffered at the hands of the apartheid forces could feel the threat waning.

The provision of basic needs is another aspect of physical safety. The government must ensure, at the very least, that basic needs, such as food, water, shelter, sanitation, medical care, and counseling, are being met. The relationship between reconciliation and economic interests will be examined in greater detail in a later chapter; but for present purposes, it suffices to note that material deprivation can indeed impair efforts to promote reconciliation. As Graeme Simpson has noted, " We can rebuild the social fabric and negotiate political settlements; but unless we meet people's economic needs, those agreements are worth very little."[26] Just as a newly democratic government's provision of services and goods can promote reconciliation, failing to do so may significantly impede it. In addition to the physical harms that directly result from hunger, exhaustion, and disease, many individuals may feel further depressed both by their inability to provide for themselves and their families and by their own lack of energy. Such depression in turn increases the risk of destructive and violent behavior. Moreover, it is worth considering dispute resolution as a distinct basic need. Laurie Nathan has argued that "conflict management is the essential, on-going business of governance," because where governmental institutions "lack the capacity to regulate competition and resolve disputes and grievances, individuals and groups may fulfil the functions through violence."[27]

A government's failure to satisfy the people's basic needs also creates a vacuum that opposition groups can exploit to destabilize a fragile government. In some cases, basic needs are provided by charities. But not all charities are beyond reproach. Some are ideologically committed to certain values that impede reconciliation, and to the extent that individuals rely on these organizations, their own efforts to move beyond the trauma and divisions of the past may be thwarted. In some situations, militias and even terrorist groups can provide food, shelter, or medical care more effectively than the government. Hamas and Hezbollah are classic examples of this phenomenon, as are warlords who continue to wield power throughout Afghanistan outside the capital.

The consequences of this dependence on illegitimate groups are deleterious to individual healing and to social reconciliation for several reasons. First, the conditions that the group may impose on access to necessary services might further traumatize or humiliate those people who are in need. Often the provision of these services by these types of groups ensures dependency and patronage and impedes social cohesion. Second, provision of services by illegitimate groups may nurture allegiances and loyalty to the factions which should have been directed to the central government. Having these basic needs met by the government on an even-handed and nonpartisan basis, on the other hand, can contribute to the sense of control and empowerment that is necessary for healing to begin.

While establishing a safe environment is, as Herman says, one aspect of promoting safety, another is helping survivors develop a feeling of control. Herman explains that "naming the problem" is a critical part of healing. Here, the government can help by acknowledging the human rights violations of the past and by designating them as such, rather than condoning or ignoring them. Acknowledgment should extend not just to the wrongs committed by a predecessor government or opposition groups, but to the new regime's own wrongdoings. A government that takes responsibility for the wrongs it has committed against its citizens will promote individual empowerment and will contribute to the sense of no-return, the thick line between the previous regime and the present one. (Acknowledgment is discussed in Chapter 6.)

Another aspect of naming the problem is making it safe for citizens to report the crimes or horrors that they witnessed or endured. Governments need to allocate resources to sufficiently and independently investigating crimes of the past. Far too often this is not given the priority it should have. Moreover, many police investigators may not have the political will, proper training, or sensitivity to help a victim feel empowered to tell his or her story; this failure reinforces the power dynamic that created the trauma in the first place, to the detriment of the individual and the society as a whole. Governments seeking to promote individual reconciliation should invest resources into training police and other investigators to be effective recipients of traumatic information. This is particularly true where the trauma is sexualized.

Sometimes complex problems can be solved, or at least ameliorated, in surprisingly simple ways. Herman recounts an effort to help Norwegians who had been shipwrecked. The counselors handed out a fact sheet that contained two reminders at the bottom of the page: resist the urge to withdraw by talking to people about what happened, and don't depend on alcohol. What was striking was how many people carried the paper around in their wallets with them as constant reminders, even years after the event.[28] In most transitional situations, a public education campaign (if it is backed up by reality) can also help people feel more safe and more in control of their environment and of their lives. Information and advice should be directed not only to the survivors but to family and supporters of individuals who are trying to cope with trauma.

Mourning and remembrance. The second stage toward healing is mourning and remembrance. Nations in transition are only now beginning to understand the importance of dealing with the past. By contrast, the vast majority (if not the entirety) of psychological literature has insisted for a century that remembering the past is a necessary precondition for healing. The extreme pain, helplessness, vulnerability, and sense of betrayal that characterize trauma are so inconsistent with the experiences and values that develop over a lifetime that the event stands apart and disconnected from the trajectory of the person's life. Hence the breaking and shattering metaphors. Going back to the point of rupture, this time from a position of strength and safety, is necessary to give continuity to a person's life story. In this light, recovery itself is the process of reconciling the trauma with the rest of the person's life. Perhaps we shouldn't say "I've reconciled myself to this trauma" as much as "I've reconciled this trauma to myself." The goal is to create a "whole" self that incorporates the traumatic event.

Without this recovery or reconciliation, the two realities of the survivor's life lie in tension with one another—the trauma narrative in which evil prevails over good and in which the survivor deserves the punishment, and the healing narrative, in which friends and family can be trusted and evil is punished. A new reality needs to be constructed that reflects the principal values of the survivor, but that can also accommodate the traumatic event. The question in this model, then, is not whether to deal with the past, but how.

In many non-Western cultures, rites of transition assist in the development of a fluid life story. This can be seen particularly in the reintegration of individuals into their villages after a war or other crisis. (These are further discussed in the next chapter.) These rites allow the person to come back into the village, while in some symbolic way, leaving behind the offenses or traumas committed or endured in the past. Few of these transitions involve talking, and in some sense talking is even viewed as counterproductive; as long as the person is "cleansed," there is little need to discuss what happened.[29] One study of the truth-telling processes in Sierra Leone suggests that "indigenous purification and reintegration rituals . . . may be more appropriate to reconciliation" because "the unbearable truth of atrocities [is] partially eclipsed by the more palatable truth of remorse and desires for peace."[30]

For many prominent Western theorists, however, stories or narratives are the key to unlocking trauma. Lesley Fordred notes that by narrating events, "we link a series of actions—whether by chronology, conspiracy or psychological predisposition—into a comprehensible framework."[31] In this way, she says, "the violent event that has radically disrupted the flow of normality appears to have been predictable, and the moment of chaos that has challenged order is tamed."[32] Ben Okri has urged that when "we have made an experience or a chaos into a story we have transformed it, made sense of it, transmuted experience, domesticated the chaos."[33]

Judith Herman too notes that the "fundamental premise of the psychotherapeutic works is a belief in the restorative power of truth-telling."[34] Victims are typically silenced by their relative disempowerment at the hands of the perpetrator. In private crimes, the perpetrator often couples the crime with a threat against the victim if the truth is ever disclosed. In political crimes, the victim is silenced as well. Sometimes the threat is explicit, as when Siberian prisoners were allowed to return home on the condition that they never speak about it, publicly or privately. And the secrets were kept up through the end of the communist era, and even beyond. In other situations, the threat need not be explicit. If the dominant ideology does not recognize or accept the fact of political crimes, effective disclosure is all but impossible. No one would believe the survivors if they ever tried to tell what happened. The perpetrator, of course, benefits from the silence, both because it further disempowers the victim and because it protects against arrest. The secret is safe so long as the victim feels victimized and therefore silenced.

There may be sound physiological reasons for the emphasis on the healing power of words as well as a political explanation. Some psychologists believe that traumatic memory gets recorded nonverbally, that trauma inactivates the linguistic encoding of memory.[35] When trauma occurs, it is as a neurological matter, unspeakable, or too horrible to talk about; we are literally at a loss for words; the pain is indescribable. One South African woman, describing her son's time with his mutilated father, said he "saw his father in the worst and most unspeakable state of death."[36] There are stories of people who are so traumatized that they lose the ability to speak, not only about the event but about anything, and become mute for days, weeks, even months.[37] Victims are silenced politically because there are literally no words to describe what happened. Nomonde Calata, a South African whose husband was killed by the apartheid police when she was pregnant with their daughter, recounts the impossibility of communicating anything to her daughter about the girl's father. "It is hard to explain to her. At times, she comes and says, 'Can't you draw a picture for me? Can you say something that he said?' That is very, very hard." Retelling this, Alex Boraine writes that "The inexpressability of pain stops history in its tracks."[38]

The cure for trauma, then, is speech, both oral and written.[39] This "talking cure" transforms the trauma from a wordless memory into a story that the survivor can understand and ultimately own. Indeed, "the *physioneurosis* induced by terror"—that is, the wordlessness that is the physiological mark of terror or trauma—"can apparently be reversed through the use of words."[40]Thus recounting the terror through words can itself promote healing. (When art or other nonverbal communication is used, it is often integrated into the verbal reconstruction of the trauma.) The goal of recounting the trauma story, according to Herman, is "integration, not exorcism." That is, individual reconciliation is not a purging of the horrible event, but the integration, or reconciliation, of that event into the person's life story. Putting the pieces back together.[41]

To be healed or reconciled, is to *come to terms* with the trauma, literally to find the words. Telling a story breaks the spell of silence imposed by the perpetrator on the victim. Truth telling can reverse the disempowerment because, in the telling, it becomes the survivor's own story which she can tell in her own words, in her own way. She describes the events as *she* saw and experienced them, and describes the perpetrator not as he would like to be portrayed but as *she* saw him. Writing stories has also been found to be effective in promoting individual reconciliation, particularly when the survivors are encouraged to write not just about the factual events that happened but about their emotional responses to those events as well.[42] Therapy through "structured writing" promotes "the assimilation of traumatic memories through the transduction of sensory, affective, disorganized memories into a linguistic, coherent representation."[43]

To assist in healing is to facilitate the telling of the story: to give survivors the space in which they can speak, to listen to them, to empathize with their story. The importance of listening to the process of healing cannot be overstated. "Perhaps we should begin by being silent and listening because we do not have the first word in this matter. The victims are the only ones who can begin the dialogue when they are ready to speak," writes Jennifer Balint.[44]

But the curative powers of story-telling should not be overstated, especially in the context of extreme political violence. Something is lost when traumatic memory is converted into coherent language. Victims and survivors often "frame their testimonies in language that they themselves find inadequate to describe their experiences."[45] Language communicates, but at the same time, "it distances us from the traumatic event as it was experienced, limiting our participation in the act of remembering."[46] Even the word "violence" obscures "the reality of knives cutting through flesh, of warm blood on the pavement, of children screaming, of pain, fear, and agony."[47] Because of this, there is a sense in which "what is remembered amounts to fragments of fact, a *re*construction of past events [that] fails to rise to the level of truth."[48] This gap, this *décalage*, between experience and language should not be taken to mean that the testimony is untrue in any sense; rather it is incomplete, inadequate. Describing the testimony of victims before Sierra Leone's truth commission, Tim Kelsall writes, "Dismal though most testimonies were, what was perhaps most striking about them was not how much, but how little they seemed to move the Commissioners, the audience, or indeed myself."[49]

By telling the story, in making the trauma conform to language, the survivor loses something of herself, the part of her that was defined by the formless trauma. By hearing the story, the community may begin to understand the impact of the trauma on the survivor but it should not be soothed into thinking that it knows what really happened, how it felt, how it was experienced by the survivor or the victim. What is communicated, then, is not the traumatic event, and not even what Gobodo-Madikizela calls the survivor's "lived experience of traumatic memory,"[50] but the verbal surrogate for the lived experience of the traumatic memory. Because of the spillage that occurs in the recounting, talking must be very carefully managed if it is to serve as an effective therapy for individuals and constitute an important element of community and national healing.

Truth-telling provides perhaps the best illustration of how the individual and national reconciliation models track one another. The same elements recur whether we are talking about a survivor working with a therapist or the development of a historical narrative. Herman, for instance, describes the "flooding" technique used by the United States Veterans' Administration to help combat veterans recover from wartime trauma. The veteran tells the story of each incident of trauma in a very scripted manner. The script, according to Herman, includes the four elements of context, fact, emotion, and meaning. These correspond very nearly to the four types of truth identified by the South African Truth and Reconciliation Commission: social, factual, personal, and healing or restorative truth.[51]

At either level, the interplay between the victim and the larger community is implicit in these four elements. While it is the victim's story, he may contribute only part of the information necessary to make the story complete. He will certainly contribute the personal or emotional elements of the story, including what happened to him and how he felt about it at the time and since. But a complete understanding of the story may require mining other sources. The government may be able to provide a fuller picture of the social context, including, for instance, the extent to which others shared the same trauma, or information about the political context in which the trauma occurred. In many cases, governments' propensity to destroy documents impedes this effort.[52] This limits the ability of victims to find out about specific events and who was involved in what.

One counterexample is in Germany, where victims have had access to their Stasi files.[53] Willing witnesses who have embraced the cause of reconciliation may also fill out the picture of the context of the survivor's experience. Government or private investigators may be able to provide factual or forensic information, including for instance what happened to those who "disappeared" or who "accidentally" died in custody.[54]

The last element—meaning or healing or restorative truth—may be the most challenging if only because it cannot be readily ascertained from a single source. This dialectic element needs to be developed over time, from a constellation of perspectives. This is perhaps what reconciliation commissions or ministries can do best. Only a significant policy initiative is capable of gathering all the other elements and putting them together in a way that gives meaning to the events for the survivor and for the society as a whole. A commission can provide the response to the witness that he needs in order to give his words meaning and can create the space in which other citizens understand and continue to learn from the events. Such a process encourages the society as a whole to listen, absorb, and begin the healing process that leads to reconciliation. A faulty process that opens up the wounds without providing the support necessary for reconciliation will lead only to renewed hostility. On the other hand, having no process at all may lead to social fragmentation, because the pain and anger may never find an outlet and may ferment until they erupt. Careful planning and preparation is crucial to ensure that the process achieves its aims and objectives.

Some basic principles should be heeded if the program is to be effective. First, survivors must be allowed to talk only on their own terms. No program that *requires* survivors to tell their stories can be therapeutic. They must be allowed to talk whenever they want, if at all. And they must be allowed to tell their story *how*ever they want—including whatever details seem important to them and leaving out details as they choose. Ideally, they should choose their idiom as well. Encouraging, coaxing, or guiding is useful, though insisting or directing or making the process mandatory is not.

Second, there must be room for emotional release and understanding. Survivors should be asked how they felt, what they saw, what hurt, and what they wanted. They should be allowed to tell their story entirely from their own point of view, without regard for the perspective of the perpetrators. (Police station recounting of rape events often presents the archetypal counter-example, where the talking may be forced and is more likely to be psychologically destructive than constructive to the victim, unless the listener is particularly sympathetic and the survivor's emotional state and privacy are respected. In most situations, however, telling the story of the rape repeats the trauma, because it reinforces the power dynamic of the rape itself: the victim is required to tell the story as the police want to hear it not as the victim experienced it.) Training is especially important here for investigators, statement-takers, and counselors.

Third, there must be a response to the recounting. A survivor can not be expected to tell this painful story into a black hole. Those who hear and bear witness to the story must be prepared to enhance, or at least not detract from, the survivor's continuing need for safety and vindication. This may include helping the survivor to see some meaning in the trauma, perhaps by placing the trauma in the larger context of the political strife or even by helping her understand the motivations of the perpetrators, or by reaffirming the victim's dignity notwithstanding the trauma.

This is a particularly tricky area, both in individual therapy and in national reconciliation. In both cases, the audiences—the ones who receive the information and respond to it—have to decide where to place themselves on the continuum from complete neutrality to vindication of the survivor's experience. In the context of gross human rights abuses, the moral quandary is minimal: there is no justification for human rights abuses, and adamant condemnation of such behavior is necessary not only to vindicate and support the survivor but to promote the other goals of national reconciliation, including establishing respect for the rule of law and promoting a culture of respect for human rights. The nation must, in the words of Judith Herman, "affirm a position of moral solidarity with the survivor."[55] On the other hand, a public entity condemning the actions of its constituent members puts itself in a political quandary: to do so without any concern at all for their reaction is to court revenge and possibly to retard the cause of reconciliation. South Africa, for instance, tried to hold the balance between solidarity with the victims and condemnation of the perpetrators in part by having the TRC examine, without condoning, the actions and motivations of the perpetrators.[56] In this way, personal and national narratives were developed in tandem.

Reconnection. The third stage of the healing process identified by both Herman and Ericson is reconnection. The conventional wisdom is that individual reconciliation requires a reconnection between the survivor and the perpetrator.[57] In this view, healing is contingent on the propensity of the perpetrator to show remorse or seek forgiveness. This view, however, is increasingly being challenged, both by survivors and by the psychologists who study them. Albie Sachs, the South African anti-apartheid jurist who was a victim of political violence, argues that reconciliation doesn't require each victim to forgive each perpetrator, nor perpetrators to apologize nor the parties to embrace. That is asking too much, he says, and it is inappropriate.

To Herman, psychological healing or reconciling oneself to a traumatic past involves the perpetrator even less than Sachs's model. The survivor's "healing depends on the discovery of restorative love in her own life; it does not require that this love be extended to the perpetrator."[58] The reconnection that is the culmination of the healing or reconciliation process is a restorative love between the survivor and her social network of family and friends and the local community. The perpetrator is entirely outside this web. The survivor can be said to be healed once she has successfully excluded the perpetrator from her world, when she no longer seeks remorse or atonement or compensation or even vengeance. In fact, pining for some measure of justice from the perpetrator is in most cases futile because so few perpetrators comply; in too many cases there simply is no justice, no compensation for the harm done. Hoping for something from the perpetrator is also counterproductive: so long as the survivor is focused on the perpetrator, she continues to be defined by the trauma. Once she releases the perpetrator, she is free to move on.[59] Or, as the native American maxim goes, "You must learn the wisdom of how to let go of poison."[60]

"Paradoxically," Herman writes, "the patient may liberate herself from the perpetrator when she renounces the hope of getting any compensation from him."[61] At this point, the perpetrator becomes "uninteresting" to the survivor, even boring. "She may even feel sorrow and compassion for [the perpetrator], but this disengaged feeling is not the same as forgiveness."[62] Harold Kushner recounts in *The Sunflower* that his advice to a woman whose husband had abandoned her is to forgive, not because what he did was acceptable but because "he doesn't deserve the power to live in your head and turn you into a bitter, angry woman."[63]

While the survivor needs to let go of the perpetrator, recovery is marked by the extent to which she reconnects with her social milieu. This is especially true for survivors from certain cultures that highly value the community. "Most refugees and torture survivors came from collective cultures. Connectedness used to be, in their culture, the major natural source of support and healing. These people mostly come from collective cultures that value social bonds more than individualistic enterprises. Collective identity is as strong as if not stronger than personal identity in such cultures."[64]

In too many instances, a survivor is shunned not despite his or her ordeal but because of it. This is particularly true with rape victims, but it might be true in many other instances as well. A torture victim who provided information to his captors might be ostracized upon his release if his information in fact did or was perceived to have resulted in harm to others. A child who was impressed into military service might be alienated when he tries to return home. The victim's natural inclination to withdraw is compounded by the community's inclination to ostracize. Most successful therapy addresses this need. Indeed, most traditional village-based rituals recognized the importance of reintegration, and new therapeutic models of treatment are beginning to emphasize this as well. The "wrap-around approach," for instance, is a "holistic/comprehensive community-based process of service delivery . . . based on the principles of unconditional care and community support. Community, in this context, includes the refugee community to whom torture survivors belong and the new community of resettlement that includes majority and minority groups."[65] The wraparound approach has been used successfully in the aftermath of mass violence. Like Western versions of "support groups," post-conflict healing methods may provide survivors with access to each other, so that they can talk not publicly but among themselves and provide support for each other. This may also promote personal reconciliation, because there may be many stories that victims are willing to tell each other, that they might not be willing to share with the nation or the world. But these kinds of tellings have no less cathartic power, and to the extent that they are unrehearsed and spontaneous, they have at least as much healing power.

Often, victims are angrier at those who they feel betrayed them than at the perpetrators themselves.[66] Individual reconciliation programs need to enable the survivor to tell the community how he feels about his betrayal at their hands and give the community a chance to hear his story and perhaps even to atone for its failure to protect him. Without this entrée, the disconnection that many survivors feel can make reintegration and community-building even more difficult. Individual reconciliation is therefore necessary as a component of community reconciliation as well. (The reintegration of individuals in their communities is further examined in the next chapter.) Individuals who are traumatized and unhealed must still function in the world. The most effective programs will help individuals in their interactions with others. One counseling service operating in Namibia is attempting "to help our clients become aware of the way in which their own behaviour is linked to the social and financial problems that they are experiencing. The manner in which they attempt to cope with the traumatic experiences that they have undergone often results in self-destructive or self-defeating behaviour, or behaviour that has a negative social impact."[67] Efforts like these may be promoted by NGOs as well as by governmental agencies.

It is imperative that national governments do what they can to promote individual healing; it is not a purely private matter that governments can afford to leave to the vagaries of market forces. Healing traumatized or estranged individuals will undoubtedly enhance their contributions to the life of the nation and will reduce their dependence on the public fisc. The recommendations for reparations from the South African TRC included the requirement that the reparations efforts be "capacity-building," implicitly recognizing the importance to the nation of healthy individual constituents.

In particular, governments need to recognize that while individual healing is a precondition to good national health, the converse is not necessarily true: national reconciliation may have no effect at all on the health of individuals. The challenge is therefore on the government to develop mechanisms that will actually help individuals recover from the effects of political violence. Conciliatory acts by the national government may trickle down to the individual level, but only if they are done in public, with genuine commitment, and as part of a pattern of mutually reinforcing conciliatory acts. National acts must resonate even with those who do not participate.

In addition to indirect public acts of conciliation, there are many things governments can do to succor traumatized individuals derictly. Governments should fund the organizations that provide direct assistance to survivors. Transitional governments should earmark part of their budget for trauma or counseling centers in communities throughout the affected areas to ensure that as many people as possible who need psychological counseling receive it.

In the wake of the Chilean truth commission, a National Corporation for Reparation and Reconciliation was established to provide victims and their families medical and educational benefits, specialized psychosocial services for victims of torture, and financial reparations including a special pension. In Israel, the government pays for the psychological counseling for life of all victims of political violence. Israel, of course, has far more resources and comparatively fewer victims of political violence than many transitional nations; nonetheless, all nations should recognize that access to psychological services is of the utmost importance to individuals and to the nation as a whole.

Certain rituals and ceremonies may also have significant salutary effects. A systematic program of exhumations may be necessary for individuals whose loved ones disappeared or were killed covertly. Exhumations that are conducted under the aegis of the government are more likely to promote reconciliation than government resistance to calls to literally uncover the truth. Likewise, the facilitation of funeral rituals may have both emotional and social significance to the survivors: in addition to the feeling of closure that accompanies them, such rites may also permit widows to remarry or sons to accede to the status of head of the family as may be necessary for community acceptance and reintegration.[68]

Nations that are more far-sighted should consider funding not just primary care facilities but research institutions as well, to help the population better understand the nature and effects of political violence. It is particularly important to have research on psychological trauma that is specific to the country: the way Cambodians experienced the trauma of the Khmer Rouge is different from the way ethnic Albanians experienced the war in Kosovo, and more research needs to be conducted into the particularities of social context.

Governments can also fund, endorse, and support public education campaigns, as the new government of Bosnia and Herzegovina is trying to do. These may range from reminding people not to seek refuge in alcohol or drugs, to advising people about the availability of mental health centers, to encouraging people to talk to others about their emotions, to simply teaching about citizenship, democracy, and human rights. (Public education campaigns are discussed in more detail in the chapter on national reconciliation.)

Of all the things a government might do to promote individual reconciliation, truth commissions may turn out to be among the most effective. Many of these commissions are geared precisely toward the kinds of healing that are necessary to help individuals reconcile themselves to a traumatic event.

TRCs and Individual Reconciliation

It is not surprising that truth and reconciliation commissions have been identified as useful mechanisms for coming to terms with an atrocious past.[69] In fact, truth commissions have become so popular that they are imbued with all manner of transformative powers, only some of which can realistically be achieved, and then, for only some of the people.

Perhaps the strongest arguments that can be made in favor of truth commissions as abettors of individual healing are made in the negative. What happens in the absence of a truth commission? Failure to establish this kind of process may disregard the rights and views of victims, deny the need for a healing process, preclude recovery of the past, imagine that forgiveness can take place without full knowledge of whom and what to forgive, and fail to establish human rights values as the core standard for the future. Initially, it might be noted that most transitional governments have not historically acknowledged or responded to the fact of widespread psychological trauma. When the old regime was replaced, the new regime would simply announce the changes that had occurred, but would not provide the space in which individuals could try to understand what had happened. The turn toward truth commissions is one measure of recognition of the need for psychological healing.

Governments that do recognize the imperative of individual healing have tended to mimic the therapy-centered approach of Western Europe and the United States by supporting trauma centers or other mechanisms for psychological counseling. These methods permit individuals to talk and release the pain that they feel, but they provide no context or structure to help people understand what happened. The information flows from the individual out, but the survivor receives no cognitive or psychological support.

Postcommunist Germany provided an unusual variation on this. There, information did flow in both directions, but in ways that were parallel rather than interconnected: when the Stasi files were released, information flowed from the government to the people, giving them a chance to learn what had really happened during a forty-year period. Armed with this information, the people themselves created their own opportunities to talk, and talk, and talk. But because the government itself did not address the psychological impact of the release of the files, there were no sinews linking what the government had done with how people felt. The government and the people were speaking in mutually unintelligible languages, and sometimes even at cross-purposes: the government spoke of state security and control of dissidents and the people spoke of betrayal and vulnerability. A well-designed commission can integrate the government's perspective and the information it possesses with the experiences of private individuals, thus producing a cohesive narrative that encompasses both public history and private stories.

At their best—and they are getting better all the time—truth and reconciliation commissions promote healing at the individual level insofar as they are designed specifically to meet the psychological needs of trauma survivors. Those in operation in East Timor and in Ghana, for instance, were specifically charged with helping individuals reconnect with their communities. This may also explain why, by and large, reconciliation commissions are more likely than trials to help victims recover. Commissions focus on the feelings of the victims, while trials focus on the motivations of the perpetrators. Typically, victims have a very limited role in the criminal justice system and are sometimes excluded entirely. When victims pursue criminal justice, they delegate to the state their right to obtain redress or justice. But even in those rare instances when a trial results in a conviction and a lengthy prison sentence, the survivor's healing depends more on her own release than on the perpetrator's commitment.

Nonetheless, the two modalities are increasingly converging. Some courts have ordered perpetrators to pay damages or reparations to the victim. Because the payment is seen as acknowledgment, it can assist the recovery process. So far, these types of payments are still rare, though they could be used effectively in many more cases. On the other hand, there is a tendency of commissions to follow trial processes. The South African TRC and its progeny emphasize the connection between the victim and the perpetrator, particularly in the context of amnesty hearings. This model depends largely on the participation of the perpetrator to make amends, atone, show remorse, or at least come to the table to share information. Archbishop Tutu's begging Winnie Madikizela-Mandela to apologize for her crimes during a TRC hearing broadcast live epitomizes this tendency. On this account, atonement by perpetrators is necessary for victims to forgive.

As will be discussed in the next chapters, this is not necessarily a welcome development. It would be wise for governments developing reconciliation programs to follow the approach that Judith Herman has developed for individual reconciliation, focusing entirely on the victim's health, even at the expense of the perpetrator.

TRCs have the potential to promote both cognitive and psychological healing because they trade both in information and in emotional support, and do this in a way that embodies the two-way communication that is necessary for healing. It is now commonplace to recognize that, as has been said about the Sierra Leone Truth Commission, its "mandate has both fact-finding and therapeutic dimensions."[70]Through their investigations and hearings, TRCs can reveal information about the society's past to illuminate the context in which individual trauma occurred. They can also provide opportunities to survivors to explore and explain their own feelings and experiences. The exchange culminates in a permanent record of the public historic experiences of the nation and the private emotional experiences of the people. Through TRCs, victims across the political spectrum have a credible and legitimate forum through which to reclaim their human worth and dignity.

To provide the cognitive healing that is needed, a commission must be able to gather information. Many survivors feel that they cannot move forward unless they actually know what happened to their loved ones. This is especially true in cases where people were "disappeared" or died under suspicious circumstances. TRCs that have been most successful in obtaining information about the past have had extensive investigatory powers over materials that would be in the government's hands, including the power to hold hearings, subpoena individuals to testify, and subpoena documents. They might also have direct access to government officials pursuant either to legal authority or to the Commissioners' own personal authority. Commissions should also have financial resources to allocate to investigation. To the extent that they are independent, TRCs should have more inclination and more authority to pursue these sources than governmental ministries or departments. Moreover, commissions should have the means to learn from private individuals as well. They should have the legal and financial capacity to take statements from individuals throughout the country and, where appropriate, in foreign countries. They should be able to conduct their own investigations in order to corroborate stories told by survivors or perpetrators.

Some TRCs have focused on the role of certain sectors of society in promoting or mitigating the violence. The South African TRC held hearings on the role of the media, the churches, and the medical and legal professions, among others, in the perpetuation of human rights abuses under apartheid.[71] The Peruvian TRC examined the role of the educational system, the churches, and the trade unions, among others, in perpetuating or alleviating the violence during its mandate period.[72] In addition, governments have increasingly allowed exhumations to be conducted by truth commissions.

Most notably, commissions gather information from the victims and survivors themselves; victim stories are the stock in trade of most TRCs. The commission should provide a forum in which survivors can talk comfortably so that their stories can come out clearly and truly. The victim's story contributes to the narrative that the new regime is creating, and in so doing it promotes cognitive healing. In telling his side of the story, the survivor contributes the personal, narrative, and emotional components of the story; he is literally making history. Together with the other forms of truth—the forensic or scientific, the historical or contextual—the survivor and the commission can piece together a whole and coherent (even if morally reprehensible) story. A TRC can provide what can be called a new "mental schema" by providing the survivor with information that helps to explain what happened and why. For instance, Australia's policy of forcibly removing aboriginal children from their parents would seem like simple kidnaping from the perspective of the children and their parents; learning the political context in which it took places serves to explain, though not at all to excuse. It provides a backdrop in which events of immeasurable inhumanity can at least begin to be understood, though not condoned. Since victims of political violence have experienced first hand the excesses of the political regime, true reconciliation may be said to happen when the personal and the political are merged and understood as one multifaceted narrative.

In addition to cognitive healing, TRCs can also provide psychological healing to victims and survivors. One aspect of this is the tension between forgetting and remembering, or as people are wont to say, between too much forgetting and too much remembering. Priscilla Hayner begins her study of truth commissions by asking one survivor, "Do you want to remember, or to forget?"[73] But the question poses a false dichotomy. As her Rwandan interlocutor realizes, these choices provide no choice at all. The horror can't, and shouldn't be forgotten, lest it be repeated and probably for other reasons as well. But neither should it be remembered in its rawness and entirety: "we must forget the feelings, the emotions that go with it. It is only by forgetting that we are able to go on,"[74] he says wisely. As the experience in Germany with the release of the Stasi files showed, endless uncanalized talking does not necessarily yield the release that wounded people seek. Thus, if a new government wants to help survivors of trauma heal, it can promote talking but must do so in a careful and well-structured way.

Because they operate at both the national and the individual level, TRCs turn out to be very effective ways of providing context for memory and trauma. First, TRCs invert the power dynamic. By their very existence, TRCs prove that the balance of power has shifted and that she who was oppressed in the old dispensation is empowered in the new. As one deponent in the East Timor process said, "My small village is in the hills where you can't even drive a car. No leaders ever come to see us. But today, with the grace of God, the CAVR has opened a way for us women to come to the table and tell our stories to the nation."[75] Indeed, the Timorese process "gave victims a unique opportunity to speak directly to national leaders when National Commissioners asked them if they would like to give a message to the nation." Because the hearings were broadcast on television and radio, the "victims' words went into communities and homes throughout Timor-Leste. . . . The hearings therefore placed ordinary people at the centre of the national debate on healing, reconciliation and justice."[76]

Second, TRCs' ability to receive and disseminate information provides victims with the context they need to heal. The narrative that the TRC develops can form the framework for recognizing which parts of the traumatic memory should be retained for some future use, and which parts should be discarded because they simply carry with them too much pain and too little learning. The information can provide the context for understanding the meaning of the event, and this can help transform a victim into a survivor, in her own eyes. She can then face the events head-on, and remember them constructively, on terms that empower her, rather than as unwanted intrusions in the quiet of the night. To put it another way, the context provided by a TRC can help a victim return to the place where her soul was lost to retrieve it, on her own terms, from a position of relative empowerment. TRCs also vindicate survivors. By reflecting the morality of the change in regime, TRCs exemplify the morality of the victim rather than that of the perpetrator. They thereby can confirm the survivor's previous fundamental sense of good and evil which the trauma might have upset. By inviting the survivor to tell her story and by listening to and recording her story, TRCs transform it from hidden shame to part of the permanent record of the founding of the new nation.

The extent to which a TRC can in fact promote healing for individuals within the nation depends largely on its informal design features. (The more formal design features will be discussed in the chapter on national reconciliation because they implicate national policy.) These informal features are rarely addressed in the commission's legal mandate and are therefore most often left to the discretion of the commission itself.

Often, TRCs can choose whom to invite to testify and under what circumstances; care should be taken to invite witnesses who are willing and are prepared to tell their story. The physical space should be designed to enhance the healing effect of the telling of the story.[77] For instance, a commission may choose to hold hearings in a town hall or a gymnasium rather than in a courtroom; only in extraordinary and clearly explained circumstances should they be held in places that are associated with the malevolence of the previous regime. The commissioners might sit in a semicircle or on a mat rather than on a raised dais, or on the floor if that is the local custom. The witness may be encouraged to sit near a friend or relative. The commission may dispense with the taking of an oath (although this may affect the seriousness with which the testimony is received by some sectors of the community). Commissioners will need to decide whether the witness will be led through her story (and by whom) or whether she will be permitted simply to tell the story entirely as she sees it. They will need to decide how to address the witness, and in what language. Will tissues and water be available? Will there be breaks if the testimony is particularly difficult to give? The South African and East Timorese commissions provide two distinct models for others to follow; the former was more formal, the latter more participatory and village-based.

Since TRCs offer two levels of palliation—individual catharsis and national history—putative witnesses are likely to respond more to one than to the other. Some individuals may seize on a TRC as a vehicle for personal healing, without significant attention to the public or historic aspect of the commission's work. These people may have strong feelings about how their stories are used and may fear manipulation by the commission. Others may want to participate in order to contribute to the national narrative, even if they are indifferent to the therapeutic value of testifying. These people may want to testify in camera or with assurances of anonymity. Concessions to individual needs might be particularly relevant if survivors are young or especially fragile. In all events, telling the story should always be voluntary, and the survivor should be allowed to opt out at any time. If the commission has the survivor's permission to publish the story, it should, to the extent possible, let the survivor speak for herself and minimize filtering it.

Reconciliation for Children

Children are affected by war in a variety of ways. At worst, they are made to participate in acts of war. They are rendered orphans by war. They may also be victims (particularly sexual victims) of the lawlessness that pervades wartorn areas[78] and of the famine, disease, poverty, and displacement that so often accompany wars. Witnessing horrific scenes, including the deaths of siblings and parents, will also have continuing psychological repercussions. Even children who are not the direct victims of warfare are often war's secondary victims because the adult role models that children need are themselves wounded. They are the victim's victims. Children living near traumatized adults have to deal with rage, alcoholism, polarized and unpredictable behaviors, and other kinds of social dysfunction.

Although much research has been done on the effects of war on children, there are insufficient social resources available to assist children. Counseling and therapy models that are developed for adults should recognize the distinct needs of children. While story-telling remains an important aspect of child therapy, art, drama, and other forms of expression may be more useful outlets for their stories. In addition, and particularly for younger children, nonverbal therapeutic models—such as play or touching and hugging—may be effective. Although—or perhaps *because*—the child population is least able to demand the services it needs or to develop them on their own, NGOs and governments must pay special attention to the extreme needs and vulnerabilities of this group. Commissions in Timor and Siera Leone made recommendations specifically regarding children.

Some projects around the conflict-ridden world are using art to help children heal. One such is being developed by the Kwazulu-Natal Programme for Survivors of Violence and Drama Studies at the University of KwaZulu-Natal in South Africa.[79] It uses various art forms to aid the personal, community, and career development needed for sustainable recovery from trauma. The project also has training in basic art skills, the accessing of personal and community stories, and the symbolizing and crafting of these stories into a performance.[80] In a series of intensive healing workshops, sponsored by the Timorese CAVR, survivors of torture used art, music, theater, and dance as a catalyst for discussion and understanding. Singing and theatre games were "especially important because many survivors continue to suffer physical disability or feel constricted in their bodies after terrible physical and emotional suffering. These activities aimed to help participants to identify and celebrate their capacity to survive and their courage in rebuilding their lives."[81] In Bosnia, music has been used as therapy and as recreation, especially to help children.[82]

Other programs, aimed directly at helping children's psychological needs, include hospitals and therapeutic centers. Camps for young people in wartorn societies have also become quite popular in recent years. These types of camps bear a remarkable similarity to one another, though their locations are as varied as their constituencies. Mixing peace studies, reflection, and bonding activities, they are designed to encourage youngsters to follow the path of peace rather than of war when they go back home by introducing them to members of the "other" group, and by helping them to understand their own feelings of pain and anger that result from the conflict. In this way, today's children may become tomorrow's "agents of peace."[83] Programs like these need to be encouraged, and publicly funded, to ensure that the neediest children may benefit from them.

Most important, it is essential for transitional governments to recognize that programs aimed at national reconciliation will not normally help individuals to heal. Governments must develop and implement special initiatives to help survivors of trauma recover and become productive and healthy members of their communities. It is the relationship of victims and survivors to their communities to which we turn our attention next.

Chapter 3
Reconciliation in Community

Ubuntu ungamntu ngabanye abantu
People are people through other people
    —Xhosa proverb

My humanity is caught up, is inextricably bound up in yours. We
belong in a bundle of life. I am a human because I belong. A person
with ubuntu . . . belongs in a greater whole and is diminished when
others are humiliated or diminished, when others are tortured or
oppressed, or treated as if they were less than who they are.
    —Desmond Mpilo Tutu

Western thought distinguishes what to many people around the world is
indivisible. The idea that an individual is separable from her community
may be incoherent to many people. Even more, to suggest that she may
have interests that are distinct from, and even at odds with, her community may seem incomprehensible. The African idea of *ubuntu*, which has
become so popular in the reconciliation literature, reflects the indivisi-
bility of individuality and community by actually defining the individual
through her community. In most of the world's cultures, "I am," as Archbishop Tutu says, "because I belong,"—not, as Descartes posited, because
I can engage in the exceptionally singular act of thinking. In Timor Leste,
the "concept of individual identity is closely entwined with the individual's
sense of belonging to a community."[1] There are, of course, hints in Western culture of the interrelatedness of humanity, perhaps most prominently
in Martin Luther King, Jr.'s Letter from the Birmingham Jail: "Injustice
anywhere is a threat to justice everywhere. We are caught in an inescap-
able network of mutuality, tied in a single garment of destiny. Whatever
affects one directly, affects all indirectly."[2] This network of mutuality makes
reconciliation at the group level indispensable.

While Western thinkers and strategizers recognize the importance of
community reconciliation, they nonetheless tend to privilege the individual

over the community, believing that if the individual is healthy, the group will be too. Alternative models assume that the individual cannot be healthy unless the group is. Here, attention is paid to strengthening bonds between and among individuals, which, in turn, conduces to individual healing.[3] This may entail bilateral reconciliation, as between the victim and the perpetrator, or it may involve reintegration of the individual within a broader social setting. We consider each in turn.

Bilateral Reconciliation

In common parlance, reconciliation most often refers to relationships between two persons or things. The *Oxford Student's Dictionary* defines it as "to become friendly with a person after a quarrel." But in transitional contexts, use of the term "quarrel" will often be a profound and insulting understatement. Is our general understanding of reconciliation too weak to address situations where the divisions between people are not simple quarrels but gross violations of human rights? And even if we adopt the dictionary definition, it is very hard in the transitional context to assess the success of a reconciliation program in terms of whether former foes have "become friendly" again. Does it mean they socialize together, or does it simply mean they refrain from killing one another?

Interpersonal reconciliation is the level at which the larger society begins to take note of reconciliation. It produces the best visuals—the hug, the handshake. Polls are taken of how much interpersonal reconciliation has occurred and newspaper articles are written about it when it does occur and, perhaps more sensationally, when it does not. But the polls can be misleading. First, it is not clear what the appropriate benchmark is: should the exercise be measured against people's expectations (in which case it is bound to fall short, simply because unchecked expectations can run so high) or against people's needs, in which case the prospects for success seem brighter: people are more likely to demand and receive what they need in order to get along minimally with their neighbors. Second is the problem of time. While polls are impatient and demand to see the results while the public's attention is still focused on the problem, reconciliation may take months or years. As a result, polls that purport to measure the extent of reconciliation at a given moment may actually impede reconciliation by indicating its failure before it has had time to germinate.[4] Third, it may be easier to explain why it doesn't happen than why it does. In most cultures, it is easier to recognize and accept the refusal to forgive than the willingness to forgive. In fact, bilateral reconciliation between private individuals is far rarer than its opposites—distance, mistrust, or aggression.

Interpersonal reconciliation, which has one foot in the private realm and one foot in the public, often happens imperceptibly, defying easy measure and clear documentation. Little by little, neighbors begin to speak to one another; they begin to trust each other in smaller and then in progressively more significant ways. They can speak to each other without the pain overwhelming them, and eventually their relationship may become functional again, though it may never "become friendly," as the dictionary demands.

Perhaps one of the most dramatic examples for the potential of interpersonal reconciliation occurred in the aftermath of the fall of the Berlin Wall, during the first phase of the reunification of East and West Germany. This was a veritable Petri dish for bilateral reconciliation, where the hundreds of thousands of people who had been spied upon by operatives of the state security system could confront the hundreds of thousands of people who had spied on them. Here, the spying was done personally, by and against people who knew each other intimately—sometimes even husbands and wives. But, unlike the genocide in Rwanda or other examples of violations of human rights at the personal level, the spying was not violent, and in many cases yielded no official negative consequences whatsoever. Many people did not know whether or not they had been spied upon: in the first couple of years after the fall of the wall, more than one million people applied to see their files, approximately three times as many as the number who actually had files.[5] In Germany, if reconciliation was possible, it was only because of the nature of the injury, which consisted primarily of a deep sense of betrayal and shock, rather than sadistic threats to life and limb.

In Germany, *auferbeitung*—the working through of the past—at the interpersonal level was largely a nongovernmental affair. After East German dissidents and their West German allies insisted on the preservation and opening of the Stasi files, the government passed a set of laws that would regulate access to them. The unobtrusively named Federal Law on Archives, passed in December 1991 and amended in March 1992, created the Gauck Foundation, which oversees the preservation, sequestration, and dissemination of the 122 *kilometers* of Stasi files. The simple fact of the opening of the files "shattered many lives in East Germany," as these records revealed how friends and family members had been spying on each other.[6] "In the short-term, this process of discovering the truth about the past and reckoning with its implications is likely to make the process of reconciliation much harder, creating internal tensions between truth and reconciliation. Yet," Kamali says, "it is a necessary step in the longterm reconciliation process—without acknowledging and addressing the truth, the effects of these abuses are likely to fester."

Seeing what was in the files, although painful, would facilitate discussion between "spier" and "spied upon" based on facts rather than on unfounded accusations or unjustified denials. Hard information, albeit subject to interpretation, can be the starting point for discussion and can form the common ground that is necessary for interpersonal reconciliation.

Approaching the issue of reconciliation this way created the conditions in which reconciliation could happen without forcing upon anyone the obligation to reconcile. It is possible that reconciliation would have happened even if Stasi files had not been publicly available, although that is much harder to imagine. Access to the files allowed people to see what was and what *wasn't* in the files; it permitted them in many cases to put their fears to rest upon seeing that people they might have suspected actually did not spy on them or provided no harmful information.

Beyond providing the forum—literally the space in which people could come to see their files—the government did not involve itself in the work of interpersonal reconciliation. It did not invite people to see their files, or encourage them to expiate their guilt at having collaborated. Kamali characterizes this approach as one that is "predominantly individualized." To get truth and reconciliation, she says, "each individual had to seek it for herself or himself. This process started by requesting one's Stasi file and often ended up by personally confronting one's friends and family members who had collaborated with the Stasi to try to come to terms with the betrayal. As a result, many 'kitchen table' discussions did take place, but no national cathartic attempt at regular sessions of hearings as in South Africa."[7]

This defies the conventional wisdom, which is that governments need to make extraordinary efforts to bring people into the reconciliation process. In South Africa, the Truth and Reconciliation Commission not only invited victims to participate in the process, first as witnesses during the Human Rights Violations hearings and then as opponents to amnesty during the Amnesty hearings, but it affirmatively sought them out through its field offices and in association with local nongovernmental organizations that assisted the TRC by providing information about local conditions and past events. During the hearings themselves, the TRC and in particular its leader, Archbishop Desmond Tutu, entreated, cajoled, and in some cases literally begged individuals to reconcile with one another. In Germany, the government seemed indifferent to whether or not interpersonal reconciliation between husbands and wives, employers and employees, or friends happened at all. In South Africa, the emphatic prompting of bilateral reconciliation seems to suggest that the government felt the success of its transition to ride, at least in part, on the ability of survivors and perpetrators of gross human rights abuses to reconcile. And this insistence was not always welcome. Even individual witnesses sometimes vehemently resisted the Commission's efforts to foist reconciliation and forgiveness. One witness responded that "she could not—

and that the Commission could not and should not ask her to do so, nor offer forgiveness for her."[8]

The opening of the Stasi files also gave people a starting point, some way to access the process of reconciliation, and a way of doing this on their own terms at their own pace. They could see the files whenever they wanted, and confront their informers whenever and however they wanted. Many observers of that time in Germany seem struck by how energetically many Germans embraced the opportunity to work through the past. Tina Rosenberg notes that "The Stasi was an obsession for many Germans."[9] Rosenberg describes the rounds of conversations between the *Täter* (the spies) and the *Opfer* (the spied-upon) as being almost endless, from the kitchens, to the coffee shops, to the conference halls, to the television shows, and back to the kitchens. Talking, and talking about talking, and then talking about that.[10]

But to what end? It seems that while many Germans have done *aufer-beitung*—they have worked through or at least confronted the past—the relationships that were torn apart by the Stasi were not put back together again by talking. In most cases, the collaborators failed to satisfy the victims' needs for repentance.

Even once the curtain is drawn and the reality is revealed, perpetrators across the globe have an uncanny way of deflecting responsibility. Some still don't understand, even after the world has changed around them, that what they did was wrong. They believed then and they believe now that they were fighting the good fight, against communism in some countries and for it in others, and against dissenters, insurgents, and other social misfits everywhere. Perhaps this is the kind of conditioning Archbishop Tutu warns about,[11] but whether or not it is, many perpetrators continue to feel genuine righteousness about what they did. In any event, they did not follow the moral pendulum when it swung toward the new world order.

In other cases, the perpetrators do come forward, but their apologies seem hollow. *I didn't know. Everyone was doing it. I didn't give any information they didn't already have. I was scared; they threatened me. I needed the money. I was trying to change the system from the inside. I didn't mean to kill him.* These are not the kinds of apologies that make victims open their hearts. And yet, they are genuine in the sense that the perpetrators really believe them. By the time these explanations are given, there is no purpose to lying, there is nothing to lie about. But still, reconciliation cannot be fully achieved, not because there is active animosity between victim and perpetrator, but because there is no common ground. The perpetrator can't accept responsibility for the wrongfulness of the action, and without that, the victims can't forgive. As Rosenberg says, "the general didn't translate into specifics. The victims wanted the spies to admit everything, accept responsibility for ruining the lives of their victims, and commit themselves to new values. The spies wanted the victims to listen, forgive, and maybe even renew their friendships with their informers. People would understand how they had come to collaborate and would begin to create a more democratic society. . . . This was not, to say the least, what took place."[12] And yet, it would be wrong to be judgmental of the nonrepentant, if for no other reason than that it is so pervasive that it seems more a part of the human condition than an embarrassment to it. It is the very rare perpetrator who truly comes to see the error of his ways. (The attitude of many perpetrators toward apology is explored in Chapter 6.)

In perhaps the most tragic instances, there is what seems to be genuine repentance, and still there can be no reconciliation. In South Africa, police warrant officer Jeffrey Benzien had boasted that he was "Cape Town's most successful torturer" and that most people could not stand his torture for more than 30 minutes. He subsequently applied to the TRC for amnesty. During his hearing, he described his methods in detail, at times remembering specific aspects of a victim's situation. Finally, Tony Yengeni, one of his victims, put the ultimate question to him: "What kind of man uses a method like this one of the wet bag, to other human beings, repeatedly and listening to those moans and cries and groans and taking each of those people very near to their deaths? What kind of man are you?" But Benzien could only say he didn't know. "If you ask me what type of person is it that can do that, I ask myself the same question."[13]

It is hard to imagine that Yengeni, or anyone else in the room, was fully satisfied with that response. Although the scene suggests the inversion of power under the new regime—Yengeni was by that time a prominent member of the new Parliament—in fact reconciliation was stillborn. Benzien simply could not palliate Yengeni's wounds. Moreover, it is possible that, far from helping Yengeni, the exchange revictimized him. "In their efforts to discredit the witness to challenge his application for amnesty they reproduced themselves as victims."[14]

Perhaps quite a few were downright furious when they heard that Benzien had been granted amnesty because he had in fact complied with the requirements of the statute of giving full and true disclosure of the facts of politically motivated violence. No showing of remorse was required under the terms of the statute (although arguably Benzien showed some measure of remorse). And yet, Benzien's testimony is poignant because it reveals one of the most difficult truths of the entire enterprise of reconciliation, particularly in instances of gross human rights abuses. There simply are no answers. A person can apologize, can tell the truth, can even be remorseful. And yet there are no answers that truly satisfy the need to understand how one person can torture another. If, as is frequently said, reconciliation requires coming together or change by both parties, then

Benzien's testimony (if it can be taken as genuine), bodes ill for interpersonal reconciliation: even at their most contrite, perpetrators cannot as a rule provide the kind of explanation that victims need in order to move on.

In other instances in the TRC, however, true reconciliation can be said to have taken place. But even these situations do not indicate the transformation on which reconciliation is said to depend. In his book *Coming to Terms*, Martin Meredith describes one instance, which he considers to be "one of the most memorable acts of reconciliation the TRC was to witness"—an encounter between Abobaker Ismail, the master bomber, and one of his victims, Neville Clarence, an air force officer who had lost his sight in a bombing. But as Clarence's words make clear, this reconciliation didn't require change, or time, or the TRC—it required only the right individuals. After Ismail's amnesty hearing, Clarence said to reporters, "I came here today partially out of curiosity and hoping to meet Mr. Ismail. I wanted to express the feeling that I never held any grudges or bitterness against him. It was a wonderful experience."[15] That he refers to him as "Mr." and that he "never" held any grudges or bitterness reveals far more about Clarence's character than about the effectiveness of the TRC in transforming foes into allies.

Another survivor—whose wife was gunned down in a church—says to the murderers: "I want you to know that I forgive you unconditionally. I do that because I am a Christian, and I can forgive you for the hurt that you have caused me, but I cannot forgive you the sin that you have done. Only God can forgive you for that."[16] This is deeply moving testimony, but as the survivor's reference to his Christian faith reveals, it is not a moment of transformation but a moment of character. Tim Kelsall's study of the Sierra Leone reconciliation process is similarly revealing. He describes the testimony of the perpetrators as "unrelenting blandness" with the exception of one witness "who gave a comparatively full account" of what he had done, and even apologized for his actions. This witness, however, was already enrolled in a rehabilitation and counseling program with a local NGO; his forthright testimony, then, was less a result of the TRC commission than of his own previous commitment to righting the wrongs of the past.[17]

Does reconciliation only work when a victim is predisposed to forgive? If so, do commissions and the like have any *transformative* potential? Indeed, the far more typical response is exemplified by the mothers of some of the "Guguletu 7," a group of young men who were gunned down by the apartheid police. At the start of the amnesty hearing, one mother threw a shoe at the perpetrators.

In rare cases, instances of genuine reconciliation did emerge in the TRC process in South Africa. Pumla Gobodo-Madikizela centers her book *A Human Being Died That Night* on the forgiveness offered by some of the survivors of violence committed by Eugene de Kock. De Kock was known as "Prime Evil" for his leadership role in countless killings committed in the name of apartheid. During the TRC process, he apologized, showed remorse, and contributed significantly to the success of the TRC by providing full accounts of many of his crimes.[18] Pearl Faku, whose husband was murdered by de Kock, responded to his apology with, as Gobodo-Madikizela describes it, "the fullness of her humanity," saying that "I hope that when he sees our tears, he knows that they are not only tears for our husbands, but tears for him as well. I would like to hold him by the hand, and show him that there is a future, and that he can still change.'"[19]

Examples like this are few and far between and, as Gobodo-Madikizela indicates, they may not be examples of bilateral reconciliation, as much as extensions of personal reconciliation. In cases like this, victims are not forgiving the perpetrator, as she says, "for being so malicious, so perverted, so indescribably wicked as to have committed this abhorrent act." Rather, they are expressing a change that has occurred within themselves. "When forgiveness is granted, it is a choice the victim makes to let go of the bitterness. This usually occurs when there has been a change in the way the victim relates to his or her trauma"[20] (as was discussed in the previous chapter), and not in the way he or she relates to the perpetrator. This change may be prompted by therapy, by the passage of time, or as in the case with de Kock, by his own decision to give the victims the truth and remorse that would release their pain.

Given that some people cannot move from their oppositional stances, while others are always open to reconciliation, perhaps the task of the government is to minimize the numbers in the former group, nudging them toward the latter group. While the German model didn't necessarily produce reconciliation, it is likely that it at least abetted it, providing individuals with some of the resources necessary to make reconciliation possible. Yet, even though people were armed with information, they still lacked the psychological wherewithal to be able to confront their spies or their victims and were in many instances unable to reach common ground. Perhaps that is why those few people who did understand how to speak the language of reconciliation were so successful that they took their show on the road and even—as if just to prove that the forces of capitalism had prevailed over socialism—were able to make money and earn fame working through their past—professional reconcilers, as it were.

But the majority of Germans simply did not know what to say when confronted with someone from the other side of the Stasi divide. Should victims insist on apologies? Should collaborators try to explain themselves? Should they try to repair their relationship—to make it once again what one side thought it was before but what the other side knew it never was? Although the German government was probably right to abstain from promoting a particular form of reconciliation, the country might have benefited from help from third parties—perhaps nongovernmental organizations that could have helped structure the debate and could have given some psychological and contextual guidance to those who were trying to work through their past. They could, for instance, suggest talking points or questions that either side might ask or think about. They could also indicate what appropriate expectations might be. *(Don't expect to feel better; don't expect complete contrition; don't expect the Tater to show remorse, even though he or she might feel it. Do expect them to hear you out.)*

Within non-Western social structures, there are examples of bilateral reconciliation that appear to be much more effective. An example is the Empowering for Reconciliation (Pemberdayaan untuk Rekonsiliasi) program in Indonesia. This program seeks to achieve reconciliation in three steps. First, the two or more people concerned must acknowledge the injustices that have been perpetrated on the victim(s). This acknowledgment does not entail agreeing or seeing the issues in the same way as the others view it, but it means acknowledging that experience from the standpoint of the others as an injustice to them. The parties listening to what they have done do not "speak out defensively or to try to justify themselves."[21] The aim of the process at this point is for them to appreciate and be aware of the facts and the feelings from the standpoint of those communicating and for them to acknowledge these. After this step has occurred and the injustices acknowledged, the process focuses on how to "make things as right as possible between us."[22] To make reconciliation possible those involved need to work out a response and result which is satisfactory to all. The final step is the need to obtain clarity about the future. What are the outlook and expectations toward each other in the future? This process of establishing future commitments is very constructive in the process of empowering for reconciliation.[23]

The formal structure of the Indonesian process provides a context in which people who seek to reconcile with one another can do so. Western society, which tends to minimize the importance of bilateral reconciliation, does not have such structures in place. In the West, people who want to work through the past or reconcile—as many did in the former Soviet countries—have no templates or constructs within which to work; they are more or less on their own. The loneliness of victimhood is compounded by the loneliness of failing to come to terms. By helping to structure the dialogue and establish appropriate expectations, governmental authorities or NGOs can lay the common ground from which reconciliation can grow.

This guidance not only would help individuals to understand how to achieve reconciliation between themselves and others, it might also provide a language for reconciliation that reflects people's experiences. TRCs, for instance, can mark out the beginnings of a language of reconciliation, one that recognizes that torture and rape are never justified and that a victim is also a survivor; one that locates forgiveness and narrative truth at the center of public policy, and vengeance outside of it; one that acknowledges that systematic oppression and killing of people because they are disempowered, poor, or ethnically different constitutes gross violations of human rights, whether it occurs on a large or small scale. In Germany, by contrast, the public face of reconciliation was on television and in public forums created by entrepreneurs, limiting the likelihood that the developing language would be progressive or truly transformative.

The failure of language is characteristic of transitions throughout the world. The first instinct is to divide the populace, to mark the perpetrators while giving succor to the victims. Legislation seeking to promote reconciliation is often polarized, with perpetrators conceived as debtors and victims as creditors. But the reality is always more nuanced, and far more complicated. As Inga Markovits has written, "In real life, the distinction between Stasi perpetrator and victim was often blurred. Stasi contamination could reach far and wide, and someone might have been a perpetrator in some section of his life while he was a victim in another."[24]

The distinction between perpetrators and victims, and between leaders and ordinary people, suits well the lawyer's inclination to see the world in absolute contrasts of black and white. However, an "either/or" approach—while perhaps useful for the law's preoccupation with drawing lines between right and wrong, guilt and innocence, debits and credits, and the like—is not particularly useful for historical analysis or social reconstruction. For instance, the legal assumption that former East German citizens in their interactions with the Stasi were either perpetrators or victims of secret police machinations clashes with everyday socialist reality, in which many people, in many ways, both cooperated with and undermined the state's claim to totalitarian control.[25]

This problem is pervasive in states transitioning from totalitarian regimes, where it is virtually impossible to distinguish between those who should be held morally culpable for propping up communist regimes and those who should not, because they only acted in small ways that were insignificant except in the aggregate. But the problem is not limited to these situations; it resonates to a significant degree in many other transitional situations. It is true in South Africa, where the ANC, which held the moral high ground in the struggle to end apartheid, committed some brutal atrocities of its own. It is true in the Balkans, as well as in Rwanda, where neighbors turned upon neighbors, friends upon friends, and many people saved some people while killing others. It is true in Iraq, where an indeterminate but large number of people supported the Baath regime— some under duress, some willingly, and many in between. Perhaps the conditions that pervaded in Latin America are sufficiently distinct that legislation drawing bright lines between the good folks and the bad folks would be justified: in most Latin American countries, the population at large, or portions of it (such as indigenous people, dissidents, or intellectuals) were victims and in no way perpetrators of gross human rights abuses, while the military or government officers were perpetrators, and by and large, in no way victims. But even in Latin America, where in some cases there were choices, there is the difficulty of assigning moral blame to many of the most common acts that sustained the prior regime—the low-level spying, the acquiescence in the oppression of others, the willingness to turn a blind eye.

A polarized approach to dealing with the past that assumes that the wheat can be separated from the chaff is inaccurate both as a political and as a psychological matter. In some situations, victims are able to see in perpetrators not just their capacity for evil but also their basic humanity. They may be able to understand why the perpetrators acted the way they did; they may even feel sorry for the perpetrators, as one of Eugene de Kock's victims did. Pascal Khoo Thwe, in his memoirs of being in a rebel camp on the Thai-Burmese border, describes one Burmese student who was arrested in Thailand. "They put him in jail, hoping that someone would come and bail him. But no one turned up. His jailer was a sympathetic man, and the student happened to have a skill much prized in Thailand—he was an excellent masseur. So every evening he gave his jailer a thorough and expert massage, and the jailer in turn brought him clothes, fed him, taught him Thai, and even gave him pocket money."[26]

Even more surprising is Jeffrey Benzien, the South African torturer, who conceded that he had suffocated Ashley Forbes with a wet bag on several occasions, but he also remembered that Forbes liked Kentucky Fried Chicken, the first time Forbes had seen snow, and how they had barbecued one night, as they drove around the country together "on an investigation." During his testimony in the amnesty hearing, Benzien said to Forbes: "You, I can remember especially, because I think that the two of us after weeks of your confinement really became quite close. I may be mistaken, but I think we became relatively, I wouldn't say friends, but on a very good rapport."[27] (Mr. Forbes does not seem to have responded.)

It is possible that in some situations—perhaps more than we realize—victims and perpetrators do not see themselves or each other as exclusively as "other." They may also see each other as human beings who are in horrible situations or doing horrible things, but human beings nonetheless. It may be that the sharp dichotomy between good and evil does not always resonate in the experience or the emotions of the individuals on either side of the bars.

Reconciliation systems that depend on a sharp divide between victims and perpetrators may therefore fail to resonate in people's experiences.

"Every day," says Aniceto Guterres Lopes, Chair of the East Timor Commission for Reception and Reconciliation, "we must work our canvas in shades of grey. Painting in black and white in this context is for dreamers only. And we must find a way forward from this grey into the light."[28]

To avoid entrenching this dichotomy which is at least simplistic and at most false, Mahmood Mamdani suggests that laws intending to promote reconciliation should operate under a different conceptual framework. Rather than adopting the retributive model of assigning everyone to either victim or perpetrator status, the law should focus more on who the beneficiaries of the past practices were, regardless of their moral responsibility. If the focus is less on perpetrators and more on beneficiaries, then the debate is less about retributive justice and more about social justice, according to Mamdani.[29] The discourse should not be in the language of guilt and shame but the language of reconstruction. Perhaps this new language will help those who experienced the trauma from different sides find common ground.

We might even go farther than Mamdani and suggest that the language of reconciliation should not attempt to divide at all. In shedding light on the past, and seeking explanations and understandings for the harms done, the language of reconciliation might ultimately recognize that oppressive regimes harm everyone, though obviously in different ways and in differing degrees. With that in mind, we might prefer to focus on building up constructive relationships and on ensuring the extinction of the old oppressive ways, rather than on examining the ledger of good and evil in the past.

Community Reconciliation

Many reconciliation rituals that are indigenous to cultures around the world involve the building of community bonds, without any reference at all to justice being done. For instance, in some parts of Uganda, perpetrators of terrible human rights abuses stick their right foot into a freshly cracked egg which permits them to restore themselves to "the way they used to be" because the egg represents innocent life. They then brush themselves "against the branch of a pobo tree, which symbolically cleanse[s] them . . . [and by] stepping over a pole, they [are] welcomed back into the community." Confession, apology, and atonement are also components of the reconciliation ritual.[30] Not only do these kinds of rituals enable the returnee to cast off the ties of the past, but, by participating in the ceremony, the community "publicly obligate[s] itself to reconcile with the perpetrators."[31]

Often, reconciliation rituals extend to the nonearthly community: in some traditional settings, reconciliation processes are "seen as a reestablishment of relationships between people and also with their God and spirits—who were regarded as witnesses and active participants."[32] In many rural communities in Africa and elsewhere, the living need to reconcile with the dead by appeasing their spirits in order to prevent or quell earthly disturbances like illnesses, nightmares, and bad luck. This can be done by performing a ritual or having a proper burial, with or without the dead person's body.

In some cultures, courts provide the structure in which community reconciliation can flourish. But their role in the community can be very different from what it is in the industrialized world. In the Pedi culture of Southern Africa, for instance,

The court takes great pains to reconstruct the cause of any dispute, to show individuals who are not accused how their actions may have given rise to the complaint, and frequently advises the accused that he may have a counter claim. The court always enquires whether the disputing parties have tried to come to a mutual settlement beforehand, and frequently refers a case back to the families involved to attempt by private discussion to resolve their dispute. The accent is always on arbitration rather than on punishment, and the legal institutions of the Pedi have the characteristics of a number of agencies for arbitration on various levels.[33]

Communities throughout Africa continue to adopt this approach to this day, even for crimes associated with modern warfare. "At the heart of African adjudication lies the notion of reconciliation or the restoration of harmony. The job of a court or an arbitrator is less to find the facts, state the rules of law, and apply them to the facts than to set right a wrong in such a way as to restore harmony within the disturbed community. Harmony will not be restored unless the parties are satisfied that justice has been done."[34] In Mozambique, for example, "virtually no attempts have been made to hold anyone accountable for the many heinous crimes committed during the war through official war crimes trials or tribunals."[35] And yet, Mozambique is often held up as a transitional justice success. While Mozambique has not emphasized retribution for past crimes, it has introduced local popular tribunals whose task it is to mediate conflicts within the community. The tribunals are aimed at achieving reconciliation, not punishment.

Perhaps the ideal in many countries with deep ritualistic culture is to benefit from both truth-telling and ritual. Tim Kelsall has written that, in Sierra Leone, where days of commission-sponsored truth telling culminated in a community reconciliation ceremony, the ceremony did not underline the state of affairs that the truth had brought into being; rather, "it is more plausible to view the entire five days of the hearings as a ritual building to the climax of the final ceremony, upon which the purpose of the Commission hinged."[36]

In the remainder of this chapter, we consider some of the issues that communities face and some of the programs from around the world that seem most promising in terms of promoting genuine and long-term community reconciliation.

Understanding Community

Communities come in all shapes and sizes. In the context of transitional justice, many of the relevant communities are defined by race, religion, ethnicity, or other ingrained trait. Some communities are voluntary—such as when people have choices as to where to live and which church to attend and which social circles to belong to—but many are not. Poorer people tend to have less free choice of communities. Some communities define most aspects of their members' lives, but many others do not. As communities become more entrenched, they may take up ever more space in people's lives. For instance, once a nationalist movement begins to take root, belonging to that group becomes increasingly relevant to all aspects of a person's life, defining not only which holidays she observes or which dress she adopts, but whom she marries, which language she speaks, where she sends her children to school, which shops she patronizes, and which friends she keeps. The more prevalent a community association is in a person's life, the more likely segregation will ensue between that community and its neighbors.

Most people, of course, belong to many communities at once. They may belong to a church, a trade union, an ethnic group, and a political affiliation. People may have stronger or weaker affiliations with any of these, but these choices should remain, to the extent possible, voluntary. Efforts to "kill the Indian to save the man" or to suppress religious feeling and expression (as under communism) are bound to fail, because they don't reflect how individuals actually feel and experience the world.[37] Moreover, the mere association with a community is not threatening to the nation; rather, it is the way in which the community manifests its identity. That is, it is not the fact of being a fundamentalist that is problematic; it is the fact of expressing one's fundamentalism in violence that warrants correction. Communities, as much as individuals, may exemplify the Darwinian impulse to survive and thrive, even at the expense of others. If so, then intolerance by the national government of strong community identity may produce not only decentralization but violence: communities will fight those whom they perceive to be competitors that threaten their own survival.[38] This ideology of fight-to-survive is then impressed upon the individual members of the threatened community, who engage in acts of aggression in order to protect both themselves and the larger group.

The challenge, then, is to find a way to allow the self-expression of the community in a way that neither threatens others nor impedes the development of national identity. Reconciliation among and within communities permits a multiplicity of communities but insists that none threaten the others.

The first question that arises in the context of community reconciliation is whether the contemplated reconciliation is to be within the community or between one community and one or more others. Where the dissension is internal to the community, reconciliation can be much more challenging, but also more necessary.

Repatriation and Reintegration

Intracommunity reconciliation occurs in several distinct situations. Perhaps the most common situation is where a refugee or a militant returns to a village that is not welcoming. This is a major problem in most war-torn nations, from Rwanda, to Palestine, to Bosnia. In 2004, there were more than 9.2 million refugees around the world, and in that year alone, 1.5 million refugees repatriated voluntarily to their country of origin.[39] In general, returnees constitute the poorest of populations (since those who are making a decent living elsewhere are less likely to seek to return, and when they do they are more self-sufficient). Getting people to return may involve not only the logistical difficulties of moving people from one place to another, often across international borders, but psychological obstacles as well. The problem of refugee returns in Bosnia has been particularly challenging. Branko Todorovi, a member of the coordinating committee for the Bosnian Truth and Reconciliation Committee, has said that "In order for somebody to be able to return, the person must feel accepted in his or her former environment and he or she must feel equal like the others living there."[40] In Bosnia, the failure of political and international efforts to provide for legal and constitutional equality for all citizens "has revealed the cruel fact that ethnic divisions are still very strong, and that fear and mistrust still pervade the people,"[41] according to Todorovi. In Bosnia, the right of return has been central to the postwar process under the Dayton agreement, in part because it has been viewed as a form of justice: if the refugees cannot return, then the communities remain ethnically homogeneous (or "cleansed"), and the nationalists will have won the peace, even if not the war.[42]

The flip side of the refugee problem occurs when former fighters return to a village. In Cambodia, many people still bear resentment, hurt, and anger against those who fought for the Khmer Rouge. "They make me sick with memories," says one woman when she sees the village chief and his associates drive by her house. During the war, he had been responsible for having her husband executed and imprisoning her and her children.[43]

In Timor Leste, a fairly elaborate procedure has been developed at the grassroots level to ensure the effective integration of returning soldiers into the community. This involves preliminary meetings with both sides' representatives on the border between East and West Timor, culminating in the arrival of the returnee in the village amid publicity and under the auspices of local political leaders, and ending in a traditional ceremony.[44] These processes have developed largely in the vacuum left by the failure of the national reconciliation process to reach down into the villages.[45]

In all wartorn and warworn societies, many individuals at some point decide that reconciliation, difficult as it may be, is preferable to continued anger and hostility. The comments of Dennis Bright, Commissioner for the Consolidation of Peace in Sierra Leone are illustrative: "After ten years of brutality and insanity Sierra Leoneans are now exhausted and frustrated with violence." He concluded, as previously noted, that for people whose main priority is to "live like normal human beings, they are even willing to reconcile with those who were hurting them yesterday."[46]

But this is much easier said than done. Where community reconciliation efforts are not viable, the government may decide to relocate returnees in other locations. This minimizes community tension, but it may impede individual and social healing by exacerbating the returnees' sense of alienation and reinforcing the homogeneity of the village. To some extent, this has happened in parts of Rwanda, where returnees have been placed in new villages and been given reeducation.[47] Rwanda's repatriation of refugees into identified villages may have long term negative consequences as it may allow or even foster mistrust between members of the different ethnic groups. In fact in 2000, the UN High Commissioner for Refugees commented that "Hutu returnees continued to be subject to a high level of control and the reintegration process seems to be proceeding very slowly. In such circumstances of increased segregation, there seems little hope of ethnic reconciliation and an integrated society."[48] The situation has not much changed since then.

Some conceptions of reconciliation have developed at least theoretical responses to the problem of reintegration. Public shaming, for instance, has been considered by some theorists to constitute an integral part of the returning process, a sort of rite of passage that compels the returnee to come to terms with the damage he or she caused and forces the community to come to terms with the need to accept the returnee.[49] This theory was partially adopted by the South African Truth and Reconciliation Commission, which argued that the statutory requirement imposed on applicants for amnesty to fully disclose the truth about their involvement in politically motivated human rights abuses constituted a form of public shaming that would follow them back to their communities, segregated though they might be. Stigmatization is also part of the transformation rituals that are common throughout the world.[50]

There are limits, however, to the ability of shaming to facilitate reintegration. Where the community supports the returnee (as when Afrikaners return to their still segregated communities), there will be little opportunity for shaming. On the other hand, where the returnee is not of the predominant culture in the community, shaming might be excessive and for that reason also be ineffective.

The gacaca courts in Rwanda take a slightly different approach. These community courts derive from the traditional legal system and have been in use for centuries, but have been revived and reshaped to accommodate the government's dire need to prosecute accused genocidaires. Like the Pedi tribal law, gacaca emphasizes group relations rather than individual rights. The accent is on restoring relationships as well as the reconciliation of groups. Gacaca has the potential to promote community reconciliation in several ways.[51] First, the participation of the general public as investigator or prosecutor or trier of fact is meant to foster cohesiveness among the residents of the community. From the standpoint of the defendant, a local, very public trial may constitute a form of public shaming in and of itself. Second, the public's commitment to the trial (wrought by their own participation) enhances the legitimacy of the process and may promote the sense of justice and faith in the rule of law in Rwanda. Third, and most important from the standpoint of reintegration, the penalty assessed is assumed to have been endorsed by the public generally. Thus, a gacaca court decision to allow the defendant to move back to the community is more likely to be accepted by the current inhabitants. Fourth, the gacaca tribunal may exact a concession from the defendant in exchange for the right of return. This evidences the returnee's bona fides and it materially enhances the quality of life of the community members generally and perhaps of the victim's family specifically, which in turn helps them move on. However, there is growing criticism of the gacaca approach. Evidence suggests that many Rwandans do not trust the courts and have boycotted them, that some judges have ignored the rules of these courts, and that thousands have fled to neighboring countries fearing false accusations and unfair trials. The long-term impact of gacaca remains to be seen.

Wherever there has been a cleavage in the village, where some villagers identify with the victims and others with the perpetrators, some affirmative measures of reconciliation are probably necessary in order to demonstrate the returnee's own commitment to reconciliation. The villagers are likely to accept the returnee only if they believe that there has been a change of heart and that he or she can truly be trusted.[52]

Timor Leste has also developed a transitional model of reconciliation that, while relying on traditional values, is modified to suit the modern imperatives of the postwar situation. Unlike gacaca, the Timorese model operates as a variation on reconciliation rather than on justice. The national reconciliation commission (Commission for Reception, Truth and Reconciliation, known by its Portuguese acronym CAVR) sponsored several programs to facilitate community reconciliation, in particular, the reintegration (*acolhimento*) of soldiers and refugees back into their communities. The principal venue, the Community Reconciliation Program (CRP), "combined practices of traditional justice, arbitration, mediation and aspects of both criminal and civil law."[53] Like the Rwandan gacaca process, the CRP emphasizes community participation and deals only with less serious offenses because community members said that they could not reconcile with those responsible for more serious crimes until they had been prosecuted.[54] But the CRP is far less structured than gacaca, "allowing flexibility for the inclusion of elements from local traditional practice."[55] The elders of the village (as well as the ancestors) are present at the proceedings along with the deponents, victims, CRP panel members, and other interested members of the community. Proceedings would typically open with traditional rituals and a collective prayer to promote a "spirit of concord."[56] When the deponent told his story, participants were not allowed to interrupt; when he or she was done, the victims and community members would have the chance to speak and ask questions. Then the panel would moderate a discussion among the parties to develop a "Community Reconciliation Agreement," which would describe the "acts of reconciliation" the deponent would undertake to demonstrate commitment to the community. Acts would take the form of an apology, a symbolic fine, or an act of community service, singly or in combination. Parties would confirm, through the reading of animal entrails, that the truth had been spoken. Upon mutual agreement, the proceeding would end with a summary of the day's events and a "moral teaching presented on the theme of togetherness."[57]

Acts of reconciliation ranged from the traditional (wrapping negative acts in a coconut to be buried in a forest and presenting the community with a fresh coconut, representing positive acts) to the symbolic (contributing a sacrificial animal to be enjoyed at a communal feast), to the constructive (repair of buildings or tree planting over a period of three months), to the compensatory (including cash, livestock, textiles, and ornaments). Some victims simply demanded a genuine apology. In general, the Commission found that the acts were significantly less onerous than they had expected, though they ranged from region to region.[58]

Overall, the system seemed to work well to help formalize the reintegration of people back into their community. As Guterres Lopes, Chair of the CAVR, explained, "The spiritual and cultural practices of particular regions can be used during hearings and negotiations, give additional meaning and force to the process, in addition to giving the relevant communities a larger sense of ownership and participation."[59]

In Mozambique, the process of reintegration has been even less centralized. There, the reintegration of former soldiers into their communities is accompanied by a relatively formal ritual that helps the individual overcome his military identity and become a civilian again, announce and give thanks to the spirits that the lost sheep has returned, and reconcile with the spirits of the people whom the soldier killed. The returnee asks for forgiveness and shows remorse. There are also occasions where former enemies or their families are brought together to go through rituals of cleansing to achieve reconciliation, which may include washing or burning the effects of the previous activities. Compensation might also be given to the families of the dead.[60] These rites of transition allow the returnee to put the past behind him and to emerge into the village as a new person. In some versions of the ritual, the returnee is literally forbidden to look back as he leaves the site of the ritual and enters the village.[61]

One report on Angola found that many people had turned to their communities for "conselho," or advice or consolation.[62] However, this is not always possible, because when war "routinely targets the social fabric, community structures may not be able to fill their customary role as a source of support and adaptation."[63] According to the report, Angolan communities were actively encouraging returnees and helping them to cast off memories of loss and war. This was viewed as appropriate, even though it may seem contrary to Western notions of letting the survivor develop his or her own responses to the trauma.[64] Although processes like these can and do operate throughout the world without any governmental support, many would be enhanced if a legitimate central government lent them authority and logistical support.

Whatever its particular features, a national program of repatriation must begin with attention to the emotional and psychological landscape of the village, and to the effects that repatriation will have on the community, particularly where disproportionately large numbers of people return. The importance of effective reintegration programs can not be overstated. In Timor Leste, for instance, the United Nations Development Programme noted in 2003 that "concern for security dominates the mood in political circles, and it may have serious repercussion at the local level, where people who participated in militia activity in 1999 are feared again, especially if they have not effectively reintegrated into the community."[65] Effective reintegration programs can contribute significantly to regional stabilization and productivity; their absence can engender restlessness and can make the community susceptible to opportunistic attacks of divisive politics.

These forms of amends are seeping into Western culture, where they are being incorporated into victim-offender reconciliation programs that are sprouting throughout the English-speaking world to manage criminal responsibility. In the Asian context, as well, Upendra Baxi has noted that a solution is sought "which maximizes social harmony or abates group conflict or tension. Reconciliation of parties through compromise and consensus characterizes decisions."[66]

Peaceful Coexistence

Another form of community reconciliation arises when the makeup of the community's population has not changed but the people have. In many communities throughout the world, people of distinct ethnicities live side by side in peace for generations or centuries. For a variety of reasons, war breaks out, and the erstwhile friends and neighbors can now no longer speak to one another. When the fighting is over and the peace accords have been signed by elites in some distant city, how do the people within each group learn to live together again?

Again, traditional cultures may offer some guidance. Many have developed rituals that signal the renewal and strengthening of bonds between the various elements of the society. In East Africa when there was serious conflict among the Turkana, the elders would call a traditional peace conference to repair the broken relationship and revitalize the process of healing. The meeting would be

open-ended so that all the participants had time and opportunity to air their views. The meeting would be held in a "carnival" atmosphere, punctuated with stories, songs, dance, proverbs, etc. The name of God and the spirits would be invoked during the meeting. A bull would be slaughtered and its blood collected and sprinkled into the air as a way of binding the community to the peace covenant. As a gesture of reconciliation the whole group would eat the meat together. Thereafter, feasting, singing, dancing and celebration would continue for several days. The whole society would thus be part of the agreement and anybody who violated it could suffer some calamity.[67]

Similarly after bloody conflict between the Luo and the Maasai of Kenya,

negotiation and reconciliation would be arranged by the elders with rituals to solemnise the occasion. The elders and the "whole community"—women, children and the youth would assemble at one point along their common border. A makeshift obstacle consisting of tree branches would be created along the border and the warriors would place their spears over it. A dog would then be slain and cut in half and its blood sprinkled along the border. Then, mothers would exchange babies with the "enemy" group and suckle them. The warriors would also exchange spears. Prayers would then be offered by the elders and a profound curse pronounced on any one who attempted to cross the border and create havoc to either side. After such an agreement it would be almost impossible for the two sides to fight again. This was a form of creating blood brotherhood.[68]

In modern Western cultures, the peace conference among leaders is the preferred method to reconcile diverse elements of a common social structure. And yet, as the failure of so many peace accords demonstrates, vows taken by leaders don't necessarily transfer to the people. Notwithstanding the existence of signed accords, people may nonetheless continue to fight or at least to resent one another.

In some cases, where fighting is persistent, policymakers may be compelled to consider the viability of partition. Where the parties are divided by deeply held beliefs—whether based on religion, history, or other inviolable articles of faith—positions on both sides tend to entrench themselves, making compromise less likely. In these cases, the two communities may separate out, and may, out of fear of the future or too-strong memories of a distant past, not desire to mix at all. In these difficult cases, temporary partition might be the best solution, providing people with a sort of "cooling off" time before real reconciliation efforts can reasonably be expected. As John F. Kennedy is said to have commented about the erection of the Berlin Wall in 1961, "a wall is better than war." Thus, the Dayton peace accords, ending the war in Bosnia in 1995, mandated that regions and even towns be partitioned to create ethnic enclaves and to deter interethnic mixing. As unappealing as this was, it may have been necessary to avoid continued violence. Partitions, however, can only lead to reconciliation if they are temporary. Indefinite or permanent partitions entrench intracommunity divisions by preventing the kind of social intercourse that conduces to reconciliation.

Partitions may be actual walls, like the Berlin Wall or the walls along the green line in Israel, or the "peace lines" that separate Catholic and Protestant neighborhoods in Northern Ireland. Or they may simply be a no-man's land, like the DMZ separating the two Koreas. The less penetrable partitions are, the less likely they are to conduce eventually to reconciliation, like the national borders dividing Ireland and Kashmir. Dividers that are intended to eventually dissipate should be marked from the outset as temporary, and it should be clear to all what the milestones along the way of the barrier's disappearance are intended to be. But if reconciliation is to happen, the separation must at least be porous, in order to capitalize upon opportunities for interaction. Both sides should make efforts to understand and talk to each other to find common ground and accept each other's presence in their day-to-day lives.

Like individual reconciliation, community reconciliation does not in all circumstances require government intervention; sometimes the exigencies of proximity and mutual need may over time assuage the pain of the wartime period. However, also as with individual reconciliation, governmental (and nongovernmental) programs can usually spur the healing process.

Some of the most effective community reconciliation programs promote reconciliation only indirectly. In these programs, participants do not discuss their attitudes toward each other; rather, participants build houses, make food, quilt, provide medical care, learn computer programming, or engage in some other activity. Almost anything can form the basis of an emerging relationship, so long as the activity takes place in interethnic environments. The idea is that these experiences will, over time, foster a sense of solidarity and community among the participants. For instance, the United Nations Development Programme in Kosovo has developed the community mobilization reconstruction method, in which village leaders motivate the people to work together on reconstructive projects. Accordingly, "Kosovan Serb, Kosovan Albanian, and Kosovan Roma/Ashkali/Egyptian communities will be brought together to reconstruct houses for each other";[69] those who have already received governmental assistance will build houses for those who are still waiting. Norway has recently launched a program to support culture and sports in the Great Lakes region of Africa. The purpose of the program is to promote peace and reconciliation, on the theory that sports and culture are both indirect avenues to reconciliation.

Other programs address community reconciliation head on. In Timor Leste, the CAVR worked with communities to create "sketch maps" that indicated where events had happened in a community. A particularly useful tool where people are illiterate, the maps "recognised both the depth of community experience of violence and the rich East Timorese oral tradition. They were initially created as a research tool in the Commission's truth-seeking work, but were soon acknowledged as valuable occasions for developing community understanding and healing."[70] The version of events developed in this way, which was authoritative within the community even if not scientifically accurate, provided a starting point for future investigations and the basis for recommendations to the national government for compensatory or reparatory programs.

Community Reconciliation Projects

Community reconciliation can also be stimulated by ad hoc, nongovernmental organizations, many of which rise up from the ashes of conflict. There are literally thousands of groups working toward reconciliation at any given moment in the countries of the world. It is impossible to know exactly how many, partly because new groups emerge and older groups become obsolete or merge with each other, and partly because groups join forces with others or work under the auspices of umbrella organizations.[71] These groups are often effective in promoting community reconciliation because they grow organically from the community itself; often they understand the needs and the vulnerabilities of the community better than national or international organizations.

Many such groups see themselves as primarily devoted to other issues—such as the reconstruction of the social fabric, disarmament, conflict prevention, peacebuilding, improvement in the material lives of the poor, rehabilitation—but these issues are invariably integrally intertwined with reconciliation, and no clear line can be drawn between organizations that promote peace or economic development in conflict situations and reconciliation. In 2002, Timor Leste's first year of independence, that country boasted approximately 200 nongovernmental organizations (out of a population of less than one million), and most of these engaged in the hard work of reconciliation and reconstruction.

The preeminent human rights group in Afghanistan, for instance, the Revolutionary Association of Women of Afghanistan, is both a political and a social organization. For decades, it has been preaching a message of democracy, tolerance, and secularism, but increasingly it has added social projects to its agenda, including schools, hospitals, and assistance to refugees. While it does not explicitly endorse a message of reconciliation, its underlying values are indistinguishable from those entailed in most conceptions of reconciliation. Its educational program, for instance, includes a section on "partnership values" which teaches students to "encourage listening to the ideas of others" and "respect teamwork and focus on the success of common goals."[72] In Russia, Memorial[73] has dedicated itself to "the establishment of a list of the names of all victims and the publication of these names; the clarification of the places of burial of the deceased, and the establishment of memorial signs on these burial places."[74] Since its founding in 1992, it has already published several "Books of Memory" containing information about several hundred thousand people who were victims of Stalinism.[75] Memorial does not speak specifically of reconciliation, but clearly its basic goal—"to look for the path to the past for the sake of the future"—is consistent with the goals of most of the common understandings of reconciliation.[76]

For obvious reasons, most of these groups operate in the conflict area itself. Organizations of this type vary widely in nature. Some, like the Argentine group Madres de la Plaza de Mayo, are grassroots organizations and emerged out of frustration or anger either at the repression or at the successor government's failure to palliate the wounds of repression. Some arise simply out of the need to talk and to seek or provide support to others suffering the same fate. Many of these grassroots organizations are not heavily funded and may be very local in nature, more like a support group than an NGO. In some cases, however, funding is not as much of a limitation, particularly if the institution is affiliated with a notable personality. The Arias Foundation for Peace and Human Progress, for instance, was funded largely from the proceeds of the Nobel Prize awarded to its founder, Dr. Oscar Arias, former president of Costa Rica. Sometimes these organizations are established as rebel collectives during the time of repression but in the new dispensation they become engines of reconciliation. Alternatively, they may be established in the new dispensation, in the space created by the transition.

Groups, like people, will adapt to the social geography of the conflict that they seek to manage. For instance, in Israel and Palestine, there are such deep rifts between the two groups that reconciliation may mean one thing in Israel and quite another in Palestine. Groups like the Jerusalem Link attempt to bridge this cultural gap by coordinating the activities of political and activist groups on both sides.[77] Other groups emphasize educational reconciliation. The Peace Research Institute in the Middle East is developing a set of teaching materials that reflect both the Israeli and the Palestinian historical narratives, without compromising either. Rather than trying to merge them, they published each narrative along one side of the page, leaving space for children to write their own thoughts in the middle.[78]

Reconciliation organizations may also benefit from association with long-standing institutions, such as labor unions, churches, political parties, and other corporate entities, and these, in turn, pervade civil life. Where the repression thrives on the failure of institutions, people are doubly victimized, first by the repressive regime and second by the loss of faith in institutions around which they had built their lives. Carlos Acuna and Catalina Smulovitz point out that, when the military junta took control in Argentina in 1978, "the sheer magnitude of the repression and the lack of action on the part of political parties, trade unions, the church and the press left citizens helpless."[79] Worse, the institutions that people trust might actually be complicit in the violence, as was the case in Rwanda, where thousands of Tutsi sought refuge in churches which in many cases betrayed them and in some cases even actively participated in their slaughter.

But sometimes, these same institutions may provide succor when the repression is over. In many Latin American countries, churches have been instrumental in supporting human rights and insisting that justice be done. The Archdiocese of São Paulo in Brazil, for instance, was responsible for that country's first truth commission report. In other countries, trade unions have been especially active in the promotion of reconciliation, particularly from the standpoint economic interests.

Some people approach community reconciliation from the inside and the outside simultaneously, and directly and indirectly at the same time. Art is the quintessential example of an approach to reconciliation that transcends these categories. Artists may create art that is obviously about conflict and reconciliation, but its impact on its audience may be indirect and not explicit. There are numerous examples of the use of art for this purpose throughout the world.[80] Stephen Broadbent's statue of reconciliation depicts two people hugging.[81] Australian artist David Boyd has painted reconciliation, also as an embrace. The Guernica Museum in Spain has had an exhibit entitled "Art Towards Reconciliation."

Some art challenges conventional notions of reconciliation. South African artist Sue Williamson, for instance, has a series entitled "Truth Games," which "attempts to consider the role of the Truth and Reconciliation Commission in the healing/not healing of post-apartheid South Africa through a series of interactive pieces. Each piece pictures an accuser, a defender, and an image of the event in question."[82] Superimposed on the images are words from the TRC process. The catch is that the words can be rearranged by the viewer, resulting in new phrases that change the "truth." Williamson explains that "By mediating through art the information offered for public consumption in the mass media, I try to give dispassionate readings and offer new opportunities for engagement. Art can provide a distance and space for such considerations."[83]

Some art forms, particularly the performing arts, actually engage the public in the act of reconciliation. Dramatists in Nepal, for instance, have brought what is known in English as "conflict theater" to villages around the country. In Nepali, it is called "Kachahari" theater, which refers to the village gathering or place where peasants would come to seek justice or resolve community conflicts. Now, this traditional community "court" has been transformed into a theater. A group of actors visits the village and learns about some of the difficulties that the oppressed of the village encounter. At the performance, they fictionalize the conflict, then, in the middle of the story, they pause to ask the audience what the actors should do next or how the situation should resolve itself: "the world of drama creates a space where it is legal to see one's imagination acted out."[84]

Playback theater is a variation on this theme; here the entire story is audience-driven, as audience members tell their own stories, which are then acted out by the troupe. Playback theater now operates in approximately 30 countries and is used primarily to assist in reconciliation in situations of political conflict. Sometimes, local lore from the contending cultures is woven into the play. After the play, children can explore how they felt and what the scenes evoked in them. Seeing the scenes acted out often gives the audience members a perspective they would not otherwise get: the victim actors have dignity that the perpetrators would not have previously recognized, while the perpetrator actors have motivations and a humanity that would not otherwise have been apparent to the victims.[85]

Art functions as reconciliation just as reconciliation functions as art. Art is used as a gateway, to give people access to their own emotions. It is used as a teacher to explain the roots of conflict and the manifestations of it. It is used as a therapist to help people understand their own feelings better. It is used as facilitator to help people talk and listen to one another. Nonetheless, as with any form of reconciliation that is not entirely indigenous to the conflict, outsiders must be careful in how they express the conflict and portray the real actors in the real-life drama of everyday life in conflict-ridden places, lest it devolve into what Babu Ayindo of the Amani People's Theater in Kenya has called "facipulation"—that is, not only facilitating the healing dialogue but manipulating it as well through the "subtle imposition of a pre-set agenda."[86]

Art is becoming an increasingly important way to articulate the issues surrounding war and conflict and, in its positive aspect, reconciliation. A number of groups are now sponsoring art and monitoring how art is involved in the reconciliation project. These include the Legacy Project, which is in the process of building "a global exchange on the enduring consequences of the many historical tragedies of the 20th century," and the Center for the Study of Art and Community, whose project "Art & Upheaval: Artists at Work on the World's Front Lines" documents the efforts of artists involved in reconciliation and peace in conflict areas throughout the world.

One measure of the success of a reconciliation program is the extent to which it opens up space for others to engage in further acts of reconciliation. In South Africa, the TRC paved the way for these types of efforts in that country by holding hearings on how the various sectors of society participated in, perpetuated, and promoted apartheid. It also made recommendations in its 1998 report on how each of these sectors could prevent their constituents from participating in human rights violations in the future. The Commission considered the role of the media, the churches, the medical and legal professions, and business.[87] These hearings revealed the true extent of collusion by prominent institutions in sustaining apartheid. Prompted by the culture of reconciliation fostered by the TRC, the University of Cape Town apologized for its medical school's involvement in the death (or coverup of the death) of Steven Biko, among others. The Medical Association also apologized for its role in apartheid.[88] However, many groups that undoubtedly participated in the maintenance of the apartheid system have so far chosen not to apologize.

In the United States, a country not known for reconciliation,[89] there has been increasing attention to the role that certain companies played in the perpetuation of slavery and segregation, and with it an increasing number of examples of corporate reconciliation. For instance, a school in Georgia has established a scholarship fund for the descendants of people who were prevented from attending because they were black. A newspaper in Connecticut has apologized for having run advertisements for slaves 150 years ago. The nation's largest insurance company, which had insured slaveowners against the loss of their slaves, has apologized for issuing such policies.[90] These measures are few and far between,[91] but taken together they signify the ultimate undeniability of past events, and they express the need for change. Moreover, they model the spirit of reconciliation that others can follow or adapt to their own circumstances. Again, there is a role for governments here, should they choose to promote reconciliation. Laws requiring, for instance, disclosure of an organization's participation in oppressive practices, or requiring set-asides, training programs, scholarship funds, or providing for tax incentives for particular types of charitable contributions, can contribute meaningfully to community healing and reconciliation.

In Spain, the public and private spheres mutually reinforced each other's desire to "reactivate memory," according to Madeleine Davis. In part as the result of the work of the NGO, Asociación para la Recuperación de la Memoria Histórica, and in particular the exhumations of mass graves of people killed during the Civil War and the Franco regime, a rich discourse on the past developed throughout Spanish civil society. The exhumations received extensive media coverage, which gave rise to debate in academic circles, which in turn produced "a spate of new books on various aspects of the war and the dictatorship . . . , while a major exhibition in Madrid, opened by King Juan Carlos . . . focussed on the history of those forced into exile." Davis reports that "this reactivation of memory at the social level also began to receive greater support from some politicians and regional authorities," producing, in turn, more commissions and official resolutions.[92]

Communities in Transition

If civil society is "taken to comprise the associational sphere of social life situated between markets and states,"[93] then communities are the building blocks of civil society. They are where people meet, where their closest ties and strongest bonds are. They are often the source of people's sense of identity. But communities can be the locus of evil as well as of good. In Rwanda, some churches were communities of hatred and death; in Cambodia, communities denounced their own members. In East Germany, there was a community of spies, in El Salvador of death squads, in Bosnia of rapists. In every country, there are associations of people dedicated to promoting racism, repression, and ethnic or religious hatred. Communities in transitional societies are particularly important because they sit precariously on a pivot point, between a repudiated past and a hopeful future. The challenge of post-conflict societies is to ensure that their most prominent communities are dedicated to democracy, the rule of law, and the respect of human rights, rather than to hatred and oppression.

While indifference from the national government does not necessarily doom a program, in general, programs are most likely to be successful if they operate with the blessing or the support of the legitimate governing authority. Ideally, the relationship between the government and the communities is cohesive and mutually reinforcing. The government may (often at the behest of communities) create the space in which reconciliation can happen, and may offer a language, and set the moral tone for reconciliation. But translating those government acts into reality for people is the work of the communities.

Chapter 4
National and International Reconciliation

> We tend to vest our nations with conscience, identities and memories as if they were individuals. It is problematic enough to vest an individual with a single identity: our inner lives are like battlegrounds over which uneasy truces reign; the identity of a nation is additionally fissured by region, ethnicity, class and education.
>
> —Michael Ignatieff

Both the words "national" and "reconciliation" pose particular practical and conceptual problems. First, the idea of nationhood often refers to an ethnic identity—"first nations," the Kurdish nation—whether or not a formal state exists that reflects that identity. In this book, we use the word in its more common variety, to refer to the state (as in the nation of Israel, the French nation, or the United Nations). But that hardly removes the ambiguities. Even in this context, the word "nation" generally connotes a centralized government that controls a defined territory. It implies that the people within that territory self-identify as members of the national polity (even if they also self-identify in other cultural, ethnic, or regional ways). This is the norm throughout much of the world, but it is certainly not true everywhere. In fact, the countries in which reconciliation is an issue are disproportionately countries that do not fit the dominant paradigm of nationhood.

In some countries, the central government is so weak that it can barely be realistically said that a nation exists. Rather, the territory that purportedly makes up the nation is broken up into distinct regions, populations, or political or economic interests, and the people within those territories enjoy no overarching common identity. It may be a state from an international and legalistic point of view but cannot claim to be a nation; Afghanistan, Somalia, and Sudan are often called failed states or not states at all.

But even in strong states, segregation and alienation are pervasive. Indeed, difference and alienation are usual features of transitional societies. Peter Maas has noted that the "dynamics of fear and loathing between people of different backgrounds—ethnic or religious or economic—are not as unique or complex as we might like to believe. Violent breakdowns," he says, "can occur in virtually any country during times of economic hardship, political transition or moral infirmity,"[1] as riots in 2005 in France and Australia can attest. Sometimes, the riots do not dissipate, but escalate. In Chile, for instance, the frustrations of daily life in the 1960s and '70s polarized society to such an extent that even the public's commitment to democracy and to peaceful mechanisms to resolving political differences broke down, paving the way for the military coup of September 11, 1973.[2]

In some cases, polarization might become so extreme that it tears not just at the government but at the very nation. In Afghanistan, for instance, one might legitimately ask what it is to be an Afghan, rather than a Pashtun or Tajik. Ideally, perhaps, one would identify both with the local ethnicity and with the nationality: in some places, however, that possibility does not reflect the experience of the individuals who have strong connections to their local groupings and only the most tenuous link to the national government (which often doesn't have much to do with them either). This condition may be amplified in poorer places where people do not typically travel around the country or to the capital, or where the government may have insufficient resources to make itself felt (in police protection, in schooling, or in other government services) further from the capital.

In other places, the majority of the population may have a strong sense of nationhood, but some significant portions of the population may not. Some Basques in Spain or Arabs in Israel do not self-identify with the nation-state in which they live even though many others within the same country do. This may happen in places where the minority population is actively seeking to secede (such as Chechnya or southwest Morocco) as well as in places where it is not. In the United States, Native Americans constitute a separate nation for certain legal purposes, but they are also American citizens. Where nationhood itself is so ambiguous, the question may fairly be asked how can there be national *anything* (let alone reconciliation)?

By contrast, South Africa, typically defying the odds, has a strong sense of nationhood that may be one factor that contributed to the "miracle" of the South African transition. Reflected throughout the 1996 Constitution, this insistence on national unity is a response to the apartheid government's policy of denationalizing black people at the most fundamental level by denying them citizenship and forcing them to belong not to South Africa but to the racial enclaves within—but, important, without—the larger nation.

Even where the existence and boundaries of the nation are settled, the very idea of nationhood is conceptually complicated. Can there be a national view, a national outlook, a national attitude, or a national identity? "Even in a state that could be regarded as homogeneous by virtue of its shared history, language and religion, a common national identity cannot be assumed. While nationality can be formally and legally ascribed by a constitution or law, the task of nation-building is a more elusive one."[3]

The ambiguity of the term "reconciliation" doubles the complexity of the task of understanding national reconciliation. Reconciliation at the national level may be thought of in one of two ways. It may be the repetition of the other levels of reconciliation, reiterated sufficiently frequently and broadly that it becomes a movement that is "national" in scope. But this view is problematic, if only because it is unrealistic: given most people's resistance to change—to apologize, to forgive, to forget—a national policy that depends on myriad acts of individual transformation is unlikely to succeed. These acts simply aren't common enough to justify an expectation of cultural transformation. Even if they were, there is no evidence that individual transformations, even if frequently replicated, translate into national reconciliation. To assume they do fails to recognize the distinction between public and private reconciliation. Just as public crimes (crimes of state) are not just multiple iterations of private crimes, national reconciliation can not be equated to multiple iterations of individual reconciliation. And precisely because public crimes are in their nature distinct, the response they warrant must be appropriately tailored. For national reconciliation to occur, the state must recognize that it is an entity distinct from the sum of its parts and develop a reconciliation process that operates at that national level.

Some form of national identity is needed for a state to exist. "National identity," according to Nicholas Haysom, "is that identity which citizens share with each other, in recognition of their common destiny and their shared values."[4] If national reconciliation has any significance, it is undoubtedly to unify the people, to create some common ground that is strong enough to overcome the intranational divisions of the past.

Perhaps this is one reason why nations with relatively strong identities, such as the nations of Europe, have spent very little capital promoting reconciliation, notwithstanding the existence of deep divisions within the cultures. For instance, neither Spain after its civil war, nor France in the wake of its collaboration with the Nazis, engaged in any deep soul-searching or efforts to unify erstwhile partisans, or to seek or offer forgiveness. Despite deep cultural and political cleavages in these countries, there was relative homogeneity: to a significant extent, it meant more to most people to be

Spanish or French than to be a Fascist or a collaborator or a resistance fighter.[5] This has proven largely true in Germany, too, in the wake of re-unification. Although there are meaningful differences between East and West Germans— differences that may remain significant for generations to come— the similarities are to most people stronger than the differences. In postcommunist Europe, Jacques Rupnick has suggested that nation-building was easier where the populations are homogeneous (as in Poland, the Czech Republic, and Slovenia), than in countries with significant ethnic minority populations (as in Slovakia and the Balkan states). And countries with significant precommunist histories had an easier time invoking the past to do some of the work of unification and rebuilding than countries that had little common history to call on. While ethnic homogeneity is *not*, as Rupnick reminds us, a "precondition for democracy,"[6] it is highly useful for reconciliation. Some amount of at least *relative* homogeneity—more significant points of commonality than of difference—is a desirable ingredient for reconciliation. Fostering that homogeneity, by emphasizing the common ground, is one of the principal priorities of national reconciliation.

But herein lies the challenge. Developing a common sense of belonging among diverse peoples is fraught with difficulties: the government will need to overcome the deep-seated fears and resentments between different groups, which may have been segregated for long periods of time. It will need to establish a version of its history that resonates, to some extent, with everyone. It will need to provide enough benefits to all of the people to make it worth their while to participate in the nation-building exercise. And the stakes are high: failing to achieve a modicum of reconciliation can affect many if not all facets of national, regional, and local life. Without some level of reconciliation, the nation's valuable resources will need to be deployed on conflict management, rather than on capacity-building constructive projects. And yet, aiming too high—attempting to achieve unity at any cost—has its pitfalls as well, particularly when it requires people to slough off veils of identity to which they feel attached, or when it requires them to forgive or befriend those for whom they feel no particular attachment.

Reconciliation at the national level may be fundamentally about accommodation. It is about accepting the right of others in the state to have differing views which, ideally, should be recognized and even welcomed as part of the national debate. This may require Herculean efforts on the part of the transitional governments to invite and respect views and attitudes of groups for which they have no natural affinity. As Kreisberg has written, "Reconciliation here refers to accommodative ways members of adversary entities have come to regard each other after having engaged in intense, and often destructive struggle."[7]

In nations that do not exert such a strong pull on their citizens, reconciliation efforts are more important to help each side identify with the nation as such and to realize its stake in the nation's future. National reconciliation may be thought of as the development of a sense of national citizenship, or loyalty to the nation.[8] This loyalty would supplement, not supplant, the loyalty that individuals feel to more local communities and associations; reconciliation would thereby broaden people's allegiances to include the national, as well as the parochial.

The following sections examine various paths national governments might take to promote this sense of belonging through cultural iconography, commission reports, trials, and legislation.

Cultural Symbols

One important element in national reconciliation is the creation of a national culture. Indicia of the national culture includes everything from the nation's founding documents and manifestos to the symbols chosen for the flag and the currency. A national narrative will typically have both backward- and forward-looking elements, reflecting and fostering a "common and shared memory"[9] as well as a sense of shared destiny. The symbols of the emerging culture will communicate to individuals both within and without the society what the defining ideas of that culture are. Ideally, this common story can also teach human rights values so that the traumas of the past are not repeated. As it seeps into the collective consciousness of the people, this narrative becomes part of the cultural heritage of the nation's inhabitants. Thus, the cultural narrative is a dynamic or dialogic phenomenon that reinvents itself in the relation between the individual and the nation.

Part of the charge of the new government is to develop a cultural narrative that achieves broad assent—that is, that resonates with people on all sides of the previous conflict. In some cases, this may entail not only building the new symbology but tearing down the old, as the postwar Germans did in banning the swastika. And yet in some of these cases, despite the best efforts of the authorities, the people may continue to adhere to the symbols of the past, as do the Croats in post-Dayton Mostar who defiantly display the Sahovnica, the symbol of the Croatian state.[10]

Stories of national identity may be a one-time event or a continuing or repeating process. They should have sufficient explanatory authority to be taken seriously, but at the same time be sufficiently accessible to be accepted by a wide range of the population. Most importantly, they need to feel real, or they will be viewed as just one more layer of propaganda.

Governments contribute to the national narrative in almost all of their acts, because everything the government does is part of the nation's history and therefore part of its story. The choice of a flag[11] or a national anthem, the provisions of a new constitution, and statements by government officials about ongoing violence can all be part of the national story. They may choose new official languages (as Timor Leste did when it adopted Portuguese rather than Indonesian as its national language), and they may choose new names for places, as most countries do as soon as the first statues fall.

Among the most palpable ways for a government to establish the bright line between the old and the new is through the proclamation of new holidays. Some countries celebrate the new dispensation by observing a foundational event that brought it into being, such as Independence Day or Constitution Day.[12] Other holidays focus on tragic events of emotional significance, turning defeat into national honor. Argentina now observes Malvinas Day to honor the fallen soldiers of the Malvinas War. South Africa celebrates Youth Day on June 16 to honor the students who protested against educational conditions in what became the Soweto uprising. In fact, most nations' memorial or remembrance or martyrs' days are of this type—they honor those who have died in wars won and lost. Increasingly, nations have begun to promote reconciliation as a holiday for its own sake. In Australia reconciliation is promoted through an annual "Sorry Day" and "Walk for Reconciliation." In 2002, one day after North and South Korea agreed to restart talks on reconciliation, delegates from north and south met in Seoul to celebrate Liberation Day, the anniversary of the end of Japanese colonial rule—the most significant experience they have in common. The stated purpose of the two-day festival was to spur the movement toward reconciliation, reunification, and unity. Several nations are explicit about fostering reconciliation by naming their holidays "Reconciliation Day."

If holidays are temporal statements about the values of the new dispensation, museums and memorial sites are physical commemorations. Indeed, TRCs commonly call for the construction of memorials and museums as part of the reconciliation program, both to remember and to re-create the national history. On the other end, such sites can also speak volumes when destroyed: one of the most ubiquitous images of the breakup of the Soviet Union was of statues of Lenin being taken down, physically establishing that communism was not only dead but irrelevant in the new world order, removing or deleting a part of history. The fall of Saddam Hussein in 2003 was accompanied by similar photo opportunities.

Most holidays, statues, and memorial sites are unilateral statements from the government to the people; as such, they do not necessarily reflect what is important to the people. There are, however, exceptions to this:

in the course of many revolutions, there may develop ad hoc popular memorial sites, such as in Wenceslas Square in Prague, where during the heady days of the velvet revolution, people brought candles, photographs, and flowers to a site to recognize those who had died and to revel in the liberation from Soviet occupation.

These methods of establishing unity and sometimes reconciliation may be effective to force bonds or commonalities among the nation's people, but they are neither nuanced nor comprehensive. They simply state what the new symbols are and provide the means (days off from work, subsidized parades) for people to participate and, consequently, to invest a little of themselves into the new order. However, because such nonverbal actions can be blunt, they are as likely to be divisive as they are to promote reconciliation. In one Bosnian town, for instance, the Serbian population complained that an area in the middle of town that had, before the war, been designated for a park, was now the site of a mosque, which was certainly seen as divisive rather than conciliatory.[13]

If national reconciliation implies a national unity on the matter of the past, the general population needs to believe the same or similar facts and attribute more or less the same meaning to those facts. As Brandon Hamber has observed: "History in conflict-ridden societies is a debate and a volatile one at that. However, its volatility forces us not to ignore the irresolvable debates of history but rather to seek out ways to deal with them. It seems logical that these may be best dealt with through institutionalised and legitimate social and community frameworks."[14] In Bosnia, Jakob Finci, who spearheaded the movement for a truth and reconciliation commission there, argues that a national TRC is needed precisely because "[nationalists] from the three ethnic communities involved in the recent war propagate a history that portrays their group as the one and only victim of mass abuses, depicting the other two as evil perpetrators and monsters. Three separate war crimes commissions, dominated respectively by Bosnian, Croat, and Serb perspectives, have focused on the victimization of their own group."[15] The results can be disastrous. "For now," he says, "we have three different histories, each teaching our children that our neighbours are our enemies. Continuing like this, we cannot expect anything more than a new war in 20 or 30 years."[16] Governments can promote reconciliation and protect against future bloodshed by fusing these diverse perspectives into a unified, though multifaceted, story.

Indeed, in the last twenty years, truth commissions have become increasingly popular precisely because of their ability to forge a common history out of a conflict-ridden past. Truth commissions and trials are discussed throughout this book; in the next sections, we consider how they and the narratives they produce can contribute to national reconciliation.

Truth Reports

Like holidays and flag designs, truth commission reports can form part of a new national narrative. Unlike these other forms, however, commission reports that describe and analyze the struggle and its outcome rely so extensively on disclosure of the truth that separate sections in this book examine the relevance of truth, per se, to reconciliation in more detail. Here, we look at the ways in which narratives, in the form of commission reports, advance national reconciliation by shaping the collective consciousness of the population, and thereby encourage bonds among the new nation's citizens.

Opinions vary on how great a contribution commission reports can make to national narrative. Some people have argued that the creation of the broadly accepted narrative is the primary value of truth commissions.[17] It remains to be seen whether truth commission reports actually do create new histories as they preclude denial among the diehard defenders of the old regime in the long run.

Potentially, these narratives can form the foundation of the new, post-transition nation. They can emphasize the common ground on which all sides can agree, rather than providing fodder for continued strife. The more the narrative resonates with all sides, the more successful it will be; the more contested it is, the less likely it is to promote reconciliation. And if it appears to the public to be whitewashing or covering up for the interests of powerful parties, it can actually backfire.

Also unlike symbols and holidays, truth commission reports constitute *verbal* narratives—that is, they use written language to communicate the stories they seek to tell. This in and of itself is often a source of strife in divided nations. In many conflict-ridden zones the choice of language is heavily contested. This is true in the former Yugoslavia as well as in many countries that were formerly under the Soviet sphere of influence, as well as in Québec and other places with significant linguistic subpopulations. In these instances, a nationalist language is often *not* the state language, and the promoters of reconciliation need to consider whether their official stories will be told in the official language or in the national language of the people it seeks to reconcile.

Even where the choice of language is uncontested or resolved, the choice of words can be divisive. Are the people who fought for liberation rebels, insurgents, freedom fighters, guerillas, or terrorists? Are the people who worked for the former regime bureaucrats, pawns, or war criminals? Did people die or were they murdered? Are they martyrs or suicide bombers? Is the government operating prisons or concentration camps? These are just a very few examples among the many to illustrate the war zone of language itself.

The authority creating the commission should be clear in its goals, and these goals should determine the contours of the commission and its report. Thinking through not just the content of the report but the procedures by which it comes into being can legitimize it, increasing the likelihood that a broad range of people will accept it. If, on the other hand, it is viewed as promoting ulterior goals, people are much more likely to be skeptical and to resist its conciliatory impact.[18] Ignoring these questions by allowing the appearance of bias or partisanship enables those who would contest the report to gain traction in the public debate. If there is room in the public consciousness to challenge the independence of the commission, even evidence in the report that is indisputable (photographs of graves or prisons or scars on people's bodies) will encourage the losing side to argue that the deaths were accidental, the other prisons were better, and the wounds self-inflicted. Such challenges may be minimized by attention at the outset to questions of legitimacy and independence.

The first decision is whether the report should emanate directly from the government or from some other body. Public holidays, flags, and laws of course all come from the government, as do most truth commissions. But just as private individuals can create monuments and even holidays without government sponsorship, so can they produce truth reports. In Zimbabwe, where the government had never published the report of its own truth commission (on the ground that publication would be divisive), "two major Zimbabwean human rights organizations produced a report in 1997 that thoroughly documented the repression of the 1980s on the basis of extensive interviews with victims."[19] In Brazil, the Archdiocese of São Paulo produced a report on government abuses in response to the government's refusal to do so. Even without official endorsement, reports from such bodies, if widely and thoughtfully disseminated, can contribute to the national narrative about the past events (and can be useful in subsequent trials).

If the government sponsors the commission, it needs to decide how much independence the commission will have. The more independence the commission has, the more likely its findings will be taken as legitimate and nonpartisan. The risk to the government with an independent commission is obviously that it loses control over the content—over the specifics of the narrative—but this loss of control may enhance the narrative's legitimacy, especially in a divided society where everything is contested, and where people look for issues to contest. Other decisions, including those relating to personnel, scope of mandate, and funding, will also influence the legitimacy of the process as well as both the content of the narrative and its reception by the public. Commission independence may also be enhanced in the organic law creating the commission, through grants of discretion (e.g., deciding where and how many public hearings are held) and grants of power (e.g., subpoena power, judicial personality), limitations on government oversight (e.g., no government vetting prior to publication), and control over personnel (e.g., prohibiting termination of commissioners and allowing commissioners to elect their own chair).

Other equally important questions are typically not answered in the authorizing legislation. Will the report name names, publish photographs, assign blame for specific acts? Will the commission be permitted to editorialize, or is it exclusively a fact-finding exercise? How will the report portray the perpetrators: will it humanize them, by seeking to understand their motivations and the political situation from their perspective, or, in failing to do so, will it demonize them? How much of the victims' voices will be heard throughout the report? Australia's Stolen Children report, for instance, is replete with photographs and heart-rending testimonials of children kidnaped from their parents by government officials under Australia's policy of terminating Aboriginal culture. Testimonials like these, or like those included in the South African report, are much more likely to sear national consciousness than dry descriptions of legislative and administrative policy.

In general, there are at least four major opportunities to promote reconciliation through commission reports. In all four situations, timing is critical: the government needs to take advantage when the public mood is receptive to difficult truths and interested in learning about the past; however, if the public is consumed with other problems or otherwise not accepting of the commission's authority, it will have a harder time making people care about the commission's work.

An initial opportunity exists while the plans for the commission are developing and when personnel decisions are being made. While these can be a part of a successful commission's aura, as they were in South Africa, Timor Leste, and Sierra Leone, they quickly become irrelevant if the actual work of the commission does not meet expectations. But this stage can at least invite people to think about reconciliation.

The second opportunity is during the pendency of the commission, while it is doing its work. A commission can begin to forge the national narrative of the transition immediately, if it operates within the country, transparently, and with a modicum of media knowhow. Some commission hearings have been televised. Others have been reported widely on radio and in newspapers throughout the country. Depending on the way the commission operates—does it hold hearings in a centralized location, or does it carry out field investigation—the opportunities for public participation may vary. Whatever their form, however, the more opportunities there are for public participation, the more likely it is that the people will be interested in the commission's work. Ghana's National Reconciliation Commission, operating between 2002 and 2003, provides a good example of an open and transparent commission. According to one press report, "Crowds of people throng the refurbished chambers of the old parliament building in Ghana's capital, Accra, every Tuesday, Wednesday and Thursday to witness the proceedings of the National Reconciliation Commission. Hundreds of thousands of other Ghanaians watch the hearings live on national television. Others make do with a late-evening retransmission on TV."[20]

In Timor, the CAVR took its public information role very seriously, producing a range of accessible material during the pendency of the program, including a feature-length film in multiple languages, a photographic exhibition promoting "their dignity and aspirations," a series of books on the thematic national public hearings, and a photographic book of survivors "expressing their hopes for the future." In addition, "popular items to promote the Commission included posters, booklets, brochures and T-shirts." The weekly radio program "included coverage of many community reconciliation hearings, as well as discussion of issues arising from the national hearings and other matters relating to reconciliation."[21] This was apparently effective; during the two-day hearing on Women and Conflict, "Across Dili, in homes, market places and workplaces, people followed the hearing on television, and across the nation people were tuned into the national radio live broadcast. As one international journalist traveling in the border district of Maliana on the second day of the hearings said, 'It seemed like all of Maliana was tuned into the radio broadcast.'"

If the Commission is going to contribute to the nation's historical narrative, its work must culminate with the publication of a final report. The report should give as complete a picture as possible of the events. It should state the nature and extent of the crimes committed, names of and facts about the victims, and the identities of the perpetrators. It should be disseminated broadly (using creative mediums where necessary, including radio and the Internet) so that the entire population has access to the report.[22] With the aid of inexpensive technologies and international grants, countries are increasingly making their reports widely available, as Morocco, Timor Leste, Peru, and Sierra Leone have recently done. Ideally, nonwritten forms of expressing the content of the Commission's work should be developed, to reach the nation's illiterate population.

A surprising number of truth commission reports have rarely seen the light of day. In Uganda, there is only one known copy of the commission's report.[23] In Zimbabwe, no one outside the government has ever seen the report.[24] In Uruguay, "the commission report, although a public document, was not widely distributed, nor were its findings ever officially announced to the public." As a result, it "failed to produce a national truth," according to Barahona de Brito.[25] By contrast, in South Africa, the report was not only widely disseminated to schools and to libraries, but much of the information was available in newspapers and on the Internet. Much the same can be said for Australia's report on the stolen generations of Aborigines, which is available in most bookstores. Argentina's report, authored by noted writer Ernesto Sábato, sold very well for years after its publication. Peru's 2003 report was on the Internet within days of its publication.

The publication of the report presents a third opportunity to shape a national narrative. Usually, the commission's work culminates with the submission of its report in a public ceremony to the president or prime minister of the nation or the head of state. How that person accepts the report, what statements are made at the time and by whom, can influence how the report is internalized by the general population. The Salvadoran president completely dismissed the truth report that was submitted to him in 1993, notwithstanding the august international credentials of its authors. (So it would not have been too surprising that a sweeping amnesty law was passed five days after the report was released.) President Cristiani said that the report "failed to meet the Salvadoran people's 'yearning' for national reconciliation."[26] By contrast, Chilean President Aylwin responded to his country's report emotionally by seeking "forgiveness from the victims and stressed the need for forgiveness and reconciliation."[27] In South Africa, the first five volumes of the TRC report were handed to President Mandela in October 1998. (The last two volumes, held up by the Amnesty Committee's work in granting amnesty, as well as various court cases aimed at suppressing some of the findings that were made, were handed over in March 2003.) The week before the handover in 1998, three political parties had been to court in an attempt to stop publication or redact parts of the report. It was in this climate of tension that President Mandela said that he accepted the report "with all its imperfections."[28] The TRC process and the report itself remain contested terrain in South Africa.

Tensions surrounding the contents of a truth commission report also marred the work of the Timorese Commission for Reception, Truth, and Reconciliation (CAVR). In 2005, CAVR handed over its report to President Gusmao, who had been a strong advocate for reconciliation. Upon receiving the report, however, he urged that it not be disseminated, apparently because of disagreement with some of its recommendations. No matter how independent a commission is, politicians in both legislative and executive capacities can dilute the work of even the most dedicated commission.

Even a lackluster reception, however, may not doom a well-documented report if it is published and widely available. And even if it languishes for a while, it remains available to families, researchers, lawyers, successive heads of state, and others to revive, thereby creating subsequent opportunities to use the report to promote reconciliation. Even if the commission's capacity to contribute to the national narrative is latent for a time, it may be no less effective. We might say that the commission was simply ahead of its time and that the people eventually came to a place where they could accept the findings of the commission. It is even possible that the existence of the commission itself helped move the people in that direction, although not at the same pace as the commissioners themselves. If it is true that a principal purpose of a truth commission is to create a space in which further acts of reconciliation can take place, then it matters less when those acts occur than that they do occur.

In Canada, for instance, it took the government more than a year to respond meaningfully to the report of the Royal Commission on Aboriginal Peoples. When it finally did respond, though, it did so with a report of its own, which outlined an Action Plan aimed at renewing the partnerships between the government and the Aboriginal communities, strengthening Aboriginal governance, developing a new fiscal relationship, and supporting strong communities, people and economies. At the same time, the government announced a $350 million grant to support a "Healing Strategy" to help individuals recover from the trauma of physical and sexual abuse endured while they were students at the compulsory residential schools. In addition, the government issued a "Statement of Reconciliation," in which it directly acknowledged the injustice of the government's prior policies and the effects of those policies on aboriginal culture, and formally expressed "profound regret for past actions of the federal government which have contributed to these difficult pages in the history of our relationship together."[29] In Australia, the reception of the Stolen Children report seems to have been almost the opposite; Prime Minister John Howard's government steadfastly refused to apologize, but reconciliation between whites and Aboriginals has become a firmly entrenched part of Australian popular culture and lexicon, which recognizes Reconciliation Day, Reconciliation art, Reconciliation gardens, Reconciliation support groups, and even Reconciliation T-shirts. In 1991 Australia's Parliament voted unanimously to set up a Council for Aboriginal Reconciliation to address the country's "pervasive racial discrimination and to promote reconciliation between Aborigines and Torres Strait Islanders and European settlers."[30] The law contemplated various functions for the Council, including promoting indigenous culture and history and reconciliation initiatives, developing strategic plans, promoting open discussion forums, and making recommendations with regard to a formal reconciliation document.[31]

Thus, a fourth opportunity is in the aftermath of the report. The optimal situation arises when governments anticipate the report and prepare appropriate means to follow up on the commission's work. Even if the government acts entirely in reaction to the report—if its findings, for instance, could not have been anticipated—it is critical for the government to follow up on the work of the commission, and not just to let its discoveries lie fallow. In Chile and Canada, reports have led to reparations programs. In Argentina, the publication of the Sábato report prompted a series of prosecutions against some of those who were implicated in the report.[32] In South Africa, Spain, and Australia, reports have stimulated public debate. In these cases, the report not only highlighted the facts of the division, but actually began to develop a language in which future discourse could take place. The more robust the language, the less partisan it is, and the more useful it will be to citizens from different perspectives to talk about the divisions of the past.

Here, it may be important to distinguish between "truth commissions" and "truth and reconciliation commissions." Most commissions are of the former type, although several of the most prominent ones—in Chile, Peru, South Africa, and Timor—have at least been nominally committed to promoting reconciliation as well as to revealing truth. The distinction is not often emphasized either in the literature or by commissioners themselves. And yet, it is crucial because it affects the nature of the narrative. Is the purpose of the story simply to reveal what happened, or is to help unify people? The two aims may be synergistic but they can often be antagonistic. If the commission is solely interested in truth, it may present information unvarnished, thereby possibly impeding reconciliation. If the commission is interested in both truth and reconciliation, it may provide more of a context or balance to the same truth, thereby encouraging a conciliatory response to the truth by all sides.

It may also affect what the followup should be: should the government attempt to foster reconciliation based on the truth that was revealed, or should it allow the truth revealed in the report to be divisive? Most commissions, even those that have reconciliation in their titles or as a stated aim, tend to privilege truth over reconciliation. There is little evidence of withholding truth from reports on the ground that it would impede reconciliation. More often, truth is included even where it could be divisive. Salvadoran President Christiani's statement, then, may have been absolutely correct—that the report did not satisfy the nation's yearning for reconciliation, even though it could not be faulted for shying away from the truth.

This situation may change with the influence of the South African TRC on subsequent commissions, and with increased ability to measure "reconciliation" through polls and social science studies. The next wave of commissions may in fact subordinate truth to reconciliation, which is not necessarily desirable. The less a report says, the less there is to disagree with, but the less it is likely to contribute to the long-term peace and stability of the country.

At worst, reports are irrelevant to people's national experiences. Many of the commission reports mentioned here were peripheral, if they were known at all, to the public for whom they were at least nominally intended. The commissions get set up, do their work, issue their report, and then all too often disappear without leaving a trace in the public's mental and emotional experience. The stories these commissions tell have the potential to fashion the national narrative upon which reconciliation can be built, but they can do so only if they manage to penetrate the collective consciousness of the people.

Trials

A more common, though less explicit, way of promoting a particular narrative is through criminal trials. Trials, however, produce a very different kind of narrative from that of the truth commission. The trial's narrative is far narrower, usually focused on one individual or event (or sometimes a limited grouping of individuals or events). Its only purpose is to determine the innocence or guilt of the defendant, and therefore the narrative it produces centers on that legal question. At times, the resolution of the legal question is at odds with the common perception—it is obvious to everyone that the person was guilty, but there is insufficient evidence to convict. Many issues which, in the public mind, are related to the central issue of wrongdoing nonetheless remain peripheral in the trial— the causes of the violence, the wider net of accountability and responsibility, the consequences of the violence for the victims and survivors.

All these questions—which may be examined in depth in a truth commission—are eclipsed by the trial's singular focus on the guilt or innocence of the defendant. Moreover, the trial's polarizing nature precludes nuanced assessment of these questions: the narrative speaks only the language of guilt or innocence, of right or wrong, acquittal or conviction. For these reasons, the narrative produced by a trial may be less satisfying to many people whose experiences reflect the more complex nature of most political conflict. On the other hand, trial narratives have certain advantages over truth reports. Trial officials often have greater access to information, through discovery and subpoenas, than do truth commissioners. The evidentiary standards employed in trials are much more stringent than those used in most truth commissions and therefore may lend greater credibility to the truths they do reveal, limited though they may be. In theory, trials can uncover the truth about an event or a series of events, and the verdict ascribes to that truth a particular meaning, for instance, that the defendant actually committed the acts in question, that he intended the harm that resulted, and that those acts are wrongful and warrant punishment. The trial narrative may incorporate a certain moral judgment that is often an essential part of the national foundational narrative. It is often incumbent on the new regime to emphasize the morality of the new dispensation, by demonstrating, through public and sometimes even sensationalistic trials, that the rule of law means that no one is above the law, that human rights will be respected, and that wrongful conduct will be punished. The simple "right and wrong" logic of trials may resonate in the public consciousness in a way that is more satisfying and readily accepted than the more complex versions of truth described in truth reports. When this does occur, the trial can promote national unity by helping the population at large to understand the events according to the narrative of the trial, and it can promote national reconciliation by vindicating the public's sense that justice is being done.

It may be most useful to consider the narratives of truth commissions and of trials as complementary and mutually reinforcing, rather than in competition with one another. Each tribunal has unique institutional competencies that should be identified and capitalized upon. Many courts, for instance, have limited themselves to the prosecution of leaders and those responsible for the most egregious human rights abuses. On the other hand, truth commissions might be more appropriate venues for examining the moral responsibility of bystanders or child offenders.[33] The Chair of the Sierra Leone Truth Commission suggested that both the Commission and the Special Court were "going to the promised land, but by different roads."[34] Richard Goldstone, who chaired a commission of inquiry in South Africa before he became the chief prosecutor of the International Criminal Tribunals for both Yugoslavia and Rwanda, has said that whereas the judicial process

is essential for reconciliation to begin, it is insufficient alone to satisfy the human need for knowing the truth of a tragic series of events. In addition to criminal prosecution, it is necessary for a damaged society to arrive at a wider understanding of the causes of its suffering. For no matter how well the tribunal [International Criminal Tribunal for Yugoslavia] does its job, the scope of history is far broader than proving the guilt of a few specific individuals.[35]

Despite the abundance of formal statements endorsing the comparably beneficial contributions to peace of both trials and truth commissions, the allocation of funds to the different tribunals suggests a different story. In Sierra Leone, for instance, the budget for the Special Court was originally set at $100 million, but was scaled down to $56 million over three years. The Commission, by contrast, was initially budgeted at $10 million, but "poor donor response resulted in a reduction to less than $7 million. In the end, the TRC has been pledged less than $4 million," which has precluded the originally anticipated "robust team of internationally qualified" and properly resourced researchers and investigators.[36] The United Nations has budgeted almost a billion dollars for the International Criminal Tribunal for Yugoslavia (ICTY) since its inception in 1994 to 2004,[37] but as yet no money has been devoted to establishing a reconciliation commission in Bosnia. This stark imbalance in resources dramatically illustrates the fealty that many still have toward trials over truth commissions.

Public Education

One final method of producing a national narrative that is worth mentioning is the simplest and most direct: through a public education campaign. A public education campaign is almost the reverse of a truth commission; it is all followup and no soul-searching. Nonetheless, it can contribute to reconciliation in equal measure. It can be produced by the central authority of the government itself, by a particular ministry (such as the growing number of ministries of reconciliation), or by the office of an ombudsman, which is also becoming an increasingly popular way to protect human rights.

Under the terms of the Dayton Agreement that ended the war in Bosnia, for instance, the federal government in Bosnia established an ombudsman's office which has been particularly active in advising citizens of their rights, advocating on behalf of citizens, and generally raising the profile of human rights issues in Bosnia and Herzegovina. In South Africa, this was being done even before the transition in 1994 by groups such as the Centre for the Study of Violence and Reconciliation, who engaged in school-based education, teacher training, and curriculum development related to violence.[38] Since 1994 other types of programs have been developed, including a human rights curriculum for schools. None of which is to say that human rights problems have been eliminated in these countries; indeed, it is virtually impossible to assess the effectiveness of such campaigns. In only the most extraordinary situations will they result in significant changes in attitudes or behavior among the population—and where such changes do occur, it is difficult to determine the role the campaign played.

All these methods of producing a national narrative—whether directly through reports of commissions, or indirectly, through criminal or civil trials or through the work of government departments—share many traits, even though they are diverse in their provenance, structure, and level of government control. Whatever the source, a narrative designed to promote reconciliation may, if successful, provide the common ground on which people throughout the nation can begin to recreate relationships with one another. They can begin to understand that what happened to each of them individually happened to all of them collectively in one way or another and in this way, can begin to speak of a shared history and a shared future.

Beyond Narrative

There are also other less textual, more symbolic ways in which governments can promote reconciliation at the national level. Leaders and others can, and frequently do, engage in actions that are meant to promote reconciliation. These actions do so not by explaining the importance of reconciliation, nor even by explaining how reconciliation is possible. Rather, leaders who engage in such acts lead by example. By showing the public that they are willing to be conciliatory, they suggest that the public can and should be as well. One important implication of this is that while interpersonal reconciliation (between victim and perpetrator or between victim/perpetrator and community) cannot be imposed on behalf of someone else, national reconciliation can. A leader may apologize or grant forgiveness on behalf of his or her people, whereas in bilateral and community reconciliation each person must be presumed at least to acquiesce in the act of forgiveness, whether publicly or privately, expressly or not.

A simple handshake between former enemies is perhaps the best known symbol of reconciliation at the national level. Other acts of similar nature include the signing of a peace accord, the terms of which may not be known to the general public but the fact of which demonstrates the willingness of the leaders to do business with each other. In some cases, stepping down from office may promote reconciliation, if the leader is an ineluctably divisive force.

Some acts of reconciliation are purely symbolic and purely unilateral. Abraham Lincoln, on hearing of the surrender of the Southern states, ordered his band to play "Dixie," the southern anthem. When Australian Prime Minister Gough Whitlam ceremonially returned a parcel of land to an Aboriginal group, he let some soil fall through his fingers into the waiting hands of the tribal chief. Nelson Mandela may have made the strongest impression when he wore a South African rugby jersey at the 1995 Rugby World Cup, hosted and won by South Africa. This event was the first major international event held in South Africa in the post-apartheid era and has been labeled a hallmark event in the politics of reconciliation and identity formation in the new South Africa.[39] Likewise, Australia's selection of Aboriginal track star Cathy Freeman to light the Olympic cauldron at the 2000 Games was lauded as a proffer of reconciliation.[40]

The problem with symbolic actions, though, is that there is no necessary correlation between how great the symbolism is and how deeply it penetrates into the culture. It may be clever and politically astute and wildly popular, at least momentarily. But it does not necessarily create common ground strong enough to support long-term, deep national reconciliation.

To what extent does reconciliation among elites actually promote national reconciliation? Nelson Mandela showed that it could. His deep commitment to reconciliation and his own experiences that would test the limits of that commitment persuaded millions of people to follow his example and shaped the national psyche of the New South Africa (if such a thing could be said to exist). Michelle Bachelet of Chile—another victim-turned-president—may also promote reconciliation by her very presence as well as by her actions. But these may be the exceptions that prove the rule that reconciliation among elites is rarely transformative of the larger society. Few leaders are actually willing to model *genuine* reconciliation. Certainly the norm is for leaders to reflect the popular will, rather than transform it.

The limitations of conciliatory actions at the leadership level have led to increased attention to what may be called participatory reconciliation—reconciliation that includes and involves wide segments of the public. Whereas the first generation of truth commissions operated largely behind closed doors, the current batch is characterized by a high degree of public participation and transparency, such as in South Africa, Sierra Leone, Timor, and perhaps Bosnia. Rwanda's gacaca courts are a prominent example of participatory justice, as contrasted with the exclusive (even if nominally open) nature of domestic and international criminal tribunals.

But at this level, too, the results are mixed. In any divided society, Fanie du Toit has written, "Individuals who seek to encourage reconciliation processes . . . have to convince others to give up promises of tangible, short-term rewards for long term benefits such as peace and stability."[41] And yet, it is not at all clear how much contact between individuals across social divides actually affects the rest of the communities. Du Toit argues that those who position "themselves in the no-man's-land between opposing groupings—or constantly mov[e] between these spaces from one side to the other— . . . have a powerful effect on both sides. They are fearless explorers, repeatedly returning to tell fresh tales about the 'others'."[42] But the reality is that these "explorers" seem to have little impact on the larger society, which goes about its business in more or less segregated ways. Those who travel from one side of the chasm to the other are at best ignored and at worse excoriated for the betrayal they symbolize. People who have contact with "the other" are also more likely to consider their contact aberrational and not representative of the rest of the group.

What seems to be needed is a critical mass of intergroup contacts that eventually wear down the resistance of each side. Thus, the growing number of government ministries and NGOs that are dedicated to reconciliation is a welcome development in this regard. These institutions can help individuals within groups reach across divides and can encourage intergroup communication and activities.[43] One of the newest of these, in the Solomon Islands, was mandated by the Townsville Peace Process that quelled the violent rebellion in the late 1990s. It is mandated to "engage

youth, women, churches, NGOs and other civil society groups to participate in the peace process" and to "initiate dialogue with renegade factions
of the former Isatabu Freedom Movement so that they accept and be
involved in the Peace process."[44] It is especially concerned with the reintegration of the 30,000 internally displaced persons and 5,000 soldiers
into their communities and with the setting down of arms by militants in
order to ensure civil peace. It has contracted with an NGO, the Community Reconciliation and Reintegration Project, to promote community
involvement in reconciliation and development programs.

Whatever form these measures take, governments seeking to achieve
a meaningful measure of national reconciliation need to commit to long-
term investment. This can take the form of institutions designed to follow up on the work of the commissions (such as the Chilean Corporation
for National Reconciliation), or government departments, or ongoing
decentralized programs. They should be well-funded and well-publicized
and have the continued endorsement of the central government.

Programs like this have great potential because, consistent with most
people's experiences, they link multiple levels of society: most people see
themselves as both members of a local community and members of a
larger nation. A reconciliation program that operates only at one level is
less relevant because it omits important facets of people's lives. The Solomon Islands approach ensures that the reconciliation projects have the
official endorsement and funding of the national government but reflect
the values and needs of people within their local communities.

It is worth remembering that, in many situations, national reconciliation is impossible without attention to foreign countries. Many of today's
civil conflicts transcend borders, with insurgents getting funds or support from other nations, or irredentist claims pulling the titular nation
apart. Peace in Iraq, the Congo, the Balkans, and Cambodia will necessarily entail inquiry into the role of foreign nations in the perpetuation
of warfare and civil strife. But even in these situations, reconciliation is
primarily a domestic affair. It must come from within the society, or not at
all. In contrast, the next section considers reconciliation between, rather
than within nations.

International Reconciliation

Reconciliation between two or more nations is conceptually the simplest
level at which reconciliation can happen, but (or perhaps because) it is
also the most removed from the normal experience of most people. Conflicts between nations arise from territorial disputes, disputes over the
treatment of citizens, or perceived threats by one nation against another.
Rifts can deepen as diplomats are recalled or expelled, borders are closed,

and accusations are made, culminating in some cases in military hostilities. The process of reconnecting the nations is reconciliation.

The simplest cases of international reconciliation involve disputes between nation-states. Like reconciliation between citizens, reconciliation between nations can range from mere détente (trust but verify) to increasing interdependence. And in both intranational and international reconciliation, actions may be taken that will be more or less likely to conduce to reconciliation. One common action is for a country to release or exchange political prisoners. For example, after the 1971 Indo-Pakistani conflict, Bangladesh, India, and Pakistan signed an Agreement on the Repatriation of Prisoners of War and Civilian Internees,[45] in which Pakistani prisoners of war detained in Bangladesh, and accused of having committed war crimes, crimes against humanity, and genocide, would be repatriated to Pakistan without trials as an act of clemency to promote reconciliation.[46] Israel's unilateral removal of settlers in Gaza is another example of actions that could be conducive to international reconciliation.

International reconciliation is also similar to its domestic counterparts in that it may be forged either by the principals or by third parties. The United Nations, of course, often acts as a peace broker: in addition to its teams of peacekeeping troops, negotiators, and election facilitators, it has sponsored both truth commissions (notably in Latin America) and trials (Sierra Leone, Timor), and has been negotiating for years to do the same in Cambodia. The UN also supports reconciliation processes such as that in the Central African Republic;[47] likewise, the Arab League may be committing itself to reconciliation in Iraq. Independent or nonaligned nations or individuals may also help other countries to reconcile. Egypt has frequently over the years attempted to broker peace between Israel and her neighbors; China is increasingly becoming a peace broker in Asia. Foreign diplomats helped forge the Dayton Peace Agreement ending the war in Bosnia, the Good Friday Agreement ending hostilities in Northern Ireland, and the 2005 agreement ending the civil war in Aceh Province in Indonesia. When the international community is involved, it can provide many of the services a national government can provide, including space for negotiations, trials, and nonjudicial tribunals such as truth commissions, and the development of common ground between the adversaries. Sometimes the pressure is indirect: Turkey has been said to be confronting the Armenian genocide as well as its treatment of the Kurds in part to increase its chances of inclusion in the European Union, while Japan is confronting its behavior in World War II in part to help its bid for a permanent seat on the United Nations Security Council.[48]

International reconciliation, like other matters of diplomacy, is often characterized by pomp and circumstance. For example, at the same time that CAVR released its report indicting Indonesia in war crimes, the presidents of Indonesia and Timor Leste celebrated Christmas together at a mass in a soccer field on the island of Nias. This took place notwithstanding the severe continued tensions between the two countries over the failure of prosecutions in Indonesia (discussed further below). The show is said to be important for the citizens of all the nations involved and for the world community. In addition to the peace accords, the establishment of diplomatic missions, and visits of by heads of state to each other's countries, there may also be other less elitist measures that are more likely to affect the lives of the citizenry. These might include educational and professional exchanges, increased transnational traffic of local goods, services, and cultural products, establishment of sister cities, and increased opportunities for foreign travel.

International reconciliation is not, in most cases, as emotionally laden as it is at other levels, in part because it is more abstract and in part because those who would resist reconciliation need not participate or even accept it; most citizens will not be substantially affected by international reconciliation one way or the other. They will be more affected by the end of the war than by the fact that, after the war ended, the countries reconciled. Overall, if international reconciliation has any effect on a nation's citizens, it is likely to be positive, as the nation is welcomed back into the world community. Thus, Libya has in recent years worked to rehabilitate itself in order to be able to participate in world affairs. Efforts to bring North Korea back into the fold have increased recently at all levels, from diplomatic roundtable discussions, to family visitation programs.

Increasingly, former colonial powers are attempting reconciliation with their erstwhile possessions, indicating how deeply the culture of reconciliation is becoming embedded in worldwide consciousness. Belgium, for instance, having fueled the flames of Tutsi-Hutu tensions as the colonial power, took the lead in international prosecutions of Rwandan genocidaires when those tensions erupted there in 1994. Pursuing other avenues, Germany has attempted reconciliation with Namibia. The hundredth anniversary of the German slaughter of 65,000 indigenous Namibian people—most notably the Herero—prompted an apology by the German foreign minister in 2004, but the apology failed to satisfy Namibians because it placed blame on the individual commander rather than on German policy and denied that the slaughter was a genocide at the time it was committed.[49] In 2005, Germany launched a reparation program, pledging $25 million for development and reconciliation "in order to heal the wounds left by the brutal colonial wars of 1904 to 1908."[50] Although these funds are to be dispersed by a committee and would be used for development projects in areas mainly inhabited by Herero, Nama, and Damara people, many Namibians are disappointed that the program does not appear to include participation by or even consultation with the local people.

In Indonesia and Timor Leste, the call for reparation and reconciliation has not taken a century, as in the German-Namibian situation, but here too the efforts by the former colonizers are not as salutary as might at first appear. In 1999, Indonesia established an Ad Hoc Human Rights Court for human rights violence in East Timor, but as mentioned earlier, very few convictions resulted. Indeed, Human Rights Watch called it a "whitewash:" "Indonesia's political leaders have created an atmosphere of impunity for these trials . . . [and] . . . Indonesia has failed in its promise to hold the military accountable for the atrocities in East Timor."[51] By 2003, only twelve people had been prosecuted, and of those ten were acquitted, nine of them Indonesian military and police personnel. The only two convicted individuals were from East Timor.[52] These facts obviously dampen the trials' effectiveness as an engine of reconciliation.

In 2005, Indonesia tried again, with the creation of a Commission of Truth and Friendship to achieve reconciliation between the two countries and learn what occurred during Timor's transition to democracy.[53] Indonesia has refused to indict senior leaders, including General Wiranto, who was named by the Indonesian Human Rights Commission as responsible for the 1999 violence[54] and some soldiers responsible for the commission of human rights abuses in East Timor have subsequently been promoted. Statements by the former president of Indonesia, Megawati Sukarnoputri, that many of the military leaders involved in the violence in East Timor were "national heros" and urging the military to "carry out your duties and responsibilities in the best possible manner without having to worry about human rights abuses"[55] have also not assisted the process of reconciling the two nations.

Colonial era human rights abuses and slavery to remain highly contested issues in the international reconciliation project, as seen in the World Conference against Racism, Racial Discrimination, Xenophobia and Related Intolerance (WCAR), held in 2001.[56] Quite a considerable part of the World Conference was devoted to these themes. The WCAR declaration recognized that dealing with these issues was being done "with a view to closing those dark chapters in history and as a means of reconciliation and healing."[57]

Individual countries on both sides of the Atlantic have also attempted to deal with the slave trade. The president of the Republic of Benin, Mathieu Kerekou, has said that "We owe to ourselves never to forget these absent ones standing among us who did not die their own deaths. We must acknowledge and share responsibility in the humiliations."[58] Benin has argued that the loss of millions of Africans has led to a lack of development and prosperity. A visit to central Africa by U.S. President Clinton also prompted acknowledgment of America's role in the slave trade.

In increasing numbers of cases, it must initially be determined whether a conflict is national or international in dimension. Northern Ireland and Bosnia present two complex situations where the underlying question is what the national boundaries are, or should be. In Northern Ireland, some constituencies favor remaining within the United Kingdom, while others favor separation from the UK and envelopment within the Republic of Ireland, others favor independence from both, and still others favor more flexible, semiformal relationships with both the UK and the Irish Republic. Thus, the question of identity within Northern Ireland is inextricably linked to its relationship to other countries.

Postwar Bosnia presents similar problems. Again, some individuals within Bosnia favor the creation of a strong, independent Bosnian state, where relations with other parts of former Yugoslavia (such as Croatia, Serbia, and Montenegro) would be akin to any nation's relations with its neighbors. However, some Croatians within the Federation of Bosnia-Herzegovina favor much stronger ties (or actual integration) with Croatia (the project of Herceg-Bosna), while some Bosnian Serbians (both in Republica Sprska and within the BiH federation) wish to be annexed to Serbia. In southeastern Europe, the problem is complicated by the tenuous location of boundaries, both between Bosnia and its neighbors and within the Federation of BiH. In both Bosnia and Northern Ireland, however, it is clear that the question of national identity cannot be separated from the question of cross-national relations, and the latter must necessarily be settled before the former can be nurtured. The inverse problem arises when nations nominally within the state seek to secede. Sudan's Interim Constitution of late 2005 provides for a referendum on secession of the Southern States in six years. This problem of "stateness" is explored more fully in Chapter 8.

In even more complex cases, conflicts arise where minority populations within one nation claim support from other countries. The Serbs in Bosnia, the Protestant Northern Irish, the Hutu in the Congo, all have ties to nations outside their "host" (Serbia, England, and Rwanda respectively). This, of course, radically alters the balance within the host nation by making the minority much more powerful—in terms of money, arms, and international visibility—than they would be without the "protector" state.[59] For instance, tensions between Serbs and Croats in Bosnia are likely to increase when Serbia makes strong claims to unite under one flag Serbs who live inside Bosnia. The situation inside Bosnia is made even more volatile by the claims from Croatia made toward its nationals living inside Bosnia. Only the Bosniaks have no nation-state to buttress their negotiating power (as they were made painfully aware during the war). Thus, those who attempt to promote reconciliation *inside* Bosnia must also consider the political situation outside its borders. This external dynamic can also be seen in France's response to its former colonies: France's support of one side or the other of the conflicts in Rwanda in 1994 and Côte d'Ivoire in 2004 will affect the prospects for reconciliation among the locals. The plight of the Roma and the Bosniaks in Europe and the Kurds in the Middle East illustrates how an ethnic minority that has no claim to a protector nation can be substantially disadvantaged. Nonetheless, even in these situations, there may be cross-border interests that affect the overall balance of power. For instance, Romas all over Europe have attempted to organize themselves in order to press their claims in several European countries, while the Kurds in Iraq have allied themselves with the Americans so as not to be at the mercy of the majority of Arabs in Iraq.[60] It is so common throughout the world for outside nations to support their cross-border nationals or allies (materially, militarily, or morally) that *every* domestic conflict involving different ethnic groups should be scanned to determine the extent to which an international dimension exists.[61]

The role of foreign nations is increasingly coming under scrutiny as domestic transitional processes get under way. Writing about the prosecution of former president of Chad Hissène Habré, Miriam Aukerman says: "This case is much more complex than the role of Habré. There is the role of France that supported him. There is the role of the United States that supported him. If we are to judge Hissène Habré, we have to also judge those who supported him."[62] Indeed, at the end of 2005, Habré was arrested in Senegal for possible extradition to Belgium or trial by the International Criminal Court or a tribunal set up by the African Union.

Truth commission reports have also increasingly examined the role of foreign influence in their domestic struggles. Recent reports from countries as diverse as Chile, Timor Leste, and South Africa have recognized the impact of the U.S.-Soviet Cold War on their domestic politics.[63] Reconciliation between these states as well as others who are blamed for various human rights abuses may also be necessary.

Governments embarking on reconciliation programs must recognize that reconciliation can and should take place on multiple levels simultaneously. These levels are distinct and require distinct mechanisms to be effective, but they are interrelated. National governments can contribute to reconciliation on every level, both by funding programs that promote reconciliation at the various levels, and by engaging directly in programs that promote national reconciliation, such as truth commissions. But the particular nature of the transition in each country—and the ways in which the populations of each country experienced the rupture that defined the previous administration—must dictate how each new government will allocate its reconciliation resources.

Part III
Reconciliation's Inner Logic

Chapter 5
The Costs of Reconciliation

> What would you say if your favourite bicycle was stolen one sunny afternoon, and six months later I came to you and said, I'm the one who stole your bike. Now I'd like to be your friend? How would you respond? At the very least, you might want me to say that I'm sorry. You would certainly be justified in wanting me to return your bicycle, You might or might not accept my offer of friendship. You might even want me to be prosecuted and punished for theft. What if I hadn't stolen your bicycle but your home and land? What if I had killed your child? . . . How then would you respond?
> —Laurie Nathan

Reconciliation holds the promise of an end to violence and a new beginning. It may augur added reverence for human rights, for the respect for the rule of law, and respect for one another, a culture in which individual and group differences are worked out through dialogue and friendship rather than conflict and strife. But can it really deliver on these promises? And even if it can, what are the costs? What must people give up in order to achieve the new order? What do they lose when they gain reconciliation?

Reconciliation has its detractors, and in this chapter we consider some of the major criticisms that have been leveled against it. In general, those most likely to resist reconciliation are the victims; the perpetrators are more likely to embrace any possibility of reconciliation, seeing it often as the alternative to punishment. But even perpetrators may resist reconciliation, if they view it as coopting them into a new "rainbow" nation of which they want no part. In some circumstances, therefore, perpetrators may view reconciliation as denying them their due. Toward the end of the chapter, we consider these arguments. The purpose of the chapter is not to convert reconciliation skeptics into true believers; rather, we aim to examine the reasons for reconciliation skepticism and, in some cases, to suggest ways of reconceptualizing both reconciliation and its costs to make reconciliation more appealing and its costs more tolerable for both sides.

Lack of Principle

At the most general level, the argument is often made that reconciliation is unprincipled, in the sense that it is not guided by any overarching values such as justice or equality or liberty. On this view, as Jonathan Allen says, truth commissions (and reconciliation programs generally) "are merely political compromises, institutions spawned by an unprincipled negotiation of a transfer of power. Justice becomes the casualty of a political calculation."[1] This is often true. In many cases, reconciliation is a pragmatic response to a complicated political quagmire. When regimes are replaced, the old guard does not simply disappear. Perhaps some die in battle, or emigrate to undisclosed locations, but the majority of people who kept the old regime running remain in the country to bear witness to the transition, sometimes taking on prominent roles in the new dispensation, sometimes fading into the background. In Iraq, many Baathists were needed to help rebuild. In Afghanistan, many former Taliban leaders found their way into the new government of Hamid Karzai. (The women's group Revolutionary Association of the Women of Afghanistan has denounced Karzai's "reconciliation" policies as treasonous to human rights and democracy and has argued that the absence of progress and of human rights is because the Karzai government found it more "beneficial to join hands with the most notorious and filthy faces" than to distance itself from them.[2])

The first question facing the new governors is what to do with "notorious and filthy faces," particularly if they participated in or were responsible for gross abuses of human rights, as is often the case. Wholesale prosecution is often too expensive and, in a fair system, retribution (in the form of long-term incarceration) is not guaranteed. Some countries have nonetheless tried this, but the efforts have not been very successful. Ethiopia pursued thousands of perpetrators and Rwanda hundreds of thousands, but in neither case did fair trials result in convictions. Other countries, such as Cambodia, Namibia, Zimbabwe, and to a lesser extent South Africa have ignored the crimes, but that has not enhanced those countries' human rights records either. In Guatemala, although prosecutions were recommended by its TRC, none have occurred. As more and more governments at the turn of the century have faced this quandary, they have turned to reconciliation as the major goal for their societies in transition.

When adopted for lack of better alternatives, reconciliation appears unprincipled. It simply looks like the least offensive of the evils, and not a very attractive one at that. Like others, Graeme Simpson has recognized that "There are undoubtedly times when all countries may have to sacrifice legal principles in the name of political pragmatism—in order to end wars or to achieve peace," but, he says, "so long as this is done with scant regard for its impact on the credibility of the criminal justice system and of criminal justice processes, we breathe life into the culture of impunity which is a foundation stone of criminal behaviour in any society."[3]

To those who argue that reconciliation should be rejected because of the absence of principle, there are two basic responses. The first accepts the premise that reconciliation is unprincipled but argues that absence of principle is not grounds for disqualification. The second rejects the premise and recasts reconciliation as a highly principled option.

First, the argument that reconciliation is desirable, even though it constitutes a political, rather than a principled, response recognizes that political transitions are products of the marriage between pragmatism and idealism. Democracy, by definition, functions not along unwavering lines of principle but along axes of compromise and consensus. What carries the day is what a majority wants that day, not what it committed to yesterday. It is inherently messy, as many people have found after they struggled so hard and sacrificed so much for the principles of equality or liberation. "We fought for liberation, and all we got was democracy" is the catchphrase of many transitional societies.

And transitional politics, even more than normal politics, are marked by political exigencies. Those who wielded power in the previous regime may have been ousted but often still retain significant power, in political, military, economic, and ideological forms. The new regime does not come in because good prevails over evil, but because the forces of democracy finally garnered enough support, from inside and outside the country, to oust the forces of despotism. The change may result from a violent overthrow of the old regime or from peaceful populist movements that erode the authority of the old regime. Either way, it results from shifts in *political* power. Lack of principle, therefore, should not disqualify a governmental program. Moreover, the leaders who gained prominence during the struggle and who become the founders of the new regime are rarely naive idealists: they are careful strategists who understand the need for political compromise and negotiation. Nelson Mandela, Vaclav Havel, Lech Walesa, Hamid Karzai, Xanana Gusmao of Timor Leste, and Michelle Bachelet of Chile are examples of people whose effectiveness was enhanced not only by their commitment to their cause but by their political acuity. Many leaders of the former Soviet socialist republics who were communist leaders before perestroika and democratic leaders afterward display the same talents for knowing when to emphasize principle and when to favor pragmatism. President Sanguinetti of Uruguay put the choice bluntly: "What is more just," he asks, "to consolidate the peace of a country where human rights are guaranteed today or to seek retroactive justice that could compromise that peace?"[4]

In transitions, moreover, nothing can be taken for granted. Almost every foundational decision is contested, from the status of minority groups, to the status of the head of state, to the allocation of power between the civilian and military authorities, to the balance of power between the federation and its constituent parts. All these decisions, and all the minor ones as well, are the subjects of dispute that get resolved only through extensive negotiation and compromise. None are resolved simply by recourse to some abstract principle. Their resolution reflects the balance of power (political, economic, and military) among the contending forces, as it waxes and wanes through the negotiating period.

In many cases, reconciliation is part and parcel of this pragmatic approach. In the transitions of Latin America, for instance, where the prior military regimes still wielded significant power (and control of the military ordnance) for years after the transitions occurred, reconciliation was a precondition to a peaceful transition: the military leaders withdrew from power only on condition that they be given amnesty.[5] The civilian leadership was forced to accept this deal to get the handover of power and often in order to avoid civil war. They often promoted the deal as reconciliation to save face. But it was never really about reconciliation, per se. It was about power. If the new regime had held the balance of military power, reconciliation would not have emerged. Even in South Africa, the same might be said. Would there have been a need for a reconciliation campaign if the forces of apartheid had not been so powerful throughout the transitional period? As Stuart Wilson argues in the South African context, "The language of restorative justice and societal reconciliation was mere window-dressing for a process meant to help consolidate the political gains of transition for the incoming government by ensuring that there would be no serious attempt to undermine the new dispensation by those, of whatever political hue, keen to avoid prosecution for their apartheid-era crimes."[6] In this view, reconciliation can be seen as "a political sop aimed at masking moral defeat."[7]

Jonathan Allen responds, on behalf of "skeptical critics," that "this amounts to making a virtue out of necessity—or more correctly, out of a particular (and perhaps mistaken) judgement concerning necessity."[8] And that may be true. Much depends on the accuracy of the assessment that the old guard continues to be a threat. If they are receiving the benefits of reconciliation because they are friendly with the new regime, then reconciliation is nothing more than a tool in the ongoing collusion between human rights abusers of the past and the present. But where the old guard is a genuine threat to the establishment of order and rule of law in the new regime, the new government may be forgiven for trying to develop effective ways to contain that threat. In these instances, reconciliation may be less costly, more peaceful, and ultimately more effective than any alternative.

Even aside from its pragmatic appeal, reconciliation might be defended as a foundational value. As such, it accords with other values of the transition, including respect for individual dignity and promoting a culture of human rights and of community integrity. Viewed this way, those who insist that the new dispensation be built on principled foundations can include reconciliation within their pantheon. Reconciliation may be an inherent good in that it reflects the values of peaceful co-existence in a diverse community. This ought to be fundamental value of any nation transitioning from warfare and conflict. If the new dispensation is going to work, and work peacefully, it will require that former adversaries learn to live with one another.

What makes the South African example so compelling is that reconciliation was promoted there as both a pragmatic *and* a principled response to the postapartheid period. It was the best of the alternatives, given the cost and uncertainty of high-profile trials, the lack of information about the gross human rights abuses, and the desperate need to avoid interracial and political violence.[9] But it was also a principled way for South Africans to understand the horrible realities of apartheid and to mark an emphatic departure from the values of the prior regime, by committing themselves to a new set of foundational values which included reconciliation.

Injustice

The argument against reconciliation is made stronger when content is given to the absence of principle. For instance, it might be said that the principle that is lacking is the principle of justice and that to promote reconciliation is to sacrifice justice. Here, it is necessary to define the terms of reference. If "justice" means retributive justice[10] and "reconciliation" means amnesty, then the argument must be accepted: a perpetrator who is given amnesty for his or her crimes will not be tried and will therefore escape punishment. For many people—victims and others—this is patently unjust. As one commentator said about his country's situation, "Reconciliation has never been assumed in Argentina, and there is a resistance even to the suggestion of reconciliation taking place under current conditions."[11] Argentineans were in no mood to grant their tormentors impunity. The same has been true in Rwanda, where it was said that while reconciliation would be nice, they preferred justice, and reconciliation could wait.[12]

Reconciliation in the sense of impunity may exact even higher costs than simply the absence of retribution. In some circumstances, it may entail the absence of the rule of law. One of the cardinal goals of any transitional government is to establish the rule of law. This means in general that both in appearance and in fact each person will be held accountable for his or her own actions, that actions have consequences, and that similarly situated people will be treated equally. This is critically important in transitional situations for several reasons. First, only where there is rule of law can there be safety; safety is important intrinsically and because it is a precondition for reconstruction. Second, the new government's legitimacy often rests on its distance from the prior regime, and one of the principal ways for the new government to distinguish itself is by assuring that law—and not raw power—governs in the new system. Third, rule of law is important because transitional moments are also foundational moments and the rule of law is the cornerstone of stability in modern times. If reconciliation is merely a mask for impunity, then its lack of principle is indeed problematic.

But both justice and reconciliation may be understood to have broader meanings. Justice is not simply trying and sentencing wrongdoers; it could be conceived of more broadly, as setting things right, or correcting an imbalance, or making one whole again. In some views, reconciliation and justice are incompatible because reconciliation cannot set things right. In fact, reconciliation assumes a parity where in fact none exists: it treats perpetrators and victims as comparable, as both living on the same moral plane, when in fact one chose to torture, rape, or kill and the other did not. Many people, and especially those who have been victimized, want justice and view the failure to punish as a denial of the original injury. They do not want their perpetrators to be treated as though nothing happened or as though they are morally equivalent. Doing so is profoundly *un*just, as Aristotle recognized long ago.

Reconciliation is more likely to be accepted if it can separate these two strands: a reconciliation program may avoid punishment but it must not appear to condone the actions of the perpetrators. "Reconciliation," Russell Batman explains, "does not replace or exclude justice. However, it is also unacceptable to make it totally subject to satisfying justice's legal requirements. Reconciliation builds the foundation of commonality, which makes it possible for justice to be done in the spirit of openness and acceptance of the other in the interest of our common future. Reconciliation replaces the culture of revenge, not the culture of justice."[13]

The relationship between justice and reconciliation is further examined in the next chapter. Here we only note that reconciliation and justice need not be mutually exclusive but may, as it were, be reconciled.

Concession

Insofar as reconciliation entails an end to the struggle, victims and survivors may be reluctant to stop waging their battle. This may be especially true if they do not believe that they have obtained sufficient gains from the other side, as where, for instance, the leaders are ready to negotiate and concede before the rank and file is. This may manifest itself in several ways.

First, those on one or both sides of the struggle may want to continue the struggle. They may feel that the laying down of arms is not yet appropriate, as a matter of principle or political strategy. Second, there may be psychological or personal reasons for resisting reconciliation. If reconciliation entails closure, they may have to give up the part of themselves that is defined by the struggle against the other; they may fear losing themselves if they lose the memory of the trauma.[14] Some people may come to believe the very reason why they were made to endure such hardship was to fight against the other, so they are unwilling to give up the fight. Though the feeling may be a negative one—experienced as anger or hatred—they may feel that maintaining that stance keeps them and the memory of their loved ones alive.

The specific terms of the reconciliation program in any given society may also pose a problem for some people. In South Africa, for instance, the TRC Act required that perpetrators fully disclose their participation in their politically motivated crimes, but it did not require remorse, restitution, or any other act of atonement. Indeed, for some, including Nobel laureate Wole Soyinka, this is a fatal flaw of the South African process.[15] Justice, Soyinka explains, assigns responsibility, and few will deny that justice is an essential ingredient of social cohesion—indeed justice constitutes the first condition of humanity, he says. And even as justice is not served by punishing the accused before the establishment of guilt, neither is it served by discharging the guilty without evidence of mitigation—or remorse.[16] As one commentator wrote about Argentina's transition, "the political discourse of reconciliation is profoundly immoral, because it denies the reality of what people have experienced. It isn't reasonable to expect someone to reconcile after what has happened here."[17] In this sense, reconciliation comes perilously close to collaboration, if not collusion, with the perpetrators.[18]

South Africa's decision to not demand remorse from amnesty applicants or, more generally, from any of those perpetrators who would participate in their country's reconciliation process, may indeed be seen as an inexplicable oversight or injustice.[19] But the choice can also be seen as actually enhancing the integrity of the process. Avowals of remorse and regret are much too easy to fake; they can be proffered for the wrong reasons, particularly when there is material benefit to appearing remorseful. They can be said in ways that are only minimally sincere and seem inadequate to the victims. Because it is impossible to secure true and valuable remorse, it might be argued, remorse should have little to do with a meaningful reconciliation process. On the other hand, inviting—without demanding—

acknowledgment of responsibility and remorse honors both the victims and the perpetrators. And it provides a window through which to see where remorse does *not* genuinely exist. This might be disappointing, but it is one indicator of the true extent to which the population remains divided and the victims remain at risk.

Nor did the South African TRC process require restitution of any kind from perpetrators or even that reparations be paid before amnesty was granted. While amnesty has been accorded to thousands of perpetrators, black South Africans wait: most were not determined to be "victims" within the terms of the TRC's mandate, and of those who were so designated, most have received little financial benefit to date. The state has paid only a small fraction of the nominal amounts recommended by the TRC. This inequality continues to cause much bitterness and resentment and is reinforced by the continued enormous inequalities in the standard of living between blacks and whites in South Africa.

Unfortunately, this is true throughout the world. In Latin America, some years after the truth commissions, little has changed, and economic disparities are as bad as ever and in some cases worse. (This may explain the current Latin American trend toward new truth commissions as well as toward leftist governments.) Marginalized groups still often feel marginalized, and those who lived well under the oppressive regimes continue to live well under democracy. In Guatemala, some victims have been able to achieve compensation through the Inter-American court while many millions of indigenous people believing that they were subjected to genocide have received nothing.[20] Transitions in Africa and in postcommunist Europe reveal the same story.

In other situations of reconciliation, victims may feel that they are expected to offer forgiveness for deeds that they find unforgivable. If reconciliation is built on this requirement of forgiving unforgivable crimes, or forgetting unforgettable trauma, then it can not be healthy for the victims.[21] For all these reasons, reconciliation is being offered on behalf of many who do not necessarily feel that they are getting much quid for their quo.

All these other choices can legitimately be criticized, but they can also be defended either on grounds of some hidden deeper principle or by the tug of political imperatives or at the very least by carefully constructing the reconciliation process so that it alleviates rather than reinforces the burdens already borne by the large victim classes of so many transitional societies.

Ensuring that victims are represented in the negotiations to create the reconciliation process may alleviate some of these difficulties. But this leads to other practical and conceptual problems: how much of a right do the victims, per se, have to dictate the terms of the reconciliation? Can the victims insist on terms that are sufficiently onerous as to defeat reconciliation? And how can the law reflect the multifarious values or needs of a disparate group of victims: some victims may insist on remorse while others may be happy to forego remorse but insist on reparations or restitution. How can the law accommodate all these quite reasonable demands?

And what if the demands are not reasonable but nonetheless real? In many cultures throughout the world, the proper response to violence is violence, not peace. Generations of cultural and religious training may instill in some victims a strong desire for vengeance and retribution. Those who seek to promote reconciliation need not submit to this view but they should acknowledge the strength of the feeling in their communities and present their program of reconciliation in a way that will respond to the real desire of some to continue to commit violence, by either channeling or quelling it.

The Past

Quite a bit more complicated is the feeling that victims may have that reconciliation requires them to give up on the past. The language of reconciliation is almost invariably about the past: working through the past (*auferbeitung*), let bygones be bygones, the need for closure, forgive and forget, settling accounts, "like the accountant's job of reconciling conflicting claims before closing a ledger book."[22]

The analogy between reconciliation and closing the book may be initially appealing, but it is problematic. Two questions immediately present themselves. First, is closing the book even possible, especially for individuals, or societies, recovering from deep trauma? Second, even if it is possible, is closing the book desirable?

For many people, forgetting the past is not a realistic possibility. Pumla Gobodo-Madikizela describes how survivors of trauma conflate past and present when they talk about their trauma. "'Here *is* my son,'" says the woman whose eleven-year-old was shot moments after running out of the house to go to school. "With a gesture of her hand she transformed the tragic scene from one that happened more than ten years earlier to one that we were witnessing right there on the floor of her front room," Gobodo-Madikizela says.[23]

But it is not just the language that conflates past and present; it is the deeper memory. Here, we should not say that memory of the trauma impedes reconciliation, but that it challenges reconciliation. "When torture has been committed, no 'healing truth' can redeem the past, and the memory of horror, the only experience unchanged by recollection, cannot be shared. [It is like] a debt that can be acknowledged yet remains impossible to settle."[24] The memory is so searing that no amount of restitution or compensation will ease the pain of the memory or will help the past recede into the past.

For survivors of profound trauma, the past, as William Faulkner said, "is never over; it isn't even the past." Long after the traumatic event has ceased, victims continue to wear the past in the bodily scars and chronic pain they retain from having been tortured, in the recurring nightmares they endure, in the fear they live with every day, in the sadness of losing a son or a daughter, or more than one. Time does not heal all wounds. Victims often live in what Lawrence Langer has called durational time—time that is past but is still felt and experienced as real and present even decades later.[25] In a small survey of Cambodians conducted nearly a quarter century after the end of the Khmer Rouge, 58.75 percent said that they continue to think about their experiences in the 1970s and 60 percent of respondents said it made them sad to talk about their experiences under the Khmer Rouge.[26] For survivors of trauma, the past is always present. A reconciliation plan that depends on putting the past away is not realistic and is simply doomed to fail.

Moreover, survivors in these situations might in fact resist letting the memory recede. Memory might be the only thing that survivors feel they have to hold against the perpetrator class or for themselves. Memory might be "the ultimate form of justice."[27] Clearly skeptical of the desirability or the possibility of closure, Wole Soyinka asks: "Are we then perhaps moving too far ahead of our violators in adopting a structure of response that tasks us with a collective generosity of spirit, especially in the face of *ongoing* violations of body and spirit?"[28]

For many people who struggled for change, the very reason to fight—the raison d'être of the transition—was to open up the past, to resist obscuring the past. Where the oppressive regime of the past was largely defined by suppression, repression, silencing, and denial, the new day is envisaged as a place where people can speak freely and openly about what happened. If the new dispensation then requires them to close the book, it perpetuates the attitude and even the crimes of its predecessor. Even proposing that victims give up their experience of the past may raise difficult moral questions.

Even if it were possible, forgetting the past entirely is not likely to be desirable. As was discussed in Chapter 2, many psychologists will say that understanding the past is critical for emotional healing. Philosophers will say that those who do not remember the past are condemned to repeat it. Thus, the cries of "Lest we forget" and "Never again" demand that we keep the past alive in the present and for the future.

Each culture may have a slightly different relationship to memory and to the past, as generic concepts. European cultures, for instance, may be more prone to longer memories: inside Europe, people were not particularly shocked that the battle cry for Serbian nationalism in the late twentieth century was rooted in the need to settle fourteenth-century scores. In Northern Ireland, and many other countries in transition, school children report that history is the most important subject they learn in school. Understanding history is not only relevant for school children but important for the wider society: it is essential to finding a more inclusive and acceptable version of the past that reflects the experiences of all the constituencies. In the late 1980s, the failure of the historians to accurately tell the history of Stalinism (and of the deportations in particular) was a significant rallying cry for many Lithuanians as they sought to liberate themselves from communism. In some cultures, history may even outlive the people in whose name it is recorded: in Cambodia, for instance, many people continue to support a tribunal to judge the Khmer Rouge to allow the souls of those who died thirty years ago to finally rest in peace.

At the other extreme, there are cultures in which the past has been rewritten so many times that memory has essentially become worthless. The communists were particularly adept at overlaying new meanings onto the past. Many elderly who have lived their whole lives in Eastern Europe have lived under a succession of regimes, each one erasing and rewriting the past that came before.[29] In African cultures, by contrast, where many meaningful traditions are likely to be carried on orally and where transition and adaptation is integral to survival, people may place less emphasis on the wrongs done in the past.[30] Even here, however, the memory of some tragedies—like the slave trade or the German genocide in Namibia—remains relevant and is periodically reactivated by anniversaries or other public events.

There are also more structural and less personal reasons to attend to the past. The past often plays an instrumental role in transitional times. It is the springboard for the future.[31] Aniceto Guterres Lopes, who chaired the Truth, Reconciliation, and Reception Commission of East Timor, explained the relevance of the past to the Commission's work in this way:

The very essence of the Commission's work is to assist transformation. The fabric of our social relationships has been destroyed. Our work is to transform our experience of the dark of yesterday into a positive tomorrow. In doing this we must first remember the past, look at what has happened and face the painful truth. Then we will use this truth as a solid base for our transformation, for the reconciliation of our differences. We will learn from our history, and the lessons will help us to prevent mistakes being made in the future.[32]

It is only if we "recognize the injustices of our past," as the 1996 South African Constitution states in its preamble, that we can create a better future. Rather than "forget and reconcile," many victims would prefer to "deal and heal."

If the victims score a point in insisting that the transition cannot lock up the past and throw away the key, the other side scores a point in insisting that the role of the past in the present and future must be limited and carefully defined, lest it overwhelm. As one Chilean official said, "It is very difficult to walk forward safely when you are looking backward. Probably you will fall on something."[33] In this view, if reconciliation focuses excessively or disproportionately on the past, it impedes progress. If victims stay anchored in the past, they remain in the place where there is the deepest divide between themselves and the perpetrators. Obsessing on past crimes prevents victims from understanding the perpetrators and prevents the perpetrators from rehabilitating themselves in the eyes of the victims. Elizabeth Kiss notes that "the past" can become an indulgence and an obsession, playing into our capacity for "scab-picking curiosity." "A little forgetfulness," she says, "might be in order."[34] As an empirical matter, as well, it is not at all evident that the past retains sufficient prophylactic powers to prevent the recurrence of crimes. Despite the outraged calls to remember the Holocaust, genocides have occurred in each decade since the 1940s, including our own.

And this is how the debate on reconciliation is played out. All too often, reconciliation discourse falsely pits the past against the future.

But the question is not whether to remember or forget the past, or whether to privilege the past or the future, since both can be useful.[35] Nor can it be stated in quantitative terms: there is no precise balance point between too much remembering and too much forgetting.[36] The real question is *how* to remember the past. As Archbishop Desmond Tutu put it, "We could not make the journey from a past marked by conflict, injustice, oppression, and exploitation to a new and democratic dispensation characterised by a culture of respect for human rights without coming face to face with our recent history. No one has disputed that. The differences of opinion have been about how we should deal with that past: how we should go about coming to terms with it."[37]

If the challenge is *how* to remember the past, we might want to ask the antecedent question: for what purpose do we remember the past? In other words, what function will the past play in the new environment? It might be for purposes of keeping alive the fire of anger or revenge or to vindicate the victims. If this is the case, then any memory can be divisive. Memories of victory—like the Protestant marchers in Northern Ireland commemorating the 1689 Battle of the Boyne that established Protestant hegemony there—can keep the fires of ethno-chauvinism burning just as effectively as memories of defeat, as the Serbs demonstrated when they called their countrymen to arms to vindicate their defeat in the Battle of Kosovo, six hundred years earlier. Commemorations of martyrs can have the same effects.

Alternatively, referring to the past might show what *not* to do in the new system: we keep the torture museums open so that people never forget what unchecked power leads to. Another use of the past is to maintain continuity with certain aspects of people's history. In Lithuania, which had a long and proud pre-Soviet history, the first signs of change came with the restoration of medieval symbols and place names. In the Spanish transition after the death of Franco, people reached back to the country's long grandiose history rather than its more recent divisive past.

Or, learning about the past might help people understand how things could have gone so horribly wrong. The Chilean Truth Commission wrote: "The Commission believes it must take into account the situation of the country leading up to September 11, 1973. That situation led to a break in our institutional life and a deep division between Chileans which made it more likely that human rights would be violated."[38] This use is more complex and requires more explanation and understanding. If this is the purpose of keeping the past alive in a particular society, it should be done not only through museum exhibits, but through reports and education programs. Indeed, Timothy Garton Ash, among others, has argued that history lessons are the most important way to teach people how not to repeat the past.[39] Many countries, of course, don't heed this advice. In Cambodia, history textbooks have entirely omitted the period between 1975 and 1979, and only recently are new textbooks with accounts of the genocide beginning to be used in classrooms.[40] In Bosnia, the way history is taught—and *whose* history is taught—is a particularly contentious issue, given the fractured nature of education in the post-Dayton state. Turkey has yet to acknowledge its responsibility for the genocide of Armenians in 1915, and in fact tried to prosecute Orhan Pamuk, a best-selling author, for having talked about it.[41]

In answering these questions, decisions must be made on how much, and what parts, of the past should be retained and perhaps even celebrated, and which parts given less focus and even, perhaps, what aspects of the past should be discarded. It may be useful to think of this as a process of packaging: trying to determine exactly what size and shape the past should assume in the new regime, what space it should take up in the present consciousness.

For instance, we might start by asking what *size* this "Past Box" should be. Should the past loom large in the new regime or should it play only a minor role? If we choose the first option, we are rooting the new dispensation firmly in the experiences of the past, and the past comes to shape and define the present and future. Symbols of the new regime would be taken from the past: the Red Hand of Ulster, the Battle of Kosovo, the

Confederate flag in the United States, the apartheid government flag, all centuries-old symbols that keep the fervor alive today in various parts of the world. National anthems would emphasize former glory or former struggles. Like others in Latin America, the Paraguayan anthem is characteristic of the genre: "For three centuries a reign oppressed / The unhappy peoples of America, / But one day, their anger aroused, they said: / 'An end to this!' and broke the reign." By contrast, the vast majority of the new European anthems are solidly forward-looking. Consider Kyrgyzstan's, adopted in 1992, the chorus of which is explicitly forward looking: "Come on, Kyrgyz people, Come on to freedom! Stand up and flourish! Create your fortune!"—which is exactly what they did in March 2005.[42] Of course, few people take literally the words of the national anthem (or even know them). But they can be indicative of how a new government wants to present itself and the extent to which it wants to root popular consciousness in the struggles and glories of the past or in the hopes for the future.

In addition to the size, we might also ask what *shape* this Past Box should be: what should it contain, and how should the elements of the past be placed in the box? For instance, should the crimes of the perpetrators be remembered? (Probably.) Should the motives of the perpetrators be remembered? (Perhaps). Should the organizations that nurtured the perpetrators be retained? (Probably not). Answering questions like these will help those in the new generation decide what lessons should be learned from the past, which will be critical in the new regime. But navigating through these questions may be difficult, partiuclarly where the meaning or even the underlying facts about the past are contested. In Rwanda, where the Tutsi and the international community consider what happened in 1994 to be genocide, the perpetrators of which are criminals, some Hutu consider it a civil war, the combatants of which should be treated as soldiers or freedom fighters. In the former Yugoslavia, interpretive disagreements are also at the heart of any understanding of the breakup of that country. For some, it was a war that represented the natural breakup of an unnatural coalition of nations that had been forced together under the terms of a treaty. For others, it was Serbian aggression against a legitimate state. Resolving these fundamental issues is a necessary part of the groundwork of reconciliation.

Another consideration about this Past Box is *where* to place it. Does it go in the front parlor, where everyone will see it and becomes a prominent feature? Should it be not just enshrined in the national anthem but emblazoned on the currency, carved into the stone of buildings, and perpetuated in the names of streets, airports, and dams? Or should it be tucked away in the attic, where it can be accessed when necessary but ordinarily won't affect the goings-on in the rest of the house? This option might be chosen as long as fundamental questions about the past are still contested. If the controversy over who the heroes and villains were of the previous regime still rages, as it does in Bosnia under the Dayton accords or in Northern Ireland until the dust has settled on the Good Friday agreement, then it might be best to let those disputes simmer down. Over time, some of the most significant issues might become less contested, and some of the partisans of each interpretation might soften their views and become more accommodating. In order to give everyone time to reconsider their positions, it might be necessary to neutralize the issue by removing names and symbols that are divisive. In Bosnia, where *everything* is still contested, the Office of Human Rights has forbidden the display of the Sahovnica (the red-and-white checkerboard Croatian symbol) and other symbols of Greater Croatia, including crucifixes and images of Franjo Tudjman. Rather, "all public buildings . . . should only display Federation symbols and insignia of 'a neutral or inoffensive nature.'"[43] There, it might be useful to designate the central parts of town as areas where no nationalist or religious iconography can be displayed, in order to provide a space where people from different groups can feel comfortable meeting and doing business.

Sometimes, language itself can mask deep divides in a culture. War or genocide? Terrorist or freedom fighter? The status of leaders of mass movements may be similarly contested: was Ariel Sharon a war criminal or Israel's last best hope; and what of Yasser Arafat? Those who would encourage reconciliation should consider how the language they use affects the survivors of trauma. In Rwanda, there is significant resistance to the very term "reconciliation" insofar as it connotes forgiveness, particularly on behalf of those who were massacred. Other terms, like "justice" and "peace building," may be more acceptable and, as Greg Duly explains, "reintegration" becomes a more useful substitute. "Its usefulness is in its neutrality and in its double meaning conveying at one and the same time, the need, after such massive displacements since 1994, for Rwandans to physically reintegrate—as in resettling and reestablishing a physical presence, and the need to emotionally or psychologically reintegrate—as in the need to embrace value systems such as tolerance, acceptance, inclusion and cooperation."[44]

And even after the fact—sometimes long after—disputes are common over language, even over the most fundamental facts, as the industry of Holocaust deniers demonstrates. In the case of the Holocaust, of course, the deniers are a small minority who have barely made a dent in the generally accepted understanding of the events of World War II. But where events are less determinate, and both sides have stronger claims to the historical evidence, contesting the past makes reconciliation all but impossible: it narrows, and sometimes completely eliminates, the possibility of common ground.[45]

Furthermore, one might ask, how well does the Past Box fit into its present surroundings? Is the past an intrusive annoyance, or is there continuity between past, present, and future? To a large extent, the role of the past will depend on the nature of the transition. Where the transition constitutes a complete break with the past (as, for instance, in transitions from colonial status to independence or when communism abruptly collapsed), the predecessor will figure less significantly and most eyes will be focused on the future—or people will reach back to an earlier, halcyon past.[46] Where the transition is fluid (as, for instance, where a democratic government succeeds a military power or a ceasefire takes years to implement), many of the structures, institutions, and values of the past may retain vitality in the future, though some may be modified, or dormant values from the past may be resurrected. In many countries of South America, for instance, the transitions in the 1970s and 1980s did not rupture the past so much as open new chapters in the nation's continuing history. In many former Soviet republics, most Westerners expected the break to be abrupt, but the reality has been more complicated: while many in these countries instantly embraced western values (especially as manifested in admission to the European Union), many of those same people also held on to certain attachments to communist systems and to communist leaders. The fact that these countries function more or less successfully—particularly in Southeastern Europe and in the Baltic states—is evidence that there need not be a formal break between past and present but that a society can accommodate both, in its own unique blend.

But when a nation overhauls itself as thoroughly as South Africa did in 1994, every element of the past had to be tested for relevance and usefulness in the future; those that were found to be irrelevant to the new nonracial and nonsexist South Africa were unceremoniously discarded (to the chagrin of a more than a few Afrikaners). Not even the country's geography was spared. Even here, however, the past is useful as contrast. The purpose of revisiting the past, in this construct, was to build up South Africa on a sound moral basis, as Minister Dullah Omar said in introducing the TRC legislation, in contrast to the apartheid regime.

Answers to these questions might evolve over time. Emilios Christodoulidis says that law is, after all, about stabilizing social expectations; if the same is true of reconciliation, we might envision a continuum along which the past becomes less and less intrusive into the present and the future, though it can never be completely effaced, nor should it be. Movement along the continuum will depend on the extent to which a society transforms, and the extent to which the previous cleavages remain and reinforce polarization and division. If the social base is changed and the nation develops, and the differences between groups are not seen to benefit and privilege some groups at the expense of others, then there is a greater possibility of advancing reconciliation. These are the questions that must be addressed in any state reconstruction or reconciliation plan. But the answers to the questions are unlikely to be determinate or clear. Even within a single society, answers are likely to vary across regions, generations, and classes. Even some individuals may well feel internally conflicted about how to resolve these questions.

Ineffectual

Perhaps the most searing of the criticisms against reconciliation is that it is ineffectual. Huge amounts time, thought, planning, and political and fiscal capital are spent promoting reconciliation and, in the end, the ins are still in and the outs are still out, the poor are still poor, the rich are still rich, and the survivors are still struggling to survive.

Pat Dodson, an Australian Aboriginal, explained his ambivalence about participating in the Corroboree 2000 at the Sydney Opera House (a huge reconciliation event) in this way: "I think many Australians will think they've done something, but they won't be sure what it is they've done and be confused about why indigenous people are still concerned that there are matters of an unfinished nature to be pursued."[47] To many people, reconciliation can seem at best ineffectual, most likely patronizing, and at worst a distraction from the more important business of improving the quality of living of minority populations within a culture. While white Australians have embraced reconciliation with enthusiasm and wish their government would do more, many Aborigines have expressed skepticism about the whole enterprise of reconciliation. Peter Fisher of the Kuku Yalanji people sees the problem this way: "Reconciliation? We don't understand this sort of thing. They keep changing it. We don't change it. We live with nature, our culture, that's all we live. European people destroying everything to buggery. They blaming us for cutting one tree to build a house and that. Europeans can be very mean and very greedy."[48] In the end, all the talk does not amount to much.

Reconciliation's origin in the real, messy, and turbulent politics of the transitional nation makes it difficult to achieve in any society with deep-rooted conflicts. And the more people expect of reconciliation—as a panacea, a stabilizing force, a fundamental value of peace and harmony—the less it seems to deliver. The proposals discussed in chapters eight and nine of this book are aimed largely at defusing this criticism of reconciliation, by showing how reconciliation efforts can in fact bring about change.

Chapter 6
Truth, Forgiveness, and Justice

There are crimes which men can neither punish nor forgive.
When the impossible was made possible it became unpunishable,
unforgivable absolute evil which could no longer be understood
and explained by the evil motives of self-interest, greed, covetousness,
resentment, lust for power, and cowardice; and which therefore
anger could not revenge, love could not endure, friendship could
not forgive.

—Hannah Arendt

Certain assumptions are treated as givens in the reconciliation literature.
It is taken for granted, for instance, that truth leads to reconciliation, that
forgiveness is a necessary element of reconciliation, and that reconciliation and justice must be traded against one another. And yet, a moment's
reflection reveals that the conventional wisdom should not be taken for
granted.

How these concepts actually interact and reinforce each other, or detract from one another warrants careful attention, in part because each
term is elastic and elusive, and in part because the precise relationship
among the concepts is variegated and complex. Take, for example, the
relationship between reconciliation and truth. Most people—particularly
those who are involved in postconflict reconstruction—argue that reconciliation is impossible without a full accounting of the truth; unless the
"beast" of the past is confronted, there can be no moving forward, they say.
But others have questioned this wisdom: they argue that far from being
indispensable to reconciliation, the truth can actually be an impediment to
it. *The more I know about you, the less I trust you.* This is particularly true where
justice is unavailable: the more truth is known, the more people are likely
to clamor for justice, and its absence is likely to impede reconciliation.[1]

Add to this the complex nature of truth and it becomes clear that simple answers are in short supply. Will warring parties ever agree on what

the truth is? Will they even agree on the kinds of evidence needed to establish the truth, or the levels at which truth is relevant? Since many divergent points of view are legitimate, the most we could say at the outset is that truth does not invariably lead to either reconciliation or renewed conflict; rather, the disclosure and dissemination of truth can open up a space that justice or forgiveness *might* fill. The challenge is to enhance the capacity of truth to lead to reconciliation.

This chapter considers in more detail the nature of truth, forgiveness, and justice in the context of transitional justice. The questions are whether they are indispensable, tangential, or irrelevant to the promotion of reconciliation, and under what circumstances can they be made to advance reconciliation.

Truth: The Road to Reconciliation?

Revealing the truth is said to be necessary for reconciliation because it exerts a transformative power over all stakeholders: the public at large, the victims, and even the perpetrators.[2]

First, it is worth noting that there may be an obligation under domestic or international law to tell the truth. This right is sometimes subsumed under the more general right to free expression, though in some constitutions and international treaties it is identified as a right in and of itself. The international nongovernmental organization Article 19 has found that there is a growing body of international and comparative jurisprudence confirming an obligation on governments to provide the public with certain types of information.[3] Article 19 maintains that there is a "right to know the truth" which is contained within the right to "seek, receive and impart information" which is guaranteed by Article 19 of the Universal Declaration of Human Rights. (There is a similar "right to receive information" in Article 9 of the African Charter on Human and Peoples' Rights, as well as in many domestic constitutions.)

Whether or not legally required, truth can be useful in times of transition. The very fact that the truth of the previous regime is being revealed and discussed demonstrates a shift, if not a complete upset, from the previous regime. Most oppressive regimes are characterized not only by their brutality, but also by a code of silence that enshrouds policies of violence and methods of control. Just as a common criminal might threaten his victim with further abuse should the truth come out, secrecy usually shields crimes of state. Secrecy associated with violent regimes interferes with democratic processes of self-government, and thereby injures the public generally. This secrecy might be mandated legislatively, secured by threat or strict enforcement, or might result from well-understood expectations on all sides. In some places, this is taken to extremes, as where expressions of sympathy or grief are themselves punished. Revealing, disseminating, and discussing aspects of the truth therefore signal the obsolescence of the previous regime and the establishment of a new culture of transparency and accountability. Arming the population with knowledge and understanding can enhance the quality of democratic decision-making.

More particularly, revealing the truth is said to help victims. Secrecy imposes special burdens on the victims. The victims, who are injured in the first instance by the actual violence, are doubly victimized by the secrecy that denies their experiences. What Hannah Arendt wrote in the wake of the Holocaust is generally true of most oppressive situations: "anyone speaking or writing about concentration camps is still regarded as suspect; and if the speaker has resolutely returned to the world of the living, he himself is often assailed by doubts with regard to his own truthfulness, as though he had mistaken a nightmare for reality."[4] For victims of official violence, society's denial of the truth may contribute to their self-doubt, shame, and even self-loathing as much as the original violence itself. Revealing the truth may help restore the victim's feeling of "worth and dignity," especially where the principal injuries suffered by the victims are psychic. (By contrast, where the victim endures long-standing physical or material injury, vindication, *without more*, may not be as effective a palliative.) It has also been argued that finding out the truth is a precondition for providing redress for the victims. As one of Eugene de Kock's victims in South Africa said, the only thing she really wanted was for him "to confess. I want him to sit in front of that cassette recorder and tell me what he did—not just to me, everything, to everybody—and then have him write it out in his own handwriting and sign it and I would keep a copy forever—with all the information, the names and dates, all the details. That's what I want."[5] Government actions that promote truth can demonstrate to their own populations and to the world that they want to move forward on the basis of an honest appraisal of the past.

A society can allow the real stories to be told by writing a truthful official history, or by opening up space in which victims can tell their own stories or, most beneficially, through a combination of public and private efforts. Each type of truth can make an important contribution to reconciliation: the official truth, it is said, "acquires a mysterious quality that is not there when it was merely 'truth'"[6] The victims' truth vindicates the victims by providing the general public with the basis for believing what the victims have known all along.

Together, multiple truths can reinforce one another. First, the existence of each kind of truth makes the other kind more likely to come out: victims are more likely to feel comfortable telling their stories if the government is supporting them through official corroboration, and the government is more likely to engage in its own inquiry if the victims are already talking, thereby creating the political imperative. Second, each level of truth enhances the credibility of the other: an official report makes victims' stories more likely to be accepted and provides a structural context for the subjective experiences of the victims, and the victims' stories make the official report more believable and ensure that the public understands not just the events but the ramifications of those events on their neighbors and comrades.

If one side of the truth coin vindicates the victim, the other side punishes the perpetrator. Human Rights Watch has held that "the most important means of establishing accountability is for the government itself to make known all that can be reliably established about gross abuses of human rights," including the identities of the victims, and the identities of the perpetrators at all levels, from those who designed the plans, to those who carried them out, to those who aided and abetted in their implementation.[7]

Holding the perpetrators accountable sometimes leads to their prosecution in criminal courts, as happened to some extent in Argentina as a consequence of the Sábato commission report. At the very least, disclosing and disseminating the truth about the actions of a perpetrator exposes him to shame and obloquy. As Aryeh Neier has written, to reveal the truth is "To identify those responsible, and to show what they did, is to mark them with a public stigma that is a punishment in itself."[8] This can be done in different ways, including the naming of the perpetrator either at a hearing or in a truth commission report. Even the threat of revealing a perpetrator's name may prompt him to come forward with more information, fearing greater exposure or prosecution if he does not.

In Sudan, for example, when conflict erupted among the Nuer, local elders called a traditional peace conference. Bethuel Kiplagat described the process: "Each day the people would gather around the elders as a 'community in discussion.' . . . What mattered was getting the truth out—according to Nuer philosophy and religion, the only way to bring about reconciliation and healing. Women played a key role as guardians of truth. If during a hearing a person omitted to tell the truth, the women would threaten to shame him by revealing what they knew."[9]

While stigmatization is potentially a powerful punishment (with both retributive and deterrent dimensions), there may be limits to the effectiveness of shame-as-punishment. Public shaming "presupposes a moral reference group that most perpetrators avoid by isolating themselves happily in their own ethnoracial enclave with similar beliefs."[10] If the perpetrators and victims live apart, then the moral sanction associated with the truth that is likely to prevail among the victim class is unlikely to permeate the perpetrator's social community. In South Africa, for instance, where the apartheid system forced (and its legacy continues to force) blacks and whites to live apart, perpetrators of both races are able to "isolate themselves happily" within their own closed communities without the shame of facing their victims.

Where victims and perpetrators live in mixed groups, however, stigmatization of the perpetrator may be mitigated by other factors. In many cultures, and for many kinds of crimes (particularly sexual crimes), dissemination of the truth is more likely to injure anew the *victim* than to punish the perpetrator. Revealing the fact of a rape can result in the social ostracism of the victim, her inability to marry or command respect in the community, or even death. In Rwanda, for instance, it has been reported that female victims of sexual abuse have been reluctant to participate in the gacaca process. "As sexual violations are widely considered unforgivable, and their consequences insurmountable, there is widespread belief among both men and women that recounting experiences of sexual violence will only block community reconciliation and aggravate community tensions."[11] In South Africa also, women were reluctant to testify before the TRC on the sexual violence they had suffered and very few did. To avoid this problem in Sierra Leone where sexual violence constitutes a significant portion of human rights abuses,[12] the TRC statute allowed anyone to provide information to the Commission anonymously.

The example of sexual violence highlights the ambiguous place of truth where the community is divided on the question of the moral status of the crime. The argument that truth vindicates the victim and punishes the perpetrator assumes a common morality that roundly rejects the perpetrators' actions. It works in places where the moral code is both pervasive and emphatic in its repudiation of the wrongs done. Where moral consensus does not exist, however, the dissemination of the truth may not only fail to advance reconciliation, but can actually impede it.

Similarly, truth is often said to have a deterrent effect: disseminating the truth changes the moral climate by undermining the mental foundations that justified criminality, thereby preventing its repetition in the future.[13] This can only happen, however, if the truth, once widely known, is definitively repudiated. Too often, past abuses are known but are accepted by the populace. Perhaps they are viewed as not that harmful (as is often the case with violence against women), or they are accepted as an inevitable and reasonable cost of security. In these cases, the truth acts not as a deterrent but to legitimate past abuses. It can even act as precedent and as justification for future abuses.

If disclosure of the truth does not invariably serve the ends of justice, perhaps it is useful as a predicate for forgiveness. As a psychological matter, it may be necessary for people to have a clear understanding of what happened before they are able to offer forgiveness. This requirement is repeated in truth commission hearings throughout the world: "We may eventually decide to offer amnesty to some or all of our former oppressors, but before we forgive, we should know what evil we are forgiving, and who caused it."[14]

A full accounting of the truth may be necessary for forgiveness as a legal matter as well. A person can give up the right to prosecute someone only if she knows the extent of his wrongdoing. In the community reconciliation process in Timor Leste, for example, reconciliation was sometimes deemed not possible because during the process it was discovered that the offender had done more than was originally understood.[15]

Another major contribution of truth to reconciliation is that it can limit or reduce the deniability of past crimes. As Michael Ignatieff has said, the process of truth-telling narrows "the range of permissible lies" that the perpetrators can tell.[16] Indeed, this is said to be the major contribution of truth commissions to reconciliation, although eliminating deniability can be accomplished in other ways as well. After World War II, for example, the Allies required "Germans to watch documentary films of concentration camps as a condition of receiving rations."[17] Whatever the medium, once the evidence is disseminated and widely accepted—the theory goes—no one can deny the extraordinary violence that was deemed necessary to maintain the previous system, no one can deny that people who had simply "disappeared" or who had "committed suicide" while in custody were in fact killed by the government. But the German example provides its own refutation: in an open and democratic system, where no one "owns" the truth, there are few truths that cannot be denied, either contemporaneously or in future generations.

These arguments suggest a certain circularity to the truth debate. If the community to which the truth is disseminated shares a common sense of morality and an agreed-upon view of the events surrounding the transition, then the "truth" can insinuate itself comfortably within that preexisting narrative. But where there is no consensus on the morality of the fundamental questions (*Was it a war or a genocide? Was everyone equally guilty of excess or can the victim class be reliably distinguished from the perpetrator class? Was torture widespread or was it exceptional?*), then the "truth" that is officially revealed is unlikely to bring people together. Instead, it may foster deeper divisions. One reason why this point is rarely discussed in the literature is precisely that, among the devotees of truth and reconciliation, there is widespread consensus on the basic human rights values.

Under certain conditions, of course, revealing the truth may be the engine for reconciliation. In Australia, for instance, there is broad consensus about the moral meaning of the White Australia policy that resulted in the kidnaping of thousands of Aboriginal children and their placement in institutions or with white families for the purpose of Europeanizing and Christianizing them. Recent efforts to examine this have been said to encourage among some a sense of "shared history" between the whites (who were largely ignorant of the policy's grossest abuses but whose parents and grandparents supported its general goals) and the aboriginals (who were largely ignorant of both the extent of the abuses and the particular fate of family members under the policies). Far from setting matters to rest, the truths that have been revealed as a result of public and private efforts have opened up more spaces in which Australians of all stripes have come together. Addressing the truth has resulted in greater understanding among white Australians of the past experiences of Aboriginals and of their present claims for cultural identity (and social support). Rejecting their school-taught lessons that Australia was "terra nullius" when the whites arrived, many whites are now coming to value the contributions that Aboriginals have made in the country. The "shared history" made possible through attention to the past becomes the harbinger of a common destiny.

The circumstances in Australia furnish the best possible conditions for the promotion of reconciliation—a generally liberal public, a tiny minority of people in the (therefore non-threatening) victim class, few perpetrators still alive to be punished or shamed (and therefore few people with a large stake in resisting the dissemination of the truth), and a prevalent morality that soundly rejects legalized racial oppression. Almost no one in Australia now maintains that the policies of the past were good, and few would argue publicly that they were justified even at the time they were promulgated and enforced.

But these conditions are unlikely to exist in countries that are still recovering from racial, ethnic, religious, or ideological warfare. And even in Australia, where many white Australians fully endorse "reconciliation," there is little chance that political or judicial mandates will meaningfully change the economic or political balance of power in any way that might threaten them. Where land claims have been made, for instance, they have been rejected or minimized by all branches of government.[18] On issues of redistribution of wealth and resources, the Australian public is still very divided. The truth in Australia is not able to *create* common ground where there is no popular consensus, but it can at least reduce the contested ground.

Victor's Truth

The principal problem with the proposition that truth leads to reconciliation is that "truth" on most important issues is not objective and not nearly as neutral as we would like it to be. The actual import of the truth depends more on whether it is believed to be true than on whether it in fact happened. If a truth, once pronounced, were invariably accepted, then it would be much more likely to conduce to reconciliation. But the truth has simultaneously too little substance and too much substance to be so readily accepted by the public and by the elites.

The first problem is simply the impossibility of ever recounting the truth accurately. Even if one wanted to convey the reality of the past, how can the packaged "truth" about an event ever do justice to the events themselves? The retelling is necessarily partial, both in that it is incomplete and in that it is biased. It can never exactly recreate reality, because too much is lost in the translation between the event and its retelling. The facts, as Hannah Arendt wrote, "must first be picked out of a chaos of sheer happenings (and the principles of choice are surely not factual data) and then be fitted into a story that can be told only in a certain perspective, which has nothing to do with the original occurrence."[19] It is not necessary to be a philosopher to understand this. It is only necessary to have read the official truth about an event in which one has personal knowledge and recognize the gap between the reality as experienced and the truth as told. The tables in truth commission appendices indicating numbers of tortures, of deaths in custody, of disappearances can never even approximate the actual experience of those whose lives are converted into numbers. No truth on paper will ever really reflect the experience of suffering and surviving of the individuals listed or those unlisted. And the more vivid individual experiences are—especially experiences of violence—the less the paper truth can capture the reality.

Truth is impossible to tell for additional reasons as well. The same event can—and sometimes must—be told in many ways at once. The South African TRC recognized four kinds of truth—narrative, historical, forensic, and social—and attempted to tell its story on all these levels at once.[20] Similarly, in writing about reconciliation in Australia, journalist Michael Gordon "came to realize that there were four layers of truth about the state of Australia's first people" and that to "stop at the first layer is as dangerous and deceptive as to tell a lie."[21] The first layer is "what I saw with the naked eye." The second layer is no less real, but cannot be seen. It is "a conspiracy of abdication, mostly unwitting but sometimes deliberate, by governments big and small, by bureaucracies, by administrators and by leaders, white and black."[22] The third layer is in the "history of the treatment of Aboriginal Australians."[23] The final layer is, simply put, "prejudice."[24] Far from being ephemeral or malleable, truth in these conceptions is palpable, multifaceted, and complex. To fail to recognize the different levels or dimensions of its substance is to fail to tell the truth.

Combining these two features of truth—that it is so difficult to convey at all and that to be conveyed accurately it must be told in multiple dimensions at once—leaves most facts (and certainly most important facts) subject to interpretation. "Truth alone is never enough to guarantee reconciliation," wrote Wole Soyinka. "It has little to do with crime and punishment but with inventiveness—devising a social formula that would minister to the wrongs of dispossession on the one hand, chasten those who deviate from the humane communal order on the other, serve as a criterion for the future conduct of that society, even in times of stress and only then, heal."[25]

Clever politicians are quick to recognize that choices in interpretation may be either favorable or inauspicious to the present regime. The truth is therefore open not only to interpretation, but to manipulation. The more important an event, the more likely it is to be transformed, from fact to opinion if bad, or from opinion to reified fact if useful. Thus, while there is undeniably a very strong impulse to tell the truth, there is also an unavoidable tendency to "tell it slant."[26]

Methods of Disseminating Truth

In general, there are three major ways in which the "truth" can be revealed and disseminated in a post-transition society: through the dissemination of files or documents, through a commission report, or through a trial or a regime of trials. If facts are known to people in the private sector, a fourth route may be the unofficial dissemination of information in newspapers, books, art, and other media. In any given society, these can occur singly or in combination. In Sierra Leone, for instance, a special court and a truth commission operated side by side to produce a fuller understanding of the truth than either could have done on its own; a similar set-up is under discussion in Cambodia.[27] A government may make public the information it has at its disposal while also providing support for the arts to spur public awareness. In fact, it is unlikely that any one mode can, on its own, produce a full and true accounting.

Publishing files or official documents is the most direct way of disseminating truthful information about the actions of the prior regime. It has the advantage of producing accurate, unvarnished truth, leaving interpretation to the general public. Nonetheless, decisions will invariably need to be made about the timing of the publication, the order in which documents are released, the amount of documents to be released. In many cases, the sheer volume of documents may require discretionary judgment about which ones to make public.[28] All these choices can have political consequences, so that the simple release of unadulterated documents may not appear as objective as originally thought. For instance, whether documents are published verbatim in newspapers or whether their contents are summarized may affect the public's interpretation of the facts. Restricting access to the documents to the victims or subjects rather than allowing public dissemination or availability for research purposes may privilege privacy concerns over other values.[29] One final difficulty with the dissemination of documents is that in some cases it is impossible. Where the perpetrators saw the transition coming, a campaign of document destruction can interfere with efforts to let the primary materials speak for themselves; publication of the remaining documents may distort the story of the prior regime.

Where documents alone cannot convey the whole story, a government may want to establish a commission to promote "truth" or "truth and reconciliation." State practice is increasingly accepting of truth commissions. In cases where prosecutions have not been undertaken and amnesties have been granted, some sort of alternative mechanism has been established, usually a truth commission and provision for reparations and compensation.

Truth commissions are often accepted as means of satisfying the duty to investigate public crimes. As disseminators of truth, commission reports have certain advantages over the alternatives. First, unlike mere document dissemination, reports provide context for the information they reveal. Second, unlike trials which are devoted to serving justice, commission reports have no other master: their raison d'être is the truth. (When truth is combined with reconciliation as the focus of the commission, the project gets more complicated. As we noted earlier, there may be a tendency to compromise the truth in order to promote reconciliation. To date, however, few commissions have emphasized the differences between truth on the one hand and truth and reconciliation on the other; in both cases, commissions seem to emphasize the disclosure of the truth—perhaps on the untested assumption that reconciliation will inexorably follow.)

The relationship between truth commissions and trials has been discussed at greater length in Chapter 4, in the context of the creation of the national narrative to promote national reconciliation. Here we simply note that no uniform rule governs that relationship. In some cases the truth can lead to trials, as it did in Bolivia, Ethiopia, and Argentina. But Priscilla Hayner has argued that these situations are exceptional and there is no obvious correlation between truth commissions and prosecutions.[30] In South Africa, it could in fact be argued that the opposite relationship existed. The trial of Eugene de Kock—and in particular his extensive testimony naming names and identifying deeds—was a spur to the TRC: the information revealed at the trial prompted putative defendants to apply for amnesty, the applications for which, in turn, produced mountains of additional information at the TRC about the crimes of the apartheid apparatus.

In the end, it appears that truth commissions and trials make complementary contributions to the elucidation of the truth. Truth commissions may provide a fuller, more holistic account of the past. However, judicial truth, having been tested by the rules of evidence, emerges with a certain legitimacy (assuming the legal system enjoys legitimacy within the society). Trials arrive at a single truth—easier for the public to grasp but quite possibly at the expense of the nuances of complex reality: ironically, in the pursuit of a verdict, trials may ignore both the victim's and the perpetrator's truths. Both vehicles for ascertaining the truth can, but do not necessarily, promote the basic values underlying most transitions, namely consolidating democracy and establishing the rule of law. But whether either of these actually advances reconciliation is another matter.[31]

The External Critique

Even if it were possible to discern, describe, and disseminate truth, there remains the question of whether such truth in fact conduces to reconciliation. The answer might be yes, but not without qualification. First, as we have noted, the disclosure of "truth" might in fact do more harm than good in some situations. "If we publish the files as some people have suggested," one Romanian government official has been quoted as saying, "there could literally be something worse than a civil war with friend turning against friend once they find out what is contained in them. In some respects, truth as well as justice was a threat to democracy."[32]

Even if there is no civil war, disclosure of the truth may still not promote reconciliation. In Poland, James McAdams reports, the general population's attitude was at best ambivalent. So many Poles were communists that when the lists of names were released after the fall of the Iron Curtain, everyone found that they had been named. Attention to the "truth" about the past—that many Poles officially supported the communist party—led not to reconciliation between those who supported and those who didn't, but to repeal of the laws requiring naming and then to the constitutional invalidation of the laws.[33] The situation in Czechoslovakia was similar, also culminating in the abandonment of lustration. In South Africa, "as the [TRC] finished its work, a poll reported that two-thirds of South Africans felt that the commission's revelations had only made them angrier and contributed to a worsening of race relations."[34] No civil war, but no reconciliation either.

Truth may not invariably produce reconciliation, but it is difficult to make the case *against* truth in any seriously strong terms. Truth commissions are unlikely to cause "a situation to become worse."[35] According to Priscilla Hayner, "Even with unexpectedly explicit and strongly-worded reports, the overall impact of each truth commission has generally been positive, often reducing the tension and increasing national reconciliation, and perhaps increasing the understanding of and respect for human rights issues by the general public and political leaders alike."[36] But even if TRCs are capable of making meaningful contributions to society—and there are reasons to believe that they do—the reasons for this may not relate exclusively to the curative power of truth. Countries that sponsor truth commissions are more likely to have committed themselves to reform. (Ethiopia, Rwanda, Mozambique, and so far Iraq and Bosnia are all examples of countries that have deliberately chosen *not* to pursue truth through truth commissions.)

When a government does commit to a program of truth-telling, it needs to consider several important issues. It needs to make decisions about the process, the timing, and the quantity of the truth to be revealed, as well as its quality. It also needs to determine if there will be ancillary government-sponsored programs to reinforce the government's own attitude toward the truth that is being revealed.[37]

Another issue concerns how much truth. Just as there may be temporal limits to effective truth-telling, there may also be limits to the quantity of truth, to the amount of detail that may profitably be disseminated. The Ethiopian experience could test the limits of a public's tolerance for pure, unadulterated truth. As Wole Soyinka has written, "Never was mass murder more meticulously bureaucratized; the records reveal a rare punctiliousness of executive psychopathy—a total contrast with the arbitrariness of the Idi Amin regime, for example, or the Mobutu. The hour, the methods of dispatch, the disposition of the victims, and the disposal of their remains are recorded, the details of torture as well as measures of reprisals against colleagues or relations who dared exhibit signs of sympathy or grieving."[38] Would the publication of such a tome, cataloguing each abuse, serve the cause of reconciliation? There may well be particular cultures in which nothing less than the *whole* truth will do, but the question should always be asked whether this particular culture is one of them.

Related to this question is the issue of qualifying the truth. When do the facts speak for themselves and when do they need explanation, qualification, and contextualization? Again, the answer will vary from place to place and from time to time. In some situations—such as perhaps where even the new government does not enjoy substantial legitimacy—it may be more prudent to present the facts with little government editorializing. Thus, when the government of East Germany collapsed, and many people who had lived under the Stasi regime might have had little faith in either their old government or the new Western government, the government may have acted in the best possible way by simply opening the files up to the public without any elaboration and letting the public ascribe whatever significance they wanted to specific facts found therein. The government of South Africa, by contrast, which enjoyed tremendous good will during the Mandela presidency, had sufficient legitimacy to provide its own version of the "truth" about the apartheid years.

The lesson to be learned from this intricate web of issues is that there are few universal rules in this area that apply to every nation in transitional situations. In some countries, the truth is better avoided, at least for a time; in other countries, it is best confronted as early as possible directly through truth commissions, or indirectly as through trials. In most countries, we would argue, it is best to mediate the truth so that it can be received by the populace in a larger context, although there may be situations where it is best to let the truth speak for itself and let the citizens provide their own context for the facts.

Finally, a government may want to consider what will be presented alongside the "truth." If the truth is in fact terrible, simply proffering it without the promise of justice, or the hope of forgiveness, in one form or another may redouble the pain.

Forgiveness

In their extreme forms, forgiveness and justice constitute two opposite reactions to the promulgation of truth. With forgiveness, the common humanity of perpetrator and victim entails embracing the perpetrator back into society's fold. With justice, the perpetrator is punished, isolated, ostracized, and *alien*-ated—his difference from the victim and from society is confirmed by a sentence: incarceration or even death. In forgiveness, the perpetrator is separated from his deed, while in justice he is defined by it. And yet, reconciliation—as a practical policy—is not comfortable at either extreme: it does not require that perpetrators of the grossest human rights abuses be embraced like brothers and sisters, but neither does it allow a society to deem them so monstrous that they are beyond the human pale.[39]

If forgiveness is about embracing others, it is of course legitimate to ask whether "reconciliation or forgiveness are even possible after massive human rights violations."[40] But the many instances of forgiveness throughout the world even under the most astounding circumstances suggest that forgiveness is at least possible and, for some, it is indispensable. A lot is packed into the simple phrase "I forgive you." In the next sections, we pull it apart, focusing on the subject, the action, and the object of the sentence in that order.

Who Can Forgive

There is, of course, no simple, uniform answer to this question; different people, different traditions (both secular and religious) will find different ways to approach the issue. Some would say that forgiveness is only for God, and not people, to do. Some would say that if that is true, on earth, only priests can forgive, but those through whom God does not speak cannot forgive. Others believe that God speaks through everyone and therefore anyone can forgive. In some traditions, only the victim can forgive the offender. In this view, murder—any murder—is unforgivable because it leaves no victim to confer forgiveness.[41] Still others see forgiveness as a purely secular affair, a decision that one person makes privately toward another.

Throughout the literature, forgiveness is presented sometimes as a weakness, and sometimes as a strength. If forgiveness is "cheap" or "easy," it can carry with it "the possibility of condoning, rather than constricting, the spread of evil."[42] In this view, forgiveness should be withheld or at least bartered only for a very high price. Many Jewish writers have held this view in the context of forgiveness for Nazis or Nazi sympathizers. As Cynthia Ozick reminds us, "Forgiveness can brutalize," because "Whoever is merciful to the cruel will end by being indifferent to the innocent.'"[43] Thus, *refusing* to forgive is what takes strength. As André Stein has written, "the opposite of not forgiving is neither cruelty, nor wallowing. It is a way of healing and honoring our pain and grief."[44] In this view, when "damaged people are urged to 'forgive,' they are further harmed because they are put under pressure to suppress or amend their anger."[45]

But for many others strength lies in the capacity to forgive.[46] Consider the story of Tomas Borge, a Nicaraguan Sandinista who was captured by the contras and brutally tortured. After the war, when a judge gave him the opportunity to confront and pass judgment on his torturer, Borge responded, "'My punishment is to forgive you.'"[47]

Forgiveness is both a sign of strength and a builder of strength. It is the refusal to give in to resentment, anger, or hatred.[48] Forgiveness can empower the victim; indeed, it may be the *only* empowering aspect of the relationship between victim and victimizer. South African writer Pumla Gobodo-Madikizela explains this inversion of power as follows: "For just at the moment when the perpetrator begins to show remorse, to seek some way to ask forgiveness, the victim becomes the gatekeeper to what the outcast desires—readmission into the human community. And the victim retains that privileged status as long as he or she stays the moral course, refusing to sink to the level of the evil that was done to her or to him. . . . 'This is what it means to be human,' [forgiveness] says. 'I cannot and will not return the evil you inflicted on me.' And that is the victim's triumph."[49]

While this version of forgiveness is to be aspired to because it signifies neither condoning nor weakness, Gobodo-Madikizela also reminds us that victims who have been disempowered by the perpetrator, and perhaps by a broader system designed to oppress them, are unlikely to have the emotional wherewithal to offer forgiveness from the standpoint of strength. "Some of the victims who encounter perpetrators cannot make that psychological leap and recognize that the tables have turned, that now the power is theirs to demand what is rightfully due them."[50] This is especially likely when the social context of the oppression has not significantly changed—where those who were victimized in the past remain poor, disenfranchised, and disadvantaged in the present (particularly vis-à-vis the perpetrator and those in his class).

If forgiveness is permissible, is it ever mandatory? *Must* victims forgive their oppressors? Must all relationships be restored? Sometimes, it might be best to allow some distance between former adversaries, particularly where power imbalances persist. An appropriate distance might allow the victim to develop the capacity to protect himself and to enhance his life independent of the perpetrator.[51] Forgiveness may require the kind of individual healing that is examined in Chapter 2.

Although stories in which victims choose to forgive are impressive and make good headlines and even better pictures (a handshake is a photo opportunity; the decision not to shake hands is not), many victims, when given the choice, abstain. In South Africa, it has been reported that "At the end of each statement, commissioners would ask the witnesses if they could forgive the perpetrators of the crimes they had experienced or seen. A few would say they could, but many remained silent. Telling their stories was their main purpose in coming to the commission, not forgiving their oppressor."[52] The willingness to forgive the perpetrator is simply beside the point for some people. And because the decision to forgive is so intensely personal, forgiveness (unlike amnesty) can never be mandated by law.[53]

While the law should not *require* people to forgive their adversaries, the government may, nonetheless, encourage forgiveness by promoting a culture of reconciliation. This "institutional support" may help victims realize that forgiveness is an option and may suggest avenues for achieving forgiveness. The absence of institutional support, Gabriel O'Malley argues, forces the victim to "choose between forgiveness and insatiable anger. Those who are unable to overcome the anger that flows naturally from victimhood are forsaken, given no support which could keep them from falling headlong into vengeance which may consume them."[54] The efforts of government and of other prominent institutions in the society to promote forgiveness, *as one option*, might be crucial for those for whom forgiveness is salutary but who need social prompting or affirmation to achieve it. These may come in the form of radio and television programs and newspaper articles, or seminars and classes, depending on the needs and habits of the community. But institutional support should never be so emphatic that it risks sliding into coercion or real social pressure to forgive.

Forgiveness, even when it does occur, does not invariably lead to rec-onciliation. It is most likely to be effective where the victims and perpe-trators have economic, social, or cultural reasons to come together other than for the sole purpose of forgiveness. Otherwise, forgiveness may not actually bring people closer.

What Is Forgiveness?

The second task is to discern the precise meaning or meanings of for-giveness. For many people, it has a strong moral component. For Donald Shriver, it begins "with memory suffused with moral judgment."[55] Often, forgiveness is suffused not only with moral judgment but with religious judgment. The discrepancy between different religions' views of forgive-ness can be seen most clearly as between Christian and Jewish faiths. Simon Wiesenthal's volume *The Sunflower* vividly illustrates the different concep-tions of forgiveness. In this remarkable book, Wiesenthal recounts an expe-rience he had when he was an inmate in a concentration camp. A young SS man who lay dying sought his forgiveness for a horrendous act: he had once herded families into a building, locked it, and set it on fire, so that everyone inside died. Wiesenthal listened compassionately to the man's story but ultimately left in silence, unable to offer verbal forgiveness. Decades later, the story still haunts him, and he presents several dozen prominent thinkers with the question of whether or not he should have forgiven the SS man. Many of the respondents who wrote from a Jewish perspective supported Wiesenthal's silence on the theory that the Jewish God is not a forgiving one, while the respondents who wrote from a Chris-tian perspective tended to advocate forgiveness even in this most extra-ordinary of circumstances. "If asked to forgive, by anyone for anything, I would forgive because God would forgive," wrote Theodore Hesburgh.[56] Had any contributors written from a Muslim perspective, it is likely that they too would have advocated forgiveness on the same ground: in the Qur'an, Allah is understood to be all-forgiving.[57]

Invoking religious ideology renders reconciliation appealing to many but problematic to others. Where societies are religiously homogeneous (such as, for instance South Africa or some Latin American countries), religious language and iconography can make reconciliation seem famil-iar and accessible. In Timor Leste, the reconciliation process fused to-gether elements of Catholicism as well as the diverse traditional religions in the various communities. But in many transitional nations, such as Bosnia, Ireland, or Iraq where the fault lines were largely defined by reli-gion, religion is a divisive, rather than a unifying force. Invoking religion, then, may carve deeper divides, appealing to some in their comfort zone but alienating others. Even where there is relative religious homogeneity, moreover, the strength and the content of religious identity vary from person to person, so that reference to religion is likely to have varying effects on the public.

If reconciliation is a process, we might say that forgiveness is the last step in that process. But there may be other things we can do short of forgiveness in those situations where, for one reason or another, forgiveness is impossible. Compassion offers one alternative to the dichotomy between forgiveness and vengeance. Like forgiveness, compassion rejects seeing the perpetrators as monsters, as outside the pale of humanity; it means recognizing the other person as human, and therefore as worthy of compassion. Unlike forgiveness, however, compassion does not require identifying with the perpetrator; you don't need to condone their actions. With compassion, you don't need to get too close. You don't need to speak. But compassion is not an endpoint; it allows for the possibility of forgiveness at some future date.

Compassion has none of the strings that attach to forgiveness. Anyone can do it, and it can be felt toward any other person; even the most despicable human being may be worthy of compassion simply because he is a human being. One can feel compassion toward a murderer without betraying the victim. Far from identifying with him, we feel compassion precisely because we would never want to be in his place. When the Dalai Lama met a Tibetan monk who had spent eighteen years in a Chinese prison in Tibet, he asked him "what he felt was the biggest threat or danger while he was in prison. . . . he said that what he most feared was losing his compassion for the Chinese."[58] Perhaps compassion is the aspect of forgiveness where the strength resides.

An even smaller step towards forgiveness might be termed "recognition." Recognition has at least three meanings. It might mean to affirm, approve of, or accept the legitimacy of the other, as a government "recognizes" the rightful leader of another government. In this sense, when a victim "recognizes" a perpetrator, she might be doing nothing more than acknowledging that he has a place in the same society as she, that she accepts his place in the community. This does not require either forgiveness or compassion, but merely acceptance and nonaggression. This sense of recognition operates in both directions, however. Victims also want "recognition" from the new government, from the perpetrators, or from society at large. In Timor Leste, victims testified to the CAVR that they wanted their names recorded, they wanted to be heard—they wanted the government to recognize the harms they had endured.[59]

Another sense of "recognize" is to see something familiar. This gets us closer to the sense of forgiveness that requires the victim to "recognize" herself in the perpetrator, or to recognize the perpetrator in herself. Pumla Gobodo-Madikizela spent months interviewing Eugene de Kock—known as "Prime Evil" for his leadership role in the atrocities of apartheid. When she left Pretoria, she writes, "I was afraid, not of the memory of the evil schemes that were concocted in that city but of my own empathy for de Kock."[60] It is precisely the familiarity of the perpetrator that is frightening to some victims, or would-be victims.

If we deconstruct the word, a third sense of "recognize" emerges. In this sense, we "re"- "cognize," that is, to understand in a new or different way. This is the transcendent aspect of forgiveness, which entails seeing the perpetrator not for what he has done, but for what he is and could become. Long and Brecke, in their study on reconciliation events after war, place great emphasis on reframing identities. "Each party has to restore a sense of self and a sense of the other that are different from those of the war years. In the end, the parties must see themselves and the other camp in a more holistic and valued way."[61] If a Cambodian survivor can see her camp commander not as a brutal sadist, but as a desperate farmer who simply wanted rice for his children, there is the possibility of reconciliation.

The focus on reframing identity suggests a new way of thinking about forgiveness. Traditionally, forgiveness is equated with forgetting, wiping the slate clean, closing the books.[62] Many victims oppose forgiveness on this ground: they do not want to, or can not, forget what the perpetrator did, and they therefore abjure forgiveness. In this sense, forgiveness is past-looking. But, increasingly, scholars are suggesting that forgiveness is not about forgetting the past but about reframing it: understanding what happened as about the relationship of the perpetrator to his deed and allowing a transformation of that relationship. "Reframing does not do away with the wrong itself, nor does it deny the wrongdoer's responsibility for it, but it allows us to regard the wrongdoer in a more complete, more detailed, more rounded way."[63] It enables the perpetrator to separate himself from the deed so that we can see that the "murderer insofar as he, a person, may be more than anything he ever did,"[64] as Arendt explained. By separating the doer from the deed, we transcend the deed and are able to forgive the perpetrator without condoning the evil that he committed.

This reorientation focuses forgiveness toward the future. Indeed, this is the very sense in which Archbishop Desmond Tutu has argued that, as the title of his book says, there is "No Future Without Forgiveness." Ironically, it was Tutu's emphasis on forgiveness during the South African TRC hearings that made it a prominent element of the reconciliation landscape, but that, at the same time, led critics to claim that forgiveness's religiosity made it inapplicable to the secular work of nation-building. As previously mentioned, he has also been criticized for insisting on forgiveness by those who interpreted his entreaties as forced forgetting. But while Tutu's understanding of forgiveness is undoubtedly rooted in his faith, his justification is purely secular and pragmatic. Forgiveness, he says, is "practical politics."[65] "In the act of forgiveness we are declaring our faith in the future of a relationship and in the capacity of the wrongdoer to make a new beginning on a course that will be different from the one that caused us the wrong."[66] This turns the common understanding of forgiveness on its head: it is necessary to deal not with the past but with the future.

Throughout the literature, there are hints that forgiveness is, ultimately, about movement or change. The perpetrator must travel from the emotionally safe zone of self-justification to the unknown territory of the victim's world. The victim must be able to proceed from the past to the future—a procession which in some situations can be unimaginably difficult. When the perpetrator does manage to "knock at the door" and the victim does manage to respond, Gobodo-Madikizela calls it "a powerful transfer of inner realities" between perpetrator and survivor.[67] The basis of this transfer is, as Tutu explains, "an act of faith that the wrongdoer can change."[68] Gobodo-Madikizela and Tutu each emphasize different aspects of the forward-looking nature of forgiveness. For the former, it is a valuable concomitant to personal healing; for the latter it is also necessary for nation-building.

Who Can Be Forgiven?

The third part of the inquiry into forgiveness concerns the offender. Are there perpetrators who can or should not be forgiven? What must an offender do to merit forgiveness? We might begin, again, with reference to religious conceptions of forgiveness. Again, there is a division: some, as we have seen, would say that God forgives everyone, while others take a more limited view of God's forgiveness, believing that forgiveness is possible only under certain conditions, such as, for instance, where the sinner has repented or atoned for the sins. Assuming that there are limits, we might consider what they are.

At the outset, it is worth noting that many perpetrators do not seek forgiveness. One study of the Czech Republic found that although almost half of the respondents had met their perpetrators informally after the transition, only 4.5 percent had received an apology.[69]

This may come about for a variety of reasons. Perpetrators might recognize the victim's power in forgiveness and choose not to endow their victims with such control over them. Arguing that forgiveness entails moral judgment, Donald Shriver writes that "for this very reason, alleged wrongdoers are wary of being told that someone "forgives" them. Immediately they sense that they are being subjected to some moral assessment, and they may not consent to it."[70]

Perhaps a more common reason for the failure to ask, or call, for forgiveness is that perpetrators—with alarming regularity—feel no guilt or remorse at what they have done. Consider the following trial testimony that took place at the end of World War II:

Q: Did you kill people in the camp? A: Yes.
Q: Did you poison them with gas? A: Yes. . . .
Q: Do you know the Russians will hang you? A. (Bursting into tears) Why should they? *What have I done?*[71]

The defendant admits the facts but recognizes no connection between himself and the crimes.

This can happen for one of several reasons. For many people, although they are willing to "own" their actions, they do not understand that their actions were wrongful. This has been extensively documented in the case of the Holocaust. "Thus thousands, and perhaps hundreds of thousands of Germans who participated in and committed genocide and crimes against humanity returned to their homes and to quiet, peaceful lives, without their consciences ever bothering them, without ever feeling any remorse. Certainly these people do not need to be forgiven by anyone, not by the victims and not by God."[72] But the Holocaust is by no means unique in this regard. While "Experience shows that the great majority of Nazi criminals felt no regret for their actions," "The same is true for the perpetrators of other atrocities, in other totalitarian countries, or even today, in former Yugoslavia: concentration camp guards, like their superiors, judge themselves not guilty."[73] Hannah Arendt recognized this as well, explaining that "this new type of criminal, who is in actual fact *hostis generis humani*, commits his crimes under circumstances that make it well-nigh impossible for him to know or to feel that he is doing wrong."[74] The kind of indoctrination (or what Tutu called "conditioning") that made commission of the crime possible in the first place also immunizes the perpetrator from guilt about it once it is over.

A different reason for failing to feel remorse or guilt is that offenders often distance themselves from their actions, resulting in what was called "inner emigration" in the context of the Holocaust: "those people who frequently had held positions, even high ones, in the Third Reich and who, after the end of the war, told themselves and the world at large that they had always been 'inwardly opposed' to the regime."[75] Although the claim of "inner emigration" is likely to be met with some skepticism, it applies to people who genuinely—though not always objectively reasonably—believed that they had no choice or that they were actually helping the cause from the inside. *If I hadn't been there, someone much more brutal than I would have done it.* In some cases, these inner emigrants in fact did alleviate some pain (by forging passports, by letting someone pass, by allowing a mother to hold her child momentarily for the last time), but the evil that they did invariably outweighs the good in most people's assessment. Nonetheless, from the standpoint of "readmittance," this group may constitute the more likely candidates: they at least know the difference between right and wrong (even though they place themselves on the incorrect side of the line).

A final reason why one who is responsible for wrongs may fail to seek forgiveness is that while he acknowledges the deed, as well as his responsibility for the deed, he believes that he was more victimized than the putative victim. Marie Smyth has observed that in Northern Ireland "there is a tendency on the part of diverse groups and individuals to claim victimhood. This willingness is not matched by a corresponding willingness to own responsibility, in relation to the hurts and harms that have been done in their name, or that we have inflicted directly by our own actions."[76] This claim of victimhood, with no concomitant acknowledgment of responsibility makes the peace process "lopsided, immature, unstable, and the process of reconciliation is impossible." This observation has relevance for most societies: as a general rule, claiming harm is much easier than acknowledging it. Because the propensity to claim victimhood impedes not only the possibility of forgiveness, but the possibility of justice as well, it is discussed in more detail in the following section on justice.

If there are perpetrators who do not seek forgiveness, we must consider whether that refusal aborts the whole forgiveness process. Is the "call" for forgiveness necessary? Again, there is disagreement, between those who would require the perpetrator to make the first move and those who would not.

To Nicholas Tavuchis, "A proper and successful apology is the middle term in a moral syllogism that commences with a *call* and ends with forgiveness."[77] The call is essential and must entail some expression of sorrow and regret.[78] In Islam, for example, asking for forgiveness from God is one of the three requirements of forgiveness, along with "recognizing the offense itself and its admission before God" and "Making a commitment not to repeat the offense."[79] In Judaism, the offender must obtain forgiveness from the victim before asking the same of God. "Judaism believes that it is only through human interaction that the victim can best be healed and the wrongdoer most profoundly changed."[80] To South African writer Pumla Gobodo-Madikizela, "there must be something in the perpetrator's behavior, some "sign" that invites the victim's forgiveness. The most crucial sign is an expression of remorse."[81]

On the other side are those who, like Archbishop Tutu, say that the offender's actions instigating the forgiveness process are desirable but not necessary. "If the victim could forgive only when the culprit confessed, then the victim would be locked into the culprit's whim, locked into victimhood, whatever her own attitude or intention. That would be palpably unjust."[82]

The difference of opinion is explainable by different conceptions of forgiveness. Those who view "the call" as indispensable tend to see forgiveness as being about two opposing sides coming together. As Lazare explains, "What makes an apology work is the exchange of shame and power between the offender and the offended. . . . In acknowledging your shame you give the offended the power to forgive. The exchange is at the heart of the healing process."[83] In this view, both sides need to act so that they can meet in the middle; otherwise, the exchange is off-balance.

If, on the other hand, forgiveness is about victim empowerment and healing, as Tutu and others argue, the victim should never have to depend on the perpetrator to take the first step. While neither of these views is necessarily correct as a moral or philosophical matter, the latter may have some traction for practical purposes. Given the general failure of perpetrators to seek forgiveness, it may be more effective to emphasize the needs of the victim than to rely on a sign from the perpetrator.

And then there are those who do—*but should not*—ask forgiveness. In *The Sunflower*, many of the respondents indicated their disapproval of the SS man precisely because he did seek forgiveness. As Rebecca Goldstein writes, "For had he seen the enormity of his crimes, he never would have dared to ask for forgiveness. Never."[84] Even with ordinary murder, as we have seen, some might take the view that the plea for forgiveness can only be directed at the one who isn't there, although we might also acknowledge that a murderer might yet ask forgiveness, not for the murder itself, but for the pain it caused those who are still living.

If the offender does choose to signal that he seeks forgiveness, what should he do? Three possibilities present themselves: acknowledgment, apology, and atonement. Acknowledgment is "truth-plus." It affirms the truth of the event, but adds a moral dimension in that the speaker takes responsibility for his or her part. When, for example, former U.S. President Bill Clinton visited Rwanda in 1998, he did not merely state the "truth" of what had happened four years earlier, but accepted responsibility for failing to intervene. What was important to the audience of survivors was not his statement of the facts (which they knew better than he) but his acknowledgment of their suffering and of his role in exacerbating their pain.

In much the same way, truth commissions perform only part of their function when they merely recount the history; another part is the acknowledgment of the responsibility of the government in fostering the conflict and perpetuating the injustices. For this reason, truth commissions sponsored by the official entity responsible for the atrocities have the potential to contribute more toward reconciliation than third-party truth commissions. A commission that bears no responsibility for the crimes cannot "acknowledge" them.

Where the truth is widely known (as in the Rwanda example), acknowledgment may be even more important than truth per se. As Long and Brecke have noted, "In small, densely populated societies such as Uruguay and El Salvador, few were untouched by violence and few did not know their victimizer. Thus the importance of a truth commission was not only in uncovering the truth, as was the case in Argentina or Chile, but in acknowledging it."[85] Aryeh Neier argues that the import of acknowledgment is that it "implies that the state has admitted and recognised that it was wrong."[86] In this way, acknowledgment can break the cycles of violence.[87] But acknowledgment is not a panacea either. First, like remorse, it can be faked: a strategic mea culpa can be an effective arrow in the political quiver. Moreover, acknowledgment does not necessarily entail repudiation of the crimes. One can say—and believe—*I take responsibility for my role in the genocide . . . but I still believe that the victims are vermin and deserved what they got.*

An apology may add an element that is missing in acknowledgment. Apologies not only admit the facts (in some general sense, it needs to be clear what the offender is apologizing for), and not only acknowledge the offender's role in the events, but also indicate that the offender believes the actions were wrongful. Apologies suggest that the offender would *not* repeat the actions, given the chance. Like acknowledgment, however, apologies can be either heartfelt or disingenuous.

Even heartfelt apologies are complicated, and contain internal contradictions, which may explain why they are sometimes so appealing to victims and survivors but, alternately, so profoundly unsatisfying. As Nicholas Tavuchis and others have shown, the modern sense of "apology" departs from the ancient use of the word, *apologia*, meaning an "oral or written defense."[88] An apologia used to be a justification or explanation for why a person did something. The modern sense of apology eliminates that element and, in fact, the presence of a justification or defense in an apology actually mitigates its effectiveness.[89] A justification (*It was the way I was brought up; I thought they were communists; everyone did it*) merely appears self-serving to the victim, because it shifts responsibility for the action from the perpetrator—where the victim thinks it should be placed—to the larger social context, where the perpetrator wants it. In so doing, the perpetrator appears to try to minimize his or her own moral responsibility. But the victim is not interested in mitigation. Rather, the victim wants to know that the perpetrator himself sees the action, as the victim does, as totally *un*justified. The victim will only be satisfied if the perpetrator apologizes for the action, without elaboration—that is, without *apologia*. (*There is no excuse for what I did*). But in such a case, the apology may well leave the victim feeling empty.

Feelings of vindication are complicated when the apology comes not from the individual perpetrator but from the state. In certain instances, the heads of state apologize—to their own citizens as well as to other states and foreign citizens—for actions undertaken by their own governments or by their predecessors. In Ghana, President John Agyekum Kufuor announced the establishment of a Truth and Reconciliation Commission in his maiden speech in Parliament in 2001. He explained, "Those who have been wronged need to be acknowledged, and where it is beyond human capability that those wrongs can be reversed as in the loss of dear ones, for example, the least we can do is to publicly apologise and help in whatever way we can, with their rehabilitation."[90] In Nigeria, President Obasanjo made an official apology to victims of human rights violations under past governments on the occasion of receiving the report of the Truth Commission in 2002. President Obasanjo said, "At this moment in history, I, as chief executive of the federation . . . wish to offer my full apology to all Nigerians in general, and to direct victims in particular, for all the misdeeds."[91] Unfortunately, as of 2005, that country's Truth Commission Report still had not been released, so it remains unknown exactly what he apologized for.

An inadequate apology can also have a dramatic effect. The ongoing tensions in Japan over its treatment of women during World War II illustrate the unfortunate effects of a failed apology, and Japan's refusal to pay reparations has exacerbated the ill feelings.[92] Japan's response to the women's demand for apology reflects the disjunction that can occur between the offeror and the offerees of an apology. Some have characterized Japan's response as "tepid."[93] Others defend the approach, calling continued demands for more emphatic apology "unreasonable."[94] By contrast, Japan's apology for its "colonial rule and aggression" led to a summit between the leaders of Japan and China and an easing of tensions between the two countries.[95] These examples illustrate the absence of any commonly accepted yardsticks by which to measure the adequacy or effectiveness of an apology.

Often, in fact, interstate apologies are more effective than apologies that occur between a state and its citizens, since citizens often feel a greater sense of betrayal by their own government and the government's simple words may often feel like too little too late. Apologies between states, however, can augur precisely the correct climate for a warming of relations. For example when President Stjepan Mesić of Croatia visited Serbia and Montenegro, the presidents from both countries took the opportunity to apologize for "all evils" that were carried out by their countries during the 1991–1995 war.[96] Recently, some colonial powers have attempted to apologize for acts committed during or as a result of their occupation, but, again, not all of these are successful, as the German government's unenthusiastic apology to the Namibians illustrates.[97] Belgian Prime Minister

Guy Verhofstadt on a visit to Kigali on April 7, 2000, stated, "I pay my respects to the victims of the genocide. In the name of my country and my people, I ask your forgiveness."[98]

Parties to the dispute can also provide apologies for the sake of reconciliation. In October 2003, the IRA apologized to families of those who had disappeared in Northern Ireland for the grief caused by its actions. The IRA stated it had in recent times reexamined information related to the disappearances that took place in the 1970s and that it would do everything possible to bring closure for the families.[99] In Rwanda, the Organic Law of 1996 for prosecuting genocide and crimes against humanity introduced a system whereby offenders could plea bargain if they confessed their crimes. In terms of the law the offender had to apologize to the victim.[100] Whether this has been successful in advancing reconciliation is as yet unknown, since apologies offered in order to gain advantage are less often taken at face value. In South Africa, some perpetrators gave apologies to victims during their amnesty hearings, but these were at times unsuccessful insofar as victims viewed them as artificial attempts to bolster their applications.

It is, of course, very difficult to distinguish between genuine and disingenuous apologies. Several options present themselves in response to this difficulty. One is to take the perpetrators at their word. This can be done more easily in intimate settings where victims and other interested parties are more likely to know the perpetrator and have occasion to ask him or her questions that would reveal the depth of his or her remorse. In community victim-offender reconciliation programs, for instance, participants in the program have the opportunity to speak about the offense and can thereby gain a sense of the perpetrator's commitment to reform. Undertakings may also lend greater credence to an apology.

Atonement, which is the first place where actions are mixed with words in search of forgiveness, may be useful in helping to ensure the genuineness of an apology. Even atonement, of course, is ineffective in undoing the wrong, but it can go a long way toward healing the victim or survivor because it begins to remove the doubt about the offender's bona fides. In the best examples of atonement, the offender does *something* to confirm his or her sincerity. The actions may be restitutive (returning the stolen goods) or compensatory (paying for the material damage caused or an amount that represents psychic or bodily injury) or reparative (helping to construct a house when the victim was maimed or left homeless by the events) or symbolic (sharing a cup of wine). In all these cases, the action may be backward-looking (trying to restore the person to position they were in before the wrongful event) or forward-looking (trying to improve future prospects for the survivor).

Atonement is a predicate for forgiveness in most of the world's major religions. "When a Catholic confesses his sins, . . . he not only is to tell the whole story but also to undergo penance to demonstrate his sorrow and contrition."[101] A Jew must fast and seek forgiveness from the objects of his or her sins before God will offer forgiveness.[102] In Islam, a wrong-doer may be forgiven by Allah if he repents and atones and shows his devotion by praying.

Nonetheless, whether actions are required is subject to debate. As we have seen, in some views, the perpetrator does not need to do *anything* to merit forgiveness, while in others, some show of transformation or transcendence is required. In the Timorese truth, reception, and reconciliation process, for example, an individual who wishes to be accepted back into his community must provide some kind of restitution (paying the victims in kind for the loss he had caused) or some other gift (wine or an animal to be slaughtered for a feast). This reduces—but does not eliminate—the possibility that the perpetrator is not genuinely sorry.

The most common approach, echoing that of the major religions, is that actions are necessary where at all possible. Wole Soyinka, speaking of an episode of civil unrest and rampant looting in Trinidad, explained, "If the fabric of society, ruptured by the double violence of the coup and the looting, was to be healed, there had first to be restitution. Truth alone is never enough to guarantee reconciliation."[103] In that situation, the police asked the looters to place stolen items in front of their houses for pickup, and most people did so.

The need for action is explicable on several grounds. The action has material significance since it is the first act of the penitent to return what he has taken, as the example from Trinidad illustrates. It has a moral dimension as well: extracting something of value from the perpetrator seeks to restore the balance between good and evil that was set awry by the wrongful actions. The cost to the offender may be the best way to protect the victim against repetition of the crime. But if actions *are* predicates for forgiveness, the question arises whether verbal apology is necessary or is merely superfluous. If the acts are forthcoming, they do more than the words to demonstrate the offender's good will; if the acts are not forthcoming, expressions of good will are subject to skepticism. The example of apologies from national governments from mass atrocities may illustrate the point. Although many victim groups clamor for apologies (including acknowledgment), most of these represent poor and disempowered populations (think of African Americans, or Australian Aboriginals, or African nationals with respect to the world financial and political powers, or sexual slaves throughout the world). In each case the supplicants would benefit far more from reparations, affirmative action, and structural changes in the distribution of material resources than from verbal apology, without more.[104] Thus the provision of reparations is often seen to be part of a process of atoning for the events of the past, while the failure to provide reparations can indicate the perpetrator's failure to atone for what was done. Japan's minimal payments to World War II victims are seen by many victims and their families to indicate that Japan has not atoned for the wrongs it committed during this time.[105] By contrast, the relatively generous payments the American government paid to the Japanese American victims of America's internment policy during World War II may indicate genuine atonement.

In two situations, apology may be meaningful without supporting actions. The first is where the parties have equivalent social and political power,[106] and the second (which may often be related) is where the wrong was primarily psychic or moral, but not physical or material. In this situation, actions will do little to ameliorate the injury. In any event, some have suggested that the apology must *in some way* be costly to the offender.[107]

If costliness is a requirement, the absence of coercion must be too. The tension between extracting an act of atonement that is genuine and pressuring an offender to comply with community expectations needs to be addressed. It is important to avoid a situation where offenders are identified "with evil or wrong-doing, blamed for it, and cast out from the community in order to leave the remaining members with a feeling of guiltlessness, atoned (at-one) with the collective standards of behavior."[108]

If the offender admits the fact of the deed, acknowledges his responsibility for it, and seeks to atone for it by some palliative action, he is a better candidate for forgiveness. He has shown that he has transcended the deed; he no longer wants to be identified with what he did but wants to be readmitted into the victim's community. Failing any of these risks exoneration or condoning or erasing the wrongful actions.

One way to understand the problem is to see the relationship between victim and offender as if governed by competing moral codes. The offender's actions were consistent with one set of moral precepts (that permit murder, for instance), but inconsistent with the victim's (in whose view murder or rape or torture is not permitted). When the offender asks forgiveness, he must repudiate the morality that permitted his action, and embrace the victim's morality. An apology asserts that although the perpetrator takes responsibility for the act, it does not fit within his or her morality; she repudiates her own action because, although she did it, she disowns it. This permits reconciliation because it confirms the common moral ground of the victim and the perpetrator. A failure to apologize, on the other hand, indicates that the perpetrator does *not* disown the action and, therefore, that it is compatible with her morality. Reconciliation is impossible because the victim and the perpetrator maintain opposing moral stances. Apology, then, is the perpetrator's commitment to the victim's moral code, and forgiveness is the victim's acceptance of that commitment. To ask for forgiveness is to plead for "readmission into the human race"[109] upon terms that are acceptable to the victim and consistent with his or her moral code.

This approach avoids the identity maelstrom—the troubling question about whether forgiveness necessarily entails empathy with the perpetrator on the theory that there is evil in all of us. The victim need not condone, accept, or even understand the evil deed; both perpetrator and victim can reject the inhumanity of the act while recognizing the humanity of the perpetrator.

On a societal scale, where a government has engaged in a policy of genocide—say the slave trade or ethnic cleansing—an apology from the government shows that the present government's moral code no longer accepts that policy (even though it was justified by the majority's moral code at the time it was implemented). Thus, in Chile, when President Aylwin accepted his country's TRC report, he not only "offered a formal apology on behalf of the government for the acts of its agents and begged for forgiveness from families of victims," but he also promised "reparations and special benefits for them."[110] Atonement from a government should not be seen as an admission of legal liability, but rather as an admission of the moral fallibility of the state in the past and of the commitment of the present government to moral rehabilitation.

Here again forgiveness appears as transformation, change, or a turning.[111] This turning is what permits forgiveness to function prospectively and not just retroactively, as Archbishop Tutu suggests. Turning, or repentance, is a necessary element of humanity. It is what makes humanity possible; otherwise we would always be tied to our (mis)deeds.

It is for this reason that apology and forgiveness can effectively interrupt cycles of violence. Whereas the victim and offender were previously on opposite sides of a moral line, after forgiveness, the offender has moved to the victim's side, thus minimizing the differences between them and binding the offender to the victim's moral code, where violence is not acceptable. Absent that crossover, violence can continue.

If forgiveness is ultimately about morality, the question arises whether law is at all relevant to the issue. In some sense, law is entirely irrelevant to, and inconsistent with, forgiveness: where law generalizes and is compulsory, forgiveness is individual and must be voluntary. Law can not promote true reconciliation because law eliminates the singularity of experience; legal response assumes the commonality of the past.

Nonetheless, there are things governments and governmental actors can do to promote the cause of forgiveness. Government leaders can, first of all, exemplify the willingness to forgive, as Nelson Mandela did. Second, they can encourage others to do the same. In Uruguay, the public voted for amnesty after "the Sanguinetti administration had maintained that democratic peace and stability must be paid for by forgiveness of the repressors. That appeal and the public's desire for a return to normalcy prevailed."[112] Through laws, governments can either promote or retard forgiveness. Laws (including the death penalty) that insist on or permit punitive measures to be taken against perpetrators—that essentially bind the perpetrator to his or her wrongful actions—will retard the cause of forgiveness. But legal processes that permit the perpetrator to transcend his deed and atone for his wrongful actions will encourage forgiveness by allowing victims and society at large to "reframe" the offender in a new light. It is worth noting, too, that often forgiveness operates in a legal vacuum. Where a formal system of laws applies, forgiveness is not likely to be a prominent feature of the landscape: the law defines what offenders can or must do to repay their debt to society, as it were. But where law does not operate formally, or it does not deal with the kinds of acts at issue, individuals are likely to find ways to permit the reintegration of the offender or, conversely, to excommunicate him from society on a temporary or permanent basis.

The relationship between forgiveness and violence confirms that forgiveness is not only a moral question; it has significant social ramifications as well, and to this extent, the law is quite relevant to questions of forgiveness. Thus, forgiveness, law, and social reconstruction all intersect. If the law permits (excessive) vengeance, violence is likely to continue. On the other hand, the law might promote (though not compel) forgiveness if it provides an alternative to private acts of revenge—either by effectively delegating punishment to the state, or by permitting some kind of partial justice. Viewed this way, forgiveness, justice, and reconciliation all serve the same goal of ending violence.

Justice

Of all the issues relating to reconciliation, justice is probably the most complex, and the most elusive. The confusion is present at every level, from the philosophical to the practical, and it exists whether justice is considered in relation to reconciliation or independent of it. Since much more can be said of justice than can reasonably be synthesized here, in this section we seek merely to raise some questions to suggest why issues of justice that relate to reconciliation defy easy resolution. The basic questions are (1) what conceptions of justice even apply in most transitional situations, (2) whether as a practical matter justice (as so conceived) can be achieved, and (3) what the relationship is between justice (as so implemented) and reconciliation is or ought to be.

At its most abstract, justice is often thought of as a balance. If an injustice weighs down one side, a countervailing act sets the balance right. This "an eye for an eye" approach is the classic form of retribution, where the wrong done by the perpetrator is inflicted back on him or her.[113] This is reflected in the death penalty and other harsh forms of punishment. But this can be a "sterile sort of justice that is far less satisfactory than breaking the cycle of violence or vengeance once and for all."[114]

Another version of the balance focuses not on the nature of the wrong but on the injury to the victim. Equilibrium means rehabilitating the victim. As applied in transitional politics, this version means that "The successor state seeks to recognise those who were rendered legally and politically invisible, those put outside the protection of the law and forced below 'the threshold of moral vision'. To make them 'morally visible' is to bring them back into a moral relationship, to socially reintegrate them."[115] Restorative justice largely reflects this conception of the role of the state in correcting past wrongs, and it may have more success in ending cycles of violence.

In some cultures, justice is symbolized as a wheel, connoting motion or progress; evolution. This different conception of justice may reflect the different position that some nations have with respect to the provision of justice. In stable, liberal cultures, justice is taken to be the norm; if an injustice occurs, it is aberrational. The justice system will correct it, thereby returning the society to the status quo. In other cultures—and this is particularly true in divided societies—it is understood that justice is an aspiration continually to be striven for, a process to be committed to, but not a status that has been achieved.

Even so, none of these conceptions of justice apply easily to transitional societies. What can it mean to "correct" centuries of slavery? What kind of "good" can be balanced against a genocide or mass violations of human rights? How can one turn the tables on totalitarianism? Any effort to seek a formula for justice in transitional settings is likely to end in frustration and futility.

In both transitional and mature democracies, justice has many faces. The goals of justice can be retribution, correction, redistribution, or restoration, among other things. Justice can apply to an individual or to a community. It can be material or psychological. Sometimes, these various conceptions of justice can be mutually reinforcing: insisting that someone who burned a house help to rebuild it can be punitive, as well as corrective and restorative. (We discuss economic justice in Chapter 8.)

The multiple goals of justice can also conflict with one another, raising difficult issues of policy and fairness. Many transitional countries do not have sufficient resources both to distribute resources through broad economic policy and to pay reparations to a relatively few number of people. Elazar Barkan has shown how the selection of one of these competing goals literally at the expense of the other manifests the new nation's evolving identity. "By selecting deserving victims and undeserving victims," Barkan writes of postcommunist Europe, "legislators and governments rewrote the national identity and favored one national story over another."[116] This Hobson's choice between broad economic justice and individual reparations grants has also stalled South African efforts to promote justice. Similarly, a transitional national government is likely to have to choose among retributive justice (by allocating resources to criminal trials) and restorative justice (by allocating resources toward truth commissions or capacity-building initiatives within communities) and distributive justice (by allocating resources to education and infrastructure). Few countries can afford multiple forms of justice, even with international help. Recent efforts at both retributive and restorative justice include Timor Leste, Cambodia, and Sierra Leone, though the populations in these countries remain desperately poor.

In addition to the internal contradictions of justice, transitional justice is especially elusive because, in most situations, the preceding *in*justice is so layered and multifaceted. It is virtually impossible, in many transitional societies, to figure out which wrongs can or must be righted and how to go about righting them. Unlike the situation in ordinary times in presumptively just societies, where the injustice is the aberration and therefore quickly and neatly cabined, many transitional societies are *defined* by injustice. Injustice is pervasive and sweeping, and yet palpable and personal. People witness, are wounded by, or participate in multiple brutal acts of injustice. How can justice even be conceived of when 20 percent of a people are killed or die of unnatural causes, as in Cambodia in the 1970s, Rwanda in the 1990s, or Sudan today? The remaining 80 percent are certainly not unscathed, but are deeply scarred by the systemic brutality. They demand some form of justice, but it is difficult to imagine what justice looks like in these situations. The only certainty is that justice in Sudan or Rwanda or Cambodia is something quite different from justice in Bosnia or the Democratic Republic of Congo, and all of these will be quite different from justice in Eastern Europe and in Latin America.

Moreover, in most situations, *in*justice is multidimensional in that it is experienced by the same people both as discrete acts of violence, witnessed or endured, and as structural inequities that result in famine, disease, and psychological wounds. Justice, then, must be both personal and systemic. Injustice is also temporally multilayered, in the sense that, most often, recent injustices arise not out of calm and peace but out of previous systems of injustice. War in the Great Lakes region of Africa is the direct successor to centuries of colonialism and Cold War political injustices. Communism in Eastern Europe came on the heels of fascism or in response to feudal forms of injustice. Is it even possible to imagine doing justice for the crimes of successive unjust regimes? Sometimes the unjust regimes followed one another with such rapidity that the same individuals were subject to successive injustices. At other times, victims of one injustice became the perpetrators of the next, as in Rwanda and Uganda. Can any present government untangle all the threads to begin to devise a conception of what justice means in any particular country? Where is the baseline against which justice and injustice are measured?

Justice assumes a status quo ante to which the nation seeks to return. Like law, justice depends on continuity, predictability, and regularity. Everyone should be treated the same and everyone should be treated tomorrow as people in the same situation were treated yesterday. By definition, however, transitions interrupt and indeed *reject* the past as a baseline. Whatever justice means in transitional countries, it is probably the antithesis of what came before, rather than the continuation of it. It is not sufficient to adjust the scales; they must be entirely recalibrated. Nations in transition are therefore often disabled from looking to their own past to define what justice means to them; they must either borrow from somewhere else or make it up as they go along. Either option risks losing the indigeneity and consistency that is normally associated with justice. In many countries, for instance, borrowing from Western conceptions of criminal justice (including principles of due process and prohibitions against the death penalty) are inimical to the local culture; a regime of trials that insists on these procedural and substantive features is unlikely to result in the healing and closure that justice is expected to bring.

Many conceptions of justice are ill-suited to the transitional context for an even more complex reason. Justice tends to connote a duality: it pits victims against perpetrators, right against wrong, the deserving against the undeserving. But the palette of transitions consists not of black and white, but of an infinite number of grays. Systemic violence typically succeeds by coopting masses of individuals, of whom some would not naturally be predisposed to violence and others would actively despise the very regimes they were forced to support. For example, in the Guatemalan civil war, the state achieved "mass indoctrination by co-opting, requesting, or forcing large sectors of Guatemala's institutions or private citizens into carrying out many of the state's repressive tactics. Even Guatemala's justice institutions became coconspirators through their toleration and encouragement of these acts by refusing to enforce and sometimes even by obstructing the rule of law."[117]

Victims in these circumstances become the very perpetrators they hate. Black overseers were made to enforce discipline against slaves; Nazi concentration camps functioned with the help of Jewish kapos, the Khmer Rouge depended on the willing assistance of thousands of citizens who sold their souls for rice for their families. These individuals are as much victims as perpetrators, though they undoubtedly perpetrated unjust acts.

Another common form of coopting is military conscription, which gives men, women, and increasingly children a stake in a system they might otherwise abhor. In Guatemala, this was done by militarizing much of society, so that people throughout the country were made to actively participate. In addition, "the state purposefully created and legalized paramilitary structures, whose members were sometimes encouraged or forced by the military to torture, kill, and rape members of communities perceived to pose a threat to society." The national police in Guatemala, as in many countries, was also militarized, and many members carried out grave human rights violations recorded during the war.[118]

The word "perpetrator" therefore embraces significant gradations of culpability. What of those who were too fearful to act but truly wanted the destruction of the "other"? Bystanders who silently witness violence are generally not responsible in law for the crimes committed, and in most situations they are not held morally accountable either. Nor are those who, through political and moral support, sustain an unjust regime, such as in Germany under Hitler, in America under Jim Crow, in South Africa under apartheid, and throughout colonial Africa. At the other end are those who for whatever reasons chose to participate in the carnage, either because of ideological commitment to the cause, psychological weakness, material gain, or for other reasons (including, often, delusions of power and grandeur).

As the category of "perpetrator" becomes less distinct, it merges with the category of "victims." "We have to accept the uncomfortable truth," writes Dilip Simeon, "that the ubiquitous language of brutality has pushed victims and perpetrators together into a seamless whole."[119] The absence of boundaries raises difficult legal questions (concerning for instance principles of command responsibility and duress) and moral questions (are they responsible?) as well as factual questions (could they have said no?). These complex questions are all in some way relevant to the central problem of reconciliation: if we judge all those who have perpetrated vicious deeds too harshly, we might impede the progress of reconciliation and healing. Even more striking perhaps than victims acting like perpetrators is the fact that perpetrators often take on the mantle of victims. Hannah Arendt was one of the first to recognize this phenomenon. She writes in *Eichmann in Jerusalem*: "So that instead of saying: What horrible things I did to people!, the murderers would be able to say: What horrible things I had to watch in the pursuance of my duties, how heavily the task weighed upon my shoulders!"[120] Indeed, after the war, many Germans felt so victimized by the Allied bombing campaigns that they compared their own situation with that of the Jews.[121] "In the West German political and cultural system," Barkan says, "Germans were the victims of the war."[122] But the phenomenon is by no means limited to postwar Germany. For example, a study of Bosnian legal professionals from all sides of the conflict reveals that "universally individuals identified their national group as victims."[123]

Of course, in many cases, the feeling of victimhood did not result from the conflict but rather preceded it; the conflict confirmed and emphasized the prior sense of vulnerability. Minority populations are fearful of the majority, agrarian populations feel oppressed by the sophisticated urbanites, those who have been oppressed are all too often angling for a fight. The conflict manifests the perpetrators' feeling of victimhood, and does nothing to alter it. Indeed, it is often the feeling of victimhood that is the rallying cry for the new terror. "Many of our favorite symbols and fables are attached to a grievance, either artificially or intrinsically. It would seem that the very act of self-definition conjures up injured innocence and righteous grief."[124] Whatever the outside world thinks of the atrocity of one side's actions, that side invariably sees itself as the victim of someone else's atrocity. This victim-association risks becoming the defining feature of the group's sense of self—even a "source of pride."[125] Victim ideology is often a deliberate political tactic designed to foster cohesiveness among some or all of the parties to the conflict. It is wise, therefore, for those who seek to foster reconciliation, to take seriously the feelings that perpetrators often have of having been victimized; those feelings are real, whether or not they are reasonable.[126]

For example, it has been argued that one reason why Abraham Lincoln's Gettysburg Address was so phenomenally effective is that Lincoln was able to harness the sense of victimhood that the entire country felt and convert it into energy for rebuilding the country. According to Robert Meister, Lincoln "lifted Americans above the unendurable cycle of guilt and recrimination by imagining the United States as a nation in recovery. He moved us from a sense of being unwilling perpetrators of evil to the recognition that we are all "victims" to the common national identity of "survivors."[127] Rather than entrenching the divide between the North and South, the whites and the blacks, the slave-owning and the slavery-abolishing, Lincoln, in this view, was able to unite all Americans under the banner of survivors dedicated to the promise of liberty and equality.

While this moral vision is appealing, and may have allowed the southern United States to admit defeat, which in turn laid the groundwork for reconciliation, it was not without cost. It was, as Meister points out, "a form of amnesty"[128] that did not entirely truthfully reflect the reality for all the members of society. In any liberation struggle, some people are *in fact* more victimized than others, and the failure to recognize differences in the degree of entitlement may ultimately retard the cause of reconciliation. If there are tangible or psychological benefits to victimhood, the slaves were unlikely to want to share them with the slaveowners, nor the Jews with the Germans, nor the Tutsi with the Hutu, nor the Bosniaks with the

Serbs. Those who are more victimized and less culpable than others are likely to resist official efforts to unite everyone under the same banner.

Nonetheless, the essential fluidity between the categories of perpetrator and victim may render the most prominent form of justice—criminal justice—inapposite. Where the perpetrators are ubiquitous and indistinguishable from the victims, trying the former for the benefit of the latter is incoherent.

And yet, criminal trials are viewed by many as the "centerpiece of social repair."[129] Academics tout the benefits of trials to palliate the birth pangs of new regimes,[130] and successor governments seek to justify a regime of criminal trials against their predecessor. Trials have become increasingly popular in transitional settings, whether domestic, international, or hybrid. Indeed, it is utterly unremarkable for a victim of a crime to insist that justice be done, and for the political community to feel obligated to respond to the victim's plea by prosecuting the alleged perpetrator. In some conceptions, it may even be required, as failure to prosecute may be seen as collaboration.

Criminal trials, *at their best*, can promote a number of values in transitional times—some or all of which overlap with reconciliation, including establishing rule of law, punishing the perpetrator, and providing closure for the victim. The problem is, however, that criminal trials are rarely at their best. This is true in mature democracies and even truer in transitional societies. Trials often fail to meet expectations for both practical and deeper conceptual reasons. The practical reasons are easy to fathom: transitional governments rarely have the economic resources (let alone the political power) to prosecute wrongdoers of the previous regime to the full extent of the law.[131] Even where trials do occur rarely are more than a handful of people tried. In Argentina, for instance, the truth commission was said to have paved the way for trials both by uncovering evidence of crimes and by setting a moral climate in which trials *had* to take place.[132] But the facts tell a less rigorous story. Of 481 military officers indicted, 11 were convicted. "Menem pardoned 277 people, including 40 generals awaiting trial for human rights abuses, lower-ranking officers, and members of guerrilla groups."[133] In Cambodia, the octogenarian leaders of the Khmer Rouge are only now beginning to face the possibility of trials.

And in many cases, those who are tried are acquitted for lack of evidence. In Hungary, the Parliament tried repeatedly to pass laws that were constitutionally acceptable, and when they finally did (or thought they did), only two trials were held for crimes committed during the suppression of the 1956 uprising, of which one ended in acquittal and the other resulted in a 5-year prison sentence. In the end, even that conviction was overturned because the law used was still held to be constitutionally defective.[134] Post-unification Germany and many other countries have similar records. Tina Rosenberg has estimated that "Even when taking into account every single Latin American dictatorship-turned-democracy, the total number of security officials who served or are serving significant terms for torture or murder probably does not reach double digits."[135] Despite numerous efforts, in numerous jurisdictions, to prosecute Pinochet, he seems impervious to the criminal justice system.

Trials can fail to achieve the goals set for them for deeper reasons as well. For instance, the "truth" that trials reveal is typically partial, limited to the facts of the case and by the evidence permitted. The bigger picture often remains outside the trial's focus. Additionally, that so many politically related trials result in acquittals for lack of evidence suggests that judicial truth and factual truth do not always correspond to one another.

By focusing on a particular defendant, trials are said to be useful for individualizing guilt; they prevent one side from saying that "all" Hutu, or Afrikaners, or Germans were guilty and thereby interrupt the cycles of revenge. But if only Hutu or Afrikaners or Germans are tried, the propensity to generalize guilt is increased. (But if members of both groups are prosecuted, the government seems to be putting both sides on the same moral plane.) On the flip side, trials collectivize innocence,[136] which may or may not reflect the actual reality. While it is usually true that not *everyone* within a group committed atrocities in the same degree, and therefore not everyone should be equally castigated (and some should in fact be honored for their resistance), it is also true that the men and women who get tried rarely acted alone; they were effective only because they had significant support networks within their government or organization and within the population at large that stood by and watched. The binary and limited nature of a trial's truth invariably renders it partial and fundamentally diminishes the ability of trials to contribute to social repair or reconciliation.

Individualizing guilt may have the additional effect of turning perpetrators into scapegoats at best or martyrs at worst.[137] This is true whether or not defendants are given the opportunity to grandstand, as Slobodan Milosevic did at the ICTY. Milosevic not only attempted to vindicate his own actions, but to impugn the integrity of the tribunal that was prosecuting him. Saddam Hussein followed suit, grandstanding, attacking the legitimacy of the trial and of the regime behind it, and at times dramatically walking out altogether. This effort to turn the tables hardly serves the cause of justice, though the defendant's challenge to the process might ultimately enhance its legitimacy.

One final reason for the inability of criminal justice to accomplish transitional goals goes to the heart of the reconciliation project. Fletcher and Weinstein suggest that one of the main reasons for the failure of criminal trials (and in particular of the ICTY) is that respondents on all sides of the Bosnian war expected either too little or too much of the tribunal. For those who were not especially affected by the actual violence of the war, the trials in the ICTY were of only marginal value. As Fletcher and Weinstein note: "Those removed from the violence placed a higher priority on postwar economic development."[138] For these people, social and economic justice would be of far more significance than retributive justice. For most of the population, healing means jobs and safety, not a tribunal nearly a thousand miles away putting a few perpetrators behind bars.[139] Reconciliation for these people would have to be more comprehensive and holistic to be effective for this large sector of the population.

For those who were close to the violence, the trials took on a wholly different meaning. These people had a much stronger sense of the meaning of the war and its significance to their own lives. They wanted trials to establish accountability, but only for crimes committed against *their* group.[140] They expected the trials to vindicate *their* understanding of the truth and to reflect *their* national experience. Their priority was not the disclosure of some objective or generally accepted account of the events, nor was it justice, nor even closure. Rather, they wanted the trial to reinforce their sense of victimhood.[141] War, politics, and justice were all viewed as tools to achieving a political goal.

Domestic trials fared no better than their international counterparts. In Mostar, Bosnia, efforts were made to try war criminals in the newly created domestic courts of the Federation of Bosnia-Herzegovina, with the blessing of the ICTY. Five Croats and as many as 23 Muslims were charged, but only a few surrendered, only two were tried, and both of those were acquitted. Both trials, which were to take place in 2000 and 2001, "rapidly unraveled" as witnesses withdrew and defendants had to be released for lack of evidence. "A newly formed judiciary in a deeply divided town, in a deeply divided region in a deeply divided country," Sumantra Bose concludes, was clearly not the appropriate venue for experiments in criminal law. "Far from fostering the cause of truth and reconciliation, the trials exposed the deeply opposed perceptions in the town regarding what happened in Mostar, and who was responsible."[142]

Self-identification as "victim" raises a paradox with respect to trials. While outsiders may see this phenomenon as blurring the categories of victim and perpetrators (and thereby rendering them less significant and rendering trials less apposite), the view from the inside suggests the opposite. People around the world call for "justice," but they do so because they want to see themselves or their side vindicated. What separates them from the perpetrators is not a blurry line or a gray zone, but a deep and unbridgeable chasm. To those who see themselves as victims, there is little identification with those they classify as perpetrators; there is no empathy or sense of common humanity. The call for justice is a call for punishment, usually harsh punishment. In a survey of southern (mostly Shi'a) Iraqis conducted by Physicians for Human Rights in the summer of 2003 (shortly after the U.S. invasion of Iraq), nearly all who were asked said they wanted "justice."[143] However, as the report explains, "the mode of justice most commonly cited was Iraqi courts (24%) and religious courts (23%) that often apply an 'eye for an eye principle.' In addition, another 15% of respondents listed execution, torture, hanging and revenge killing as appropriate modes of justice."[144] While these modes of "justice" may follow the rule of law (as defined by local customs and laws), they do not appear to be modes that would promote reconciliation. Instead, they would further entrench the division between those who see themselves as victims and those whom they see as perpetrators.

This difference of opinion between the theorists who see no distinction between victims and perpetrators and little utility in even using this dualistic terminology, and those who experience warfare as the violent manifestation of the unbridgeable divide between victims and perpetrators, reflects the current worldwide response to political violence, which seems to be moving in two directions at once. On the one hand, never has there been so much attention to promoting reconciliation; on the other, never have there been more opportunities (or more demand) to prosecute criminally those who are deemed responsible for war crimes and other crimes of state.

This insistence on justice-as-vindication by those who self-identify as victims risks undermining efforts at reconciliation, in large part because they operate from opposite assumptions. Justice-as-vindication deepens the gorge between the sides, often by demonizing the other, whereas reconciliation tries to insist on a common humanity. In order to promote reconciliation, justice needs to be conceived as something other than a tool for vindicating each side.

Although criminal prosecutions occupy the main stage in any discussion about transitional justice, there is very little evidence one way or the other about their contributions to reconciliation or justice.[145] Fortunately, trials are by no means the only avenues to justice. A less punitive form of retribution may be lustration, widely tried in some of the former communist countries. Lustration seems to achieve many of the goals of criminal trials (individuating guilt, establishing a truth, bringing closure) without the costs (due process is not necessary). In practice, however, it has not earned a very good reputation. In his book on restitution, Barkan argues that lustration failed both in its weak form (as evidenced for instance in postwar Germany) and in its strong form (as in postcommunist Europe).[146] Lustration affects many more people and therefore penetrates society much more than criminal trials, which are often nothing more than sideshows.

It therefore depends on a real, not just conceptual, schism between the victims (in whose name lustration is imposed) and the perpetrators (who alone pay the penance). But as we've seen, this does not reflect the reality of many societies. Moreover, it exerts a heavy cost on rebuilding when the leaders and experts of the old regime are neutralized in the new.[147] If justice is conceived in its broader sense, having corrective and redistributive dimensions, it can entail restitution as well as broader economic and social initiatives aimed at righting the wrongs of economic inequities. Justice is most likely to overlap with reconciliation when it is conceived most broadly. Thus, reconceiving it as "social justice" may prove most fruitful.

The South African TRC emphasized the mutually reinforcing relationship among three concepts: reconciliation, ubuntu, and restorative justice.[148] This version of justice not only operates between the individual perpetrator and his or her victim(s), but concerns the entire community. Ubuntu, as noted earlier, is the African idea that people exist through others. "A person with ubuntu," explains Archbishop Tutu, "is open and available to others, affirming of others, does not feel threatened that others are able and good, for he or she has a proper self-assurance that comes from knowing that he or she belongs in a greater whole and is diminished when others are humiliated or diminished, when others are tortured or oppressed, or treated as if they were less than who they are."[149]

In some ways, ubuntu and the standard Western view of crime coincide: in both, crime is viewed as social deviance that needs to be eradicated, and in both the community is adversely affected by the crime. But there is a profound difference in the ways in which the two approaches would resolve the problem of crime. In the Western view, the criminal is held individually responsible; his or her punishment entails removal from society, thereby leaving the remainder of society pure and healthy. With ubuntu, the emphasis is on *social* repair or reconstruction. "Social harmony is for us the *summmum bonum*—the greatest good," says Archbishop Tutu.[150] Indeed, the South African interim constitution specifically distinguished between ubuntu and victimization, calling for "understanding but not for vengeance, a need for reparation but not for retaliation, a need for *ubuntu* but not for victimisation."[151] This version of justice is therefore much more likely than retribution to contribute meaningfully to reconciliation initiatives.

Finally, there is the question whether justice, in any form, is really necessary for reconciliation. There are certainly examples of countries that, upon transition, made no attempt to correct the injustices of the past. Spain is the paradigmatic example, but other countries have followed suit, including Mozambique. As a matter of realpolitik, some of the countries of Eastern Europe, such as Poland and Romania and the Baltic states, may also fall into that category. (Of course, there are also many postcommunist countries, particularly further east, that can be said to have not yet transitioned.) Given the empirical evidence indicating that in at least some of these countries peace has ensued and democracy has largely been consolidated, the choice to "do nothing," must be treated as a viable alternative that is appropriate in certain circumstances. But upon closer inspection, it becomes clear that many of these nations did not "do nothing." They engaged in deep and sweeping reform measures including (but not limited to) adopting constitutions, reforming their economies, and installing political processes to promote democratic governance. Mozambique developed a system of community courts to help deal with intra-community violence. These programs of structural reform make it quite clear that, from a reconciliation standpoint, it cannot be said that they did nothing. Rather, it is more accurate to say that they chose systemic reform rather than justice as a means to the same ends. These kinds of reforms are further examined in Chapter 8.

Although it is difficult to imagine reconciliation emerging out of a climate of injustice, in many cases, it must. In many instances of transitional "justice," there is no justice—either because there are no trials, or the trials don't produce convictions, or perhaps because there can be no justice for some of the most horrendous crimes that attend political transitions. Yet it is nonetheless necessary for reconciliation to rise up out of the ashes. People must learn to live with each other even though (or because) the state is not accepting the responsibility of ensuring peace. In these cases, reconciliation and justice cannot be interdependent; reconciliation must evolve even in the absence of justice.

Perhaps a modicum of justice—and some measure of truth—are ways for both sides to put something on the line to show the necessary commitment to move forward. At best, it has been observed, that some form of *partial* justice may be necessary for reconciliation to take root.[152] *I might back out of it if I think you will but if you show your bona fides, I will too.* Viewed this way, truth and justice, like forgiveness, are perhaps more important for the contribution they make to a better future, rather than for their utility in understanding the past.

Chapter 7
Reconciliation Redirected

Acolhimento involved people embracing each other as East Timorese, of coming back to our selves, living under one roof, after many years of division and violence. . . . *Acolhimento* grows from an appreciation and celebration of our rich cultural heritage. This heritage includes our traditional culture that was suppressed for so many years, as well as our experiences of colonialism, war and occupation. It is a way to help us accept the many dimensions of being East Timorese, living with what we have been through, and creating a society that includes all of us.

—CAVR Report

The Many Variations of Reconciliation

Reconciliation means different things to different people. For some it has only a religious significance while for others it relates to all facets of life. For some it is about returning to the past, to "a stage where there was conciliation."[1] For others it is about a better future, about building "a new and constructive relationship between the perpetrators and the victims based on shared principles of justice, equity, and mutual respect."[2] For many, it is about integrating the past and the future.

The process of reconciliation is also contested. For some it is a goal to be accomplished while for others it is "a shared and painful ethical voyage from wrong to right."[3] John Paul Lederach writes that reconciliation is about opening "up the social space that permits and encourages individuals and societies as a collective, to acknowledge the past, mourn the losses, validate the pain experienced, confess the wrongs, and reach toward the next steps of restoring the broken relationship."[4] For some it is about peace, or justice, but most writers in the field do not distinguish among these distinct strands, characterizing them instead as part of an undifferentiated whole.

Indeed, anyone surveying the practice and literature of reconciliation will notice that it "diverges . . . on whether reconciliation is an end or a means, an outcome or a process; whether it is politically neutral or unavoidably ideological, and the extent to which it is conservative or transformative in orientation."[5] It is certainly ironic that a word that is fundamentally about cohesion can have so many different and at times competing meanings. How can reconciliation ever be achieved when there are profound disagreements as to what it even means? If some are expecting reparations and others justice and still others don't want to think about the past; if some want to live together while others want exclusive rights, then how can reconciliation be accomplished? How can we move in the right direction if we don't know which direction to go in?

Without a proper definition (that is either universally agreed upon or at least culturally acceptable), it is impossible for governments to plan effective reconciliation programs or to determine whether a program succeeds in promoting reconciliation. And this is frustrating both for the people and for the government. The people will always be wondering whether the emotional and fiscal investment was worth it. The government will never be able to show it was. No one will ever believe that the objective was accomplished if it was never made clear what the objective was.

In this chapter, we survey some of the most common understandings of reconciliation and, picking out the best parts of each, we develop a new conception of reconciliation.

Bringing People Together

Reconciliation is typically characterized as the coming together of two things. In religious parlance, it is the rejoining of man and God, though in most other contexts the two sides of the balance are equivalent. A popular accounting glossary, for instance, defines reconciliation as "the adjusting of the difference between two items (e.g., balances, amounts, statements, or accounts) so that the figures are in agreement."[6] The goal here is to match the two items and to eliminate the difference between the two, as when your debits equal your credits.[7] Ultimately, this equalizing results in perfect unity; at the end of the accounting period, there is a single number that reflects the balance. Reconciliation has the same meaning in the context of lawmaking, where bills passed by different houses of a legislature must be reconciled to produce a single unified version that each legislator votes on. Out of the many, a single one emerges. Reconciliation as unity.

To some extent, this may be a useful metaphor for political reconciliation, since it connotes equality among the parties. It also reflects the idea of change that is immanent in many conceptions of reconciliation. Numbers, like people, have to "adjust" in order to achieve a balance. Eventually, after sufficient adjustment, the items lose their distinctive identities and merge into a new whole. This may be what the postgenocide Rwandan government means when it says that in Rwanda there are no Hutu or Tutsi, but only Rwandans.[8] One American jurist said "In the eyes of government, we are just one race here. It is American."[9] In this view, reconciliation occurs as the boundaries between the different groups erode and their distinctive qualities meld together.

But this version of reconciliation may be too extreme for many people in politically diverse societies. W. E. B. Du Bois noted more than 100 years ago in regard to African Americans, that "In this merging, [the African American] wishes neither of the older selves to be lost. He would not Africanize America, for America has too much to teach the world and Africa. He would not bleach his Negro soul in a flood of white Americanism, for he knows that Negro blood has a message for the world. He simply wishes to make it possible for a man to be both a Negro and an American"[10] Many people who identify not only with a national entity, but with more parochial interests as well, be they religious, ethnic, or otherwise, have no particular desire to give up their distinct affiliations. Their identification with subnational groups remains important to them, and never more so than in the wake of a divisive event like a genocide or a civil war. This is in fact the least auspicious time to expect people to give up their subnational affiliations.

Another model for reconciliation which might be more fruitful comes from the familiar terrain of family law. Couples divorce because of "irreconcilable differences"; if they decide to stay together, we say they have reconciled. Here again, the partners are moving, coming together after a quarrel or separation. One may acknowledge wrongdoing and commit to change; the other may forgive and commit to greater understanding. Unlike in the banking metaphor, marital reconciliation does not require the two sides to give up their identity—the marriage still entails two distinct parties—but it may require them to compromise on something that seems essential to them.

These two models reflect the most common approaches to political reconciliation. In fact, almost every dictionary definition of reconciliation assumes a new bilateral relationship accomplished by movement on both sides. (The religious sense of reconciliation, by contrast, which demands change from one side—the penitent—to permit embrace by the other side does not have as much traction in the political context because it is unilateral and absolute.) Political reconciliation tends to be conceived of as rapprochement of former adversaries, requiring compromise, if not sacrifice, from both parties. How much rapprochement, how close the former enemies need to get, depends on the particularities of each community within the transitioning state. The most common definitions of reconciliation tend to vary only in how much change they insist on from the parties and how much synthesis they provide in return. Thus, they can all be marked along a continuum, from a minimum of tolerance and peaceful coexistence to a maximum of a national hug. To take South Africa as an example, it is quite clear that, ten years after the first democratic election, there is relatively little racial violence, which means that some degree of peaceful coexistence has taken root. However, it would be a stretch to say that blacks and whites now love each other (if such a thing were possible at a societal level). In other countries, such as post-Dayton Bosnia, the two goals seem almost mutually exclusive: the segregation that maintains coexistence prevents any deep emotional bonds from developing between the ethnic groups.

The first stop along this definitional continuum would be refraining from killing one another. After a war, civil war, or genocide, what has been called "nonlethal coexistence" may be the most that can be expected of people.[11] It is certainly the least that can be expected of reconciliation. In terms of measuring reconciliation, it does not matter whether killing stops because of a change of heart, a commitment to the rule of law, respect for human rights, or simply exhaustion, as long as the ceasefire is stable and long-lasting.

As we've noted previously, ending violence might require some kind of physical separation. Indeed, every nation is separated even from its friendly neighbors by a border precisely to prevent conflict. A border can simply be a large space between the parties, such as a demilitarized zone, across which no one may cross, or a physical wall or fence. Walls have, of course, been used for millennia to keep parties separate. The wall being constructed in Israel in the early twenty-first century to keep out the Palestinians is simply a modern version of the tactic used by the Qin dynasty in China to keep out the Huns and the hedge built in the seventeenth century at the Cape of Good Hope by the Dutch to keep out the locals. But if walls, fences, hedges, and borders can reduce violence by keeping adversaries separate, they do nothing to promote more robust versions of reconciliation. Separation impedes common ground.

Not all boundaries are made of bricks and mortar. Laws that prohibit mixed marriages, that mandate segregated housing, that allocate jobs and schools by race, religion, or ethnicity are as effective as walls as separating people. These measures also impede reconciliation because they prevent people from getting to know one another. Similarly, cultural climates that make social integration unthinkable can be as effective as barbed wire fences. But neither physical nor psychological walls work in the long run. There are always those who want to break down the barriers, whether by marrying someone from the other group or taking a sledgehammer to the wall. Moreover, groups within a society rarely agree on the erection of physical, legal, or de facto walls: invariably, the walls represent not just separation but exclusion. They incarnate one group's hegemony over the other group, and subordination is invariably unstable.

The next stop along the continuum might be termed "peaceful coexistence," or what the Poles called "a minimum of fraternity."[12] Thus, Maria Ericson defines reconciliation as "a positive and sustainable peace between people."[13] This stage would necessitate the demolition of walls and boundaries so that the parties can live next to one another in peace. In this vein, the Chileans use the term *reconvivencia*, "living together again."

This is slightly stronger than "nonlethal" coexistence because it assumes not just the absence of killing but also a positive aspect of a prevailing peace and the possibility of a relationship between the two parties. It means that people "have become able to put aside feelings of hate, fear, and loathing, become able to put aside views of the other as dangerous and subhuman, and to put aside the desire for revenge and retribution."[14] That expectations at this stage are still rather minimal makes it more realistic for many societies than the more evolved versions of reconciliation discussed below. A minimalist view does not mean that the people from different groups must befriend each other, but it does mean that they should not scorn or avoid each other. Tone Bringa writes that "once people again live together or side by side, they find ways of approaching each other. There are subtle gestures such as the Croat neighbor who decides to buy her milk and cheese from a returning Bosniak villager."[15]

For those who accept the minimalist position, democracy creates conditions by which people can agree to differ without killing one another.[16] Democracy requires a commitment to peaceful resolution of differences and a respect for those with whom we disagree. Or, as Shriver has suggested, "democracy is at its best when people of clashing points of view argue far into the night, because they know that next day they are going to encounter each other as residents . . . "[17] Peaceful coexistence should be the goal for reconciliation in many places where violence tore through communities and disrupted the flow of daily life, such as in many parts of the former Yugoslavia, Cambodia, Timor Leste, and central African countries like Sierra Leone, Liberia, Sudan, and Côte d'Ivoire. It is particularly apt where policies of the previous administration reconfigured communities according to some political principle. In the immediate post-Saddam period in Iraq, for instance, the most that can be expected of the relationship between Kurdish families who were removed from their homes and the Arab families who were relocated there is peaceful coexistence. In these situations, families with significant differences are *forced* to live next to one another—sometimes even in the same houses. This proximity demands a certain fraternity, manifested at least by a tacit agreement not to harm each other, and the seeds of a common purpose and tentative steps toward the emergence of a community. But demands greater than that should not be made; we should not expect friendship or affinity between such people, at least not in the short term. Most countries choose not between tolerance and love but between tolerance and war, and tolerance is always the better choice.[18]

Nonetheless, in many divided societies, a richer version of reconciliation is possible and should be expected. Some countries may seek to instill deep respect, comradeship, and even affinity between parties on opposite sides of a political conflict. With robust peace-building initiatives, this can even exist in the midst of war and conflict.[19]

This form of reconciliation requires a personal commitment on the part of each individual to treat the other with respect. This may entail forgiveness and atonement, and the setting aside of differences. It means building a new relationship based on shared understanding and values. The reconciliation literature provides myriad examples like this: erstwhile soldiers reintegrating into a welcoming community,[20] victims and perpetrators speaking to another in the course of a TRC hearing, widows' groups from all sides of a conflict coming together in shared grief or to help in community projects. The goal here is in fact friendship or solidarity between former enemies.[21] One example of such reconciliation took place in Australia's Northern Territory, in a meeting between mining company executives and Aboriginal leaders. Tensions were high, because the executives were perceived to care only about money while the Aboriginals were thought to care only about land, and common ground was difficult to detect. "Two very different perspectives of life. It was only when one of the other mining guys said to [one of the Aboriginal leaders], 'We're two grandfathers,' that it started to become human, that there was a basis for discussion." When agreement was reached, it was attributed to the two sides having recognized each other's common humanity.[22]

At a social level, this type of interaction among people from different groups can produce a kind of cultural integration that hybridizes both elements. Parliament House in Canberra, for instance, which symbolizes white Australia's domination of the continent, also contains many representations of indigenous cultures. Many people use both Western and traditional medicines to treat physical ailments, and religion as practiced in many parts of the world represents a hybridization of colonial and traditional practices. Commercial integration may be the most common instance of people from diverse cultures interacting with one another. Eventually, if the culture is sufficiently integrated, a new culture may emerge that partakes of both elements but is distinct from either, as is the case with the world's many creole cultures. "The surest and most lasting forgiveness and reconciliation is when the descendants of the evildoers and those of the victims bind themselves into a collective and unbreakable unity—into a family, a tribe, a people, a nation."[23] This is a process, however, that can take generations or centuries. In most transitional countries, the goal of nascent governments will undoubtedly stop short of this.

Most of the literature focuses on efforts that psychologically, emotionally, and sometimes physically move people from distant and opposed points toward each other. Community reconciliation programs that are designed to bring people together by engaging them in a common project (building a house, bringing food to prisoners, sewing a quilt) are particularly effective at this, because they create the incentives that are sometimes necessary to bring people in: participants who are not naturally inclined to reconciliation may nonetheless join in order to get the quilt sewn or the house built. They permit each person to develop relationships with former enemies at his or her own pace. They help shift the focus of people's attention from destruction to construction, from selfish impulses to community needs, from past to future. This shift suggests a new path, a new identity for the community, and a new framework for the relationship: where there had been killing and rape, there are now a new school and better access to water supplies.[24] (See discussion on these types of projects in Chapter 3.)

But often parties are too far apart to be pressed together even with the most well-intentioned programs. In badly divided societies, it is possible that some individuals will have the fullness of heart to overcome their differences, but it is unlikely that this will be possible for significant numbers, and it certainly can not be demanded of all. There is too much variation within any large society to expect all inhabitants to respond the same way to the prospect of reconciliation. While some may take to it instinctively, it might be frightening or unwelcome for others; people will need different amounts of time to accept the idea, and perhaps different kinds or amounts of incentives. In many cases, there will be too little interaction with people from the other group to form the basis of a relationship. In other cases, hatred and divisions will be too deep to overcome. Perhaps the most dispiriting aspect of the twentieth century is the increasing tendency it revealed toward not just genocide but fratricide. In these situations, friendship between victims and perpetrators is not to be expected as a matter of public policy.

Often, then, anything more than bare tolerance, at least initially, may be unrealistic. Whether because of continued hatred, or ubiquitous feelings of victimhood, or psychological intransigence, or perhaps even inertia, rapprochement is not always easy to come by in transitional situations. Given the difficulties, how many resources should be expended in trying to get enemies to become friends? Or to get parties to give up some of their separate identity to achieve greater unity? If individual transformation is unlikely, the question becomes: is reconciliation possible in the *absence* of compromise?

Shifting the Paradigm

One way out of this difficulty is to focus not on the individuals within the society, but on the society itself. Some people have defined reconciliation as nothing less than nation-building or establishing a lasting social order or creating a new moral order or restoring a moral order that existed before it broke down.[25] These versions of reconciliation focus on reconstructing the entire society, from a political, economic, and social perspective, rather than on the psychological and emotional attitudes of the individuals within the society. Here we should focus more on the relationship between the individual and the nation, and less on the relationships between individuals.

Here again, reference to conceptions of reconciliation from outside transitional justice may provide a useful heuristic. When a person tries to reconcile two distinct ideas, the goal is to find a theory that accommodates both. For instance, judges in legal opinions often try to reconcile two competing ideas—such as the value of free speech and the dignitary interests of would-be victims of racist speech. They cannot change either value: free speech really is important, but so are the feelings of the victims. The judge will not try to force a compromise by having each side give up a little. Rather, the judge will find some overarching theory that allows both to flourish as they are (such as adhering to the values of a free and democratic society.[26]) Similarly, promoters of reconciliation need to develop some new vision of the conflict-ridden society that allows everyone within the nation to flourish, *as they are*. As the United Nations Development Program explained in the context of Bosnia-Hercegovina (BiH), "Serbs and Croats see the challenge as being [to develop] a BiH that represents all its constituent peoples."[27]

This understanding has roots in the cognitive sciences. The theory of cognitive dissonance is that a person seeks to reduce or eliminate the inconsistency between two pieces of information.[28] Conflict arises out of the disjunction between two items, and will remain or perhaps increase until a way to reconcile them is found. In this view, the purpose of reconciliation is said to be to avoid "the confusion and misapprehension which must result unless the conflict is reconciled or abated."[29] The reconciliation is the overarching idea that accommodates both: while the items have not changed, the disjunction—the source of the conflict—has disappeared because the new principle suits both comfortably.

This version echoes a shift that has also been noted in criminal law in many countries, with the recent attention to restorative justice. Restorative justice does not demand the exclusion or banishment of the criminal, but rather develops a social and moral environment that both accommodates the needs of the victim and acknowledges the harm done by the perpetrator. Neither side has to compromise, because there is room for both.

This evolution in criminal law has come about because of the growing recognition that the social context in which a crime was committed is relevant to understanding, and correcting, criminality. Likewise, public policy makers should recognize that social context is relevant to understanding and correcting violent conflict. It should be clear that parties are far more likely to resolve their disagreements violently if they are poor, if there is no stabilizing government presence or if the government presence is ineffectual, corrupt, or biased. Conversely, parties are far more likely to find peaceful, nondestructive means of resolving their differences if they have a stake in the system, thereby making the cost of violence too great to bear. The new emphasis is on the social context in which the fighting occurs, and the new goal is to reconstruct the social context so that both parties prefer to invest in the new social order rather than destroy it.

In the context of transitional justice, this might be a more fruitful approach to reconciliation, given the profound practical, legal, and psychological obstacles to trying to transform parties on either side of a fault line. In reasoning, reconciliation involves finding an overarching principle that applies to both items. In politics, reconciliation would involve finding a new national identity capacious enough to embrace all the competing groups within the polity. This new identity might emphasize equal treatment, respect for human rights, a commitment to the rule of law, or democratic governance, or something else. A new government that embraced these values would promote reconciliation not by forcing parties to move closer together but by providing a new conception of the state to which all parties are committed.

It is quite possible that even the more familiar uses of reconciliation—such as in family law—are fundamentally rooted in this idea: couples reconcile perhaps not so much because both agree to compromise; rather, they are willing to compromise because they both commit to a redefinition of their marriage. Likewise, it might be that programs that promote reconciliation through other activities (making quilts, trading in markets, building schools, etc.) are effective not so much because participants learn to trust each other as because they all share a commitment to the success of the joint enterprise. The critical relationship is that of the participants *to the enterprise*, not of the participants to one another.

The focus ought to be on the restructuring of the society and the development of community. This includes addressing issues of language, political participation, economic equity, and reform of judicial, police, military, and educational institutions. It would include developing a national narrative that would reflect and respect the values and experiences of all the different groups. It would include recognizing the criminality and immorality of acts that were committed in the past, without condoning them, but without marginalizing the actors either.

Conceptualizing reconciliation as reshaping society as a whole rather than focusing on the relationship between enemies accomplishes several things. It emphasizes the structural aspects of reconciliation and deemphasizes its psychological aspects, thereby minimizing the idiosyncratic implications of individual circumstances and sensibilities. Efforts to promote bilateral reconciliation can feel competitive to those involved—a zerosum game. This is more likely to impede reconciliation than to promote it. For instance, a victim who feels pressured to forgive a perpetrator is as likely to feel disempowered as strengthened. A perpetrator asked to make amends by asking forgiveness or showing remorse often feels that the imposition is burdensome and unfair. The same thing can happen on a classwide basis, as when the perpetrator class is asked to make amends through redistributive policies, such as affirmative action or luxury taxes: these, too, can produce feelings of unjust burden, as if the amends are a concession to an undeserving group, which in turn produces greater tension and conflict.[30]

Focusing on social structure rather than on individual relationships enlarges the space in which law can fruitfully operate because it occupies the realm of policy rather than psychology. The new luxury tax may seem more palatable even to those burdened if they are committed to the vision of the new society and they see the tax as a contribution to the new society, not as a payment to the victim class.

Because its gaze is broader, this form of reconciliation does not demand agreement on specific aspects of the past; rather, it forges agreement on a broad vision of the future. Instead of insisting on change for the sake of reconciliation, broadening the focus achieves reconciliation for the sake of change in the future. Reconciliation becomes a means to an end. In particular, it doesn't demand either that victims forgive or that perpetrators atone or be punished or that beneficiaries of prior injustices provide restitution for their ill-gotten gains. Instead, this kind of reconciliation looks at how the society can be structured to promote the values common to an inclusive democratic state.[31]

For example, the question of whether a perpetrator is entitled to forgiveness is one that frustrates many reconciliation efforts, since people within a conflict are likely to have radically different views about it. But refocusing the inquiry toward the future dissolves the problem. If changes in the culture dramatically reduce the opportunity for oppression, then would-be perpetrators don't have the chance again. In the new, reconciled culture, the people will not tolerate the use of violence for political gains. For the same reason, divisive questions about justice and punishment become less important when the dominant paradigm has changed. It matters less that the perpetrators of the old regime are punished than that they are neutralized, disempowered. The new cultural values eclipse problems of forgiveness and punishment.

The process of redefining the culture closely mirrors the theory of paradigm shifts in scientific revolutions, elucidated in Thomas Kuhn's groundbreaking book, *The Structure of Scientific Revolutions.*[32] Kuhn maps the process of how the paradigms that govern scientific research come into crisis and are eventually replaced by new paradigms. Each stage closely parallels the world of political revolutions.

The stage before the paradigm shift, writes Kuhn, "is regularly marked by frequent and deep debates over legitimate methods, problems, and standards of solution, though these serve rather to define schools than to produce agreement."[33] These frequent conflicts about legitimacy are comparable to the pretransition phase in the life of a nation, which is often characterized by increased polarization and the breakdown of normal politics. In Chile, for instance, the Report of the National Truth and Reconciliation Commission explains that in the decade preceding the 1973 coup, "political life continued to make its way within at least an apparent shared adherence to the democratic rules of the game. Most of the population supported democracy, despite the numerous and varied issues in dispute. Over the course of the 1960s this adherence began to wane."[34] This withering adherence to the democratic rules of the game resulted in increased polarization and eventually in the use of violence to achieve political goals.

In politics—as in science—this pre-shift stage may last for centuries, until the conflict actually reaches a boiling point. In Guatemala, the UN-sponsored Commission for Historical Clarification concluded "that the structure and nature of economic, cultural and social relations in Guatemala are marked by profound exclusion, antagonism and conflict—a reflection of its colonial history" and perpetuated since its 1821 independence.[35] "Due to its exclusionary nature," the report continues,

the State was incapable of achieving social consensus around a national project able to unite the whole population. Concomitantly, it abandoned its role as mediator between divergent social and economic interests, thus creating a gulf which made direct confrontation between them more likely. . . . Thus a vicious circle was created in which social injustice led to protest and subsequently political instability, to which there were always only two responses: repression or military coups. Faced with movements proposing economic, political, social or cultural change, the State increasingly resorted to violence and terror in order to maintain social control.[36]

Kuhn argues that, though scientists "may begin to lose faith and then to consider alternatives, they do not renounce the paradigm that has led them into crisis." In science, a paradigmatic theory is "declared invalid only if an alternate candidate is available to take its place." If no more appealing substitute is available, the old paradigm lingers on, even if it fails to solve real-world problems. In other words, in science, the shift from one paradigm to another is more or less instantaneous.[37]

Some political transitions follow this path, with the emergence of the new marking the obsolescence of the old. Thus, the Czech Republic's transition from communism to liberal, democratic capitalism is referred to as a "velvet revolution," in the sense that the shift from one paradigm to another was smooth and seamless. The same is true of Hungary and the Baltic states. South Africa's transition from apartheid to "rainbow nation," though a bit bumpier, is still considered "miraculous" because there was relatively little bloodshed at the moment of transition (compared to what might have been expected).

But these are the exceptions. Most of the current transitions are far bloodier and less definite; they do not follow the scientific model. In most political transitions, the old paradigm is abandoned because it fails to correspond to most people's reality. But no new paradigm is available to replace it. It is during this interregnum that violence erupts. This distinction between scientific and political revolutions helps to explain why reconciliation is a necessary concomitant to the latter.

In most political transitions, violence outstrips the transition to a new paradigm by a substantial margin. One can see the many instances of continued fighting, over generations, as examples where the old paradigm wore out but no alternative paradigm presented itself. Think of, for example, the Democratic Republic of Congo after Mobutu's departure, or Northern Ireland that has fought for decades because of the failure of political consensus. Iraq after the fall of Saddam Hussein might furnish another example: in the first few years after the Baathist capitulation, Iraq could have gone in any number of directions—a Western-style democracy, a strong federal state with significant protection for minority groups, a Shi'ite theocracy, an Arab nation inhospitable to Kurds, a multicultural nation in which all have a voice. As long as any result is possible, each group within the polity has significant incentive to fight in order to ensure a place at the table. In addition, the costs of abstention are great, since exclusion and disempowerment at this foundational moment have long-term consequences. The stakes are so high that they are literally worth fighting for and the country slides ineluctably toward civil war.

Furthermore, in these times of political instability, normal processes of daily life are interrupted and the normal opprobrium against using violence to achieve material or political gains is diminished and, in any event, unenforceable. Spoilers may come to have added prominence, as do militias in the Great Lakes region of Africa, or the insurgents in Iraq, or the warlords of Bosnia and Afghanistan.[38] The acceptability of violence in these times is both a cause and a symptom of the lack of connection between the people and the nation. In the chaos that marks the failure of the old paradigm, anything can happen. Even where violence has come to an end—as in Bosnia, Liberia, Cambodia, and Rwanda, to name just a few—the ceasefire often occurs for reasons other than broad acceptance of a new paradigm. It comes about because of the imperatives of international politics, or a new government installs itself, or perhaps simply exhaustion on the part of the combatants. Whatever the reason, the ceasefire often exists without a governing paradigm.

These transitions are much less successful. In the smoother transitions, the future is waiting in the wings to take over as soon as the opportunity presents itself; in the remainder of cases, the future has not yet been written. The prevalence of violence in political (as opposed to scientific) revolutions makes healing a necessary element in political transitions.

One effect of violence at transitional moments is that it tends to keep people locked in the past, unable to see the future, unable to accept the new paradigm. Healing is necessary because it opens people up to the possibility of the future. It is the ability to move on. Although neither truth, nor justice, nor forgiveness constitutes reconciliation in and of themselves, they all contribute to healing by releasing people from the past, each in their own way. To the degree to which people are healed, they are receptive to a new paradigm.

When the tools provided by the old paradigm are no longer capable of solving relevant problems, Kuhn writes, a crisis is the indication "that an occasion for retooling has arrived."[39] Retooling, then, becomes the job of reconciliation initiatives. What these programs can do—perhaps even more effectively than bringing people closer together—is to provide a new "fixation point"[40] on which all the members of the community can focus. Kuhn describes the process as a "reconstruction of the field from new fundamentals, a reconstruction that changes some of the field's most elementary theoretical generalizations as well as many of its paradigm methods and applications."[41] In particular, this process of reconstruction involves "handling the same bundle of data as before, but placing them in a new system of relations with one another by giving them a different framework."[42]

This last description has important implications for the prospect of political reconciliation. The object here is not to change the "bundle of data"—the fixed points in any society—but rather to construct a new system of relations, a new framework that changes their relationship to one another.

There is no specified content to the new paradigm, except for one thing. To achieve this shift or "cultural leap"[43] the society needs, more than anything else, to repudiate the salient values of the previous regime. How that repudiation occurs is not as important as that it must occur in a true and deep way. In one country, repudiating past abuses may be most effectively accomplished by a series of trials, while in another country, amnesty conditioned on remorse, truth, or restitution may be more effective. In one society, forgiveness may be the strongest antidote to the past abuses, although remembrances, in the form of commemorative holidays or memorials, might be more relevant elsewhere. In some places, repudiating the past might have nothing at all to do with the past; instead it might entail the establishment of new schools and significant investment in agricultural programs or emphasizing multiculturalism. Truth commissions might be essential, but they might also be beside the point. There is no universal prescription for repudiating the past. But in every case of successful transition and relative reconciliation, the new government has emerged out of a widely shared agreement to reject the most oppressive values of the past. "Rather than simply condemning the abuses committed by their predecessors, both the post-communist governments of Central Europe and the post apartheid regime in South Africa have clearly based their own legitimacy on an emphatic denunciation of the very nature of the previous regimes."[44]

Likewise in Morocco, where King Mohammed VI's speech accepting the Final Report of the Equity and Reconciliation Commission demonstrated an understanding of the role that reconciliation can play in the transition from the past to the future. He called the moment a "decisive" one "constituting a bright line in our historic journey. We say, in effect, our farewell to the half-century that has passed since independence, with all the successes, reversals, and hopes that accompanied the process of putting in place a modern state. But it's also the moment at which we prepare, with the help of God, to embark on the challenge of building a Morocco of unity, democracy, and development."[45]

Here politics has something to learn from science: the best way to repudiate the past is to replace it with a new paradigm. Social stability must rest on more than mere denunciation of the past; it requires some substantive content that redefines the present and the future. "The government of a nascent democracy," Michel Feher has written, "should be primarily invested in facilitating the cultural evolution of its constituents,"[46] that is, in helping constituents progress from past to future.

Study of historical as well as current transitions reveals a wide range of new paradigms, but the feature they all share is a new, forward-looking focal point. Robert Meister has suggested that America's transition in the wake of the Civil War was facilitated by President Abraham Lincoln's vision, as articulated in the Gettysburg Address. "The forward-looking Lincoln (the Lincoln we commemorate) lifted Americans above the unendurable cycle of guilt and recrimination by imagining the United States as a nation in recovery. He moved us from a sense of being unwilling perpetrators of evil to the recognition that we are all 'victims; to the common national identity of 'survivors.'"[47]

But Lincoln did not stop at simply recasting the divisive war "between the states" as a national tragedy; he sought to "replace the moral logic of victim/perpetrator with the moral logic of common survivorship and collective rebirth."[48] In this collective rebirth, Lincoln rededicated America to certain principles—that all men are created equal, and that "this government of the people, by the people, and for the people shall not perish from this earth."[49] "The end of the story," writes Meister, "is *unity* rather than the autonomy of victims and perpetrators."[50] Collective rebirth (which, like forgiveness, permits people to start over) and common commitment to fundamental principles gave Americans a focus beyond the divisive issues of slavery, states' rights, and the meaning of the war. This united Americans behind the challenge of rebuilding the nation and rededicating themselves to the fundamental principles that defined them as a people. It is likely that this produced reconciliation between Southerners and Northerners far more than any program of truth and reconciliation or of forgiveness could have done. Since consensus on the past could not be forced, it was Lincoln's genius at Gettysburg to forge consensus on the future.

Modern nations that have transitioned relatively successfully (meaning that the post-transition phase is marked by relatively little violence and produces relative political stability) have also found a way to draw the people's attention to some new vision, be it material or psychological. They have proposed a new paradigm or a set of ideas that together form a new national identity.

The Spanish transition toward democracy after the death of General Francisco Franco provides an interesting example if only because so little was done to promote reconciliation, per se, and yet the transition and post-transition period was not nearly as volatile as was broadly expected. Indeed, it was Spain's least bloody transition of the twentieth century, but it was also the only one "that did not call prior regime leaders to account."[51] What made the Spanish people begin to get along with another after a horribly bloody civil war and four decades of divisive repression? One explanation might be found in the broad commitment that many Spaniards shared to a particular vision of post-Franco Spain.[52] This vision was characterized mainly by stability and centrism. Although the population was divided on issues relating to the Civil War and Franco, Paloma Aguilar has noted the "overwhelming desire of Spanish society to see a peaceful and gradual change and even to pretend that it had forgotten the past rather than call anyone to account."[53] Under these circumstances, national reconciliation would be promoted neither by trials nor by commissions, but rather by promoting stability and gradual liberalizing reforms in the future. This was the vision on which most Spaniards agreed. Focusing on the future at the most volatile period of transition is not to suppress the past but to postpone the most divisive issues until the country is strong enough to withstand the tensions thereby produced.

In the 1990s, the Czech Republic tried a program of lustration to deal with its past. But the program is widely viewed as a failure, and "its repercussions on the national psyche [were] often divisive."[54] Its failure to unite may be explained in part because, as a backward-looking phenomenon, it focused on the divisions within Czech society, rather than on the values that might unify all Czechs. In these circumstances, it is possible that the nation's commitment to becoming a modern, democratic market economy, replete with industrial privatization and a full-blown tourism industry, might prove to be a much more effective way to diffuse the tensions between former communists and former anticommunists than lustration, reparations, or trials. Entering the European Union and attracting international investment may turn out to be the better elixir to restore the nation's health. Viewed in terms of paradigm shifts, it is the new, shared commitment to a market economy that supplants the divisions of the past.

The same can be said of several other Eastern European countries and the Baltic states, where few if any meaningful efforts were made to punish communist operatives or redress harms done under the previous regimes. In many of these societies, the elements of the past that were dredged up were selected precisely for their unifying potential, and divisive events of the past were ignored. In Lithuania, the focus at the time of transition was on the medieval kings and princes who created the great power Lithuania once was. More recent history was also used to unify people, as emphasis was placed on Lithuania's interwar independence and the wrongs committed by the Stalinist regime against the Lithuanian people as a whole, particularly with regard to the massive Baltic deportations to Siberia.

In Hungary, Gábor Halmai and Kim Lane Scheppele argue, the transition was characterized as a "rule of law revolution."[55] Ironically, a cornerstone of this emphasis was the Constitutional Court's insistence on continuity between past and present. The new legal system, the Court held, gained "binding force" because it was "enacted in a procedurally impeccable manner, in full compliance with the old legal system's regulation of the power to legislate." In substance, then, "there is no distinction between 'pre-Constitution' and 'post-Constitution' law."[56] Hungary was able to distinguish between repudiating the past (which it did not do) and repudiating the *values* of the past, which it did through commitment to the rule of law. This commitment was most obviously manifested, as Halmai and Scheppele describe, by the creation of the Constitutional Court, its investiture with unusually broad powers of judicial review and, importantly, by the respect that the government and the public gave to the Court's judgments, unpopular though they might have been. "If the new democratic polity is to fully repudiate the anti-democratic one of the recent past, then the best way to do so, in the Hungarian view, is to refuse to be tempted by having the power to use power against its enemies." This emphasis on constitutional rights, rather than on non-democratic or even democratic power, "provides the moral backbone of the policy."[57] This broad vision of a new Hungary defined by its commitment to the rule of law and to procedural justice might have given Hungarians a focal point that all could ascribe to without giving up any strongly held views about the guilt or innocence of former communist public officials or indeed of their neighbors. Disagreement on the subject of communism was outweighed by consensus on the value of due process.

As in Thomas Kuhn's conception of the process of scientific paradigm shifts, repudiation of the past does not occur unless a substitute is available. This was the case in many Eastern European and Baltic states, where the first stirrings of perestroika in the mid-1980s opened up space in which nationalists throughout the region began to imagine greater autonomy and greater nationalist identity, so that when the Soviet Union did collapse, in the early 1990s, new leaders—with new ideologies and backed up by emergent civil society—were ready to take charge.[58] At exactly the same moment that the past was repudiated, the present and future vision were available to replace it.

South Africa managed to avoid revenge killings by black people largely because of the moral leadership of the African National Congress, and to avoid violent efforts by whites to destabilize the nascent government largely because of the profound commitment of so many South Africans to the development of a new "rainbow" nation. One of the first acts of the transitional period was the adoption of the interim Constitution of 1993, the preamble of which announces "a new order" that will be open to "all South Africans" (unlike the colonial and apartheid states, which had excluded black South Africans from the polity) and "in which there is equality between men and women and people of all races" and in which "all citizens" shall enjoy "fundamental rights and freedoms." The postamble makes the paradigm shift explicit: "This Constitution provides a historic bridge between the past of a deeply divided society . . . and a future founded on the recognition of human rights, democracy, and peaceful co-existence."[59]

The clarity with which the new replaces the old is critically important in political transitions. Whereas it may be intellectually disorienting to some to have a science without a paradigm, a political regime without a paradigm is a crucible for chaos. In Northern Ireland, fighting continues until a new vision of that place emerges that captures the hearts and minds of the Northern Irish. The same can be said of other places around the world that seem to be in a state of perpetual war, including the Congo and even Israel and Palestine.

The paradigm-shifting framework is appealing in part because it helps to explain why some transitions are velvety while others seem forever mired in blood. It also explains the link between abstract ideas of national narrative and national consciousness on the one hand and people's lived experience on the other in a way no other theory of reconciliation does. "A paradigm governs, in the first instance, not a subject matter but rather a group of practitioners. Any study of paradigm-directed or of paradigm-shattering research must begin by locating the responsible group or groups."[60] What is significant here is not only that the paradigm is a new idea, but that the paradigm *changes the perception* of the people who operate under it. When a scientific paradigm shifts, the scientific community now sees the same objects differently; the same planets and the same sun are seen to bear a different relationship to one another. Likewise, when a political paradigm shifts, the political community now sees the same objects (here, other people) differently: people who were once enemies are now coparticipants in the new democratic experience. People who were once "the other" are now fellow citizens. A paradigm acts as a kind of cognitive umbrella that unites all those who are protected by it in a shared cognitive experience.

The new paradigm may be promulgated by the government expounding a new vision for the country (particularly when there is strong leadership). Or it may emanate from the people, demanding new rights and norms (Romania, Georgia, the central Asian Soviet republics, and to some extent in Serbia, where mass demonstrations led to the peaceful changing of the guards, or in Australia, where the people have demanded reconciliation with aboriginals notwithstanding the government's resistance). Or—and perhaps this is the best alternative—it comes about from the dialectic between the private and public spheres, each reinforcing and elaborating upon the initiatives made by the other. This may describe some of the relatively peaceful ways in which the combination of perestroika and Soviet withdrawal allowed civil society to emerge. However it comes about, the paradigm shift is complete when the people's perceptions have fundamentally changed.

This attitudinal change is one reason why paradigm shifts may have greater long-term benefits than other reconciliation models. Once the perception has truly changed, the likelihood of reversion is minimal. The clarion call of "never again" is most likely to be secured when a new framework governs people's perceptions of their neighbors and of their relationship to the new country. New governments can encourage this attitudinal change by ensuring that all the constituent groups have a real stake in the future of the community.[61]

Some common threads can be teased out of these diverse national experiences, although it remains critically important to remember that each country's new identity must be created to suit its own particular experience. The substantive content and methodological approaches of each country's new redefinition will be unique, though certain threads may be useful to other countries.

Spain's experience (and to some extent that of postliberation France) suggest that nations with longer and richer pretransition histories are at an advantage in the post-transition period: by rallying people around a common history, language, and culture, they can transcend the divisions of the immediate past. This process contributes to a *relative homogeneity*: a sense that the ties that bind are stronger than those that divided. Thus, regardless of where they stood in the preceding conflict, there is a sense of belonging to the same whole because, at the end of the day, they are all made of the same stuff. Newer nations, like South Africa or the Czech Republic, can still accomplish the same goals, but have to work harder at it.

Another contributing factor is strong leadership. Such men as Vaclav Havel in the Czech Republic and Nelson Mandela in South Africa can be useful in embodying and modeling values of the new dispensation. That these men were strongly identified with the resistance or opposition during the pretransition phase may be an important, but not indispensable, factor. Their immense personal charisma and their ability to envision and then implement a path to the future were probably more relevant to their success. In Hungary, that visionary leadership was embodied not in a person but in the institution of the Constitutional Court.

Perhaps what is most important is that the new paradigm be recognizable as a coherent plan that is both imaginative enough to attract adherents and realistic enough to keep them. As one Australian aboriginal complained, "Aboriginal affairs is littered with scenes of horses without saddles, of cows with bridles."[62] Governments that try to be too many things to too many people rarely satisfy their constituents. At least not in the long run.

In the end, all these countries—as well as many others, to be sure—have redefined what it means to be a citizen of that country. To be Australian now no longer means to be white; it may mean to be Aboriginal or to feel a part of both cultures. To be Guatemalan is also to be Mayan, and to be Mayan is also to be Guatemalan. To be black in South Africa means to be a citizen of South Africa, and the identification of who is "African" needs to be reconfigured. It may not be as much about sharing a history, but about sharing a sense of destiny. The country now moves forward on a new trajectory with all its constituent parts.

A Common Destiny

The joint commitment to a common purpose may be the most vivid manifestation of reconciliation within a nation. When all (or at least most of) the diverse groups share a common vision of the fundamental values of the country, we may begin to say that reconciliation is occurring. As the United Nations Security Council put it, reconciliation in South Africa had not automatically emerged at the conclusion of the work of the Truth and Reconciliation Commission "but was continuing to develop with the building of a nation based on shared values and a common destiny."[63]

The key here is not necessarily that the groups, or their constituent members, are getting along better with one another but rather that the various groups are all committed to the same or similar values. In the context of the political transitions of the late twentieth and early twenty-first centuries, most of the transitions are from oppression toward democracy. Typically, therefore, the shared values would relate to the establishment of a functioning democratic order within the country. They might entail an exclusive commitment to the democratic rules of the game, which means that "the overwhelming majority of the people believe that any further political change must emerge from within the parameters of democratic formulas."[64] In a reconciled state, groups may seek to promote their own interests, but not at the expense of the common political framework. Thus, a group that loses an election must submit to the will of the majority in the name of stability and democracy rather than insist on its right to govern. Commitment to the democratic rules of the game does not necessarily mean happily accepting defeat; resort to courts or other legitimate dispute-resolving institutions is acceptable, and the government has a responsibility to ensure the viability and availability of such institutions. But it does preclude resort to violence as a dispute-resolution mechanism.

The next chapter details how governments can promote adherence by all constituencies to the democratic rules of the game.

Part IV
Reconciliation
Reconstructed

Chapter 8
Politics and Money

Reconciliation is only possible after oppressive structures of economic and political injustice have been torn down; after power, rights and responsibility are no longer the privilege of the happy few, but shared by all.

—J. Celliers Breytenbach

We talk about the fault lines in divided societies in terms of ethnic, religious, racial, or even ideological differences. So-called "tribal" wars in Africa are manifestations of primordial aggression between peoples who have hated each other since time immemorial; ethnic cleansing in the Balkans is the intermittent settling of scores, played out over centuries and at the cost of millions of lives. But a closer look at civil tensions reveals that identity-based fault lines invariably mask deprivations of economic and political power. Identity conflict arises out of a complex social arrangement often involving one or more of the following: "an increase in repressive measures by states against distinct ethnic minorities or against ethnic dissidents; the failure of democratic mechanisms for negotiation or power-sharing between ethnic political actors; the emergence of essentialist ethnic ideologies and tightly knit ethnic political 'vanguards'; the rise in racist and xenophobic postures among the population; increasing economic and political disparities between ethnic groups; and legal arrangements designed to favour one ethnic group and exclude others."[1] These imbalances in political and economic power are far more significant than the length of one's nose or whether a pencil slips through one's hair.

In Northern Ireland, where the "Troubles" are always described as tensions between Catholics and Protestants, the impulse toward violence is not explainable in ecclesiastic terms. People are killed not because one group adheres to the tenets of the Pope and the other does not, but because the Catholics demand the same economic opportunities and the same degree of political participation and control that Protestants have enjoyed and that have been explicitly denied to them. In Kosovo, differences in economic and political power between Kosovar Albanians and Serbs explains much more than differences in identity per se. The same is true in the Democratic Republic of the Congo (DRC) and throughout central Africa, where access to citizenship and other civil and economic rights are allocated on the basis of identity.[2] The genocide presently occurring in Sudan may be rooted in conflict over the distribution of oil, as is, to a large extent, the chaos that followed Saddam Hussein's removal from power in Iraq.

Over time, the significance of the reasons for the original conflict may wax and wane: what starts out as an insurrection to control resources devolves into an policy of removing the people who stand in the way of that control, which eventually metamorphoses into ethnic conflict. Indeed, because identity is one of the easiest ways for leaders to gain support for a violent conflict, they often exploit insignificant differences among groups simply to gain political and economic advantage.[3] While identity-based differences "are not the primary cause, they acquire an independent force that makes peacemaking difficult."[4] This is as true of civil war as of international conflict: cross-border invasions to control the diamond mines of the DRC, for instance, have turned into ethnic wars between groups who live along the DRC's borders. Indeed, the failure to recognize the underlying socioeconomic causes is one reason why outsiders are so often perplexed by the tensions that tear insiders apart: outsiders cannot tell the difference between the two groups, whereas insiders, aware of the root causes of the dispute and the continuing oppression, will kill over those differences.

Divided societies are divided precisely in that one group denies the other equal access to human rights—the right to housing, employment, education, protection against arbitrary arrest and detention, and in the worst cases, the right to life. One group secures these rights for itself but not for "the other." The fact of these deprivations is often more significant for the victims than the fact that they ostensibly occur for reasons of identity.

That said, simple economic benefits will rarely be sufficient to mark a real change in the power relations of the people. As the final report of the Moroccan Equity and Reconciliation Commission explained, reparations for victims of human rights abuses are essential but insufficient. "There is also an essential element of reforms aiming to put in place guarantees of non-repetition and building for the future. In a process aimed at restoring confidence, we should not, therefore, reduce the concept of reparation to simple material disbursements or state benefits It is also necessary to re-establish the victims, as citizens, in all their rights, including the right to participate in the reforms aimed at reinforcing the rule of law."[5]

The challenge for reconciliation, then, is not to remove the differences between the two groups but to ensure that everyone within the society, regardless of their identity, may participate fully and equally. Full and equal participation, in turn, depends on a constellation of political and economic opportunities that must be made available to all citizens within the polity. The provision of what Jack Donnelly calls "equal concern and respect"[6] is the task of reconciliation. To advance it, governments must proceed along both political and economic axes at once in order to promote both political and economic equality. Political equality entails the right to vote and to participate in the political life of the nation on the same basis as others. Material or economic equality entails the ability to enjoy a standard of living that at the very least does not interfere with the opportunity of political participation.

Increasingly national and international actors have come to recognize the integral role that political and economic reforms play in securing peace and entrenching stability in divided societies. As a result, almost every transition of the last quarter century has entailed the adoption of what has been called market democracy—a hybrid of liberal economic reform and republican electoralist strategies.[7] In this chapter, we explore to what extent and under what circumstances these twin reforms can promote reconciliation. Since in most cases political restructuring is prior to economic reform, we address political issues first.

Politics as Reconciliation

Reconciliation, as we have seen, does not require assimilation. Nor does it require integration, absorption, or even unification. But it does require cooperation. For reconciliation take root, the various constituencies of the state must agree to cooperate within a single political structure. Cooperation, in turn, depends largely on the willingness of partisans to treat each other as equals, enjoying equal measures of power, and entitled to equal measures of respect. This means accepting the right to be heard, the right to disagree, and the right to take legitimate and legal steps to resolve differences. These are the minima of a functioning democracy.

For those seeking to promote reconciliation, the major task for a new government is to develop a system that creates, fosters, or encourages both real and apparent equality among all members of the polity.

A political system must encourage the maximum number of people from a broad range of sectors and communities to participate in the processes of governance and to respect the outcomes of those processes. By doing so, diverse individuals and groups can become loyal to the state, even while maintaining their parochial identities. As the OECD has explained, "Broad acceptance throughout society of the legitimacy of the state and the credibility of the institutions of governance is a key aspect of forging such a civic spirit. When . . . ordinary men and women are involved in the political process, resort to violence to effect political change is obviously less likely. Efforts to support participation, democratisation, and peacebuilding, through strengthened institutions of governance, are clearly interlinked."[8]

We leave to the political scientists the daunting task of designing political structures. Since our focus is reconciliation, we concern ourselves only with one slice of the larger complex of issues: what features of a political system are most likely to conduce to reconciliation and what features are most likely to retard it?

We begin with the largest questions. What are the contours of the state? What structures within the state facilitate reconciliation?

The Structure of the Nation

Boundaries and the Legitimacy of the State

"Wars of the late twentieth century," Kalevi Holsti writes, "are not about foreign policy, security, honour or status; they are about statehood, governance and the role and status of nations and communities within states."[9] Often, they are about the ultimate problem of statehood: identifying the appropriate boundaries of the state. Where lines are drawn on a map can have ramifications for centuries. Decisions made at the 1884–1885 Berlin Conference continue to have life-and-death repercussions for millions of Africans. These arbitrary lines still exist only because they are too difficult to change, and certainly not because they reflect the actual affiliations of the population, either then or now. This is what Linz and Stepan describe as the "stateness" problem:[10] "When different segments of a polity have radically different notions" of the appropriate boundaries of the state, in terms of either territory or citizenry, "the legitimacy of the sovereign unit itself" comes into question.[11] This question must be resolved prior to any other; it is, as Bose says, "logically prior" to any other issues concerning the make-up of the state. Unfortunately, in many cases, it is also "insoluble within the framework of democratic theory."[12] That is, the different and exclusive claims each have equivalent legitimacy in moral, historical, or theoretical terms.

The stateness problem cuts across multiple dimensions. It is not only a political problem in which the territory of the state and the definition of citizenship are contested. It manifests itself also as a hermeneutic problem in which the meaning of the past in both personal and historic terms is contested. In Bosnia, for instance, how the new state *should* be defined may depend on the nature of Yugoslavia before and during its breakup.

If Serbia and Croatia were distinct from Bosnia (and if, by extension, Serbs and Croats are distinct peoples from Bosniaks), then the legitimacy of the old Yugoslav framework is contested, and then there is no intrinsic reason to assume they should all be joined now under one national roof. If on the other hand, Yugoslavia, as such, was a legitimate entity, and the war of the 1990s was an internal civil war among different factions within the same nation, then the greater Bosnia project has a stronger historical basis.[13] It is not easy to determine which of these claims is correct, nor is it easy to determine which frame of reference or which theoretical construct provides the appropriate logic for resolving these competing claims. It is not even easy to identify the logical starting point for the analysis.

A significant separatist or secessionist movement within a country may create a stateness problem if its members challenge the right of the state to incorporate their section within it. In Bosnia, a significant number of Serbs and Croats reject the very fact of the Bosnian state and seek to adhere to Serbia and Croatia, respectively. (Only the Muslim Bosniaks have no irredentist claims.) Palestine clearly has a stateness problem because its location and boundaries, and indeed its very existence, are contested. The Kurds, the Basques, the Acehnese, and the Québecois may all create stateness problems for the states in which they currently live (from the other perspective, Iraq, Spain, Indonesia, and Canada may all create stateness problems for themselves if they do not sufficiently accommodate the demands of the groups within). And, Linz and Stepan note, "the greater the percentage of people in a given territory who feel that they do not want to be members of that territorial unit, however it may be reconstituted, the more difficult it will be to consolidate a single democracy within that unit."[14] The December 2005 legislative elections in Iraq may illustrate the point. "By all appearances," wrote Edward Wong in the *New York Times* from a town in Kurdistan, "the elections for national parliamentary seats might as well have been about Kurdistan and Kurdish dreams. Iraq, or the idea of Iraq, seemed as distant as the moon."[15]

The opposite side of the secessionist coin is ethnic cleansing—when one group (with or without the backing of the state) decides that another group is no longer welcome within the state. This, too, creates a stateness problem, as the civic and territorial boundaries of the state are contested: can there be a Rwanda that includes Tutsis, the Hutu asked themselves. Can Yugoslavia include non-Serbs? Can Croatia include Serbs?

A weaker form of this, but one that nonetheless raises significant stateness questions particularly from the standpoint of reconciliation occurs when one group decides that another group may stay, but not on the same terms as others. The group selected for discriminatory treatment may not have the same educational, occupational, political, or other rights as others in the same state. Slavery, apartheid, and other forms of discriminatory legislation are all instances of this form of the stateness problem. In its worse instances, it challenges who is a citizen of the nation and what it means to be a citizen. In South Africa, blacks were literally members of the state, but politically excluded, lacking citizenship and all other rights. In the Baltic states, the meaning of citizenship had to be reassessed when Soviet troops left but ethnic Russians stayed. (Curiously, the denial of rights to women has never been thought to raise the stateness problem, though certainly discrimination, disenfranchisement, and oppression against half of a population ordinarily would.)

The resolution of stateness problems is essential for both humanitarian and political reasons. First, if one group within the polity decides that another should not be included, there are very few options available to the excluders, particularly when they are supported by the institutions of the state. As Linz and Stepan argue, "If the titular national [that is, the national group that is empowered with the attributes of statehood] actually wants a truly homogenous nation-state population, a variant of the 'ethnic cleansing' formula is too often a tempting method."[16] As the recent histories of Sudan, Bosnia, Northern Ireland, and many other countries make clear, the failure to resolve the stateness problem can too easily lead to bloodshed. By contrast, Linz and Stepan are at pains to point out that resolving the stateness problem, as Spain deftly did by inclusion, and as the Czech Republic did by exclusion, can avoid bloodshed. Failing to resolve the stateness problem can also stymie the political transition. Linz and Stepan argue forcefully that stateness problems must be resolved before democratization can be initiated and consolidated. The "democratic process presupposes a unit. *The criteria of the democratic process presuppose the rightfulness of the unit itself.* If the unit itself is not [considered] proper or rightful—if its scope or domain is not justifiable—then it cannot be made rightful simply by democratic procedures."[17] In other words, as they show, only a state can bestow or define citizenship, which is necessary for the exercise of democracy. Democracy will not, on its own steam, resolve the stateness problem.

Layered Sovereignty

We start with an observation, and then a hypothesis. First, we observe that most people, in most parts of the world, are comfortable with multiple levels of identity. Rather than suppressing all but one, or privileging only one, most people would rather integrate these various identities and live with them simultaneously. The hypothesis is that a political model that realistically reflects and enhances people's sense of their own multiple identities is more likely to produce in state loyalty, stability and reconciliation than a model that attempts to counter or channel them. This observation—that most people are comfortable with, and indeed seem to *prefer*, multiple identities—may require some elaboration. The basic point seems fairly intuitive: people identify by their gender, their sexual orientation, their race, their religion, their class, their interests, and along many other axes. Some of these identities overlap, while others are more stratified. People identify in terms of locality (or tribe or clan), regionality, nationality, and even supranationality. Some aspects of identity, at some times, are more controversial than others.

This principal point has several corollaries. First, people have different degrees of commitment to their multiple identities. For some, their political ideology or religion is extremely important; for others it is not. In Northern Ireland, for instance, one person might be devoutly religious, but apolitical; another may rarely go to church but may be a committed unionist. Another corollary of this principle is that attitudes toward identity may change over time, even though identity does not. Ethnicity, for instance, may not be important to many people living in a multiethnic state until a nationalist movement makes it the defining attribute of personhood.

The point, however, should not be overread: the argument is not that there is no such thing as a minority because everyone is simultaneously part of minorities and part of a majority. Though this is true, people may nonetheless partake of minority status if they self-identify with minority groups or if they are identified with the minority group by society. Thus, within any given society there may be, and usually are, bases of identification that accord some people minority status. The challenge for divided societies is to minimize the burdens borne by those in the minority, thereby equalizing and enhancing the opportunities and assets of the population as a whole.

In terms of vertical loyalty, it may generally be true that for many people around the world, their strongest loyalty is to the smaller community rather than to the state. Secessionist and nationalist movements are built on this fact. If forced to choose between the local and the state, most people would choose the local. This is particularly true if the state appears to be or is in fact weak; in such a case, many people will find their emotional home among those most like them in cultural, linguistic, or ethnic ways. Thus, the engorging effects of civil war on nationalist identity.

Because people are comfortable with multiple levels of identity, and because identification with these levels is variable and individual, the state should not ask people to choose among them, both because it does not accord with people's experience and because it may lose adherents. A Kurd is more likely to develop loyalty to Iraq if she can be both Kurdish and Iraqi; she is less likely to do so if the price of admission to Iraq is her Kurdish identity. The state should instead provide spaces in which multiple identities can coexist. The peace agreement ending thirty years of civil war in Aceh province in Indonesia recognized this reality. The Free Aceh Movement—which had been seeking independence—finally gave up its claim when the Indonesian government agreed to allow local political parties who could run candidates at all levels of government. The peace agreement essentially reframed the problem: it created a new identity that allowed people to be both Acehnese *and* Indonesian, thereby reconciling their loyalties to their region and their nation.[18]

Languages and language usage have often been flashpoints for conflict.[19] Some argue that a single language is a prerequisite for national reconciliation (on the reconciliation-as-unity theory). Yet it has become clear that in many instances states can become stronger by recognizing multiple national languages. Canada and South Africa are examples of countries with multiple official languages. Other states recognize some languages at regional level to grant status to it, such as Belgium and Spain.[20] Many modern constitutions—including Spain's and the interim constitution in Sudan—impose on the state the affirmative obligation to develop and protect minority languages. Allowing multiple languages can promote reconciliation by allowing people to express their identity in multiple ways. As Linz and Stepan note, Finland was able to craft state loyalty notwithstanding a sizeable Swedish population because it "made Swedish one of the two national languages and granted broad citizenship rights." The Swedish minority, they note, "easily developed loyalty to the democratic state of Finland while retaining important Swedish cultural institutions, which were recognized as legitimate by the Finnish state."[21] This remains a challenge for many postcommunist countries with respect to sometimes sizable Russian populations.

As a general rule, then, a system that permits, or encourages, an individual to feel at home both in her region and in her state is more likely to engender that citizen's loyalty. We therefore next consider how systems can be structured to encourage multiple levels of belonging.

Federalism and Devolution

A single national electoral system works well where the population is homogeneous and not divided along any fault lines. This type of system also works well when there is a national government that is elected regionally, or in constituencies, in proportion to the population's make-up in a region. But significant groups that do not constitute national majorities could be marginalized if the power is exercised exclusively at the national level in general elections. Some form of power-sharing structures would promote reconciliation by expanding the reach of the state to all important constituencies.

This can be done in a variety of ways, from proportional representation in national bodies, to nongeographic devolution of political power over specific issues (such the Hungarian experiment in minority self-government for the Roma) to collective decision-making in both legislative and executive bodies (as in the seven-member executive council in Switzerland) or a power-sharing executive structure (as in Bosnia under Dayton and the interim constitution in Sudan), to parallel rights for diverse cultures (as in Belgium). Another mechanism used in many countries is having two or more houses of parliament, whose make-up is attained along different lines, increasing diversity and representativeness. Veto rights or the need to attain super-majorities are another way minority and other interests can be protected. Yet another is to give nonelected sectors (such as the military, environmental, or agrarian interests) a say either directly or in an advisory council whose views are taken into account.

Another approach is to ensure representation either at the regional or local level, resulting in some form of "layered sovereignty."[22] While this seems an obvious choice in many instances of divided populations, it presents many difficult questions about *how* the power is shared: what powers are in whose hands, and which powers are more significant, both as a formal matter and in practice. Countries around the globe have developed a range of responses to layered sovereignty. At one end of the spectrum, nations secede or proclaim independence, as Rhodesia did in the 1960s, as Pakistan and Bangladesh did, and as more recently as the nations of the former Soviet Union did, as well as countries in central Europe including Croatia, Slovenia, and Slovakia. These are fully independent nations (notwithstanding the overarching control which the European Union exercises over those in Europe). But there are also many variations that fall short of absolute sovereignty.

There are states that are independent in almost every respect, such as Greenland, for whom Denmark exercises control over foreign affairs. There are many nations that are members of a larger commonwealth, such as the 53 states that form part of the British Commonwealth, and Puerto Rico that is associated with the United States commonwealth. These relationships also vary. In some cases, particularly the British Commonwealth, the relationship is purely diplomatic, whereas in other cases the parent state exercises real and substantive control over elections, currency, judicial and regulatory functions, and foreign affairs.

Within nation-states, there is also a range of autonomy allocated to various groups at the subnational level. In the United States, Native Americans who still live on "reservations" continue to be organized into tribes with a measure of real sovereignty: tribal courts have exclusive jurisdiction over certain matters; tribal economies are outside the jurisdiction of the national revenue service; and tribes wishing to negotiate with the United States have historically made treaties, just as foreign nations do.

More common are so-called semi-autonomous regions. Examples of these include Kurdistan in northern Iraq under Saddam Hussein, where the Kurdish people controlled their own police force, political parties, and election cycles and largely their own economy, as well as the semi-autonomous regions of Russia (including most problematically Chechnya) and the 31 semi-autonomous regions of Nigeria. In island nations such as Comoros and the Solomon Islands, federalism is a particularly useful way to reconcile the separate island cultures. These examples show that such relationships may be more or less contentious, and may change over time from relatively stable to extremely volatile. Latin America has also been experimenting with semi-autonomous regions to recognize the particular cultures of the indigenous population: in 1987, Nicaragua amended its basic law to allow certain native populations to adopt their own constitution and concomitantly granted some power to these tribes.[23] In the 1990s, substantial power devolved from the United Kingdom to Wales, Scotland, and Northern Ireland, although London still controls not only foreign affairs powers, but also the more significant power to tax. In Australia, where the states do not claim any degree of sovereignty independent of the national government, the central government likewise maintains exclusive taxing authority. In Switzerland, where the cantons *do* claim a significant degree of autonomy and sovereignty, the federal government likewise controls taxation, although the portion remitted to the cantons is constitutionally prescribed. In Canada, by contrast, all three levels of government (national, provincial, and municipal) have revenue-raising power, which means that each level has greater control over how public monies are spent. The range, therefore, of federal arrangements is as diverse as the number of countries: no two countries allocate power between national and subnational entities in precisely the same way. And in almost all federal systems the balance of power has required periodic, and sometimes contentious, adjustment.

Many of these arrangements were originally developed to allow regional majorities some measure of power notwithstanding the unification of the nation as a whole. In countries as diverse as South Africa, Bosnia, Iraq, and Spain, among the most difficult questions of the entire transitional period has been the vertical allocation of power. In India, group rights may ultimately threaten the integrity of an otherwise strong and stable democracy.

Asymmetrical federalism is one variation that has worked well in Spain and Canada and is being tested in recent peace agreements: in Aceh, one of Indonesia's provinces will have greater rights of political participation and control over resources at the local level; in the Sudan, the interim constitution allows the southern Sudanese to vote on secession after six years. It is appropriate where minority populations have claims that other segments of the country do not share.

The more dispersed the population, the less likely it is that federal structures will accommodate particular regional interests.[24] In such places, nongeographic methods to devolve power must be developed. Hungary has provided the world with one model with the development of minority self-government for Gypsies (Roma). As a condition of entry into the European Union, many Eastern European countries have been required to pass special legislation to protect the rights of ethnic minorities, most prominently the Roma. Hungary has gone far in this regard, creating minority self-governments (MSGs) that have some autonomous powers and some advisory powers with respect to education, media, culture, and language. Though several election cycles have already taken place, budgetary limitations have constrained the ability of the Roma community to exercise true autonomy in these areas. Moreover, self-government has not proven sufficiently robust to ameliorate relations between the Roma and the larger national community, in part because the jurisdictional boundary between MSG and Hungarian government is still subject to negotiation. The new system has in fact resulted in little reduction in racial violence directed at the Roma, or in significant improvements in the standard of living of most Roma living in Hungary.[25]

Notwithstanding its shortcomings, the Hungarian example may be most useful to suggest that creative and novel solutions should be considered within each nation or region to accommodate the various demands of the local populations. Based on local and temporal necessities, these solutions will vary in their particularities according to the specific needs of the local population. The Baltic states developed a short-lived system of dual parliaments in the transitional years to reflect disparate views on the integration, or disintegration, of these states with the communists to the East and the Europeans to the West. In each case, whether the experiments have been successful is open to debate, but the broader point seems unassailable: states need to continue to innovate in order to develop solutions that respond to the local needs for self-governance and to particular sensitivities of local populations that may have given rise to conflict in the past or that threaten conflict in the future.

The history of the treatment of the Roma in Hungary, the Native Americans in the United States, and many other populations throughout the world, illustrates the fundamental tension in ethnic rights between integration (which often means loss of culture, language, and ultimately identity) and segregation (which often means deprivation of civil, political, social, and economic rights). Few countries with sizable minority populations have managed to avoid excesses on either side. Integrationist policies such as affirmative action can spawn genuine, though not always reasonable, fears and resistance among the majority population that can feel threatened. Segregationist policies, on the other hand, can overemphasize differences between majority and minority populations, which can tend, in extreme situations, toward dehumanization and ultimately genocide.

Likewise, autonomy is important to promote individual dignitary interests and collective self-determination, but it can frustrate the national reconciliation project by cutting the autonomous off from their fellow citizens in the rest of the country and from the national government itself.

Semi-autonomous federalism can provide sufficient room for the region to develop its own cultural values without the fear of being overwhelmed by the sovereign authority and perhaps can even reduce the perception that it poses a threat to the identity of the titular nation. At the same time, staying within the larger state means that *some* interaction will be necessary: the subgroup will depend on the sovereign for certain interests (those that have not devolved to the more local level), and there will be constant adjustment of the boundaries between the local and the state.

As Sumantra Bose has argued in the context of Bosnia, perhaps the middle ground between integration and segregation is some kind of cooperation. Cooperation is harder to achieve because it cannot be mandated or enforced, but depends primarily on the good will of the people involved. Yet, by structuring the federal relationship to encourage and reward interethnic cooperation, government can advance reconciliation over time as both sides learn to negotiate with one another. At the very least, this will require resolving the following questions.

- How much power will be exercised other than at the national level?
- Which powers will be exercised at other than the national level?
- Will the dispersion of power away from the center be symmetrical or will different subnational entities enjoy various degrees of autonomy?
- How many levels other than the national will be established?[26]
- How much oversight will the national government have over decisions made at other levels? (Will approval of certain measures be required?)
- How much input will the regional government have in decisions made at the national level? (Will approval of certain measures be possible?)
- How will changes to the allocation of power be made? (By referendum, judicial decision, political negotiation?)
- What is the spread of resources between the different levels, and have they been equitably distributed?
- Will there be a neutral and independent arbitrator over disputes on allocations between the levels?

At any single level of government, difficult questions also present themselves, including

- How will power be shared between the executive and the legislature?
- What safeguards will be introduced to protect against the executive's untoward usurpation of authority for his or her own particular constituency?
- Will any group be able to exercise a minority veto or some other measure to check the exercise of power, either for all issues or for some class of legislation deemed vital?
- How will the rights of women be protected? (Women are geographically diffuse and make up at least close to a majority of the voting age population; in most postwar societies, they constitute a substantial majority of the voting age population, though in no society have their social, political, and economic interests been securely protected.)
- How will the rights of all individuals who have less education and less access to public media be protected and enhanced?
- What limits will there be on the freedom to incite hatred or chauvinism?
- How will accountability be secured? What will be the terms and term limits of office-holders? What will be done to ensure that officeholders elected from nongeographic constituencies are nonetheless accountable?
- What will be the role of the courts?

How these questions are answered may reflect some of the fundamental policy choices that undergird the new government; it may force the government to confront how it conceives reconciliation and what kind of future it envisions for the new nation. For instance, is the purpose of reconciliation ultimately to integrate the nation or is it to pluralize the nation? Is the goal for everyone to share one predominant identity—presumably one that reflects loyalty to the state—or is it to create a state in which diverse groups of individuals retain important separate identities? These decisions will affect how reconciliation takes root. A carefully crafted system for a previously divided society can create significant common ground among the nation's citizens and residents, while still ensuring that members of particular groups retain their distinct identity and culture and that their interests are protected from oppression or encroachment by the state or private actors.

As always, the issue needs to be resolved in both formal and practical terms. Attention must be paid to which specific powers are allocated to which specific level. But at least as important are the ways in which power is *actually* exercised by the politicians. This may depend on variables that are determinable, such as funding sources and levels and provisions for accountability, but it may also depend on the serendipitous nature of leadership and on what James Madison called "the affections of the people."[27]

Constitutionalism and the Rule of Law

A new national government's biggest challenge is to focus on questions of governance. Good governance will enhance people's lives *and* foster reconciliation. The link between good governance and reconciliation is clear, and no transitional government can avoid the obligation. As Secretary-General of the United Nations Kofi Annan has said, "Good governance is also a component of our work for peace. It has a strong preventive aspect; it gives societies sound structures for economic and social development. In postconflict settings, good governance can promote reconciliation and offer a path for consolidating peace."[28]

This might begin with the development of a constitution. Indeed, the first accomplishment of many nations in transition is the establishment of a constituent assembly or other body with constitution-making responsibilities. Both the process by which the constitution is written and its content may have ramifications for reconciliation, and those who seek to promote reconciliation should be attuned to the demands of the nation in this regard. In some places, people may demand an open and legitimate process, as happened in South Africa.[29] In other places, such as in many of the former Soviet nations now joining Europe, attention of the people was more on the content than on the process.

In some instances, it may be useful to resurrect an old constitution until a new one has been written. This happened in Afghanistan, with the reinstatement in 2001 of the 1964 constitution, which had been abandoned after only nine years. But even an obsolete constitution may be better than none: during times of extreme turmoil and uncertainty, providing continuity by tapping into a common history and a familiar structure may be useful as an interim measure. An alternative, used in South Africa, is to adopt an interim constitution which, to some extent, governs both the process by which the final constitution will be adopted and the substantive content of the final constitution.

The constitution itself forms a part of the new national narrative and should, to the extent possible, reflect the experiences and the aspirations of all the peoples that constitute the new nation. The constitution should energetically protect individual and group rights to ensure that those who have been oppressed in the past will be safe from oppression in the future and, where appropriate, may have access to special benefits, rights, or opportunities to protect their culture. Moreover, the constitution should establish institutions to ensure the government's commitment to rule of law and enforcement of rights provided in the text. This may include courts, police, human rights commissions, reconciliation ministries, or ombudsman's offices, or other permanent types of organizations. Divisions based on race, religion, ethnicity, and other marks of difference may be formidable obstacles, and the new government needs the strong backing of an emphatic constitution and its support systems if it is to subdue the tensions that people may feel toward one another.

The Constitution should entrench many of the structural decisions discussed in the previous sections in order to protect them against excessive political manipulation. The constitution should also include reference to or enumeration of protected rights. Indeed, in most modern states, the culture of constitutionalism is most prominently identified not with entrenching structural limitations but with protecting individual (and sometimes group) rights.[30]

But as the guarantor of rights, constitutions pose certain practical and theoretical problems. First, they are not self-enforcing. Constitutions require institutions, which in turn require commitments of substantial sums of money, as well as cadres of professionals, including judges, lawyers, and clerks, who take seriously their obligation to enforce the constitutional mandates. While there has a been a sizable increase in the number of constitutions since 1989, and a concomitant increase in the number of bodies capable of adjudicating constitutional claims (from 10 in 1989 to 70 in 1999),[31] the level of funding and professionalism in each court system varies dramatically from country to country. And, of course, in nascent and war-torn countries, the levels of both are likely to be shockingly low. At the end of the Rwandan genocide, for instance, there were about fifty lawyers (mostly civil) in the entire country and only *five* judges, all without cars or offices.[32] For constitutions to become effective and meaningful, there must be not only the written document, but a living culture within the society that expects, and receives, adherence to constitutional rules and values. This may take time, but work toward that end should begin immediately.

Because a constitution's basic purpose is to constrain governmental action, it tends toward counter-majoritarianism and has a paradoxical effect on democracy. In one sense, it reduces the sphere of democratic action by withdrawing certain issues from the political process: a legislature in most constitutional systems will not have the authority to legalize torture or to permit police to enter homes without warrants, even if the vast majority of citizens want those laws. The resultant democratic deficit, however, is said to be outweighed by the value to democracy of the protections enshrined in the basic law. By preventing the legislature from limiting the rights of certain individuals or groups to vote, to obtain education and work, to reside in a place of their choosing, and so on, the constitutional system ensures that all members of the polity are treated equally under the law. The legitimacy of constitutionalism has been maintained through the ages by recourse to a range of theories, some relying, perhaps paradoxically, on democratic values and others on contemporary international human rights norms. Whatever its legitimacy, it seems to be our age's preferred response to imbalances in social power. And, ultimately, this is constitutionalism's contribution to reconciliation: because it prevents those who are well educated, well nourished, and properly housed from denying these and other basic needs to others, it diminishes the gulf between the powerless and the powerful. When effectively enforced, it can ensure that all members of the polity are treated with equal concern and respect and have equal opportunities to participate in the political and civic life of the nation.

Closely linked to constitutionalism is the principle of the rule of law. The rule of law has the potential to be an even greater equalizer. The law converts all people—with their manifold differences in talents, education, strength, charisma, money, etc.—into single units of equivalent value: each person stands before the law as an individual with the same rights and obligations as every other. Under law, neither power nor wealth nor access to arms gives advantage. This ideal has perhaps its most emphatic articulation in the Universal Declaration of Human Rights, whose very first words recognize the "inherent dignity and . . . equal and inalienable rights of all members of the human family.[33]

Like constitutionalism, the rule of law relies on cooperation, or buy-in, from the bulk of the population to pledge to treat each other with respect and to comply with regulatory and judicial orders when issued. It relies on bureaucrats within an administration to fulfill a variety of tasks that mediate between the people and the government, such as tax collecting, policing, regulating the flow of money, and so on. These functionaries should evince the strong and sustained commitment to rule of law that is necessary if the system is to provide the appearance and assurance that all citizens are equal before the law. This sense of equality is essential if reconciliation is to take root.

In their efforts to promote national reconciliation, governments may also use traditional tools of governance, which, if put to good use, can be as effective as anything else.[34] Legislation is perhaps the most obvious tool. It can supplement the constitutional order because it can be both more detailed and more flexible and nuanced. Some laws will be directed specifically at those responsible in the previous regime. These may include lustration or amnesty laws or laws permitting prosecution or civil litigation. In some cases, truth commissions have been authorized to develop proposals for legislation, but if the commission is developed at the ministerial level its authority might go further. In Spain, an interministerial commission was charged with producing "a draft bill setting out the measures necessary 'to provide the victims with proper moral recognition and satisfaction.'"[35]

Other laws may be directed at the public generally. Most people agree that the law is powerless to *require* reconciliation, but it can certainly promote it by mandating the conditions in which reconciliation may thrive. A government, for instance, can prohibit ethnic violence or discrimination, and can back up that proscription with visible and effective enforcement. It can allow all groups within its borders to vote and to enjoy language, educational, and employment rights. It can permit marriage between groups and can guarantee equal pay and status. It can repatriate former combatants. It can provide a juridical basis for asserting claims against looters or others who have wrongfully appropriated property. It can recognize rape as a form of political violence and punish it accordingly. It can encourage settlement in integrated areas and develop educational programs that help students learn to live together. It can provide a fair and equitable system for the repossession of lost property, including real property.

Economic laws can also promote reconciliation. Tax provisions can encourage (through a luxury tax) or require (through mandatory income tax) beneficiaries of oppression to redistribute some of their ill-gotten gains. Tax breaks and direct subsidies can assist in relocation and reintegration efforts. Governments can also promote reconciliation through appropriations. They can provide basic funding for a police department and a judiciary, including (re-)training programs, along with other public-protecting institutions as previously mentioned.[36] Other appropriation measures might seem luxurious to poor transitional nations, but may nonetheless be necessary, such as the funding of a reconciliation commission or a public awareness campaign. Economic inequity is examined in more detail below.

Another important step toward democracy and reconciliation may be the complete overhaul of the security forces, which are often to blame for human rights abuses. This usually requires subjecting the military to civilian control and clearly demarcating the limits of each armed force's authority. In addition, hiring and firing decisions should be made with sensitivity to all sectors, with particular attention to the overall representativeness and responsiveness of the force.

The national government, if it wants seriously to promote reconciliation and enhance the level of security in the country, needs to address the problem of crime that plagues many weak states and postconflict societies. Crime impedes reconciliation in a number of ways: it produces additional victims and perpetrators, which not only creates more trauma but may entrench prejudice and accompanying social divides which need to be assuaged. Ultimately, the insecurity produced by high levels of crime undermines public trust in the new government which is seen as powerless and not worthy of the people's loyalty.[37] All of this is true when the crime is private; it is exacerbated when the crime is committed by public officials.

Certainly, crime, and increased crime rates during a transition have impeded reconciliation in a number of transitional societies, including Bosnia, South Africa, and Iraq.[38]

Some of these measures that come under the general banner of "good governance" may be imposed by the international community and in particular by the donor sector. The IMF and the World Bank, like Kofi Annan, have increasingly recognized the inextricable link between governance and peace. Transitional nations need to negotiate carefully with these institutions in order to ensure that the policies they impose do not exacerbate poverty and lawlessness in the short term.

Democracy

For countries emerging from a civil war or periods of conflict, democracy is by far the best way of restoring state integrity and peace. Although, as practiced in most countries, it is far from perfect, no other system allows so many people to participate in the affairs of the nation on such equal footing. Whereas with authoritarian regimes, public confidence and systematic credibility revolve around the legitimacy of the entity in power, with democratization the focus of society is on the institutions of democracy. Democracy does not mean that problems will be solved, but it does mean that those in power are accountable at least periodically and that the views and voices of society will be represented in both the long and short term. It is this control over the process by the public at large that lends legitimacy within a system. For purposes of promoting reconciliation, this public participation in governance also increases the proportion of the population that has a stake in the continuing stability and prosperity of the nation.

But democratic representative government has its pitfalls as well. Token or purely symbolic inclusivity can backfire if people view it as a masquerade to further a divisive agenda. Victims' groups in particular may also view it as unjust to include in the polity those who were responsible for abuses and atrocities in the past. In Spain, for instance, one of the more controversial decisions of the transitional process was the inclusion of the communist party in the national elections. Ultimately, the population accepted this decision because the value of inclusivity outweighed the desire to isolate the fringe parties.[39] In particular, inclusion forces the parties to be more accountable and responsible and to play within the rules of the democratic game. Iraq made the decision when it allowed former Baathists on the ballots in legislative elections, though as of this writing the ultimate outcome of this decision is still being debated. The risk, of course, is that the extremists might win, as Hamas did in the 2006 Palestinian elections. Other nations have taken other routes, including banning political parties as in Rwanda or limiting the types of parties as in Turkey.

At the outset, a simple paradox of transitional democracy-building must be addressed. How can a system designed to create democratic legitimacy for future decisions itself be legitimate if it is not democratically elected? In other words, what makes the first election legitimate? At first blush, this may seem problematic, but many countries have dealt with this problem in creative and effective ways.

One possible response may simply be the utilitarian approach: it doesn't matter if the process for designing democratic institutions is legitimate, as long as the outcome is. Possibly the best example of this approach is the closed-door, elitist, exclusive writing of the American Constitution (though certainly it should be said that problems of legitimacy and meta-legitimacy were not taken quite as seriously 200 years ago in America as they are today throughout the world). A modern and less successful example of this approach is in Brazil, where the president's plan "was announced on television to a shocked nation with absolutely no prior consultation with political parties or congress."[40]

Perhaps a more fruitful response can be found in the countries that have tried to promote democratic ideals in both substance and process, from the outset. In Spain, for example, the process of transition and of establishing a constitutional democracy was led by elites but was constrained in two important ways. First, all new laws were legal emendations of prior legislation, thereby ensuring continuity. Second, major pieces of legislation were subject to referendum, thus providing prompt post hoc legitimacy. The exceptions to this were significant and strategic. The question of Spain's boundaries was not subjected to political approval. Elections were statewide, which implicitly answered the question whether Basque and Catalonia would secede. Nor was there a referendum on the monarchy, a decision that lessened the degree of dissatisfaction and dissension at the time of transition.[41] In South Africa, the African National Congress embarked on an extensive program of consultation and workshops in advance of the elections and, as in Hungary, a constitutional court played a significant role in ensuring the legitimacy of the transition.

Many countries now follow a multiphased process, developing increasingly important and long-lasting structures as the authority becomes increasingly democratic and legitimate over time. For instance, a temporary constitution might be imposed by the political victors, but it might mandate prompt elections to create a constituent assembly which in turn would draft a permanent constitution, to be ratified by the people. This process was followed in South Africa, as well as in East European countries. In South Africa, the interim constitution contained 34 principles that would control the final constitution. The Constitutional Court (which was established under the interim constitution) reviewed the draft final constitution to ensure its compliance with the 34 principles. Whatever the specifics, multiphased processes can add legitimacy and stability to the volatile transitional phase.

Elections

The touchstone of a democratic system is free, fair, and periodic elections in which parties work to gain the trust of the maximum number of people. Elections are particularly critical to reconciliation because they establish the appropriate framework for the new, post-transition paradigm. With democratic elections, the relationship of people to one another is not as important as the relationship of each individual to the state; nor is what happened in the past as important as how each person envisages the future, as reflected in his or her electoral choices. With democratic elections, the issue is reframed, so that instead of focusing on the interpersonal or intercommunal conflicts of the past, the government recognizes the equal value of each person's vote.

Although elections in themselves are not sufficient to ensure a successful transition, they are a way of inculcating values of citizenship, inviting broad participation in the life of the nation, and enhancing the sense of commitment that people feel toward the new state. As a result, genuinely free and fair elections can bring immediate legitimacy to a country in the eyes of its own citizens and the international community. Consider the 2005 election of Ellen Johnson-Sirleaf as president of Liberia, particularly in contrast to the 2006 reelection of President Aleksandr G. Lukashenko of Belarus, which was met by throngs of protesters over a period of weeks.

The difficult question is, of course, what to do when the democratic process selects representatives who are decidedly undemocratic, as happened in the Palestinian election of 2005, which resulted in a victory for Hamas. Many have argued that, outcome aside, the process of holding elections promotes democratic and participatory values. The series of elections in Iraq in 2004 and 2005 may provide one example of this. The period preceding the elections gave no reason for hope, as they were marked by terrible violence and those organizing the elections had little legitimacy within the country. Nonetheless, the elections themselves were largely unmarred, and the very fact of large-scale participation in this archetypically democratic process marked a turning point in Iraq's transition, both for many people within the country and for the international community. Each successive election saw increasing numbers of people participating and decreasing levels of violence (and in particular increasing Sunni participation). As the *New York Times* reported on election day in December 2005, "In villages and towns, in the Shiite south and in the Sunni Triangle, Iraqis streamed to the polls, some bringing their children, some pushing wheelchairs, many dressed in their finest clothes. With streets across Iraq closed to vehicular traffic, many Iraqis milled about after they had voted, looking on as their children played soccer. In Kirkuk, one Kurdish couple showed up at a polling center and married."[42] The long-term effects of these peaceful moments will not be known for years to come, but they may have symbolic value in the short term.

Electoral politics can be both a means and an end to social integration. Voting is the most direct way for individuals to engage in a common enterprise with their fellow citizens on an equal basis. The fact of a *genuine* election can unite the vast majority of a nation's citizens toward a common purpose, regardless of the actual outcome of the election. Properly run elections demand that participants (both voters and candidates) engage in the process, respect the rights of others to engage, and respect the outcome of the process, whether they are the winners or the losers. The process of elections can invite conversation, coalition-building, and mutually supportive relationships across formerly divided groups. Moreover, a well-designed and well-run democratic system will open avenues for the peaceful resolution of conflicts that arise outside the context of the elections themselves. Where people participate in an electoral process that is worthy of their respect, they are more likely to trust the system to resolve other types of conflicts, mitigating the impulse toward self-help.

And yet, in times of transition, people are most likely to feel threatened and insecure. It is at these times that they are most likely to choose extremist politicians whom they view as most likely to fervently represent their interests. They will reject the compromisers in favor of the hardliners. The politicians, for their part, often feed into this: they seek votes by appealing to racial, ethnic, religious, or tribal groups, promoting factionalism that can lead to polarization and sometimes violence. In Northern Ireland, during the implementation phase of the Good Friday Agreement, the centrist politicians, some of whom have been awarded Nobel Peace prizes for their conciliatory efforts, have been sidelined in favor of the hardliners. The same can be seen in postwar Bosnia.[43] In the first national elections in Bosnia under the Dayton Agreement, the "result was a landslide victory for candidates and parties that openly opposed reconciliation among Bosnia's ethnic communities."[44] Likewise, in the municipal elections of 1997, "only 6 percent of local council seats were won by candidates who did not exclusively represent the rights of one ethnic group." In Mostar, the hardline Croat and Serb parties were the "known devils" that were "still regarded as a necessary guarantee of their future by most ordinary" BiH Croats and BiH Serbs.[45] This is true, Bose says, even though most Croats know "in their heart of hearts" that the Greater Croatia project is a nonstarter. Thus, the appeal of hardliners is not necessarily in what they can deliver, but in what they represent. Continuing support for Slobodan Milosevic throughout the 1990s provides yet another example, as does the rise of religious parties in post-Saddam Iraq and the unexpected Hamas landslide in 2006. Politicians and parties rise to power on the basis of a predetermined commitment, namely to protect against some perceived threat of the "other." The fear spawns the hatred.[46]

Those who design and plan elections should create counterincentives in order to minimize the propensity of people to choose hardliners when they are feeling most threatened. For instance, they can structure voting districts to force candidates to appeal to a range of voters and structure legislative bodies to force coalitions. They can schedule elections only when there is relative calm and not when the feeling of threat is high.[47] Violence can undermine elections, and the ability of the populace to participate. Those responsible for elections, be it the UN or others, should encourage politicians to argue and engage and encourage voters to see that security lies in compromise, not in intransigence. And they should ensure that as broad a spectrum as possible of the population is able to participate. Voting and running for office should be open to all qualified adults, including those who would question the viability of the political process itself.[48]

Electoral engineering thus becomes critical. There are no neutral electoral systems. Each system is designed with certain interests in mind, and the degree of social integration and peace that results will depend to a large extent on the electoral choices that are made through a legitimate and inclusive process.

Types of Electoral Systems

The major challenge of politics, and particularly of forging reconciliation in divided societies, is how to protect minorities, particularly those marginalized, discriminated against, and alienated from the system in the past. Simple majoritarianism is not effective because it allows 51 percent of the population or of the government to dominate and oppress the remaining 49 percent. What is needed is some form of democratic governance that includes as many people as possible in the process, but nonetheless precludes certain oppressive actions that the majority might otherwise choose.

One option that has been urged in the last half-century is consociation. Consociation has been described as "mutual recognition and autonomy for, and power-sharing between, the different segments of a plural society."[49] Consociation ensures that virtually everyone in the electorate will have someone in the government who looks like them. But because con-sociation guarantees representation for specific previously identified groups or interests, it allows people to vote only for those particular parties that most accommodate their specific interests; voters need not join with others who are different from them. It promotes identity politics and offers no incentive for people to cooperate with one another at the local level, although it does require representatives to forge coalitions with each other if they want to govern effectively.

Consociation is to political systems what walls are to territory: it is a way to divide up the goods to keep everyone happy—for a time. Like walls, consociation ensures that each interest has space in which it can flourish. It produces a certain level of peace because everyone understands that each other group has the right to be at the table. But like walls, it does not conduce to reconciliation because it provides no incentives for coalition-building. In minimally divided societies, where people would otherwise vote across ethnic lines, it artificially entrenches identity politics; in deeply divided societies, it removes the incentive for coalition-building or even intergroup communication. As Sumantra Bose has shown with respect to postwar Bosnia, the consociational model introduced in the Dayton Agreement has not fostered mutual trust among the Bosniaks, Croats, and Serbs.[50] Indeed, it has justified communal self-segregation. In divided societies seeking to promote reconciliation, it is crucial to design systems that "encourage moderation within groups and alliance-building across groups."[51]

The preferable model has features containing some type of proportional representation. Proportional representation generally is an electoral system in which voters choose parties based on ideological interests or on the basis of racial, ethnic, religious, linguistic, or any other affiliation, and parties gain seats in proportion to the percentage of votes cast for them. Where seats are allocated on a national basis, election results represent the overall will of the voters more accurately than regional or local-level elections can. In addition, a small party that does not have enough support to win seats in any one regional election may have enough support nationally to win seats because its votes can be aggregated across regions. National tallies of votes tend to mask regional differences, for better or worse.[52]

This system is more flexible than consociation because, rather than predetermining the power allocation among the competing groups, it encourages the parties to vie for the allegiance of the greatest numbers of people. Yet, like constitutionalism, it can protect minority interests from abuse by ensuring *some* voice for minorities in the political arena. In many instances, the minority party may be necessary to form governing coalitions and may even hold the balance of power, as the Kurds have found themselves doing in the transitional period in Iraq.

Another good system for promoting reconciliation is a preferential voting system, or Alternative Voting (AV), where voters choose a first, second, and third choice. If their first choice receives insufficient votes, their vote transfers to their second choice, and so on, until one candidate receives a majority or plurality of votes. This method promotes reconciliation in large part because it reduces the likelihood that hardliners will prevail. It encourages each voter to choose someone other than or at least in addition to the hardliners, and it increases the chance of victory for candidates who sought support across lines. The candidates who catered only to the extremists within their group are likely to be eliminated in either the first or the second round;[53] the candidates who crossed lines to secure broader support, even if not as a first choice, are more likely to be successful.

Constituent governments wishing to encourage moderation and alliance-building must also pay attention to the nature and number of political parties within the system. Perhaps the most critical characteristic of a robust political system is that the parties should be based on ideas, not identity. Identity-based parties have little incentive to seek new voters and stand simply for the supremacy of their constituency's identity. Idea-based parties are more likely to be flexible in order to increase their support. This flexibility will increase the likelihood that the parties actually represent people's views and will make the system more resilient over time. In Northern Ireland, for instance, the political system is likely to be much stronger and more mature if parties based on the economy and the environment and other social and political issues begin to take the place of identity-based parties.

Second, idea-based parties are more likely to encourage reconciliation and cross-connections at the local level and among the population. Identity-based parties permit people to vote and to associate only with people most like them. They force alliance-building only at the elite level because none is possible at the local level. A Shi'a and a Sunni in Iraq, or a black and a white in South Africa, or a Protestant and a Catholic may come together in the Green Party, but they would be unlikely to come together if the only party options available were based on race or religion.

Third, idea-based parties will offer voters more real choices by allowing for subtle differences in platforms. Identity politics forces everyone who shares that identity to adhere to the group's platform, regardless of his or her degree of commitment to it and regardless of other, possibly stronger values.

Another essential characteristic of a robust political system is that it should contain numerous parties, offering voters real choices as to where to throw their political support. A system that offers voters real choices is much more likely to reflect the values of the population over time, and this flexibility is likely to enhance its stability and resiliency. This may require the inclusion even of parties that would criticize or thwart the democratic values of the system. In general, these parties must be included, and eliminated by political choice of the people rather than by fiat of the authorities.

Confronting choices about what kinds of parties to encourage is especially important in transitional situations, where the choices made on day one of the new government are likely to influence events for the next ten or a hundred years or more. Given that certain types of identities shift over time while others typically do not, the political reform should be responsive as people's political maturity develops.

Timing of Elections

Nations in transition are precarious animals; major events such as elections must be planned and organized with utmost caution. It is a truism of transitional politics that elections and violence go hand in hand. Countries as diverse as South Africa, Iraq, Cambodia[54], and Spain can all point to dramatic upsurges in violence in the run-up to transitional elections. Indeed, one mark of a consolidated democracy—a democracy no longer in transition—is that elections no longer prompt violence: if democratic governance is the only game in town, then elections, and not violence, are the means by which major policy questions are decided.

One reason for the strong correlation between violence and early elections is the general lack of trust and absence of commitment to the electoral process as a system for resolving questions about the allocation of power. Violence may be used to derail the elections completely if there is no commitment to the democratic process whatsoever. Alternatively, violent spoilers may be trying to shift the balance of power going into the election. A third use of violence is targeted, to discourage the participation of a particular group in the political process.

There is an irony that inheres in democratic processes of decision-making for transitional or ambivalent societies. For the process to be legitimate, there must be frequent elections—to ensure that representatives continue to be accountable to the electors and to enhance the opportunities of people to participate in self-governance. Yet each new election cycle provides resisters with opportunities to undermine or completely derail the process: until democratic values take root, each successive election is an invitation to violence.

Democratic nations and institutions, including most notably the United States and the United Nations, have urged early elections on recently transitioned nations on the theory that elections can establish democratic sensibilities within societies. But to many this is an "electoralist fallacy."

The reality is that, with few exceptions, elections do not a democracy make. Rather, the relationship between the elections and the society is much more dynamic, each mutually reinforcing the other. Thus, many observers have urged that elections occur only after the some social stability has been established and after there is a general commitment at both the elite and popular levels to electoral politics. Otherwise, elections are likely to "reinforce divisions and hardline politics produced by war."[55] A war produces raw and hardline feelings that disincline people toward compromise; given the competitive advantages of incumbency, early elections which validate war-time sentiments are likely to have long-term consequences that could be avoided by scheduling elections only after civil life has begun to be reconstructed.[56] The electoralists would counter that elections are needed to instill the values of a democratic culture.

Time may help to resolve this debate. Time is needed to enable previously warring factions to learn alternative methods of asserting their views and to recognize the necessity of abandoning violence, to allow grieving and wounded populations to trust those in power, and to implement educational programs to teach people how to read ballots and cast votes. Attention to the independent value of time demonstrates that transitions are not moments or bright lines, but periods or phases in a country's history. The transitional period has its own dynamics and sensitivities, pushes and pulls.

To acknowledge the importance of allowing time to elapse during the transitional phase, most transitional nations have established temporary unelected constituent assemblies. Some have adopted interim constitutions, as in South Africa, Iraq, and several eastern European countries. Others have developed interim ministries and other governmental structures meant to guide the nation through the transitional period and to dissolve within five or ten years.

Economic Reconciliation

Needs for Economic Reform

The relationship between reconciliation and economic interests is often a fundamental problem in transitional societies. As one Australian aboriginal man explained: "The reconciliation process can achieve nothing because it does not . . . promise reparation for the taking away of our lives, our lands and our economic and political base. Unless it can return to us those very vital things, unless it can return to us an economic, a political and a viable land base, what have we? A handshake? A symbolic dance? An exchange of leaves or feathers or something like that?"[57]

Material deprivation is often the source of conflict and the principal impediment to reconciliation. Economic oppression divides populations, and conduces to exhaustion, frustration, and ultimately violence. Desperately poor people have neither the time, the energy, nor the hope to participate in programs designed to foster democracy, reconciliation, or justice. Economic reform is as important as political reform, and perhaps even more so. Reconciliation is ordinarily only possible between equals, and cannot even be attempted when conflicting parties humiliate and stifle one another.[58]

Moreover, if, as we have argued, reconciliation entails the reframing of the relationship between the nation and the individual, then that reframing should be done not just through expressive and symbolic means but in material ways as well. A poor farmer is more likely to believe that she is an integral part of the new nation when her standard of living improves. Indeed, for many people, the economy is the most important, and sometimes even the *only* determinant of a successful transition or reconciliation process. As Australian Aboriginal lawyer Noel Pearson explained, "If we don't understand that 'it's the economy, stupid,' then it's just mere symbolism and fanfare and that's all reconciliation will ever be. It won't provide a real basis for inclusion."[59] In fact, the argument could readily be made that the concept of reconciliation is entirely incoherent in the absence of economic justice.

Even when reconciliation is wrapped in the garb of moral righteousness and individual dignity, the unequal distribution of wealth is often at the root of the problems. During the public hearings before the Sierra Leone truth commission, William Schabas writes, "victims have testified to horrific violations such as amputations, killings, and rapes, but when asked if they have anything they would like the Commission to include in its recommendations, they reply: free education for our children, access to medical care, adequate housing."[60] As a result, the TRC process in Sierra Leone "has been likened to a national catharsis, involving truth-telling, respectful listening and *above all*, compensation for victims in deserving cases."[61] On the other hand, in South Africa, where the TRC accomplished much, except notably the provision of meaningful reparations, it has engendered deep and bitter disappointment among the population it was designed to assist.[62]

Often, the money is not viewed by the victims as reparations or as payment of a moral debt. The demand is more basic: it is about electricity and water and paying a doctor. Economic deprivation is invariably the most significant of the wounds that struggling populations endure before, during, and after transitions because, as Pearson explains, "The sticks and stones of racism are wounds that you suffer externally. The whole welfare thing is viral. It actually gets inside you and breaks you down from the inside."[63] Given the importance of economic benefits to most victims of war, one woman's reaction to a landmark decision from Bosnia's constitutional court is understandable: "Does this mean I will receive my pension on time from now on?"[64] All that matters is the ability to pay bills and survive.

If done well, economic reform can encourage reconciliation in multiple ways. First, economic reform should diminish inequalities among the country's citizens. Bringing people together economically will also bring them together culturally, politically, and socially. A growing middle class is more likely to participate in the civic and political affairs of the nation at every level. (Middle class is used here as a relative concept, different from one nation to another, but referring generally to those who are neither so rich that their political power is assured, nor so poor that their political power is ignored.) This enriches and broadens civil society, and in turn provides people with more outlets for political activity, defusing the tendency toward political violence. A middle class also facilitates the practice of electoral politics. It is difficult and problematic to hold elections where a majority of the people are so poor or so remote that they are unable to reach the polls, to educate themselves about the candidates, or to demand accountability from their representatives. In a country where there is no middle class and a significant divide between rich and poor, electoral politics are likely to be geared exclusively toward the rich: polls may not be in places where poor people live; ballots may not be designed for illiterate voters; and candidates may not seek out the support of the poor and marginalized, even if this group constitutes a majority or vast majority of the nation's population.[65] And if a majority are disenfranchised, either in fact or by law, the result can hardly be called a mandate. Democracy requires that a significant portion of the population is committed to the political process. And the more people have to lose, the more committed they will be to the system, because the system is their best protection.

The relationship between democracy and a middle class may be circular: a government that depends for its mandate on a middle class is more likely to work to preserve that voter base. The best way for the democratically elected government to stay in power is to promote policies that enhance the standard of living for the maximum number of voters. And a government whose legitimacy increases over time is more likely to be able to provide the goods and services that people need, which will extend its mandate.

Economic reform can produce a related psychological benefit. It invites people to feel that they have a stake in the new nation, and it builds loyalty to the nation's policies and to the fact of the central government itself. People who benefit from economic reform are more likely to own land and businesses, which, in turn, encourages them to support the government's policies. These people are then more likely to pay taxes, which can take economic reforms even further. People living in outlying areas who nonetheless benefit by governmentally planned economic reform are less likely to be seduced by or dependent on warlords or other illicit power brokers. They are more likely to support national policies over their own parochial interests. This enhances the new government's authority and creates a protective cushion should other policies require sacrifice on the part of the people.[66] Choices between centralization and federalism can be counterbalanced by economic choices: empowering individuals in the one realm may lessen the need to empower them in another. In this view, redistribution of wealth is another aspect of politics: both mechanisms mediate the relationship of the individual to the state, which is what reconciliation is all about.

For economic reform to be effective, it must have two qualities. First, the reform measures must provide for relative equality among the population. While each country has a different standard of living, economic reforms must minimize the gap between the rich and the poor within the nation. The national economy must provide its services on a relatively equal basis, so that no group within the nation is severely underserved as compared with other groups. Many divided societies are divided precisely along economic lines, with benefits and privileges flowing to one portion of the population at the direct expense of another portion. If the transition exacerbates inequality, many people are likely to become disillusioned by the transitional government; they are likely to doubt that the struggle was worth the sacrifice and to lose faith in the ability of the new government to keep the promise of the revolution. This has happened in many postcommunist countries, where those who had worked the communist system to their advantage were now seen to be working the capitalist system to their advantage, and those who were marginalized under communism found themselves even more disadvantaged under capitalism. Economic reforms that reduce inequality become the tangible evidence that the state treats all its citizens with "equal concern and respect." They permit all citizens to stand in roughly the same position with respect to the civil and political institutions of the nation.

Second, the reform measures must provide for a minimum standard of living—a floor below which human beings should not have to fall. A democracy in which the vast majority of people are destitute is not likely to survive long even if the gap between rich and poor shrinks. As Linz and Stepan have explained, the state must have a "fiscal and moral capacity to play an integrating role in society and to provide basic services to citizens."[67] In other words, the government, and its services, must be present throughout the country. If the government has insufficient means to build roads and provide police protection and run hospitals and schools,

the result will undermine reconciliation efforts in two mutually reinforcing ways, as discussed earlier. The people who are underserved by the government are unlikely to develop strong loyalty and identity to the state if
there is no strong state presence in their communities, thus diminishing
the strength of national identity. Moreover, unregulated groups are likely
to step into this vacuum and provide the services that the government
should have provided; in so doing, these groups will engender loyalty from
portions of the population, thus deepening the divides. As noted earlier,
the groups that provide these services are not always altruistic, and often
have political and indeed divisive agendas that can undermine any efforts
to promote reconciliation.

Unfortunately, the reality of transitional economic policies falls far short
of the ideal. Many economic policies do not promote reconciliation and
many in fact retard it. Since the end of the cold war, reconstructive policies
have been guided by the macroeconomic approaches of the International
Monetary Fund and the World Bank which favor privatization, limited government and, in many cases, austerity measures to enhance a country's
appeal to foreign investors. In theory, marketization and privatization
policies hold some appeal from a reconciliation perspective both in form
and in substance. In substance, this economic approach may reinforce
reconciliation efforts insofar as it produces a middle class. In form, they
are the economic analogs to rule of law and to voting: they hold the individual up as the significant unit and, in so doing, allow every person to
stand in the same relation to power as every other. At least in theory, a
true market economy does not play favorites: everyone enjoys the same
opportunity to buy or sell, make (or lose) money, regardless of race, gender, political ideology, or past associations.

But the reality is quite different. In the vast majority of instances, at least
so far, these policies fail to protect the poorest and most vulnerable sections of the population (often the vast majority of the population) from
the ravages of competition and unchecked privatization. Indeed, as Roland
Paris has noted, capitalism is "inherently competitive. It inevitably creates winners and losers."[68] As a result, in most countries, levels of inequality actually increase rather than decrease in the transitional period.[69] If
the IMF, the World Bank, and donor nations want to promote reconciliation and stability, they must become more concerned with how the people of the country actually live.[70] One way to do this—as the Namibians
demanded of the Germans—is for those who impose the rules to consult
with and listen to those who have to live by the rules. Particularly in the
South, many in transitional and dependent nations see their relationship
with the donor community as fractured and imbalanced.

Even when imposed from within, the types of economic policies chosen
by a new government should be the result of democratic and consultative

processes. In most situations, significant economic reform may have to wait until the first democratically elected government is in place. The government will need sufficient legitimacy to alter the allocation of resources and sufficient institutional support to moderate effectively the competition that arises from marketization, including enforcement and subsidization mechanisms.[71]

Types of Economic Reforms

Economic reform can range from narrow restitutionary measures to a discrete group of victims, to the restructuring of tax and business law, to a rearticulation of the balance of the rights and responsibilities of the public and private sectors. It can be about righting specific wrongs from the past, or about ensuring a better future through affirmative action and broadly redistributive policies. At times the government establishes programs unilaterally, and other times they result from intense negotiation or reflect broad consensus. Whatever the formal structure, the participation of those most in need of economic reform (or their representatives) should be deemed mandatory by those in authority, but should not be compulsory for those who may not want to participate for a variety of reasons.

Restitution is the "return of the specific actual belongings that were confiscated, seized, or stolen, such as land, art, ancestral remains, and the like."[72] It appears to have a moral dimension since it is paid to the victim by the putative wrongdoer. The "wrongdoer" may be the government or it may be an individual under pressure by the government or local authority. Its moral basis distinguishes restitution from other types of economic reform, which are often purely political. Yet, even restitution is often limited to "economic damages and rarely directly addresses the loss of political freedom, personal liberty, cultural identity, or human rights."[73] Moreover, since restitution tends to be limited both in amount and in scope, it has less capacity to breach socioeconomic divides than more broad-based measures. As a result, restitution works best where it is needed least as an economic reform. In postcommunist countries, where there is less destitution and less inequality than in other parts of the conflict-ridden world, restitution has a greater chance of speaking its moral message, without having it undermined by the lack of real material change in the circumstances of recipients. (That said, the record of restitution even in Eastern Europe is by no means spotless.[74])

In his study on political restitution, Elazar Barkan argues that both the process and the result of restitution can be effective in forging new identities for both perpetrators and victims. Restitution can advance reconciliation by softening the image of both sides. In the intense negotiation on restitution between Germany and the Jewish community in the aftermath of the Holocaust, he argues, the issue of restitution was the "anvil on which to forge . . . the place of Jews and Jewish victimization in the German identity."[75] Through the process of negotiation, victims can assert themselves and demand the respect and recognition they are due. Perpetrators might reveal themselves as capable of atonement and redemption. This does not always happen, of course, but the potential exists for the negotiation over restitution to provide one avenue in which victims and perpetrators can begin to communicate and reframe their understanding of each other.

On the other hand, there is also a cynical side to restitution. It may provide disingenuous perpetrators with the opportunity to appear more benevolent than they are. This is often the case when the perpetrator's economic resources are vast in comparison with the money offered to the victim or victim class. Perpetrators, in this view, may appear to be buying the victim's forgiveness or paying for expiation: *if I give you back your bicycle, can we forget this ever happened?* Victims, for their part, might be put in what Barkan calls a "Faustian predicament,"[76] being asked to take money from the devil. They are damned if they take the "blood money"[77] and damned (or at least poorer) if they don't.

Closely related to restitution is compensation, which raises many of the same moral and pragmatic issues. Compensation might be paid in many of the same circumstances in which restitution would be appropriate, except that it is impossible to return the specific items taken. Indeed, the Universal Declaration of Human Rights requires compensation to be paid in cases of "torture or other cruel, inhuman or degrading treatment or punishment [that] has been committed by or at the instigation of a public official."[78]

Many of the victims at the Ghana National Reconciliation Commission process sought compensation for the harms caused them. A gold dealer whose gold had been confiscated said that "as a result of his detention he lost opportunity for advancement in his employment and therefore could not educate his children in secondary school, adding he now sells used clothing with his wife."[79] Before the same commission, the son of a man whose brewery had been confiscated explained: "We hold no grudge against those who tortured us, but we want the benefit of our father's sweat and toil."[80] Tim Kelsall described a similar phenomenon in the proceedings before the Sierra Leone Truth and Reconciliation Commission. "A notable feature of witness testimony," he wrote, "was that when asked by the Commissioners for their recommendations, most victims pointed to their dire economic plight as individuals (though some made more collective statements) and urged the government, or the Commission itself, to come to their assistance."[81]

Reparations are a slightly broader-based form of compensation. Whereas restitution and compensation are typically for a particular wrong committed, reparations are typically from a government that takes responsibility for a policy or set of policies or actions. There is less effort here to tie the amount of payment to the actual harm caused. Reparations represent a kind of moral accounting, where the payment represents the *fact* that harm was done, but not the amount of suffering or loss that was endured. Is the motivation for such claims moral satisfaction, or material need? In their study of the Czech Republic, Roman David and Susanne Choi Yuk-ping argue that it may be both, in that "monetary compensation acts as a proxy for justice."[82] For those who believe that the moral injustice needs to be corrected, reparations may be essential. Wole Soyinka has written that the failure of the South African process to deliver reparations was one of missing links between truth and reconciliation.[83] Likewise, Archbishop Tutu has forcefully argued that some form of compensation is essential to reconciliation. Upon the tenth anniversary of the initiation of the South African TRC, Chairperson Desmond Tutu renewed his entreaty to the government that reparations be paid to the victims of gross human rights abuses. Not only South Africa's TRC but almost every recent TRC process has insisted, at least in word if not in deed, that payment of money to victims is an essential component of reconciliation.[84]

But, like restitution and compensation, reparations are virtually impossible to secure from even the best-intentioned legislators: there are always other causes, other needs that may take precedence. For example, "The Sierra Leone TRC has no resources of its own to distribute to victims."[85] So while government officials are often heard to say that reparation or compensation is of critical importance, the money is rarely forthcoming. The outcome in South Africa is likely to be repeated throughout the world, as high-minded recommendations for reparations succumb to realpolitik and real economics.

The resistance to reparations may have many motivations. Some may not subscribe to the moral message of reparations that so often suggest responsibility if not liability. Others may agree that reparations are morally appropriate but may believe that the government's scarce resources would be better spent on programs that enhance the lives of everyone in the nation, or at least the most needy, such as on schools, roads, and housing, rather than on the targeted group of designated and proven victims. South Africa has been debating for a decade exactly how much money should be paid to whom, and on what basis. Under the TRC's narrow definition, only 21,000 individuals qualified as "victims" of apartheid, even though any common-sense count of apartheid's victims would include nearly every person of any color in South Africa. Given the narrow class of people who would benefit from reparations, the question must be asked whether reparations to relatively few people are justified on any theory, particularly if they would impede the delivery of services such as water, electricity, housing, education to the millions of people who were not deemed to be victims.

As a result of these tensions, even in the rare instances where they are paid out, reparations never involve sufficient amounts of money actually to change the socioeconomic status of the recipient. She may get enough to buy a new refrigerator, but she still won't have enough to pay for electricity to run it. The value of reparations then is mostly symbolic and thus, like restitution, is most meaningful when the victims' injuries are primarily noneconomic.

Reparations suffer from additional defects that have significant implications for reconciliation purposes. One problem concerns the putative payers of reparations. Whenever there has been a transition, those who committed the wrongs no longer control either the government or the public fiscus. Should the successor government be forced to pay for the crimes of its predecessors? When victims demand reparations, do they really want to take money from the cash-strapped government, which bears no responsibility whatsoever for the victims' injuries and may represent the victim class? The victims are clearly in need, but if the money comes from the innocent (and victimized) successor, it is difficult to see how the moral message of atonement is being communicated.

Another problem concerns the victims. Whereas restitution is paid directly to the victim of a particular crime, reparations are paid to a class of people who are recognized as having a particular entitlement. Often, because of the passage of time and the difficulty of ascertaining who was subjected to which injustice over which amount of time, the determination of the victim class is a hotly contested issue. People with similar scars from similar events are apt to be treated differently because one lacks evidence that the crime was politically motivated or because it occurred before or after the cut-off dates, or for myriad other reasons that may seem arbitrary and unjustified to those deemed undeserving. And no matter how much the government seeks to assuage the additional injury of being denied compensation, the line-drawing that reparations necessarily entail is bound to create resentment and division among groups of victims, where previously there was solidarity. Even from the standpoint of reconciliation, reparations can be problematic.

Broad-based economic reforms are likely to be more conducive to reconciliation than the more targeted programs because they are likely to be more responsive to the needs of more people. But because these cost more, and because these may be inconsistent with the demands of the donor community, these are much more difficult to secure. And even when secured in law, they are more difficult to implement. In Brazil, Linz and

Stepan remind us, the "price of legislative support was almost always an agreement not to put fiscal reform on the agenda or to give special subsidies to constituents or congressmen and governors."[86]

And yet, dysfunctional economies are especially conducive to conflict and division. Competition for access to and control of resources is likely to ignite tensions. Finding ways of growing the economy, attracting investors, and reducing unemployment is therefore fundamental. A growing economy that improves the standard of living for everyone enhances the prospects for reconciliation.

In addition, economic policies must be integrated into the broader context of the government's transitional program. For instance, where class differences are demarcated along racial, linguistic, ethnic, or other identity-based lines, special attention needs to be paid to the implications for promoting broad scale or more incremental reforms. If insufficient change is realized, tensions between the groups can mount, and the cycle of violence begins anew.

Economic reforms, no less than trials and commissions, are bound to affect people in different ways, depending on where they sit. Those who benefited from the prior injustice are likely to resist radical reform to compensate the victims of that injustice; those who were deprived in the past are obviously likely to welcome redistributive policies. As the transitional state attempts to address and redress the disparities between groups, either through land reform, tax reform, affirmative action, and other similar measures, so backlash may result.

Economic reform forces those in privileged positions to sacrifice something for the common weal. Ultimately, such reforms are likely to be most effective where, as discussed in previous chapters, those who are being asked to give something up understand that reconciliation ultimately benefits them as much as the receiving class, by helping to establish a stronger and more peaceful nation. And as with other aspects of reconciliation, an inclusive process can be just as important as a just result; consensus building with *all* stakeholders will not only facilitate the most efficacious policy, but will help build loyalty to the program and to the new nation.

Like political reform, new economic policies may be vulnerable to timing. Both economic and political reform probably require more time than the international community is used to giving. Time can assuage some of the pangs that necessarily accompany dramatic changes in a nation's structure. It is perhaps unfortunate that nations in transition must generally tackle both economic and political reform at the same time, since the aggregation of the two may have a tendency to increase the sense of fear and insecurity among some significant segments of the population. If people—particularly those who were privileged in the preceding regime—feel disempowered by the political change, they may be more likely to resist economic redistribution, and to blame the new beneficiaries of government policies for the new competitiveness. For instance, former communists in Hungary may feel disempowered as a result of the change in government, may fear loss of income or social privileges, and may be more likely to blame the Roma for the new insecurity—even though in most cases, the formerly disadvantaged, like the Roma in Europe or the blacks in South Africa, do not gain significant economic power as the result of transitions. But others may genuinely, if not entirely reasonably, feel that they do. It is not at all uncommon for racial and ethnic violence against minority groups to increase during times of economic upheaval: those who were most privileged previously feel the most threatened when the system changes and take it out on those least able to defend themselves. It can be a very difficult time for a new government with reconciliation on its agenda to ask those very people to accede to redistributive policies that are likely to only augment the sense of unfairness that they feel. Economic and political reform must be implemented with delicacy and with understanding of the diverse perspectives within the society.

Political and economic reforms are essential to a government's efforts to reframe what it means to be a citizen of a formerly divided society. In a material way, they enhance the ability of each citizen to participate in the life of the nation. In a psychological way, they increase the value of citizenship, and in a structural way, they strengthen the nation as a whole by recognizing the value of diversity and pluralism. In a symbolic way, they indicate that everyone is an equally valued member of the political community. They can in theory and in practice promote a new national collective consciousness about the meaning of the transition and the value of citizenship in the new state. On the other hand, political and economic reforms that are crafted without sensitivity to reconciliation can further divide the people of a nation and commensurately further weaken the state. An integrated and holistic approach must be adopted.

Economic and political reforms both represent what might be called super-structures. Neither in and of itself dictates the content of particular policy. But they do allow for policies to be chosen in a legitimate way by a majority of the people. In this sense, they are both capable of promoting reconciliation, because they allow people to develop a common language for resolving differences of opinion.[87] For many deeply divided and traumatized societies, the ability to disagree respectfully in the context of a political structure is quite possibly the most that can be expected of reconciliation.

Chapter 9
The Mechanics of Reconciliation

> I'm hoping people look beyond what's happening today to when
> their grandchildren or great grandchildren will be adults and
> having to live with what we leave them.
>
> —Kerry Arabena

Every country is unique. Every country has its own political, social, cultural, ethnic, and linguistic cleavages, its own history, and its own response to history. Each has different circumstances, different impetuses, different stresses and strains. For this reason, no country can replicate another's reconciliation process: what worked in one place may not work in another, and conversely, what has not yet worked may be successful in the next country. The trajectory must necessarily be tailored to the particular transitional landscape of each nation. This uniqueness should give the local designers of reconciliation processes "the confidence to realize that they are the experts on their own situation, to trust their own judgement about what will work and what will not in their context, and to use, adapt, alter or replace ideas from elsewhere."[1]

Moreover, each country has a different set of resources and assets to capitalize on, and a different set of limitations. Economic resources are obviously a huge boon to reconciliation initiatives, but other kinds of assets should not be overlooked. A country that has one or more strong charismatic leaders, a rich cultural tradition, a long history of multiculturalism, significant attachment to cultural or religious institutions, or other features that could become sources of strength and unity may find them as useful as money in promoting reconciliation. On the other side, each country approaches reconciliation with certain limitations: extreme poverty, a deeply divided or traumatized population, a long history of internecine warfare, and so on. A reconciliation program is bound to seem like empty rhetoric if "it fails to confront the specific, shifting and complex needs of the parties involved, and the limited resources available for determining and meeting those needs."[2]

In each country, the population also has a different set of needs, and the reconciliation program should be tailored to those needs. Again, these may be economic, but they may also be physical, psychological, or material. To a very significant degree, these variables will determine how the country is able to promote reconciliation.

Notwithstanding the infinite variety of approaches to reconciliation, there are certain basic premises that inhere in the very notion of transitions toward democracy. Most analysts of transitional justice emphasize the need for effective government institutions to keep the peace. Government is necessary to protect a nation's people not only from outside aggressors but from internal threats as well. The absence of a government or the presence of a weak or ineffective government allows powerful forces to prey on weaker individuals or groups without any meaningful constraints. Government is also necessary to model and enforce the rule of law by insisting that both public and private actors be held accountable for legal transgressions.

Therefore, one of the first tasks of the postconflict generation is to establish a functioning government: one with a legislature to prescribe the rules by which it and others shall be governed; an administrative bureaucracy with the capability of enforcing rules (including a respectable police force) and providing essential services including education, medical care, and housing; and a functioning and respectable judiciary which, whether comprising members of the old guard or the new, adheres to current legal and cultural norms and enjoys the power of constitutional review.

But beyond these essential predicates of reconciliation, questions abound as to the mechanics of reconciliation.

Who Should Promote Reconciliation?

The short answer is "everyone." As many individuals, groups, and institutions as possible both in and outside the country should be included in the process. Since reconciliation is an integrative process, it should embrace all prominent sectors of civil society. This includes elites as well as those involved in grassroots movements and people who have traditionally been on the margins.[3] Moreover, programs should be developed to ensure crossover participation by people in all sectors of civil society, including collaborative efforts between the public and private sectors, between educational and civic organizations, between religious and secular interests, and between women's groups and spheres from which women have traditionally been excluded.

Reconciliation is as much about perception as it is about substance. It is about the perception of the past as well as the perception of the future. What people think about the past (what Bloomfield calls the "mythology") is as important as what actually happened in the past (the history).[4] A reconciliation program that is rooted only in the forensic evidence will not be as successful as one that is also informed by the way people experienced the past and think about it. Likewise, a reconciliation program must not only be structurally sound; to be successful it also must invite the trust of the population. People must *believe in* reconciliation and *believe* that official efforts to promote reconciliation are legitimate and not simply excuses for impunity. The success of a reconciliation program depends in large part on the extent to which the public accepts the process.

The role of the media is paramount. The media may determine what issues are being discussed, as well as how people think and talk about those issues. Reports on progress being made in advancing reconciliation can go a long way in encouraging others to participate in the reconciliation process. (By contrast, media reports during a civil war have throughout the world goaded people to commit atrocities against their neighbors: in most countries where civil war has broken out and the government did own the media, inflammatory messages were an important part of the mobilization process.) Efforts to bring the media into the process and transparently opening the process to the media are therefore essential.

Other external institutions can assist in a variety of ways as well. The participation of all sectors of civil society should be encouraged because, as discussed in Part Two, reconciliation can and must take place at all levels of society. Community organizers, educational institutions, corporate interests, and the like all have an interest in advancing reconciliation and all can lend support in the form of expertise, personnel, materials, or money. Geographically defined communities can complement the national process by initiating their own reconciliation programs or participating in programs that originated elsewhere, as many groups have done in Israel and Palestine, in Timor Leste, and elsewhere. In other places, groups defined not by geography but by common interest have taken the lead in reconciliation efforts. In Mozambique, the churches drew attention to the enormous toll the civil war was taking in human lives. In Latin America, mothers did the same thing, while human rights groups drew attention to the lawlessness of the military regimes. In Bosnia and in Northern Ireland, student groups have initiated local reconciliation programs to help youth from different cultures learn to live together despite the boundaries imposed by the political elites. In Cambodia, doctors and psychologists have helped people to heal. In Rwanda, widows from both ethnic groups have banded together to feed prisoners. Individuals, on their own or as part of groups, can become the intrepid "explorers" that Fanie du Toit believes drive the "the twin processes of dialogue and development." These individuals, he says, can traverse to unknown territory and return "to tell fresh tales about the 'others'. Their more accurate and humanising tales from the 'far side,' replace superstitious, malicious and stereotypical rumours. When people doubt whether reconciliation is possible, they look to these explorers."[5]

Outsiders may also contribute to reconciliation in a country. Outside organizations, which often have significant expertise in everything from psychological counseling, to mine clearance, to creation of infrastructure should not be marginalized simply because they are not indigenous. Indeed, in many cases conflicts seem so intractable and so deeply embedded in the social structure that reconciliation can only be sparked by the torch of an outsider whose neutrality can help to defuse tensions (as the Clinton White House did in galvanizing the Good Friday Peace Agreement in Northern Ireland). Outsiders may be particularly useful in helping to "reframe" the issues. It is critical, however, that international actors not be permitted to design or implement programs without local input. Ideally, the local community, with greater knowledge of its own needs and resources and cultural attitudes of the people, would identify the needs to the international community, which may have greater programmatic and organizational capacities. The international community—including professional conflict managers and donors—has begun using development assistance as a means to promote reconciliation. According to one development task force, "This is very difficult and time-consuming work, amounting to providing conditions and opportunities conducive for communities to change their attitudes towards each other and towards integration,— nowhere an easily orchestrated or speedy matter."[6] The work is based on "limited explicit and tested thinking, both about the causes of violence and about the social dynamics of polarisation and identity formation." As a result, "Much work is needed, based on insights from the social sciences and the experiences acquired to date in the field."

The United Nations also has a role to play. For instance, it has increasingly focused attention on both direct and indirect methods of promoting reconciliation within countries in transition. It has held a number of reconciliation conferences in Somalia. It has also been a central player in the establishment of truth commissions in Guatemala and El Salvador and more recently in East Timor and Sierra Leone, to name a few.[7] In addition, the UN, especially through its Development Program (UNDP), has initiated many programs aimed at enhancing democratic governance, assisting in crisis prevention and recovery, and promoting human rights awareness, all of which are related to reconciliation. In Liberia, for instance, the UNDP envisages that through comprehensive disarmament, demobilization and sustainable reintegration, all ex-combatants will be enabled to contribute to national development and reconciliation instead of posing a threat to peace and stability.[8] In Bosnia and Herzegovina, the UNDP has developed cooperative reconstruction and economic revitalization programs and is heavily engaged in monitoring stability and growth indicators.[9] Whether the facilitators are insiders or outsiders, the values and priorities of the program should reflect, if not emanate from, the indigenous culture, to enhance the ability of the program to be accepted by the people of the culture.

Moreover, at times foreign governments (not just foreign and international NGOs) may be useful and indeed necessary to promote reconciliation within a country. China, for instance, has recently gained attention for holding disarmament talks with North and South Korea (as well as other countries). Here, China serves as a relatively trustworthy, neutral neighbor trying to stabilize the region. In 1995, the United States served largely the same function in helping Bosnia to reach agreement to end the war there. At the end of 2005, Cuba provided a neutral forum for peace talks between the Colombian government and major rebel groups. In other cases, a foreign country might be indispensable to the peace and reconciliation process: reconciliation in the Democratic Republic of the Congo, for instance, will require attention to the role that neighboring countries such as Rwanda, Sudan, and Uganda have played in exacerbating the crisis there. The South African TRC considered the role that the international community as a whole played, through sanctions, in pressuring the apartheid government to make concessions in the early 1990s, but, like many other TRCs (particularly in Latin America), it also examined the role that the Cold War politics of the United States and the Soviet Union played in maintaining a climate of repression and polarization in the preceding decades.

Finally, it is becoming increasingly common for countries to seek the assistance of the international community in supporting their reconciliation efforts, not only through loans and grants, but in other ways as well. In 2003, President Museveni of Uganda became the first head of state to seek the assistance of the International Criminal Court when he referred to it the situation in northern Uganda regarding violations by the Lord's Resistance Army (although more recently amnesty seems to have been offered).

Ironically, outsiders may be of least utility where they are most needed—that is, where the tension is the most intense. In Bosnia, for instance, where there is such a long and complex history of interethnic relations, outsiders are warned against seriously misassessing the situation, even if they think they understand it. Speaking not of reconciliation experts but of the post-Dayton international diplomatic corps in Bosnia in general, Sumantra Bose says "The lesson is that international authorities should beware of becoming unnecessarily entangled in the maze of intrigue that is Bosnian politics, and should, in particular, guard against being manipulated into becoming the tools of some factions in their struggle against other factions."[10] Bosnia, like many countries, has a long history of both ethnic interdependence and mistrust, as well as a long history of corruption and clientelism. The international community, Bose suggests, is profoundly mistaken if it thinks it can cleanse Bosnian politics of its traditional business ethic.

The government of the troubled country is as important as any player in the conflict. Indeed, it may be that "The most important role-player in the process of reconciliation is the State. Government as a collective, as well as individual members of government, play a crucial part in reconciliation."[11] But it is critically important to distinguish between what the government can, and cannot, do. It cannot insist on or require reconciliation. But it can do many things to nurture it.

First, the allocation of authority to various sectors of government may determine the extent to which and the ways in which government can act. A president who is responsible only to the people directly may have more leeway to initiate reconciliation programs by executive fiat or order; a parliamentary system where both the head of government and the head of state are responsible to the parliament may require that major policy initiatives be established only after legislative deliberation and compromise. Even where a reconciliation program could be decreed constitutionally, it may benefit both substantively and politically from legislative debate and consensus—and from the public debate that legislative processes may spur. An executive program may more likely be seen as partisan, and a president's statements touting a reconciliation program may be seen as political rhetoric. Thus, a process of inclusive consultation and obtaining widespread support for the process among elites and nonelites may be indispensable in the long run.

A separate consideration is the relationship between the executive and the military, both old and new. If the executive is perceived to be aligned with the military of the old regime, the legitimacy of its reconciliation program may be impugned and the need for political support for the program becomes critical. On the other hand, if the present military is not under civilian control, reconciliation may be all the more essential and a president may deftly use a reconciliation project to marginalize errant military authorities.

The vertical allocation of power will also affect government action: if the country has a strong federal system, where local and regional organizations enjoy significant power and the allegiance of the people, the central government will have less legal or political authority to initiate sweeping policy changes.

Assuming that the central government does have both the legal and the political authority to act, it is useful to disentangle the various ways in which governments typically do act. The most obvious way is through legislation or regulation. Second, because in most countries the government controls the greatest share of resources, government acts through allocation of funds. Third, government action can be expressive.

No government can mandate reconciliation on pain of imprisonment or fine. Yet, steps can be taken to encourage reconciliation. A government in a divided society can establish an administrative department dedicated to promoting reconciliation. Fiji, Rwanda, Somalia, Central African Republic, Côte d'Ivoire, and Australia are among the countries that have done this. These departments function in widely varying ways, but in each case the creation of a ministry demonstrates the government's long-term commitment to reconciliation.

Governments can also enact laws that specifically protect the rights of people *as members of groups*. These laws may provide affirmative protections and rights for members of certain groups, including affirmative action provisions in education, employment, and contracts. Laws that provide safe havens for groups to express themselves as such may include parade and march permits, ethnic holidays, and recognition of language, religious, and cultural freedoms. The government needs to ensure that each group has the space within the society to express itself. These laws should be supported to deter backlash by the dominant populations. Other laws may deter ethnic oppression or domination, such as regulation of hate speech and incitement, antidiscrimination and antisegregation laws, and penalty enhancements when crimes are ethnically motivated. Laws need to be rigorous in letter and enforcement. Sometimes, temporary laws (that include automatic or presumptive sunset provisions) may be useful if greater protections are needed in the short term to avert violence. Similarly, laws governing only one geographic area may be appropriate if ethnic relations are not consistent throughout the country's territory. In many cases, the new regime of laws should be supported by a public education campaign that advises people of the existence of the laws and of the government's commitment to enforcing them.

In addition to passing new laws, governments must repeal old laws that allowed conflict and distrust to fester. Structural laws that contributed to political polarization, such as those limiting the exercise of the franchise and political speech and association, should be repealed promptly.[12] Laws that contributed to social and cultural polarization, such as those prohibiting interethnic marriage or establishing separate schools and facilities for people from different groups, or in other ways contributed to a caste system, should also be repealed. However, broad scale repeal must be done with care to avoid the vacuum that political opponents can exploit if there is confusion about which laws are valid and which laws are not.

Whatever legal mechanisms governments utilize to promote reconciliation programs, the processes should be characterized by an ethos of transparency. Often, the longest-lasting legacy of oppressive regimes is distrust of government, and one of the most effective ways for transitional governments to draw bright lines between themselves and their predecessors is to operate in the open, allowing press coverage and encouraging full debate and discussion during both the planning and implementation stages of the process, as well as in its aftermath. Decisions to withhold publication or distribution of commission reports can undo all the good will that was built up over the commission's life.

Because governments typically control the lion's share of resources in most countries, allocation of funds can be a significant impetus to reconciliation. The government can fund initiatives such as ministries, truth commissions, and trials that are directly intended to promote reconciliation. In addition, the government can fund other kinds of programs that may indirectly (but equally effectively) promote reconciliation, such as the gacaca trials in Rwanda or town meetings or other public fora to discuss issues that have divided the people. Governments also can expend resources on reparations, in the form of individual grants or structural assistance (including anything from rebuilding schools and community centers to training and hiring programs to providing free psychological counseling and medical assistance). The decision to make reparation payments may result from recommendations of an independent commission. In most cases, these recommendations are not obligatory (with the exception of El Salvador), but they can provide pressure points around which the civilian society or the international community can lobby for change in the future.[13] Other forms of economic assistance to underdeveloped areas, such as tax incentives, subsidies, and private enterprise grants or low-interest loans, could also be explored.[14] These were examined in more detail in the previous chapter.

Governments may also need to expend significant resources on demilitarization and reintegration programs, which should include both material assistance to help people move from one place to another and establish homes again, as well as psychological assistance to help returnees and ex-combatants reintegrate into the daily life of the community and to help the villagers accept the returnees. These programs will differ, depending on a number of variables: whether there are a significant number of returnees to a particular locale or just a few; whether the returnee was a victim, a perpetrator, or a bit of both; whether the village is open or not to the person's return; whether the returnee is a child or adult; and whether there is a family in the village willing to assist in the reintegration process, among other things.

Some resources may be directed to programs that open up spaces in which the recipients may themselves promote reconciliation. Even relatively poor governments might decide to fund cultural programs that explore how people feel about the past. The government could also fund works projects that would simultaneously assist in material rebuilding and in helping people learn to work together. Public spaces—such as monuments, museums, and memorials—can also promote reconciliation, so long as they are inclusive and not privileging one side's experience over the other. Sometimes an open competition to design such a space can help ensure that the process is inclusive, and the result is more likely to be accepted by everyone. It may be also important to ensure that a specific space recognizes more than one group or is perceived to be to the memory of more than one group.

Law's expressive nature is inextricably intertwined with its regulatory and distributive functions. Since everything the government does communicates a message at the same time that it achieves its primary function, the government must be aware of how its actions are being perceived by the public. Sometimes this is explicit, as when the government owns, controls, or uses the major media outlets in a country to promote a particular program or priority. At other times, it is an implicit—though unmistakable—side effect of a government action. For instance, an appointment to a court or government department installs the new person in the office and simultaneously communicates to the public the government's vision for that office: the appointment of a hardliner communicates a very different message from that of a moderate, even before the appointee's first day on the job. For example, the appointment of John Garang, the rebel leader who had founded the Sudan People's Liberation Movement, as vice president of the national unity government was widely seen as a conciliatory gesture.

Likewise, a high-ranking official's decision to offer testimony to a commission can be a significant boon to the public's embrace of the reconciliation process. Modeling conciliatory behavior can promote a climate of reconciliation, as Nelson Mandela, Julius Nyerere, Vaclav Havel, and others well understood. A high-level government official who apologizes or offers forgiveness models an inclination to move forward that others might follow. These acts, like all other governmental acts, can establish, promote, and confirm social norms by identifying behaviors that are or are not acceptable and by demonstrating appropriate responses to unacceptable behaviors. All governmental acts, whether symbolic or legislative, are subject to skeptical questioning: was the act done purely for its symbolic value or is it backed up by mutually reinforcing actions and statements? A grant of amnesty, for instance, looks very different depending on whether the official involved appears to believe in the conciliatory power of amnesty or, rather, seems complicit in the crimes that are being amnestied.

Another aspect of how government expresses itself is through education. Public education is perhaps the most important way for a new dispensation to promote its values and gain legitimacy. And yet, in many conflicted countries, it is a hugely contested issue. Important decisions need to be made about both process and substance, though the categories invariably merge. Should students from different groups be integrated or separated? What language should they be taught in? Should the pedagogic style be lecture (where students are given information to learn) or dialectic (where learners are encouraged to question and analyze and view things from multiple perspectives)? Specifically, what should be said about the recent events? Should blame be attributed to one side or should responsibility be meted out all around? Should students be taught the sources of the conflict? Should they be taught that violence is ever acceptable? How should they be taught to treat the children in their classes from a different group? Will specific attention be paid in the schools to teaching multiculturalism and diversity? And likewise, what should be said about history? Who are portrayed as being the aggressors? And who as the victims? Once again, these questions will impact on the reconciliation process if not handled carefully. Making education inclusive and subjecting history to debate signals that everyone within the polity does and should have a stake in the society and that all have a meaningful role.

One final aspect of law's expressive nature that needs to be addressed is the language itself in which the government communicates. This means not just the dialect, but also the choice of words. At the outset, it may be said that the language of reconciliation is primitive. Much of the present language is the language of division and strife, us and them, black and white. But reconciliation requires the recognition of commonalities within difference, of shades of gray, of overlapping layers of guilt and innocence.

This failure of language presents difficulties at every level. Sometimes, it is not even clear what the various groups involved should be called. South Africa can hardly move toward reconciliation, it has been suggested, if people can't decide whether to use the word "black" or "African" and debate whether the whites in South Africa are "Africans." But even once the group names have been agreed upon, the language by which we promote reconciliation needs to be better developed. As we have seen, the very word "reconciliation" is entirely ambiguous, and people may have very strong reactions to it, both positive and negative, without being clear on what, exactly, it entails. The same is true for many of the issues that are related to reconciliation, such as justice and amnesty, words whose meanings can radically change depending on the often unstated context and expectations of the policy-makers.

Many words that we use not only fail to accurately reflect reality, but distort it in a way that is peculiarly debilitative to the reconciliation process. In Germany, the law opening the Stasi files referred to Opfer (victims) and Täter (victimizers).[15] And yet it is widely recognized that few fell exclusively into one group or the other. Language's predilection for dichotomization survives, thereby entrenching in the new dispensation the divides of the old. In other ways, language can retard healing. The South African Truth and Reconciliation Commission, following the statutory mandate, used the word "victim" to describe those who had suffered gross violations of human rights. But the Commission itself noted that these individuals were more than simply victims of the apartheid system; they were survivors of it. Survivor denotes a certain inherent dignity, a condition to be proud of, while victim tends to connote failure and weakness. On the other hand, "victim" can indicate entitlement, and when, during the South African TRC process, it was seen to encompass even white soldiers who were injured while defending the apartheid system, many took issue.[16]

In some cases, the repercussions of the failure of language are felt for generations. In New Zealand, a central problem between the Maori and the European populations is what it meant for the Maori to cede their sovereignty to the whites in the Treaty of Waitangi.[17] The Europeans and the Maori clearly had, and still have, a different conception of what sovereign control over territory can mean.

One major contribution that a truth and reconciliation commission can make is to begin to develop a new language that promotes reconciliation, rather than further entrenching divisions and disputes among people. For instance, where land is disputed, there should be a way to identify it that neither condones nor rejects the competing claims. Where the preceding conflict could legitimately be described as a civil war, a rebellion, or a genocide, the commission should choose (and try to popularize) language that is neutral and acceptable to all.[18]

Reconciliation will rarely, if ever, result solely from the efforts of the government. The goal is for the public sector and the private sector to engage in a partnership, each side reinforcing the message and values of the other. The government generally has more resources, more legal authority, and greater control over the media and can therefore set the agenda; the general public often has more energy and more creativity and can therefore shape and perpetuate the agenda. To some degree, this has happened in South Africa, where the initial impetus for reconciliation came from the Mandela government but the public have also appropriated the issue and made it part of their art, theater, and public discourse. In other countries, civil society takes on the mantle of reconciliation and goads the government into it.

Where Should Reconciliation Be Promoted?

Political and fiscal capital for reconciliation should be allocated where the needs are greatest and the resources are fewest. The first priority is obviously to end fighting and conflict wherever it continues. Attention should also be given to the subfissures within a society—those conflicts that may not yet have boiled over but are nonetheless simmering. These are not the rifts that gained attention or caused civil war, but they impede the development of a truly national identity. In Bosnia, enclaves of people live as minorities within larger populations; in Iraq, minority populations live within larger minority groups, such as the Assyrians and Turkmen who live in Kurdistan; throughout the United States, Europe, and the Pacific anti-immigration sentiments are on the rise, particularly where majority populations perceive their economic opportunities to be shrinking.

Often geographic distinctions within a country can produce tensions, such as between urbanites and agrarian interests. (This has been a significant factor in many of the world's most atrocious genocides, including those in Germany, Rwanda, and Cambodia.) A government's partiality toward one group or region can also exacerbate tensions, as evidenced in Saddam's Iraq, Mobutu's Congo, and many other countries around the world. It is critical in these situations for the new government to promote genuine reconciliation with all parts of the nation and to commit to allocating resources fairly and equitably throughout the nation.

When Should Reconciliation Begin and End?

"Transitional time" has its own cadence, its own meter, which, like most other aspects of the transition, varies from place to place. In a very few places, transitional time may literally be a moment—as in Australia, where it is said that the new nation came into being at the stroke of midnight of January 1, 1901. But most nations engaging in the laborious process of reconstruction and reinvention are not so lucky. For them, the transition is a period that bridges the past and the future, of varying length and amplitude.

What happens during that time is not like what came before or what will follow—it may need its own government (the self-styled "governments of national unity and reconciliation"), its own theory of electoral legitimacy (since those organizing the elections will not have democratic legitimacy), its own interim constitution, with a particular legislative authority—the constituent assembly. Laws that are in place during the transitional period may be similar to prior laws or to the future laws, or they may not—they may be enacted for the transitional period alone, containing sunset clauses upon the closure of that period. It is in fact becoming increasingly common for incipient governments to establish interim constitutions or, as in the case of Iraq, constitutions that are subject to modification during the transitional period.

The bulk of the work of the reconciliation initiatives would normally be conducted during this period. A TRC is most effective during this period—when the wounds are still fresh, and the way forward is unclear. If the conflict is ongoing, the transitional period should be used to set down the few principles on which everyone can agree, leaving to a later date the more contentious issues. This establishes at least some foundation for consensus as the process moves forward. Over time, it is hoped, agreement will be reached on more and more issues. Thus, it is always possible to begin the reconciliation process while conflict, and even violence, still rages.

In fact, people are increasingly turning their attention to reconciliation processes initiated *before* a conflict erupts. Such efforts may dampen the tension and prevent the worst excesses. Recently developed early warning systems make it possible to target resources to situations in which conflicts are simmering, in order to prevent their reaching a full boil. Many NGOs are beginning to use such systems to identify areas where wars, genocides, and other humanitarian disasters are likely to arise.[19] By recognizing the triggers or early warning signs they can intervene before terrible violence is done and before feelings have become calcified. Among the indicators of intergroup violence are increasing polarization, frustration with normal politics leading increasing numbers to resort to violence, cultural distancing, as evidenced in part by prevalence of slurs, and decreasing social interaction between the groups. Once violence becomes accepted, however, the prospects for reconciliation dramatically decline: violence, rather than discourse, becomes the chosen method to resolve disputes. Its wounds impair people's ability to participate fully in public life, and it reduces or eliminates the common ground on which people might otherwise build a conciliatory relationship. While intervention sometimes takes the form of material aid, it may also involve more conventional processes of reconciliation such as holding mediated meetings to help reduce tensions between groups. Attention from NGOs to these pre-violence indicators is crucial, because in too many cases only violence draws attention from governments or media.

Once the violence has occurred, it is difficult to determine when the reconciliation process should start or how it ought to be undertaken. While some might say as soon as possible, in many situations, where the violence is extreme, expecting many people to feel like reconciling may be unrealistic. In Rwanda, for instance, it took the government several years after the genocide even to begin to speak of reconciliation; until then it was entirely focused on ending the violence and bringing the perpetrators to justice. Cambodia has not begun to speak of reconciliation, thirty years after the fall of the Khmer Rouge. Peru had a truth and reconciliation commission more than a decade after the end of the military regime there, and Brazil may be starting one, again, decades after its worst violence. Given the recent international attention to reconciliation, countries are being pressured to focus on reconciliation earlier and earlier, but not everyone may be able to do so, particularly where the precise demands of reconciliation remain spectral.

One solution may be to start reconciliation programs in targeted and small ways initially. As the process becomes more successful and others see the benefits, it may be possible to extend it to other areas and sectors. In the Middle East, for example, even though the tensions between Israel and its neighbors remain high, there are programs in place that try to bridge relationships between small groups of Israelis and small groups of Palestinians. Obviously those who participate are self-selecting: they are moderates and are inclined toward peacemaking, seeking to distance themselves from radicals who communicate through violence. Interfaith groups as well as youth groups and women's groups are often conduits for such reconciliation processes. These programs could be helpful in themselves and as platforms for other processes in the future.

Though reconciliation programs clearly may begin at a precise time, they don't necessarily end at any particular point in time. For instance, a memorial statue is meant to survive indefinitely; an educational program should also be expected to survive through the foreseeable future, as are economic, legal, and political reforms. A commission, however, should have a precise ending date, so that people do not lose interest in its work, and it feels obligated to provide a report and a set of recommendations while the issues are still relevant. The closing down of a commission, however, should not mean the end of reconciliation efforts. Successful truth commissions (or truth and reconciliation commissions) will set the stage for future reconciliation initiatives to be undertaken by the government and civil society; they can identify the language that can be used in future discussions, and they can set the parameters for the debate—but they should not be seen as determining the existence or extent of reconciliation projects. Indeed, the success of a commission may be measured by the extent to which it spawns successive and independent reconciliation initiatives throughout society. A commission will be considered ineffectual if its work is not reinforced and continued after its life by other institutions and agencies.

Once again, the country context is crucial. Where the cleavages are deep and people in different groups distrust or even hate each other, the reconciliation program clearly needs to continue at least until some of the hardest feelings have subsided. This may take years or even generations. Such is the case, for instance, in the former Yugoslavia, where the eruptions of the 1990s had been simmering for decades or even centuries, periodically reaching the boiling point. The same is true of many ethnic wars, as in Guatemala in the 1980s and Darfur now. When the divisions are not as deep and there has been relative peace between the parties and a strong base of commonalities, the reconciliation program need not be as long term. In many South American countries, where the violence was ideological but not class-based or ethnic, a truth commission with a precise beginning and ending date might be adequate to ensure that those countries never again slide back into military authoritarianism. In between, most countries of the world might require a set of reconciliation initiatives that can evolve with the changing needs of society as it proceeds through its transitional and post-transitional stages. For instance, a reconciliation ministry that is established primarily to assist in psychological healing may find that after a period of years it should shift its focus toward promoting tolerance through education and the arts.

It is also important to note that events may retard the process toward reconciliation at any stage, and regression can occur. This could be the result of one event, such as a killing of a member of one community by another, or even a ill-considered statement by a leader of one group intended or received as a slur against another. Public reaction to such an event will require the relevant reconciliation authorities to reconsider their approach and may require them to revert back to techniques previously discarded.

A well-designed reconciliation scheme might involve several programs, initiated in stages, according to the resources of the government and the willingness of the public to support them. As the public become more open to the idea of reconciliation (and concomitantly more committed to the new dispensation), the programs might become more ambitious, building on previous successes. Implicitly or explicitly, the organizers might develop a timetable that establishes policy goals well into the future: the elimination of all discriminatory laws within two years, a TRC report within three years, the implementation of affirmative action programs within five years, decent housing for the poorest people within ten years, and full, substantive equality of opportunity for all groups within the society within twenty years. These policy goals dovetail with the progression of reconciliation identified in Chapter 7: first "nonlethal coexistence," then a minimum of fraternity, and so on. Each of these different stages will require different organizational and institutional support. For the early stages, outside facilitators, negotiators, and monitors might be necessary. As the process continues, and reconciliation begins to seep deeper into the fabric of society, the need for international or external assistance will diminish and local coordinators will emerge and stamp the process with indigenous values. There may be certain points, however, at which international participation continues to be valuable well into the future, as for instance with election monitoring and financial support.

While some people might not have the patience to wait for a generation, most, seeing the incremental progress of the government on the smaller goals, would support the long-term plan, for the benefit of their children. A staged plan also has the benefit of not requiring those who are opposed to reconciliation to support the most demanding measures right away. If time heals all wounds, it helps the victims as well as the perpetrators to acclimate to the new social system.

Reconciliation doesn't end with a flourish. When the nation's politics become normalized, conducted in deliberative and peaceful ways, and the predominant issues are not transitional, it can be said that the reconciliation programs have done their work. This does not mean that the country or the people "have reconciled," but merely that the emphasis on reconciliation gives way to the day-to-day stuff of normal politics. Now the front pages are filled with news of budget disputes in parliament or low-level corruption or local crime. The rare intergroup offense seems anachronistic and is unwelcomed by the members of *all* the communities—it loses its power to galvanize people to more violence. The upcoming election does not spur violence or tension but carries the assumption of peaceful transfers of power. This does not mean that everyone in the country has become friends, but it does mean that the country functions with acceptably low levels of division because the population is generally committed to resolving disputes peaceably. But it is impossible to determine, ahead of time, when this will come about. And it may be necessary to have reconciliation tools at the ready indefinitely should the early warning signs of tension be detected.

The process of promoting reconciliation must be a highly differentiated one: it must be localized and contextualized, and it must concern itself with both short- and long-term consequences, and perhaps even with both practical goals and idealistic aspirations.[20] Because flexibility and responsiveness are essential elements of any reconciliation initiative, they should always contain mechanisms for self-monitoring to ensure that they continue to fulfill the needs of the nation and of the communities within it.

How Do We Achieve Reconciliation and How Do We Measure Success?

Reconciliation is frequently thought of as the bringing together of two warring factions, through dialogue or some sort of activity (sports, art, community projects) in order to encourage mutual understanding. Too often, however, people involved in the conflicts view these efforts as a zero-sum game: *if she wins, then I must be losing, and the only way to ensure that I don't lose is to prevent her from winning.* Hence the sparring over the narrative of the conflict, to ensure that each side's victims become heros and martyrs. But for the "new history" to win over the skeptics, it must "persuade not only the members of the in-group who will 'benefit' from the new interpretation, but also their 'others': those whose own history will presumably be 'diminished,' or 'tainted,' by the new narratives."[21]

The most effective way to do this is to create a metastructure that reframes the issues by encompassing the range of experience, rather than forcing people to choose between *us* and *them*. This metastructure can be a narrative that creates the story of the new nation, such as the "rainbow" nation of the New South Africa, the "rededicated" nation of post-Civil War America, or the capitalist and Europeanized nations of the former communist bloc. Or it can be political, with the new nation defined in large part by institutions of democratic consolidation: regular and open elections, a free press, and public-protecting institutions. Or it can be economic, when a transitional government embarks on large-scale economic reform, including redistribution of wealth, land reform, and broadened economic opportunities for all. The metastructure may also be legal, when a nation rewrites its constitution in a manner that is both procedurally and substantively inclusive, provides for enforcement of constitutional norms, and repeals oppressive laws that entrenched social hierarchy, replacing them with legal protections against discrimination and abuse and legally mandated access to education, employment, and other basic rights. In the South African context, one view is that the new constitution "is a response to the injustice and division of the past: it establishes constitutionalism, broadens the moral community and seeks to promote national unity and reconciliation. It is, moreover, a celebration of the diversity of the land and its people; it seeks to accommodate a plurality of values and interests; it empowers the disempowered and tries to allay the fears of whites and other minorities."[22] The most successful transitions incorporate multiple metastructures, melding social, economic, political, and legal reform to create the new nation. Yet, these do not exhaust the strategies the government and civil society must use to encourage reconciliation.

Emphasis may also need to be placed on demilitarization, demobilization, and reintegration of soldiers, refugees, perpetrators, victims, and other groups. These are important for a variety of reasons, not least of which is the need to account for the weapons that are normally in circulation during a crisis. Soldiers on any side of a conflict can contribute to destabilization, perpetuate a climate of fear, exacerbate corruption, or reignite intergroup enmity if there is no strategy in place to deal with them. That strategy should be determined not by any abstract principle but by the contingencies of the particular circumstances, with careful attention to the balance between the power of the former soldiers and the needs of the emergent society. This has been a terrible problem in and outside of Rwanda, as both the Hutu interhamwe and the Tutsi RPF continue their fighting in the refugee camps, even years after the initial genocide ended. It has been a different kind of problem in Bosnia, where former soldiers have turned into local strongmen, and in post-Saddam Iraq, where the authorities vacillate between repudiating Baathist soldiers and inviting them to participate in the country's reconstruction.[23] Their crimes are obvious, but so is their expertise. Our purpose here is not to dictate how former soldiers should be dealt with, but to emphasize the need to develop and implement, as soon as possible, a coherent policy regarding combatants.

As discussed previously, the treatment of alleged perpetrators and prisoners will also affect the reconciliation process. In Rwanda, the large number of prisoners and the slow pace of prosecutions have negatively affected reconciliation for both detainees and genocide survivors.[24] As the trials are directed only at Hutus, they are viewed, at least by some, as victors' justice, thereby hampering reconciliation. Evenhandedness is clearly a critical component of any prosecution policy. In many communities throughout the conflict-ridden world, the reintegration of those known to have committed crimes or abuses is of paramount concern. Here, the balance must be struck between allowing the perpetrators to restart their lives so that they can become productive members of their communities, without at the same time condoning their past actions.

Likewise, the government must recognize and respond to the needs of the huge numbers of displaced peoples, whose lives are invariably traumatized by the conflict, even if they had not chosen to become involved. If they are not allowed to return to communities where they can begin to lead productive lives, they remain vulnerable to further attacks by armies on every side, become financial burdens on the state, and are prevented from providing for their children; failure to take care of these people wastes millions of lives, and arrests the development not just of the current generation of refugees but of future generations as well. These already victimized populations become further traumatized by the pains of being displaced and by the economic and social dependency that such displacement breeds; eventually, many people living under such dehumanizing conditions become perpetrators or victims of economic and sexual crimes. Thus, finding solutions to internally displaced persons or refugees poses extreme challenges for nations (and for their neighbors) but can not be avoided. Without resolving such difficulties the path to reconciliation remains fraught with obstacles.

One of the most intractable difficulties in the development of reconciliation strategies is determining how to measure their success.[25] While reconciliation cannot be specifically measured, certain indicators can be identified that can help to ascertain social developments and trends in attitudes. One useful method for measuring the attainment of reconciliation is a reconciliation barometer that monitors the reconciliation process. Through regular audits of actual social, political, and economic transformation, national surveys, and ongoing anecdotal analysis of sociopolitical trends, a barometer can seek to measure how a country's reconciliation process is going. Such a tool could be used for a country or a region (within or outside a state).[26]

The South African Institute for Justice and Reconciliation has established a reconciliation barometer to audit social, political, and economic transformation regularly and to conduct biannual public opinion surveys as well as ongoing analysis of sociopolitical trends. Through these measures, it can determine the extent to which South Africa is progressing toward racial reconciliation. These measures also reveal information on the views, experiences, and expectations about reconciliation held by South Africans; they indicate the extent of tangible social, material, economic, and political transformation within the society; they help people to evaluate the performance of the country's leaders and democratic institutions regarding transformation, economic redress, and reconciliation; and they inform sociopolitical analysis of past trends and forecasts of possible future trends.[27]

The most important aim of such a tool ought to be continually to identify the impact of issues and events within a society that can impede or galvanize the reconciliation process. The architects of the system must therefore be able to recognize these issues and events and then design surveys that can accurately measure them. Comprehensive measurement should address both the historical or factual reality and the public perception. For instance, if a country is moving toward economic equality at a relatively good pace, but the perception is of intransigence and failure, the barometer should identify both of those facts, so that the government and civil society can continue to address the sources of the genuine dissatisfaction. It is also critical to measure the attitudes of the range of groups and stakeholders within a society: often the beneficiaries of the oppressive regime will view political and economic transformation as being excessive while the victims view it as insufficient. The purpose of recognizing this dissensus is obviously not to determine who is right, but to help leaders appreciate the divergent views of the citizens. Moreover, some issues may be significant in one portion of the population but do not resonate with the general public. Reparations to victims' groups, for instance, or land disputes within a particular locality may significantly impede reconciliation, but only in a discrete segment of the population; nonetheless, to the extent that these issues are important to any segment, they should be recognized as significant to the leadership of the country. Thus, both qualitative and quantitative assessments ought to be made on a regular basis to evaluate the progress or retardation of the reconciliation movement.

The overall purpose of the barometer is, of course, not to identify when reconciliation has been achieved so that all the efforts can be stopped. In most countries, it is never *finally* achieved. Rather, the purposes are to identify what measures can be taken along the way to spur the process forward and to recognize where significant impediments exist so that efforts can be taken to remove them. Certainly, if it can be shown that tensions between communities have subsided and that intergroup verbal or physical violence has diminished in frequency and intensity, the participants in the reconciliation process will have something to celebrate. Likewise, the eventuation of successive fair and free elections resulting in peaceful transfers of power and the minimization of economic oppression and inequity are measurable indicia of progressive reconciliation.

Reconciliation itself cannot be seen, but certain indicators can be gleaned. In this regard, it resembles its opposite, tension. Reconciliation exists in a society when conflicts that would previously have resulted in violence get resolved through normal politics. It can be seen when a powerful interest loses an election or a vote on an important issue and accepts defeat without threatening or engaging in violence. It can be seen when companies and schools and social functions are integrated. Or when people who had previously stood on different sides of the chasm now agree with each other on some issues of public importance and agree on the importance of participating in the debate. When the society is strong enough to withstand problems and threats without disintegrating and when these problems are seen as aberrations, rather than as symbolic of larger social problems, it can be said the society is moving toward reconciliation.

Reconciliation is never achieved but is an ongoing process that nurtures itself. When reconciliation can reproduce itself without need of law, then it has become immanent in the culture. It ceases to be the centerpiece of transitional politics and becomes the backbone of normal politics.

Notes

Chapter 1. The Lay of the Land

Epigraph. Paul Gordon Lauren, *The Evolution of International Human Rights: Visions Seen*, 2nd ed. (Philadelphia: University of Pennsylvania Press, 2003), 92, quoting observers at the Paris Peace Conference, apparently attributed to Wellington Koo. For a fuller development of these issues, including fuller references, see Jeremy Sarkin and Erin Daly, "Too Many Questions, Too Few Answers: Reconciliation in Transitional Societies," *Columbia Human Rights Law Review* 35 (2004): 661.

1. In *Algeria*, the Charter for Peace and National Reconciliation was proposed on August 15, 2005 and ratified by popular referendum the next month, despite the claims of Human Rights Watch and others that the Charter creates a climate of impunity. The *Canadian* Parliament enacted "A First Nations – Federal Crown Political Accord on the Recognition and Implementation of First Nation Governments," which recognized the need for new approaches to reconciliation. http://www.ainc-inac.gc.ca/ni/prs/m-a2005/02665afn_e.html. *El Salvador* enacted a National Reconciliation Act (Decree No. 147) in 1992. The *Lebanese* Charter of Lebanese National Reconciliation (Ta'if Accord) of October 1989 is annexed to the Constitution. *Namibia* included reconciliation in its constitution and adopted a Policy of National Reconciliation shortly after independence. http://www.grnnet.gov.na. *Nicaragua*, which had had a National Unity and Reconciliation government in the 1920s, enacted a General Amnesty and National Reconciliation Law in 1990, which was later replaced with a more particularized amnesty. *South Africa*'s Promotion of National Unity and Reconciliation Act of 1995, mandated by the provision of the same name in the 1993 Interim Constitution, created the Truth and Reconciliation Commission.

2. *Chile*'s National Commission for Truth and Reconciliation issued its final report in 1992 and was followed by a National Corporation for Reparation and Reconciliation. The Report of the *Peruvian* Truth and Reconciliation Commission was finalized in 2003 and is available at www.cverdad.org.pe. *Sierra Leone*'s Truth Commission, which was established as part of the Lome Peace Agreement, operated from 2002 until 2004 when it delivered a five-volume report. The report of the *Timor Leste* Truth, Reconciliation, and Reception Commission was delivered in December 2005 and is available online at www.etan.org. The *Moroccan* Commission of Equity and Reconciliation also completed its work in December 2005;

its report is available at www.ier.ma. The *Ghanaian* National Reconciliation Commission has not yet issued its final report, as of this writing. The *Guatemalan* Commission for Historical Clarification is of an older generation, but has been very influential. It was established in 1994 "to clarify with objectivity, equity and impartiality, the human rights violations and acts of violence connected with the armed confrontation that caused suffering among the Guatemalan people" (Prologue, Memory of Silence, Report of the Commission for Historical Clarification). The Report is available at http://shr.aaas.org/guatemala/ceh/report/english/toc. html. The *South African* Truth and Reconciliation Commission has probably been the most often copied. Its report is available at http://www.info.gov.za/otherdocs/ 2003/trc/. The United States Institute of Peace and the International Center for Transitional Justice track truth commissions on their websites.

3. These include Australia, Fiji, the Solomon Islands, and Rwanda.

4. Stephen Holmes has written that "The most pressing need in these societies was social reconciliation, not collective self-laceration." Stephen Holmes, "The End of Decommunization," in Kritz, *Transitional Justice*, 1: 116, 117.

5. For Afghanistan, see "Karzai Calls on Taliban to Join Reconciliation Process," Reuters Alertnet, November 15, 2005, http://www.alertnet.org/thenews/ newsdesk/ISL144572.htm. In his maiden speech as Zimbabwean Prime Minister in 1980, Robert Mugabe called for reconciliation and national unity. He stated that his party had no intention of victimizing the white minority and that to achieve reconciliation he wanted to "draw a line through the past." Peter Stiff, *Cry Zimbabwe: Independence—Twenty Years On* (Alberton, S.A.: Galago, 2000), 27.

6. Sean Byrne and Cynthia L. Irvin, eds., *Reconcilable Differences: Turning Points to Ethnopolitical Conflict* (West Hartford, Conn.: Kumarian Press, 2000); Louis Kriesberg, *Constructive Conflicts: From Escalation to Resolution* (Lanham, Md.: Rowman and Littlefield, 2003).

7. Lusaka Protocol, Annex 6, 1 (1999), http://www.angola.org /politics/p annex6.htm. See Jeremy Sarkin, "Democratização e justice no periodo de transição em Angola," in *Conferência internacional Angola—Direito, democracia, paz e desenvolvimento* (Luanda: Faculdade de Direito, Universidade Agostinho Neto, 2001), 203.

8. Ministry of National Reconciliation and Multi-Ethnic Affairs, Fiji Government Online Portal, http://www.fiji.gov.fj/publish/m_reconciliation.shtml.

9. Daan Bronkhorst, *Truth and Reconciliation: Obstacles and Opportunities for Human Rights* (Amsterdam: Amnesty International Dutch Section, 1995).

10. Kader Asmal, Louise Asmal, and Ronald Suresh Roberts, *Reconciliation Through Truth: A Reckoning of Apartheid's Criminal Governance* (Cape Town: David Philip, 1996), 9–11.

11. See Stephen Holmes, "Gag Rules or the Politics of Omission," in Holmes, *The Passions and Constraint: On the Theory of Liberal Democracy* (Chicago: University of Chicago Press, 1995): 202 (suggesting that silence on sensitive or controversial questions can enable groups who would otherwise divide on these issues to cooperate and work together to solve common problems).

12. Dumisa Ntsebeza, "A Lot More to Live For," in *After the TRC—Reflections on Truth and Reconciliation in South Africa*, ed. Wilmot Godfrey James and Linda Van De Vijver (Athens: Ohio University Press, 2001) 105.

13. Michael Bratton and Nicholas van de Walle, *Democratic Experiments in Africa: Regime Transitions in Comparative Perspective* (Cambridge: Cambridge University Press, 1997), 238.

14. See Josiah O. Samba, "Peace Building and Transformation from Below: Indigenous Approaches to Conflict Resolution and Reconciliation Among the

Pastoral Societies in the Borderlands of Eastern Africa," *African Journal of Conflict Resolution* 1 (2001), http://www.accord.org/za/web.nsf; Anthony N. Allott, "African Law," in *An Introduction to Legal Systems*, ed. John Duncan M. Derrett (New York: Praeger, 1968), 131, 145; Jim Consedine, *Restorative Justice: Healing the Effects of Crime*, rev. ed. (Lyttleton: Ploughshares Press, 1999), 171.

15. Timothy Murithi, "Rebuilding Social Trust in Northern Uganda," *Peace Review* 14 (2002): 291, 292–95; see also Dennis Pain, *"The Bending of Spears": Producing Consensus for Peace and Development in Northern Uganda* (London: International Alert, 1997), 2, 82–83, www.km-net.org/publications/spear.doc (describing the traditional Acholi conflict resolution process).

16. "Over fifty-six per cent of the 188 member states of the United Nations Organization made major amendments to their constitutions in the decade between 1989 and 1999, the most remarkable aspect is that of these states, at least seventy per cent adopted completely new constitutions." Heinz Klug, *Constituting Democracy: Law, Globalism and South Africa's Political Reconstruction* (Cambridge: Cambridge University Press, 2000), 12.

17. Roland Paris, *At War's End: Building Peace After Civil Conflict* (Cambridge: Cambridge University Press 2004): 1.

18. Rome Statute of the International Criminal Court, art. 5, 1, 37 I.L.M. 999, 1003 (opened for signature July 17, 1998, entered into force July 1, 2002).

19. Hannah Arendt, *Eichmann in Jerusalem* (Munich: Viking Press, 1963), 276.

20. See Tina Rosenberg, *The Haunted Land: Facing Europe's Ghosts After Communism* (New York: Random House, 1995), 44–45 (discussing the contradictions that arise in the gray zone with regard to Czechoslovakia).

21. Yasser Arafat, "The Palestinian Vision of Peace," *New York Times*, February 3, 2002, 15. He continues: "Two peoples cannot reconcile when one demands control over the other, when one refuses to treat the other as a partner in peace, when one uses the logic of power rather than the power of logic."

22. "Exiled Liberians Shun Government's Reconciliation Conference," *Perspective*, August 23, 2002, http://www.theperspective.org/survey.html (quoting Marcus Dahn, a Liberian opposition politician, explaining why he would not attend the Reconciliation Conference sponsored by President Charles Taylor).

23. See José Zalaquett, Conference Presentation, in *Dealing with the Past: Truth and Reconciliation in South Africa*, ed Alex Boraine, Janet Levy, and Ronel Sheffer (Cape Town: Institute for Democracy in South Africa, 1997), 9–10.

24. See generally Consedine, *Restorative Justice*.

25. Howard Zehr and Harry Mika, "Fundamental Concepts of Restorative Justice" (Mennonite Central Committee, 1997), http://www.ojp.gov/nij/restjust/ch1/fundamental.html

26. This point was not lost on Archbishop Tutu when he chaired the TRC. See Tutu, in Truth and Reconciliation Commission of South Africa, *Truth and Reconciliation Commission of South Africa Report* [TRC Report], 1998 (London: Macmillan Reference, 1999), 1: chap. 1, p. 82, paras. 125–31.

27. (1) Argentina: *Nunca Más*; (2) Brazil: *Nunca Mais* (Archbishop of São Paulo and World Council of Churches); (3) Uruguay: *Nunca Más* (Serpaj); (4) Paraguay: José Luis Simon G., *La dictadura de Stroessner y los derechos humanos*, and Guido Rodríguez Alcalá, *Testimonio de la represión política en Paraguay, 1975–1989*, Serie Nunca Más 1, 3 (1990). The opening chapter of the recent Timorese Commission report is similarly entitled "Chega!" (meaning stop! or no more!). *Final Report of the Commission for Reception, Truth and Reconciliation in East Timor* (CAVR), http://etan.org/news/2006/cavr.htm.

28. Jamal Benomar, "Justice After Transitions," in Kritz, *Transitional Justice*, 1: 41.

29. Chilean National Commission on Truth and Reconciliation, *Report of the Chilean National Commission on Truth and Reconciliation*, trans. Phillip E. Berryman, intro. José Zelaquatt, 2 vols. (South Bend, Ind.: University of Notre Dame Press with Center for Civil and Human Rights, Notre Dame Law School, 1993), 2: 886.

30. Peruvian National Commission on Truth and Reconciliation, General Conclusions, www.cverdad.org.pe/ingles/ifinal/conclusiones.php.

31. Priscilla B. Hayner, "Fifteen Truth Commissions—1974 to 1994: A Comparative Study," in Kritz, *Transitional Justice*, 1: 225, 235, 249.

32. There are countless examples of leaders going back on their word, trying a coup again, or requiring successive agreements; one act of "reconciliation" does not necessarily deter them from pursuing their agendas.

33. Hayner, "Fifteen Truth Commissions," 229.

34. Neil Kritz, "The Dilemmas of Transitional Justice," in Kritz, *Transitional Justice*, 1: xix, xxi.

35. George Orwell, *1984* (1949; New York: Signet Classics, 1961), 32.

36. See, e.g., Rosenberg, *The Haunted Land*, xv.

37. See Jonathan Tepperman, "Truth and Consequences," *Foreign Affairs* 81 (2002): 128, 130.

38. This argument might come out differently if one takes as a given the moral imperative to punish wrongdoing and the relative moral value of democracy.

39. Dennis Bright, "The Balancing Act: The Current Situation Regarding the Truth and Reconciliation Commission Within the Broader Political and Security Framework," paper presented at the National Workshop on the Sierra Leone Truth and Reconciliation Commission, November 16–17, 2000, 16–17.

40. See Emily H. McCarthy, "South Africa's Amnesty Process: A Viable Route Toward Truth and Reconciliation?" *Michigan Journal of Race and Law* 3 (1997): 250; Jamie Wacks, "A Proposal for Community-Based Racial Reconciliation in the United States Through Personal Stories," *Virginia Journal of Social Policy and Law* 7 (2000): 207.

41. See Peter Uvin, Informal Task Force on Conflict, Peace and Development, Co-operation, OECD Development Assistance Committee, "A Synthesis and a Commentary on the Lessons Learned from Case Studies on the Limits and Scope for the Use of Development Assistance Incentives and Disincentives for Influencing Conflict Situations," in *The Influence of Aid in Situations of Violent Conflict* (Paris: OECD, 1999).

42. Martha Minow, *Between Vengeance and Forgiveness: Facing History After Genocide and Mass Violence* (Boston: Beacon Press, 1998) (discussing the choices that societies emerging from mass violence must make when deciding how to prosecute and punish perpetrators).

43. Christopher Hibbert, *The Days of the French Revolution* (New York: Morrow Quill, 1999), 241–48. Although a few people were acquitted, to call the product of this tribunal "justice" is to stretch the meaning of that word beyond recognition.

44. Gary Jonathan Bass, *Stay the Hand of Vengeance: The Politics of War Crimes Tribunals* (Princeton, N.J.: Princeton University Press, 2000), 38; see generally Bass, 37–57 for a discussion of the European response to Napoleon after his defeat.

45. Bass, 71.

46. Bass, 71.

47. Bass, 68.

48. Bass notes that, "Forewarned by this cautionary tale, Nuremberg managed

to avoid most of the pitfalls of Leipzig; but for the ex-Yugoslavia and Rwanda tribunals currently sitting, Leipzig is all but forgotten" (60).

49. See Jeremy Sarkin, "Transitional Justice and the Prosecution Model: The Experience of Ethiopia," *Law, Democracy and Development* 2 (1999): 253, 260.

50. Samuel P. Huntington, "The Third Wave: Democratization in the Late Twentieth Century," in Kritz, *Transitional Justice*, 1: 65.

51. A. James McAdams, ed., *Transitional Justice and the Rule of Law in New Democracies* (Notre Dame, Ind.: University of Notre Dame Press, 19997), 259 n. 49.

52. Mary Albon, "Project on Justice in Times of Transition: Report of the Project's Inaugural Meeting," in Kritz, *Transitional Justice*, 1: 49.

53. Rome Statute of the International Criminal Court, opened for signature July 17, 1998, entered into force July 1, 2002 art. 12, 1, 37 I.L.M. 199, 1003.

54. Rome Statute, art. 13.

55. Alexander Solzhenitsyn, *The Gulag Archipelago, 1918–1956*, trans. Thomas P. Whitney (New York: Harper and Row, 1974), 178, quoted in Diane F. Orentlicher, "Settling Accounts: The Duty to Prosecute Human Rights Violations of a Prior Regime," *Yale Law Journal* 100 (1991): 2539.

56. José Zalaquett, "Balancing Ethical Imperatives and Political Constraints: The Dilemma of New Democracies Confronting Past Human Rights Violations," in Kritz, *Transitional Justice*, 1: 203, 204.

57. Orentlicher, "Settling Accounts," 2544 n.22, citing Emilio Fermin et al., "Dictatorship on Trial: Prosecution of Human Rights Violations in Argentina," *Yale Journal of International Law* 10 (!984): 118, 149, n. 119.

58. Martha Minow has probably been the most influential in asserting this argument. See Minow, *Between Vengeance and Forgiveness*.

59. TRC Report, 1: ch. 5, 68.

60. See Carlos S. Niño, "The Duty to Punish Past Abuses of Human Rights Put into Context: The Case of Argentina," *Yale Law Journal* 100 (1991): 2619–20.

61. In the South African context, the acquittal of the former minister of defense and his co-accused had dire consequences for the nation. See Howard Varney and Jeremy Sarkin, "Failing to Pierce the Hit Squad Veil: An Analysis of the Malan Trial," *South African Journal of Criminal Justice* 10 (1997): 141.

62. For more on the problems and issues concerning the attempt to get Botha to testify before the TRC, see Erin Daly, "Transformative Justice: Charting a Path to Reconciliation," *International Legal Perspectives* 12 (2002): 73.

63. Wole Soyinka, *The Burden of Memory, the Muse of Forgiveness* (New York: Oxford University Press, 1999), 29.

64. *Philadelphia Inquirer*, November 24, 2005.

65. ICC Statute, in Kritz, *Transitional Justice* 6, preamble.

66. See Niño, "The Duty to Punish," 2620.

67. Sven Alkalaj, in *The Sunflower: On the Possibilities and Limits of Forgiveness*, ed. Henry James Cargas and Bonny V. Fetterman (New York: Schocken Books, 1997): 101, 103 (joining 31 other commentators in a symposium response to Simon Wiesenthal's *The Sunflower*).

68. See, e.g., Todd Howland and William Calathes, "The International Criminal Tribunal, Is It Justice or Jingoism for Rwanda? A Call for Transformation," *Virginia Journal of International Law* 39 (1998): 135.

69. See Ruti Teitel, "How Are the New Democracies of the Southern Cone Dealing with the Legacy of Past Human Rights Abuses?" in Kritz, *Transitional Justice*, 1: 146–53, 147.

70. See Final Report on the Question of the Impunity of Perpetrators of Human

Rights Violations (Economic, Social and Cultural Rights) by Mr. El Hadji Guisse, Special Rapporteur, Pursuant to Sub-Commission Resolution 1996/24, UNESCOR, Commission on Human Rights Sub-Commission on Prevention of Discrimination and Protection of Minorities, 49th Sess., UN Doc. E/CN.4/Sub.2/1997/8 (1997).

71. The significance of Pinochet's continuing hold on power "is reflected in President Aylwin's pre-election statements that he intended to 'reconcile the virtue of justice with the virtue of prudence, because we know the subject touches the sensibilities of very powerful sectors of the armed forces.'" Teitel, "New Democracies of the Southern Cone," 151.

72. David Pion-Berlin, "To Prosecute or to Pardon? Human Rights Decisions in the Latin American Southern Cone," in Kritz, *Transitional Justice*, 1: 82, 95–96.

73. "Any link between nonpunishment of the crimes we are considering and democracy must be premised on a concept of amnesties which are conditional in nature and which exchange the state's discretion to punish only in return for truly compelling state interests." Teitel, "New Democracies of the Southern Cone," 150.

74. Soyinka, *Burden of Memory*, 35.

75. President Menem's amnesty of military officers was made on "reconciliation grounds" as necessary to heal the wounds of the dirty war. Teitel, "New Democracies of the Southern Cone," 149–50.

76. See Hayner, "Fifteen Truth Commissions," 226.

77. Priscilla B. Hayner, *Unspeakable Truths: Facing the Challenge of Truth Commissions* (New York: Routledge, 2001), 222–23.

78. Hayner, "Fifteen Truth Commissions," 247.

79. This is where sometimes the definition of a truth commission, or what is classified as a commission of inquiry, becomes murky.

80. Hayner, "Fifteen Truth Commissions," 254–55.

81. Cf. James L. Gibson and Helen MacDonald, "Truth—Yes, Reconciliation—Maybe: South Africans Judge the Truth and Reconciliation Process," Research Report (Rondebosch, S.A.: Institute for Justice and Reconciliation, 2001).

82. See National Unity and Reconciliation Commission, Report on the Evaluation of National Unity and Reconciliation 4 (November 23, 2001), http://129.194.252.80/catfiles/2805.pdf.

83. Ministry of National Reconciliation and Multi-Ethnic Affairs, Fiji Government Online Portal, http://www.fiji.gov.fj/publish/m reconicliation.shtml

Chapter 2. The Divided Self

Epigraph: Jorge Sutil Correa, "Dealing with Past Human Rights Violations: The Chilean Case After Dictatorship," 1992, reprinted in *Transitional Justice: How Emerging Democracies Reckon with Former Regimes*, vol. 1, *General Considerations*, ed. Neil J. Kritz (Washington, D.C.: U.S. Institute of Peace Press, 1995), 493.

1. Examples of "national unity" or "national unity and reconciliation" governments include South Africa, Angola, Burundi, Fiji, and the Solomon Islands, as well as Iraq.

2. Alison Des Forges, *Leave None to Tell the Story: Genocide in Rwanda* (New York: Human Rights Watch and International Federation of Human Rights, 1999)

3. Jeremy Sarkin, "The Development of a Human Rights Culture in South Africa," *Human Rights Quarterly* 20 (3) (August 1998): 628; see Howard Varney and Jeremy Sarkin, "Failing to Pierce the Hit Squad Veil: An Analysis of the Malan Trial,"

South African Journal of Criminal Justice 10 (1997): 141 and Jeremy Sarkin and Howard Varney, "Traditional Weapons, Cultural Expediency and the Political Conflict in South Africa: A Culture of Weapons and a Culture of Violence," *South African Journal of Criminal Justice* 6 (2) (1993): 2.

4. Chanrithy Him, *When Broken Glass Floats: Growing Up Under the Khmer Rouge* (New York: Norton, 2000), 23. See further on Cambodia Terence Duggy, "Towards a Culture of Human Rights in Cambodia," *Human Rights Quarterly* 16 (1) (1994): 82–103.

5. Pumla Gobodo-Madikizela, *A Human Being Died That Night: A South African Woman Confronts the Legacy of Apartheid* (Boston: Houghton Mifflin, 2003), 90.

6. Gobodo-Madikizela, 90.

7. CAVR, April–May 2003, update, www.easttimore-reconciliation.org, 16.

8. Judith Herman, *Trauma and Recovery: The Aftermath of Violence—From Domestic Abuse to Political Terror* (New York: Basic Books, 1997), 41.

9. See Kader Asmal, Louise Esmal, and Ronald Suresh Roberts, *Reconciliation Through Truth: A Reckoning of Apartheid's Criminal Governance* (Cape Town: David Philip, 1996), 46.

10. Mark Hay suggests that personal reconciliation occurs when there is "the recognition, acceptance and affirmation of the human and civil dignity and honour of the person. It occurs when fundamental repair to human lives, especially to the lives of those who have suffered is achieved." Mark Hay, *Ukubuyisana: Reconciliation in South Africa* (Pietermaritzburg: Cluster Publications, 1998), 114. He distinguishes between personal, social, and religious reconciliation. According to him personal reconciliation deals with the restoration of the individual's humanity, whereas social reconciliation looks to the restoring of social relationships.

11. Craig Etcheson, "The Limits of Reconciliation in Cambodia's Communes," in *Roads to Reconciliation*, ed. Elin Sklaar, Siri Gloppen, and Astri Suhrke (Lanham, Md.: Lexington Books, 2005): 206.

12. See Martha Minow, *Between Vengeance and Forgiveness: Facing History After Genocide and Mass Violence* (Boston: Beacon Press, 1998), 61–66.

13. Indeed, there is a growing literature on the value of *repression*—that is, nonintervention—as a technique for healing that has been shown to be useful in some situations.

14. The ramifications of this preference are far-reaching. Although it is not necessarily the correct method in all situations, the perspective of these nations disproportionately influences the debate on healing both because of the relative abundance of literature from these nations and because of the propensity to fund and support programs that are most consistent with their own perspective.

15. Herman, *Trauma and Recovery*, 37.

16. Studies have shown that "Torture can be transmitted cross-generationally, constituting a historical trauma." Ibrahim Aref Kira, "Torture Assessment and Treatment: The Wraparound Approach," *Traumatology* 8 (June 2002), citing Zahava Solomon, *Combat Stress Reactions: The Enduring Toll of War* (New York: Plenum Press, 1993).

17. See further Ronald Paul Hill, "Blackfellas and Whitefellas: Aboriginal Land Rights, The Mabo Decision, and the Meaning of Land," *Human Rights Quarterly* 17 (1995): 303.

18. See for example CONADEP, *Nunca Más: The Report of the Argentine National Commission on the Disappeared* (New York: Farrar, Strauss, 1986); Claudio Grossman, "Disappearances in Honduras. The Need for Direct Victim Representation," *Hastings International and Comparative Law Review* 15 (3) (1992): 363; Margaret

Popkin and Naomi Roht-Arriaza, "Truth as Justice: Investigatory Commissions," *Latin America Law and Social Inquiry* 20 (1) (1995): 79; Naomi Roht-Arriaza, "Truth Commissions and Amnesties," *Latin America: The Second Generation, Contemporary International Law Issues* 92 (1999): 313.

19. Brandon Hamber and Richard Wilson, "Symbolic Closure Through Memory, Reparation and Revenge in Post-Conflict Societies Human Rights" *Working Papers* 5 (24) (2000): 97, http://www.du.edu/humanrights/workingpapers/index.html.

20. Hamber and Wilson, 97.

21. Hamber and Wilson, 100.

22. Maria Ericson, *Reconciliation and the Search for a Shared Moral Landscape: An Exploration Based upon a Study of Northern Ireland and South Africa* (New York: Peter Lang, 2001), 86–96.

23. Herman, *Trauma and Recovery*, 156–57, noting that although her taxonomy is not universal, it echoes the "same basic concept of recovery stages" that has been seen repeatedly since the time of Janet and Freud. Another book that describes a process of healing is Michael Walzer, *On Toleration* (New Haven, Conn.: Yale University Press, 1997). Walzer describes five separate stages of toleration, from the "resigned acceptance of difference for the sake of peace" to "the enthusiastic endorsement of difference."

24. Bandon Hamber and Hugo van der Merwe, "What Is This Thing Called Reconciliation?" paper presented at the Goedgedacht Forum After the Truth and Reconciliation Commission, Goedgedacht Farm, Cape Town, March 28, 1998.

25. Political violence did, however, continue at an alarming (although reduced) rate for two or three years in the Kwa-Zulu-Natal Province.

26. Graeme Simpson, "Reconstruction and Reconciliation: Emerging from Transition," *Development in Practice* 7 (4) (1997): 475–78.

27. Laurie Nathan, *Early Warning and Action in Respect of Intra-State Crises* (Cape Town: Centre for Conflict Resolution, 1998), 17.

28. Herman, *Trauma and Recovery*, 158.

29. Alcinda Honwana, "Healing and Social Reintegration in Mozambique and Angola," in Sklaar, *Roads to Reconciliation*, 97–98.

30. Tim Kelsall, "Truth, Lies, Ritual: Preliminary Reflections on the Truth and Reconciliation Commission in Sierra Leone," *Human Rights Quarterly* 27 (2) (2005): 388.

31. Lesley Fordred, "Taming Chaos: The Dynamics of Narrative and Conflict," *Track Two* (July 1999): 1. See, for example, Jamie L. Wacks, "A Proposal for Community-Based Racial Reconciliation," *Virginia Journal of Social Policy and the Law* 7 (2000): 195; Allen Feldman, *Formations of Violence: Narratives of Body and Terror in Northern Ireland* (Chicago: University of Chicago Press, 1991); Aida Gertie, *Story Making in Bereavement* (London: Jessica Kingsley, 1992).

32. Fordred, "Taming Chaos," 3.

33. Ben Okri, "The Joys of Storytelling," in *A Way of Being Free* (London: Phoenix, 1997) quoted in Fordred, "Taming Chaos," 4.

34. Herman, *Trauma and Recovery*, 181.

35. Herman, 39.

36. Gobodo-Madikizela, *A Human Being Died*, 84. The woman ends the story with the words: "since then my son has not been his normal self."

37. One woman who testified before the Ghanaian National Reconciliation Commission explained that she "lost a job as a teacher after she had lost her voice

as a result of seven months of torture by police, military and Bureau of National Investigation (BNI) officers in 1985," Testimony of Madam Elizabeth Adongo, http://www.nrcghana.org/pressdetails.php?q=2003–01–28

38. Alex Boraine, *A Country Unmasked* (Oxford: Oxford University Press, 2000), 103, citing Alex Boraine, Janet Levy, and Ronel Sheffer, eds., *Dealing with the Past: Truth and Reconciliation in South Africa* (Cape Town: Institute for Democracy in South Africa, 1997), 31.

39. Herman, *Trauma and Recovery*, 12.

40. Herman, 183.

41. The tendency to consider story-telling as a modern-day heir to the leeches and purges used to extract the evil within is strong. Herman cautions us, however, that the purpose of story-telling is integration, not exorcism. Exorcism may be symbolically appealing, but without integration into the person's worldview, it does not amount to reconciliation.

42. Joshua M. Smyth, Nicole True, and Joy Souto, "Effects of Writing About Traumatic Experiences: The Necessity for Narrative Structuring," *Journal of Social and Clinical Psychology* 20 (2001): 161–72.

43. Joshua M. Smyth, Jill Hockemeyer, Chris Anderson, Kim Strandberg, Michelle Koch, h. Katherine O'Neill, and Susan McCammon, "Structured Writing About a Natural Disaster Buffers the Effect of Intrusive Thoughts on Negative Affect and Physical Symptoms," *Australasian Journal of Disaster and Trauma Studies* 1 (2002), http://www.massey.ac.nz/~trauma/issues/2002–1/smyth.htm

44. Jennifer L. Balint, "The Place of Law in Addressing Internal Regime Conflicts," *Law and Contemporary Problems* 59 (1996): 103, 121–22.

45. Gobodo-Madikizela, *A Human Being Died*, 85. Peter Burke notes: "A way of seeing is a way of not seeing, a way of remembering is a way of forgetting, too. If memory were only a kind of registration, a "true" memory might be possible. But memory is a process of encoding information, storing information and strategically retrieving information, and there are social, psychological, and historical influences at each point." Peter Burke, "History as Social Memory," in *Memory: History, Culture and the Mind*, ed. Thomas Butler (Oxford: Blackwell, 1989), 97, 103. Language can play a critical role in reconciliation, not only in what is said, but how it is said, what is given priority, and what is left out. Also the tone used can be critical. On the role of language, see John Paul Lederach, "Of Nets, Nails, and Problems: The Folk Language of Conflict Resolution in a Central American Setting," in *Conflict Resolution: Cross-Cultural Perspectives*, ed. Kevin Avruch, Peter W. Black, and Joseph A. Scimecca (New York: Greenwood Press, 1991), 165.

46. Gobodo-Madikizela, *A Human Being Died*, 85.

47. Dilip Simeon, "A Finer Balance: An Essay on the Possibility of Reconciliation," in *Experiments with Truth: Transitional Justice and the Processes of Reconciliation*, ed. Okwui Enzewor, Carlos Basualdo, Ute Meta Bauer, Susanne Ghez, Sarat Maharaj, Mark Nash, and Octavio Zaya, Documenta 11_Platform 2 (Ostfildern-Ruit, Germany: Hatje-Cantz, 2002), 136. We would add that it also obscures the long-term consequences of war and brutality, in terms of the psychological and material damage to human beings who witness horrific scenes, live in hiding, and grow up without parents, without schooling, without food.

48. Gobodo-Madikizela, *A Human Being Died*, 86.

49. Tim Kelsall, "Truth, Lies, Ritual: Preliminary Reflections on the Truth and Reconciliation Commission in Sierra Leone," *Human Rights Quarterly* 27 (2) (2005): 368.

50. Gobodo-Madikizela, *A Human Being Died*, 87.

51. Truth and Reconciliation Commission of South Africa, *Truth and Reconciliation Commission of South Africa Report* (TRC Report) (1998) (London: Macmillan Reference, 1999), 1: 110–14. Ruti Teitel also describes truth-telling as a kind of historical justice. Ruti Teitel, "From Dictatorship to Democracy: The Role of Transitional Justice," in *Deliberative Democracy and Human Rights*, ed. Harold Hongju Koh and Ronald C. Slye (New Haven, Conn.: Yale University Press, 1999).

52. In South Africa, for instance, an extensive process of document shredding occurred in the runup to the transition. See Verne Harris, "'They Should Have Destroyed More': The Destruction of Public Records by the South African State in the Final Years of Apartheid, 1990–1994," paper delivered at the conference The TRC: Commissioning the Past, University of the Witwatersrand, Johannesburg, June 11, 1999.

53. The Stasi destruction of files prior to November 1989 was stopped only by the occupation of their offices by citizens. See Graeme Simpson, "Truth Recovery or McCarthyism Revisited: An Evaluation of the Stasi Records Act with Reference to the South African Experience," Occasional Paper, Centre for the Study of Violence and Reconciliation, Johannesburg, February 1994.

54. A useful example is the Australian Royal Commission into Aboriginal Deaths in Custody.

55. Herman, *Trauma and Recovery*, 178.

56. This balance was not always satisfactorily maintained: some argue that the process was less victim friendly than it ought to have been, and often perpetrator-focused. See TRC Report, 5: chap. 7.

57. See, for instance, Jodi Halpern and Harvey M. Weinstein, "Rehumanizing the Other: Empathy and Reconciliation," *Human Rights Quarterly* 26 (3) (2004): 561–83.

58. Herman, *Trauma and Recovery*, 190.

59. Martha Minow has written that "the fantasy of revenge simply reverses the role of perpetrator and victim, continuing to imprison the victim in horror and degradation." Minow, *Between Violence and Forgiveness*, 13.

60. José Hobday, in *The Sunflower: On the Possibilities and Limits of Forgiveness*, ed. Henry James Cargas and Bonny V. Fetterman (New York: Schocken Books, 1997), 174.

61. Herman, *Trauma and Recovery*, 190.

62. Herman, 190.

63. Harold Kushner, in Cargas and Fetterman, *The Sunflower*, 185–86.

64. Aref Kira, "Torture Assessment and Treatment," 69–70. See also Gennady I. Chufrin and Harold H. Saunders, "A Public Peace Process," *Negotiation Journal* 9 (3) (1993): 155–77; and Ron Kraybill, "The Cycle of Reconciliation," *Conciliation Quarterly* 14 (3) (1995): 7–8.

65. Aref Kira, 72.

66. Herman, *Trauma and Recovery*.

67. Penelope Curling, "Trauma Psychology in Namibia: Notes from the Field," *Traumatology* 7 (2) (2002): 91.

68. Where clinics do not exist they should be established, with properly trained and equipped staff, to assist these people in a supportive, non-threatening environment. Where the issues concern rape and other forms of gendered violence, staff should be composed of people of the victim's gender: both men and women are disinclined to talk about sexual abuse with members of the opposite sex. Confidentiality is essential, especially for women, who often report fear of reprisal

from the perpetrator or his colleagues, or that they will be ostracized by family and friends if they discover what happened.

69. TRCs, as an aspect of national reconciliation policy, are discussed in greater detail below in the section on "National Reconciliation."

70. William Schabas, "The Relationship Between Truth Commissions and International Courts: The Case of Sierra Leone," *Human Rights Quarterly* 25 (2003): 1035, 1039.

71. As far as health professionals are concerned it has been noted that "many of the individuals implicated in complicity with human rights abuses are still working in the health sector; many even hold senior positions in professional organizations and in the public health services. Their failure to 'come clean' regarding their past activities may present the most serious obstacle to reconciliation within the profession and to the success of institutional reform directed at building a human rights culture." Jeanelle de Gruchy, Leslie London, Laurel Baldwin-Ragaven, and S. Lewin, "The Difficult Road to Truth and Reconciliation—The Health Sector Takes Its First Steps," *South African Medical Journal* 88 (1998): 975. On the violations committed, see Laurel Baldwin-Ragaven, Jeanelle de Gruchy, and Leslie London, eds., *An Ambulance of the Wrong Colour: Health Professionals, Human Rights and Ethics in South Africa* (Cape Town: University of Cape Town Press; 1999).

72. See www.ictj.org for the English translation to much of the Peruvian CVR's Final Report. See www.cverdad.org,pe for the original Spanish.

73. Priscilla B. Hayner, *Unspeakable Truths: Confronting State Terror and Atrocities* (New York: Routledge, 2001), 1.

74. Hayner, 1.

75. CAVR, April–May 2003, update, 15.

76. *Final Report of the Commission for Reception, Truth and Reconciliation in East Timor* (CAVR Report), Part 10, para. 133, http://etan.org/news/2006/cavr.htm

77. The experience of Chad, where the commission had no choice but to set up in the former prison, should constitute an example *not* to be followed. By contrast, the more recent and well funded East Timor Truth Reconciliation and Reception Commission was housed in Comarca Balide, the former political prison; however, it was significantly refurbished.

78. In Uganda, for example, approximately 20,000 children have been abducted and used as soldiers by the Lord's Resistance Army's offensive against the government.

79. Hazel Barnes and Dain Peters "Translating Trauma: Using Arts Therapies with Survivors of Violence," *South African Theatre Journal* 16 (2002): 157.

80. Another project to entertain children and ease their trauma through creative expression is the "Alive Kids" project in Kwa Mashu outside Durban, South Africa. This project established in 1994 provides music, dance, and drama workshops.

81. CAVR Report, Part 10, section 10.3.3.

82. See, for instance, the Pavarotti Music Centre, operating in Mostar, under the aegis of the NGO War Child.

83. International Fellowship for Reconciliation, http://www.ifor.org/Noticebrd /Uganda/International.pdf. See also Glencree Centre for Reconciliation in Northern Ireland (http://www.glencree-cfr.ie/index.htm); Apostles of Peace in Burundi; and Seeds of Peace, operating throughout the world (http://www.seedsofpeace.org).

Chapter 3. Reconciliation in Community

Epigraph: Desmond Tutu, *No Future Without Forgiveness: A Personal Overview of South Africa's Truth and Reconciliation Commission* (New York: Doubleday, 1999), 31.

1. *Final Report of the Commission for Reception, Truth and Reconciliation in East Timor* (CAVR Report), Part 9, para. 133, http://etan.org/news/2006/cavr.htm

2. http://www.thekingcenter.org/prog/non/Letter.pdf

3. See Donna Pankhurst, "Issues of Justice and Reconciliation in Complex Political Emergencies: Conceptualising Reconciliation, Justice and Peace," *Third World Quarterly* 20 (1) (1999): 239.

4. See Priscilla B. Hayner, *Unspeakable Truths: Confronting State Terror and Atrocities* (New York: Routledge, 2001), 156 (noting polls from 1998 indicating that TRC hadn't succeeded).

5. Maryam Kamali, "Accountability for Human Rights Violations: A Comparison of Transitional Justice in East Germany and South Africa," *Columbia Journal of Transnational Law* 40 (2001): 89; Inga Markovits, "Papers of General Interest: Selective Memory: How the Law Affects What We Remember and Forget About the Past—The Case of East Germany," *Law and Society Review* 35 (2001): 513.

6. Kamali, 115.

7. Kamali, 135.

8. Hayner, *Unspeakable Truths*, 156.

9. Tina Rosenberg, *The Haunted Land: Facing Europe's Ghosts After Communism* (New York: Random House, 1995), 372.

10. Rosenberg, 386.

11. See Chapter 1.

12. Rosenberg, 390.

13. Quoted in Martin Meredith, *Coming to Terms: South Africa's Search for Truth* (New York: Public Affairs Council, 1999), 125.

14. See Michael Humphrey, "From Terror to Trauma: Commissioning Truth for National Reconciliation," *Social Identities* 6 (1) (2000): 7.

15. Meredith, *Coming to Terms*, 218.

16. Meredith, 274–78.

17. Tim Kelsall, "Truth, Lies, Ritual: Preliminary Reflections on the Truth and Reconciliation Commission in Sierra Leone," *Human Rights Quarterly* 27 (2) (2005): 371–72.

18. See Eugene de Kock, *A Long Night's Damage: Working for the Apartheid State* (South Saxonwold, S.A.: Contra Press, 1998).

19. Pumla Gobodo-Madikizela, *A Human Being Died That Night: A South African Woman Confronts the Legacy of Apartheid* (Boston: Houghton Mifflin, 2003), 94.

20. Gobodo-Madikizela, 97.

21. See Duane Ruth-Heffelbower, " Issues and Policy: Indonesia: Out of One, Many?" *Fletcher Forum of World Affairs* 26 (2002): 223, 235.

22. Ruth-Heffelbower, 223, 235.

23. Ruth-Heffelbower, 223, 235.

24. Markovits, "Papers of General Interest," 513, 535 n. 31.

25. Markovits, 529 n. 24.

26. Pascal Khoo Thwe, *From the Land of Green Ghosts: A Burmese Odyssey* (London: HarperCollins, 2002), 251.

27. Meredith, *Coming to Terms*, 127.

28. Aniceto Guterres Lopes, Acceptance Speech for Ramon Magsasay Award for Emergent Leadership, July 30, 2003, www.easttimor-reconciliation.org

29. Hayner, *Unspeakable Truths*, 164, citing Mahmood Mamdani, "Degrees of Reconciliation and Forms of Justice: Making Sense of the African Experience," paper presented at the conference Justice or Reconciliation, Center for International Studies, University of Chicago, April 25–27, 1997, 6.

30. The ritual is described in Mark Lacey, "Victims of Uganda Atrocities Choose a Path of Forgiveness," *New York Times*, April 18, 2005, A1.

31. Kelsall, "Truth, Lies, Ritual," 388.

32. Josiah Osamba, "Peace Building and Transformation from Below: Indigenous Approaches to Conflict Resolution and Reconciliation Among the Pastoral Societies in the Borderlands of Eastern Africa," *Africa Journal in Conflict Resolution* 2 (2001): 71–86, www.accord.org.

33. Quoted in R. B. G. Choudree, "Traditions of Conflict Resolution in South Africa," *Africa Journal in Conflict Resolution* 1 (1999): 9–17, www.accord.org. See also H. O. Mšnnig, *The Pedi* (Pretoria: Van Schaik, 1967), 308.

34. Anthony N. Allott, "African Law," in *An Introduction to Legal Systems*, ed. J. Duncan M. Derrett (London: Sweet and Maxwell, 1968), 145.

35. William J. Long and Peter Brecke, *War and Reconciliation: Reason and Emotion in Conflict Resolution* (Cambridge, Mass.: MIT Press, 2003), 57.

36. Kelsall, "Truth, Lies, Ritual," 386. He further explains that "The ceremony did not signify or commemorate a reconciliation that had come about by means of telling the truth. It enacted, or brought about a reconciliation, with the help of an emotional effect unleashed by its ritual form" (389).

37. It remains to be seen whether the effort of the post-genocide government of Rwanda can encourage its citizens to see themselves as Rwandans, rather than as Hutu or Tutsi. It seems unlikely that the program will eradicate all feelings of ethnic identity, but it may be an appropriate move in the right direction to counterbalance the extremism of the 1990s.

38. Michael Walzer has made a similar point with respect to nation-states: "Among histories and cultures, the nation state is not neutral; its political apparatus is an engine for national reproduction. National groups seek statehood precisely in order to control the means of reproduction. Their members may hope for much more—they may harbor ambitions that range from political expansion and domination to economic growth and domestic flourishing. But what justifies their enterprise is the human passion for survival over time." *On Toleration* (New Haven, Conn.: Yale University Press, 1995), 25.

39. "2004 Global Refugee Trends: Overview of Refugee Populations, New Arrivals, Durable Solutions, Asylum-Seekers, Stateless and Other Persons of Concern to UNHCR" (June 17, 2005), www.unhcr.org/statistics.

40. "Ways of Reconciliation in Bosnia and Herzegovina," paper delivered at Stockholm International Forum on Justice and Reconciliation, April 23–24, 2001.

41. "Ways of Reconciliation."

42. Tone Bringa, "Reconciliation in Bosnia-Hercegovina," in *Roads to Reconciliation*, ed. Elin Skaar, Siri Gloppen, and Astri Suhrke (Lanham, Md.: Lexington Books, 2005), 194–96.

43. Craig Etcheson, "The Limits of Reconciliation in Cambodia's Communes," in Skaar, *Roads to Reconciliation*, 205.

44. Dionísio Babo-Soares, "Nahe Biti: Grassroots Reconciliation in East Timor," in Skaar, *Roads to Reconciliation*, 231–32.

45. Babo-Soares, 225–49.

46. Dennis Bright, Commissioner, Commission for the Consolidation of Peace, "The Balancing Act: The Current Situation Regarding the Truth and Reconciliation

Commission Within the Broader Political and Security Framework," paper delivered at the National Workshop on the Sierra Leone Truth and Reconciliation Commission, November 16–17, 2000. Dr. Bright quoted a report of a UN Security Council Mission to Sierra Leone: "While visiting locations outside Freetown, members of the mission were struck by the deep desire of Sierra Leoneans to lead a normal life in peace and by their commitment to that objective."

47. This is an issue that needs to be resolved, as "the numbers of people forced out of farming and becoming impoverished are likely to pose a social and ethnic threat. Rwanda's history should have shown that an ethnicization of economic activities is something to be avoided if the country wants to evolve to a more peaceful future." Saskia Van Hoyweghen, "The Urgency of Land and Agrarian Reform in Rwanda," *African Affairs* 98 (392) (1999): 353, 367.

48. UN High Commissioner for Refugees Background Paper on the Human Rights Situation in Rwanda, UNHCR Centre for Documentation and Research, Geneva, January 2000. However, if the 2003 election results for president in Rwanda, which saw Paul Kagame, a Tutsi, receive over 90 percent support, are the result of a free and fair election, which some doubt, and a true litmus test of ethnic reconciliation in a country where Tutsis make up only 15 percent of the population, then Rwanda seemingly is well on the way to reconciliation. The timing of reconciliation is always an important and very difficult issue.

49. Mark Drumbl, "Punishment, Postgenocide: From Guilt to Shame to Civis in Rwanda," *New York University Law Review* 75 (2000): 1221, 1263. See further John Braithwaite, *Crime, Shame and Reintegration* (Cambridge: Cambridge University Press, 1989).

50. "While this symbolic gesture [stigmatization] does not apply to every single individual who will return to and reside in East Timor, in encounters between both sides, the anti-independence supporters who are refugees themselves usually accept the blame." Babo-Soares, "Nahe Biti," 238.

51. The courts, 673 of which began operating in November 2002, to be followed by a further 8,258 in March 2003, are meant to speed up the trials of those accused of genocide crimes, reveal the truth about what occurred, put an end to the culture of impunity in Rwanda, reconcile the Rwandan people, and strengthen ties among them. See United Nations Office for the Coordination of Humanitarian Affairs (OCHA) Integrated Regional Information Network (IRIN), Rwanda: Special Report on Hopes for Reconciliation Under Gacaca Court System, December 4, 2002.

52. See Etcheson, "The Limits of Reconciliation," 216–18 (commenting on the difficulty of determining the genuineness of a professed change of attitude but the importance of such change as a predicate for integration).

53. CAVR Report, Part 9, para. 2

54. CAVR Report, Part 9, para. 2 n.

55. CAVR Report, Part 9, para. 3.

56. CAVR Report, Part 9, paras. 68–70, 88.

57. CAVR Report, Part 9, paras. 74–86.

58. CAVR Report, Part 9, paras. 134–35.

59. Aniceto Guterres Lopes acceptance speech, www.easttimor-reconciliation.org

60. See Iraê Baptista Lundin and António da Costa Gaspar, "Mozambique: Making Peace—The Roots of the Conflict and the Way Forward," in *Through Fire with Water: The Roots of Division and the Potential for Reconciliation in Africa*, ed. Erik Doxtader and Charles Villa-Vicencio (Rondebosch: Institute for Justice and Reconciliation, 2003), 305, 320.

61. Alcinda Honwana, "Healing and Social Reintegration in Mozambique and Angola," in Skaar, *Roads to Reconciliation*, 95–96.

62. Carola Eyber and Alastair Ager, "Conselho: Psychological Healing in Displaced Communities in Angola," *Lancet* 360 (9336) (2002): 871.

63. Derek Summerfield, "War and Mental Health: A Brief Overview," *British Medical Journal* 321 (22 July 2000): 232, 233.

64. Eyber and Ager, "Conselho." See also Marten W. De Vries, "Trauma in Cultural Perspective," in *Traumatic Stress: The Effects of Overwhelming Experience on Mind, Body, and Society*, ed. Bessel K. van der Kolk, Alexander C. McFarlane, and Lars Weiseath (New York: Guilford Press, 1996), 398.

65. United Nations Development Fund, "Community Reconciliation in Timor Leste," http://www.undp.org/erd/publicinfo/ transitions/2003_04/east%timor. htm

66. Upendra Baxi, "People's Law in India: the Hindu Society," in *Asian Indigenous Law: In Interaction with Received Law*, ed. Masaji Chiba (New York: KPI, 1986), 227.

67. Osamba, "Peace Building and Transformation," 23.

68. Osamba, 23.

69. UNDP Kosovo—Conflict Prevention and Reconciliation Initiative, www. kosovo.undp.org/Projects/CPR/cpr.htm

70. CAVR Report, Part 10, paras. 210–11.

71. The Latin American Servicio de Paz y Justicia (SERPAJ), founded by Nobel Peace Prize laureate Adolfo Pérez Esquivel, and the Dutch International Fellowship for Reconciliation are large umbrella organizations that help to coordinate the efforts of more grass-roots organizations that work directly in the community.

72. RAWA, http://rawa.fancymarketing.net/policy.htm

73. Memorial, a Russian group set up in 1987 committed to "accountability" and "fact-finding" about repression in Russia as far back as 1917, has "published several books with lists of victims' names and an analysis of state policies of repression." Hayner, *Unspeakable Truths*, 21–22.

74. Burial or reburial ceremonies play useful roles in achieving closure and at times reconciliation. See, for example, Shari Eppel, "Reburial Ceremonies for Health and Healing After State Terror in Zimbabwe," *Lancet* 360 (2002), http:// www.thelancet.com/journal/-vol360/iss9336/full/llan.360.9336.health_and_ human_rights.22432.1

75. See www.memo.ru

76. Memorial says: "Our task is not to teach society, but to find the facts, collect them, contemplate them, and to publish them. What will come of this uncomfortable truth—will it be grasped by society or [will it be rejected] with disgust— this is the choice of the historical journey. It is a no less important choice than the choice of state form or economic structure," "The Historical-Enlightenment Work of Memorial," http://www.memo.ru/eng/history/intro.htm. In this way, too, Memorial echoes the basic structure of reconciliation organizations in that it seeks to promote dialogue and greater understanding, though not to determine it.

77. www.batshalom.org. "The Jerusalem Link [is] the coordinating body of two independent women's centers: Bat Shalom—The Jerusalem Women's Action Center, located in West Jerusalem, and Marcaz al-Quds la l-Nissah—the Jerusalem Center for Women, located in East Jerusalem." The two independent women's centers are autonomous and each "takes its own national constituency as its primary responsibility." The Jerusalem Link, however, coordinates efforts between the two to run programs that promote "peace, democracy, human rights, and women's leadership."

78. *Learning Each Other's Historical Narrative: Palestinians and Israelis* (Peace Research Institute in the Middle East (preliminary draft of English translation).

79. Carlos H. Acuña and Catalina Smulovitz, "Guarding the Guardians in Argentina: Some Lessons About the Risks and Benefits of Empowering the Courts," in *Transitional Justice and the Rule of Law in New Democracies*, ed. A. James McAdams (Notre Dame, Ind.: University of Notre Dame Press, 1997), 99.

80. Art has a particular place in the resolution of trauma. In her study of the psychology of trauma, psychologist Judith Herman notes that "Given the 'iconic,' visual nature of traumatic memories, creating pictures may represent the most effective initial approach to these indelible images." Judith Herman, *Trauma and Recovery: The Aftermath of Violence—From Domestic Abuse to Political Terror* (New York: Basic Books, 1997), 177.

81. Copies of the statue have been placed in Belfast, Liverpool, Glasgow, Richmond, Virginia, and Cotonou, Benin, http://www.sbal.co.uk/sbal/pages/html/rt.php

82. Another South African artist who has explored extensively the work and processes of the Truth and Reconciliation Commission through various art forms is William Kentridge. Using various art forms, including drawing, theater, puppets, film, and printmaking, as his medium of social, political, and moral commentary, he has attempted to create an awareness of the past among South Africans and encourage them to share in this responsibility. See further Michael Godby, "William Kentridge's History of the Main Complaint—Narrative, History, Truth," in *Negotiating the Past: The Making of Memory in South Africa*, ed. Sarah Nuttall and Carli Coetzee (Cape Town: Oxford University Press, 1998), 100–111. See also Jane Taylor, *Ubu and the Truth Commission* (Cape Town: University of Cape Town Press, 1998); and L. Stafford, "Arts Achiever of the Century: William Kentridge—Haunting Imagery to Talk About," *Financial Mail Millennium Issue*, December 17, 1999.

83. http://www.legacy-project.org/arts/display.html?ID'3

84. http://www.msnepal.org/reports_pubs/conflict_theatre/2.htm

85. http://www.playbacknet.org

86. *Wajibu, a Journal of Social and Religious Concern* 15 (2000), http://www.peacelink.it/wajibu/10_issue/p2.html

87. On the media, see further Anthea Garman, "The Media and the TRC: Fragments of the Truth," *Rhodes Journalism Review* (November 1997): 30; Simon Lewin, "The TRC and the Media: The Next Agenda," *Rhodes Journalism Review* (March 1990): 27. On the churches, see, for example, James Cochrane, John W. de Gruchy, and Stephen Martin, eds., *Facing the Truth: South African Faith Communities and the Truth and Reconciliation Commission* (Cape Town: David Philip, 1999); Carmel Rickard, "Church and State: The Faith Community and the TRC," *Indicator South Africa* 16 (1) (Autumn 1999): 42. On the medical and legal professions, see Jeanelle de Gruchy, Leslie London, Laurel Baldwin-Ragaven, and S. Lewin, "The Difficult Road to Truth and Reconciliation—The Health Sector Takes Its First Steps," *South Africa Medical Journal* 88 (1998): 975; David Dyzenhaus, *Judging the Judges and Ourselves: Truth, Reconciliation and the Apartheid Legal Order* (Oxford: Hart, 1998). On business, see Nicoli Nattrass, "The Truth and Reconciliation Commission on Business and Apartheid: A Critical Evaluation," *African Affairs* 98 (1999): 373–91.

88. See Tanya Goodman and Max Price, "Continuing the TRC Project: The Use of Internal Reconciliation Commissions to Facilitate Organisational Transformation—The Case of the Wits Health Sciences Faculty," paper presented at the conference The TRC: Commissioning the Past, University of the Witwatersrand, Johannesburg, June 11, 1999; Vaness Johnstone, "UCT Apologises for Role

in Biko's Death: Department Begins Reconciliation Process," *Cape Argus:* Wednesday, June 6, 2001, 8; David Dyzenhaus, "To Tell or Not to Tell: MASA Apologises for Past Apartheid Behavior," *South African Labour-Business Monitor* 1 (1) (5 July 1995): 12.

89. Eric K. Yamamoto, *Interracial Justice: Conflict and Reconciliation in Post-Civil Rights America* (New York: New York University Press, 1999).

90. Aetna, the largest insurance company in the United States, issued an apology in March 2000. See "Aetna Statement on Pre-Civil War Insurance Policies," http://www.aetna.com/news/2000/pr_20000310.htm. Aetna subsequently announced that it would contribute money to scholarships for African Americans, but the total contributed has to date been relatively minimal. See http://www.aetna.com/diversity/corporate_philanthropy.html (noting contributions totaling $32,000 over two years for medical school scholarships for African Americans).

91. There have been calls for the U.S. government to issue a general apology for the race discrimination and racism pervasive throughout the country. See Jamie L. Wacks, "A Proposal for Community-Based Racial Reconciliation in the United States Through Personal Stories," *Virginia Journal of Social Policy and the Law* 7 (2000): 195, 233.

92. Madeleine Davis, "Is Spain Recovering Its Memory? Breaking the *Pacto del Olvido*," *Human Rights Quarterly* 27 (3) (2005): 858, 873–74.

93. Jeffrey C. Isaac, "1989 and the Future of Democracy," in *Between Past and Future: The Revolutions of 1989 and Their Aftermath*, ed. Sorin Antohi and Vladimir Tismaneanu (Budapest: Central European University Press, 2000), 55.

Chapter 4. National and International Reconciliation

Epigraph: Michael Ignatieff, *The Warrior's Honor: Ethnic War and the Modern Conscience* (London: Chatto and Windus 1998), 169.

1. Peter Maas, *Love Thy Neighbour—A Story of War* (London: Papermac 1996), 121.

2. *Report of the Chilean National Commission on Truth and Reconciliation* (Notre Dame, Ind.: University of Notre Dame Press, 1993), 1: 48ff.

3. Nicholas Haysom, "Nation Building and Constitution Making," paper on file with authors.

4. Haysom.

5. This may need to change as ethnic polarization and conflict increase as backlash to immigration and contractual workers coming in from other regions, as the 2005 race riots in France.

6. Jacques Rupnick, "On Two Models of Exit from Communism," in *Between Past and Future: The Revolutions of 1989 and Their Aftermath*, ed. Sorin Antohi and Vladimir Tismaneanu (Budapest: Central European University Press, 2000), 20–21.

7. Ronald J. Fisher, "Social-Psychological Processes in Interactive Conflict Analysis and Reconciliation," in *Conflict Resolution: Process, Dynamics and Structure*, ed. Jeong Ho-Won (Aldershot: Ashgate, 1999), 83 (quoting Louis Kriesberg).

8. Karol Soltan, "1989 as Rebirth, " in Antohi, *The Revolutions*, 28.

9. Brandon Hamber and Richard Wilson, "Symbolic Closure Through Memory, Reparation and Revenge in Post-Conflict Societies," Human Rights Working Paper 5, April 24, 2000, http://www.du.edu/humanrights/workingpapers/index.html

10. Sumantra Bose, *Bosnia After Dayton: Nationalist Partition and International Intervention* (New York: Oxford University Press, 2000), 127–28.

11. The powerful and symbolic image of a country's flag is captured by Theodore Herzl, who once said: "You might ask shockingly: 'A flag? What's that? A stick with a rag on it?' No sir, a flag is much more. With a flag you lead men, for a flag, men live and die. In fact, it is the only thing for which they are ready to die in masses, if you train them for it. Believe me, the politics of an entire people . . . can be manipulated only through the imponderables that float in the air." Quoted in Sanford Levinson, "They Whisper: Reflections on Flags, Monuments, and State Holidays, and the Construction of Social Meaning in a Multicultural Society," *Chicago-Kent Law Review* 70 (1995): 1079, 1118. A flag may also be divisive, such as the Confederate flag in the U.S. or the Croatian flag in Bosnia.

12. Lithuania has two independence days, commemorating its independence first from the Russian Czar and then from the Soviet communists. Belgium has several national holidays, each recognizing a constituent nation. In South Africa, Reconciliation Day is celebrated on the day previously known as the Day of the Vow, a hallowed day for white Afrikaners who had vowed on December 16, 1838 that, if they defeated thousands of Zulus with whom they were in battle, they would religiously observe that day. Not coincidentally, the first meeting of the Commissioners of the South African TRC took place on this day in 1995. Inga Markovits has noted a similar phenomenon in postcommunist Germany, where the Bundestag uses June 17 as a symbolic date. On that date in 1953, the Soviets crushed an uprising of East German workers. Under the present regime, the Bundestag accepted the report of the first Enquete Commission to Parliament on that date in 1994 and the second report on that date in 1998, thereby "claim[ing] heirship to the early East German freedom fighters." Inga Markovits,"Papers of General Interest: Selective Memory: How the Law Affects What We Remember and Forget About the Past—The Case of East Germany," *Law and Society Review* 35 (2001): 519–20. In several of the former Soviet republics, Reconciliation Day is celebrated November 7, the day that used to honor the Great October Socialist Revolution of 1917.

13. In another Bosnian town, non-Bosniak residents complained to the federal ombudsmen that the street signs not only reflected Muslim personages, but were written in Cyrillic and, furthermore, were all green, the color associated with the Muslim minority.

14. Brandon Hamber, "Strategies for Dealing with past Political Violence in Northern Ireland, South Africa and Countries in Transition," paper delivered at the conference, The TRC: Commissioning the Past, University of the Witwatersrand, Johannesburg, June 11, 1999, 17.

15. Jakob Finci, "Revenge in the Making," *The Courier* (UNESCO), May 2001, http://www.unesco.org/courier/2001_05/uk/droits2.htm

16. Finci.

17. This is a particularly widely held view in South Africa and has been adopted by Richard Goldstone (see *For Humanity: Reflections of a War Crime Investigator* [New Haven, Conn.: Yale University Press, 2000] and Archbishop Tutu (see TRC Report, quoting Michael Ignatieff, 1: 33).

18. In forging national narratives, governments may indeed have motives other than the altruistic pursuit of reconciliation. For instance, people in the government may be trying to solidify their own positions in power. A report in this case is more likely to emphasize politics over nonpartisan truth, and is more likely to feature the exploits of the ruling class (and the elites). Alternatively, the government may seek to lionize certain members of the population, such as those who resisted or fought for the insurrection (depending on which side the government represents). The planned Bosnian TRC is expected to identify not just the perpetrators

and the victims of gross abuses, but the heroes or champions of human rights as well those who saved, helped, or fought against the rampages.

19. Priscilla Hayner, *Unspeakable Truths : Confronting State Terror and Atrocities* (New York: Routledge, 2001), 55. See further Victor De Waal, *The Politics of Reconciliation: Zimbabwe's First Decade* (London/Cape Town: Hurst / David Philip, 1990).

20. "Ghana: Focus on National Reconciliation Process," *Nigeria Journal Com,* March 4, 2003, http://www.nigeriajournal.com/ghanarecon.html

21. *Final Report of the Commission for Reception, Truth and Reconciliation in East Timor* (CAVR Report), Part 1, p. 36, para. 142; p. 34, para. 129, http://etan.org/news/2006/cavr.htm

22. Jeremy Sarkin, "The Necessity and Challenges of a Truth and Reconciliation Commission in Rwanda," *Human Rights Quarterly* 21 (3) (August 1999): 667–823.

23. Hayner, *Unspeakable Truths,* 52.

24. Hayner, 55.

25. Cited in Hayner, 54.

26. Hayner, 40.

27. Hayner, 37.

28. President Mandela said: "I therefore take this opportunity to say that I accept the report as it is, with all its imperfections, as an aid that the TRC has given to us to help reconcile and build our nation." South African Press Association, "Truth Report Handed to Mandela," October 28, 1998, http://www.doj.gov.za/trc/media/1998/9810/s981029r.htm

29. Statement of Reconciliation issued by Canadian Government, January 1998.

30. Rose Weston, "Facing the Past, Facing the Future: Applying the Truth Commission Model to the Historic Treatment of Native Americans in the United States," *Arizona Journal of International and Comparative Law* 18 (2001): 1017, 1032.

31. In regard to achieving reconciliation the Council identified communication, consultation, cooperation, and community action as methods "for achieving each of the three major steps toward reconciliation: first, looking together at the issues and recognizing the need for change; second, looking forward and agreeing to make the needed changes; and third, implementing change." Weston, "Facing the Past," 1034.

32. Aryeh Neier, "What Should Be Done About the Guilty?" in *Transitional Justice: How Emerging Democracies Reckon with Former Regimes,* vol. 1, *General Considerations,* ed. Neil J. Kritz (Washington, D.C.: U.S. Institute of Peace Press, 1995), 181, noting that "the disclosure of the truth by the Sabato commission helped to create a climate of opinion that supported the government's prosecutions."

33. See William Schabas, "The Relationship Between Truth Commissions and International Courts: The Case of Sierra Leone," *Human Rights Quarterly* 25 (2003): 1045, noting that "The view was frequently expressed by both the Secretary-General and the Security Council that the Truth and Reconciliation Commission was probably a better venue for dealing with child or juvenile offenders."

34. Schabas, 1038, citing Bishop Joseph C. Humper, Chair of the Sierra Leone Truth and Reconciliation Commission.

35. Richard Goldstone, "Ethnic Reconciliation Needs the Help of a Truth Commission," *International Herald Tribune,* October 24, 1998, quoted in Avril McDonald, "The Right to Truth, Justice, and a Remedy for African Victims of Serious Violations of International Humanitarian Law," *Law Democracy and Development* 2 (1999): 1, 5.

36. Schabas, "The Relationship Between Truth Commissions and International Courts," 1039 and n.15.

37. The ten-year ICTY budget totaled $966,683,622, with annual budgets from $276,000 (1993) and $10,800,000 (1994) to $271,854,600 (2004–5 approved). Coalition for International Justice, http://www.cij.org/index.cfm?fuseaction=faqs&tribunalID=1#q7

38. Graeme Simpson, "Truth, Dare or Promise: Civil Society and the Proposed Commission on Truth and Reconciliation," paper presented at Making Ends Meet: Reconciliation and Reconstruction in South Africa, Centre for the Study of Violence and Reconciliation, Johannesburg, August 18, 1994.

39. David R. Black and John Nauright, *Rugby and the South African Nation: Sport, Cultures, Politics and Power in the Old and New South Africas* (Manchester: Manchester University Press, 1998), 122.

40. Indeed, "sport . . . often provides a uniquely effective medium for inculcating national feelings; it provides a form of symbolic action which states the case for the nation itself," cited in Stephanus Muller, "Exploring the Aesthetics of Reconciliation: Rugby and the South African National Anthem," *South African Journal of Musicology* 21 (2001): 19, 26–27, http://www.ajol.info/viewarticle.php?id=1533

41. Fanie du Toit, ed., *Learning to Live Together* (Rondebosch: Institute for Justice and Reconciliation, 2003), 141.

42. Du Toit, 141.

43. A useful initiative in the national setting, although set up and run by an international organization is the ICTR Information and Documentation Center, known as Umusanzu mu Bwiyunge (contribution to reconciliation) in the Kinyarwanda language of Rwanda. It was established in Rwanda's capital in September 2000. The Center provides information on the work of the ICTR as well as a research library service. See Kingsley Chiedu Moghalu, "The Evolving Architecture of International Law: Image and Reality of War Crimes Justice: External Perceptions of the International Criminal Tribunal for Rwanda," *Fletcher Forum of World Affairs* 26 (2002): 21 n. 3. See also Aleksandar Fatic, *Reconciliation Via the War Crimes Tribunal?* (Burlington, Vt.: Ashgate, 2000), 81.

44. http://www.commerce.gov.sb/Gov/PresentGov.html#unit

45. Reprinted in *International Legal Materials* 74 (1974): 501.

46. Para 14–15, *International Legal Materials* 74 (1974): 501, 504–5.

47. Thus United Nations Peace-Building Support Office in the Central African Republic (BONUCA), is assisting that country's return to democracy. See Office for the Coordination of Humanitarian Affairs Integrated Regional Information Network Reports, September 2003.

48. Stephen Kinzer, "Courting Europe, Turkey Tries Some Soul Cleansing," *New York Times*, December 4, 2005, A4; Ayse Betul Celik, "Transnationalization of Human Rights Norms and Its Impact on Internally Displaced Kurds," *Human Rights Quarterly* 27 (3) (2005): 969–97; Norimitsu Onishi, "Koizumi Apologizes for War; Embraces China and South Korea," *New York Times*, August 16, 2005.

49. Between 1904 and 1908, German policy in Namibia was to shoot indigenous people on sight; those who were not killed were put in camps and used as sexual slaves, http://www.newera.com.na/archives.php?id=2697; 8623

50. Jeremy Sarkin, "Reparations for Colonial Genocide" (forthcoming)

51. Human Rights Watch Press Statement, "Indonesia's Court for East Timor a 'Whitewash'," December 20, 2002, http://www.hrw.org/press/2002/12/etimor1220.htm

52. Human Rights Watch Press Statement.

53. In addition, the United Nations and the independent Timorese government

have established processes to promote transitional justice. The United Nations Transitional Administration in East Timor (UNTAET) created Special Panels for Serious Crimes in the Dili District Court; this is a hybrid or mixed international-national judicial process to investigate and prosecute those suspected of crimes against humanity and other serious crimes that took place in East Timor before its independence. Finally, the government also established the Commission for Reception, Truth and Reconciliation (CAVR), which operated along grassroots reconciliation initiatives promoting reintegration and produced its final report in 2005.

54. Human Rights Watch Press Statement.

55. Human Rights Watch "Justice Denied for East Timor," http://www.hrw.org/backgrounder/asia/timor/etimor1202bg.htm

56. M. Bossuyt and S. Van de Ginste, "The Issue of Reparation for Slavery and Colonialism and the Durban World Conference Against Racism," *Human Rights Law Journal* (2001): 22, 25.

57. United Nations A, General Assembly Distr., General, A/ Conf. 189/YY, September 24, 2001, Original: English, World Conference Against Racism, Racial Discrimination, Xenophobia and Related Intolerance, Durban, August 31–September 8, 2001, Adopted September 8, 2001 in Durban, South Africa (final version released December 31, 2001).

58. "Prevent Genocide," *International News Monitor*, October 2002.

59. Will Kymlicka, *Multicultural Citizenship* (Oxford: Oxford University Press, 1995), 58.

60. Kymlicka notes that "Protecting the rights of a national minority under these circumstances can become a pretext for territorial aggression by the self-proclaimed protector state" (57), citing among his examples the Germany's invasions of Czechoslovakia and Poland under the pretext of protecting ethnic Germans who lived in those countries.

61. Bose, *Bosnia After Dayton*, 260–64, citing Rogers Brubaker, *Nationalism Reframed: Nationhood and the National Question in the New Europe* (Cambridge: Cambridge University Press, 1996).

62. Miriam J. Aukerman, "Extraordinary Evil, Ordinary Crime: A Framework for Understanding Transitional Justice," *Harvard Human Rights Journal* 15 (2002): 74 n. 202, quoting Babacar Sine, as quoted in Norimitsu Onishi, "An African Dictator Faces Trial in His Place of Refuge," *New York Times*, March 1, 2000, A3.

63. The Timorese Report, for instance, places blame for human rights abuses during its prolonged fight for independence not only on the United States and the Soviet Union, but also on Britain, Australia, Japan, France, China, the Vatican, and the United Nations (especially the Security Council), charging them with indifference and complicity in failing to stop Indonesian oppression and crimes against humanity over 24 years. CAVR Report, Executive Summary, 50–51, http://etan.org/news/2006/cavr.htm

Chapter 5. The Costs of Reconciliation

Epigraph: Laurie Nathan, "Healing Divided Societies: Sharing Lessons and Experiences," in *Rwanda and South Africa in Dialogue: Addressing the Legacies of Genocide and a Crime Against Humanity*, ed. Charles Villa-Vicencio and Tyrone Savage (Rondebosch: Institute for Justice and Reconciliation, 2001): 125.

1. Jonathan Allen, "Balancing Justice and Social Unity: Political Theory and

the Idea of a Truth and Reconciliation Commission," *University of Toronto Law Journal* 49 (3) (1999): 315.

2. RAWA Communiqué on Universal Human Rights Day, December 10, 2004, http://www.rawa.org/dec10–04e.htm

3. Graeme Simpson, "Rebuilding Fractured Societies: Reconstruction, Reconciliation and the Changing Nature of Violence—Some Self-Critical Insights from Post-Apartheid South Africa," paper commissioned by United Nations Development Program, http://www.csvr.org.za

4. Aryeh Neier, "What Should Be Done About the Guilty?" in *Transitional Justice: How Emerging Democracies Reckon with Former Regimes*, vol. 1, *General Considerations*, ed. Neil J. Kritz (Washington, D.C.: U.S. Institute of Peace Press, 1995), 35.

5. Chile healed its society after the fall of a seventeen-year dictatorship, not through trials, but rather through the use of a truth commission, and a limited one at that.

6. Stuart Wilson, "The Myth of Restorative Justice: Truth, Reconciliation and the Ethics of Amnesty," *South African Journal on Human Rights* 17 (4) (2001): 531, 535.

7. Susan Dwyer, "Reconciliation for Realists," *Ethics and International Affairs* 13 (1999): 81, 89.

8. Allen, "Balancing Justice and Social Unity," 315.

9. Almost all the deaths, 16,000 between 1990 and 1994, were of black people, mostly in the context of political violence between the two principal black parties, the ANC and Inkatha..

10. "The pursuit of justice does not presuppose a retributive view of punishment. It means only bringing individuals to trial who are credibly alleged to have committed crimes and are seeking a legal verdict and an appropriate punishment if they are found guilty." Amy Gutmann and Dennis Thompson, "The Moral Foundations of Truth Commissions," in *Truth v. Justice: The Morality of Truth Commissions*, ed. Robert Rotberg and Dennis Thompson (Princeton, N.J.: Princeton University Press, 2000), 22.

11. Priscilla B. Hayner, *Unspeakable Truths: Confronting State Terror and Atrocities* (New York: Routledge, 2001), 160.

12. It was also noted that the word "reconciliation" only entered the government's vocabulary five or six years after the genocide and then only in the context of reconciliation for victims. See Jeremy Sarkin, "The Tension Between Justice and Reconciliation in Rwanda: Politics, Human Rights, Due Process and the Role of the Gacaca Courts in Dealing with the Genocide," *Journal of African Law* 45 (2) (2001): 143–72.

13. Russell Botman, "Justice That Restores: How Reparation Must Be Made," *Track Two* 6 (3, 4) (1977), http://ccrweb.ccr.uct.ac.za/archive/two/6_34/p17_justice.html

14. "Letting go of these emotions, if there is nothing new in the victim's life to strengthen her or him, makes the victim feel exposed and vulnerable again" because, Gobodo-Madikizela surmises, "the emotions associated with the trauma become part of the identity of the one who has suffered loss." Pumla Gobodo-Madikizela, *A Human Being Died That Night: A South African Woman Confronts the Legacy of Apartheid* (Boston: Houghton Mifflin, 2003), 97, 96.

15. Wole Soyinka, *The Burden of Memory, the Muse of Forgiveness* (New York: Oxford University Press, 1999), 31.

16. Soyinka, 35.

17. Hayner, *Unspeakable Truths*, 160, quoting journalist Horacio Verbitsky.

18. Diane F. Orentlicher, "Settling Accounts: The Duty to Prosecute Human Rights Violations of a Prior Regime," in Kritz, *Transitional Justice*, 1: 375–416; Ruti Teitel, "How Are the New Democracies of the Southern Cone Dealing with the Legacy of Past Human Rights Abuses?" in Kritz, *Transitional Justice*, 1: 146–53, 150.

19. See also Jeremy Sarkin, *Carrots and Sticks: The TRC and the South African Amnesty Process* (Antwerp: Intersentia, 2004).

20. See further Paul Seils, "Reconciliation in Guatemala: the Role of Intelligent Justice," *Race and Class* 44 (1) (2002): 33, 59.

21. As Miriam Aukerman has said, "if reconciliation depends on forgiveness, and forgiveness depends on punishment, does the impossibility of proportionate retribution in the context of extraordinary evil render reconciliation impossible?" "Extraordinary Evil, Ordinary Crime: A Framework for Understanding Transitional Justice," *Harvard Human Rights Journal* 15 (2002): 82.

22. See Kader Asmal, Louise Asmal, and Ronald Suresh Roberts, *Reconciliation Through Truth: A Reckoning of Apartheid's Criminal Governance* (Cape Town: Mayibuye Books, 1997), 46.

23. Gobodo-Madikizela, *A Human Being Died*, 89.

24. Emilios Christodoulidis, "Law's Immemorial," in *Lethe's Law: Justice, Law and Ethics in Reconciliation*, ed. Emilios Christodoulidis and Scott Veitch (Oxford: Hart, 2001) 227, citing Jean Amery.

25. Gobodo-Madikizela, *A Human Being Died*, 89

26. Suzannah Linton, "Reconciliation in Cambodia," for Documentation Center for Cambodia (DC-Cam) (2002), http://www.dccam.org/National%20 reconciliation/chart.pdf, reprinted and analyzed in Suzannah Linton, *Reconciliation in Cambodia* (Phnom Penh: Documentation Center of Cambodia, 2004).

27. Roger Errera, quoted in Luc Huyse, "Justice After Transition: On the Choices Successor Elites Make in Dealing with the Past," in Kritz, *Transitional Justice*, 115.

28. Soyinka, *The Burden of Memory*, 14 (emphasis original)

29. Milan Kundera, *The Book of Laughter and Forgetting* (New York: Harper-Perennial 1994), 2–3.

30. Huyse, "Justice After Transition," 109, citing Ali Mazrui, "Conflict Resolution and Social Justice in the Africa of Tomorrow: In Search of New Institutions," *Présence Africaine* 308 (28) (1983): 127–28.

31. Christodoulidis, "Law's Immemorial," 209–11.

32. See *Final Report of the Commission for Reception, Truth and Reconciliation in East Timor* (CAVR), February 19, 2003, www.easttimor-reconciliation.org.

33. Jorge Correa Sutil, "'No Victorious Army Has Ever Been Prosecuted . . . ': The Unsettled Story of Transitional Justice in Chile," in *Transitional Justice and the Rule of Law in New Democracies*, ed. A. James McAdams (Notre Dame, Ind. : University of Notre Dame Press, 1997), 1 n. 13, quoting Fernando Matthei, commander in chief of the Air Force, in an October 22, 1989, interview in *El Mercurio*.

34. Elizabeth Kiss, "Moral Ambition Within and Beyond Political Constraints: Reflections on Restorative Justice," in Rotberg and Thompson, *Truth v. Justice*, 71, quoting Amos Elon, "The Politics of Memory," *New York Review of Books*, October 7, 1995,

35. At its best, "reconciliation is neither the perpetual nurturing of grievance nor the cultivation of amnesia. It requires transcendence, which implies preservation as well as negation (as in rising above, leaving behind)." Dilip Simeon, "A Finer Balance: An Essay on the Possibility of Reconciliation," in *Experiments with Truth: Transitional Justice and the Processes of Reconciliation*, ed. Okwui Enwezor,

Carlos Basualdo, Ute Meta Bauer, Susanne Ghez, Sarat Maharaj, Mark Nash, and Octavio Zaya, Documenta 11_Platform 2 (Ostfildern-Ruit, Germany: Hatje-Cantz, 2002), 147.

36. Sandra Day O'Connor, Foreword to Richard Goldstone, *For Humanity: Reflections of a War Crime Investigator* (New Haven, Conn.: Yale University Press, 2000).

37. Truth and Reconciliation Commission of South Africa, *Truth and Reconciliation Commission of South Africa Report*, Foreword by Archbishop D. M. Tutu, 1998 (London: Macmillan Reference, 1999), 1: 5 .

38. Chilean National Commission on Truth and Reconciliation, *Report of the Chilean National Commission on Truth and Reconciliation*, trans. Phillip E. Berryman, intro. José Zelaquatt, 2 vols. (South Bend, Ind.: University of Notre Dame Press with Center for Civil and Human Rights, Notre Dame Law School, 1993), 1: 32.

39. Timothy Garton Ash, "The Truth About Dictatorship," *New York Review of Books*, February 19, 1998, 40.

40. "Cambodia Keeps Lid on Dark Past," *Christian Science Monitor*, http://www.csmonitor.com/2003/0212/p06s01-woap.html; see also Documentation Center for Cambodia (DC-Cam), "Genocide Education": "By 2002, coverage of the regime had disappeared from junior and senior high school texts (the section on modern history was torn out as a result of an intra-government dispute over the treatment of the 1993 elections). No new texts were published in 2003 or 2004," http://www.dccam.org/Projects/Genocide/Genocide_Education.htm

41. Turkey's best-selling novelist, Orhan Pamuk, went on trial December 16, 2005, for having said to a Swiss magazine, "One million Armenians and 30,000 Kurds were killed in these lands and nobody but me dares talk about it." The trial caused Turkey significant embarrassment as it negotiates entry into the European Union. Olli Rehn, European Union enlargement commissioner, who oversees Turkey's entry talks with the bloc, said that the trial was a "litmus test whether Turkey is seriously committed to the freedom of expression and reforms that enhance the rule of law." Reuters, "Popular Turkish Novelist on Trial for Speaking of Armenian Genocide," *New York Times*, December 16, 2005, A10. One month later, the Turkish court dismissed all charges against Pamuk, though on a procedural technicality, thus leaving open the question of Turkey's commitment to free speech and open debate. "The Way Forward for Turkey," Editorial, *New York Times*, January 31, 2006.

42. Compare also the Czech and Slovak anthems. During the twentieth century they were joined in one song, but since 1992 each country has taken only the section that refers to it. The Czech Republic: "Where is my home, where is my home? / Water roars across the meadows, / Pinewoods rustle among crags, / The garden is glorious with spring blossom, / Paradise on earth it is to see. / And this is that beautiful land, / The Czech land, my home, / The Czech land, my home." Slovakia: "There is lightning over the Tatra / thunderclaps are striking ferociously. / Let us stop them, brothers, / (you will see that) they will disappear, / the Slovaks will revive. / This, our Slovakia / has long been fast asleep. / But the lightning of the thunder / is rousing it / to wake up" The South African national anthem takes on the compromises and inclusivity that characterize that transition. The anthem now combines two stanzas from the old apartheid anthem (one in English and one in Afrikaans) and two stanzas of the anthem used by those who were their opponents in two indigenous languages. Thus, there is now one anthem in four languages containing half from each of the two different versions. (All national anthem lyrics from www.wikipedia.org.)

43. Sumantra Bose, *Bosnia After Dayton: Nationalist Partition and International Intervention* (New York: Oxford University Press, 2000), 128.

44. Greg Duly, "Creating a Violence-Free Society: The Case for Rwanda," *Journal of Humanitarian Assistance*, http://www.jha.ac/greatlakes/b002.htm, citing Jeff Drumtra (1997); see also Jeff Drumtra, *Life After Death: Suspicion and Reintegration in Post-Genocide Rwanda* (Washington, D.C.: U. S. Committee for Refugees, 1998).

45. Christodoulidis, "Law's Immemorial," 214, argues that the present "pre-structures" the past by the questions it asks (the law being one instantiation of the present doing this). In every case, he says, "the recovered past can be nothing but reconciled with the present" (218). In each case, in the name of coherence, legal memory calls up events as relevant to its current needs of classification and as relevant to expectations of how events will be classified in the future. . . . The certainty of expectations and the exigencies of the rule of law dictate a minimization of ambiguity here that looks both forward and backward: unambiguous future, unambiguous past, so far as possible. Law is after all about stabilizing social expectations.

46. "After all, what future does not seek its point of departure in some origin in the past?" Christodoulidis, 207. If the rupture/transition is significant, the new future does not need to seek its origin in the past.

47. Michael Gordon, *Reconciliation: A Journey* (Sydney: University of New South Wales Press, 2001), 100, quoting Pat Dodson.

48. Gordon, 42, quoting Peter Fisher, Aboriginal living on Cape Tribulation of the Kuku Yalanji people.

Chapter 6. Truth, Forgiveness, Justice

Epigraph: Hannah Arendt, "The Origins of Totalitarianism," reprinted in *The Portable Hannah Arendt*, ed. Peter Baehr (New York: Penguin, 2000), 139–40.

1. As Madeleine Davis reports, "Initially, the impulse behind the activation of memory politics in Spain was toward truth rather than justice. As the campaign developed and broadened, however, demands for justice in certain senses began to be more clearly articulated." Madeleine Davis, "Is Spain Recovering its Memory Breaking the *Pacto del Olvido*," *Human Rights Quarterly* 27 (3) (2005): 858, 879.

2. This was the motto of the South African Truth and Reconciliation Commission. See further Patricia Chisholm, "Apartheid: Can the Truth Set a Nation Free?" *Maclean's* 109 (15) (1996): 28–31.

3. Article 19, Global Campaign for Free Expression, "Who Wants to Forget? Truth and Access to Information About Past Human Rights Violations" (November 2000), http://www.article19.org/pdfs/publications/who-wants-to-forget-.pdf

4. Arendt, "Totalitarianism," 120.

5. David Luban, "On Dorfman's Death and the Maiden," *Yale Journal of Law and the Humanities* 10 (1998): 115, 121 , quoting Ariel Dorfman, "Death and the Maiden."

6. Juan Mendez, Review of Lawrence Weschler, *A Miracle, A Universe, New York Law School Journal of Human Rights* 8 (1991): 8.

7. Human Rights Watch, "Policy on Accountability for Past Abuses," *Accounting for the Past: The Lessons for South Africa from Latin America* 4 (11), October 23, 1992, http://www.hrw.org/ reports/1992/southafrica/ 12.htm

8. Aryeh Neier, "What Should be Done About the Guilty?" in *Transitional*

Justice: How Emerging Democracies Reckon with Former Regimes, vol. 1, *General Considerations,* ed. Neil J. Kritz (Washington, D.C.: U.S. Institute of Peace Press, 1995), 180.

9. Bethuel Kiplagat, "Is Mediation Alien to Africa? Perhaps in Letter, But Not in Spirit," *Track Two* 7 (1) (1988).

10. Heribert Adam, "The Presence of the Past: South Africa's Truth Commission as a Model?" in *Religion and Politics in South Africa,* ed. Abdulkader Tayob and Wolfram Weisse (Munster: Waxmann, 1999), 146.

11. In Rwanda, for instance, this has happened. "Gender, Sexual Violence, and Prospects for Justice at the Gacaca Courts in Rwanda," *African Studies Quarterly,* http://www.africa.ufl.edu/asq

12. Human Rights Watch, African Division, Sierra Leone, "We'll Kill You if You Cry: Sexual Violence in the Sierra Leone Conflict" (January 2003), http://hrw.org/reports/2003/sierraleone/. See also Amnesty International, *Sierra Leone: Rape and Other Forms of Sexual Violence Against Girls and Women* (June 29, 2000).

13. Luc Huyse, "Justice After Transition: On the Choices Successor Elites Make in Dealing with the Past," in Kritz, Transitional Justice, 115.

14. See Huyse, 115 (full cite in text).

15. http://www.easttimor-reconciliation.org/

16. Michael Ignatieff, "Articles of Faith," *Index on Censorship* 5 (1996): 110, 113.

17. Elazar Barkan, *The Guilt of Nations: Restitution and Negotiating Historical Injustices* (Baltimore: Johns Hopkins University Press, 2000), 16.

18. See *The Wik Peoples v. The State of Queensland & Others* (1996) HCA 40 (December 23, 1996).

19. Hannah Arendt, "Of Truth and Traps," in *The Portable Arendt,* 554.

20. See Erin Daly, "Reparations in South Africa: A Cautionary Tale," *University of Memphis Law Review* 33 (2003): 367.

21. Michael Gordon, *Reconciliation: A Journey* (Sydney: University of New South Wales Press, 2001), 1.

22. Gordon, 4.

23. Gordon, 4.

24. Gordon, 5.

25. Wole Soyinka, *The Burden of Memory, the Muse of Forgiveness* (New York: Oxford University Press, 1999), 81.

26. Emily Dickinson summed up all of these issues more concisely than anyone else could: "Tell all the Truth but tell it slant— / Success in Circuit lies / Too bright for our infirm Delight / The Truth's superb surprise / As Lightning to the Children eased / With explanation kind / The Truth must dazzle gradually / Or every man be blind—"

27. While we endorse these developments, it should be noted that the combination of court and commission poses significant questions about the jurisdiction of each and the relationship between the two. For instance, if a detainee is being held for trial by the Special Court, may he testify before the Commission? Can, should, or must the TRC share information it has with the Special Court? In Sierra Leone, these conflicts hampered the reconciliation process that the tribunals were meant to promote.

28. This was a major problem in Germany, where miles and miles of files were found and a process to catalogue and permit access to them had to be devised. See Joachim Gauck, "Dealing with a Stasi Past," *Daedalus* 123 (1) (1994): 277–84.

29. In Germany, for instance, the files of the Secret Police were made available to anyone who believed he or she was the subject of a file, although limitations were placed on scholarly use of the files. See generally Inga Markovits, "Papers

of General Interest: Selective Memory: How the Law Affects What We Remember and Forget about the Past—The Case of East Germany," *Law and Society Review* 35 (2001):

30. Priscilla B. Hayner, "Fifteen Truth Commissions—1974–1984: A Comparative Study," *Human Rights Quarterly* 16 (4) (1994), reprinted in Kritz, *Transitional Justice*, 225, 226. See also Priscilla B. Hayner, *Unspeakable Truths : Confronting State Terror and Atrocities* (New York: Routledge, 2001).

31. Rama Mani believes that it is "an open question whether TCs are a universal good for all post conflict societies. . . . Despite the popularity and proliferation of TCs, recent evidence is ambivalent about their contribution in the aftermath of conflict." *Beyond Retribution: Seeking Justice in the Shadows of War* (Cambridge: Polity Press, 2002), 103.

32. Samuel P. Huntington, "The Third Wave: Democratization in the Late Twentieth Century," in Kritz, *Transitional Justice*, 80.

33. See Andrzej S. Walicki, "Transitional Justice and the Political Struggles of Post-Communist Poland," in *Transitional Justice and the Rule of Law in New Democracies*, ed. James A. McAdams (South Bend: University of Notre Dame Press, 1997) (describing transitional politics in Poland).

34. Jonathan Tepperman, "Truth and Consequences," *Foreign Affairs* 81 (2002): 135. See also François du Bois, "'Nothing But the Truth': The South African Alternative to Corrective Justice in Transitions to Democracy," in *Lethe's Law: Justice, Law and Ethics in Reconciliation*, ed. Emilios Christodoulidis and Scott Veitch (Oxford: Hart, 2001), 91–115.

35. "As the panels proliferate, an intense debate has broken out over whether they cause more problems than they solve, and whether they deserve international support—or condemnation." Tepperman, 131.

36. Hayner, "Fifteen Truth Commissions," 230.

37. Hayner, "Fifteen Truth Commissions," 259.

38. Soyinka, *The Burden of Memory*, 30.

39. Archbishop Tutu rejects the perpetrators-as-monsters argument for the opposite reason—that it yields no justice. "If perpetrators were to be despaired of as monsters and demons, then we were thereby letting accountability go out the window because we were then declaring that they were not moral agents to be held responsible for the deeds they had committed." Desmond Tutu, *No Future Without Forgiveness* (New York: Doubleday, 1999): 83. Hannah Arendt noted the conundrum of the Israeli triers of Adolph Eichmann: if they deemed him a monster they could not try him under normal law; but neither could they characterize him as normal or like so many others. Arendt, "Eichmann in Jerusalem," reprinted in *The Portable Arendt*, 372–73.

40. Miriam J. Aukerman, "Extraordinary Evil, Ordinary Crime: A Framework for Understanding Transitional Justice," *Harvard Human Rights Journal* 15 (2002): 40, 80.

41. Except in the unusual circumstance where a person forgives the murderer for what he is about to do, much like Jesus on the cross—although most people would decline to hold murder victims up to that standard.

42. Herbert Marcuse, in *The Sunflower: On the Possibilities and Limits of Forgiveness*, ed. Henry James Cargas and Bonny V. Fetterman (New York: Schocken Books, 1997), 208: "I believe that the easy forgiving of such crimes perpetuates the very evil it wants to alleviate"; Robert McAfee Brown, in *The Sunflower*, 121.

43. Cynthia Ozick, in *The Sunflower*, 215.

44. André Stein, in *The Sunflower*, 253.

45. Quoted in Trudy Govier, *Dilemmas of Trust* (Montreal: McGill-Queen's University Press, 1998), 199, quoting Alice Miller.

46. In the Muslim tradition, "The strong one is not he who knocks out his adversary; the strong one is he who keeps control over his temper." M. Amir Ali, "Forgiveness," published by the Institute of Islamic Information & Education, www.iiie.net, citing Imam Al-Nawawi, *Riyadh-Us-Saleheen*, trans. S. M. Madni-Abbasi (Karachi: International Islamic Publishers, 1990), 1, #45, 43. Allah is reported to have said the most honorable among his servants is "He who pardons when he is in a position of power." *Mishkat al-Masabih*, trans. Fazlul Karim as *Al-Hadis* (Lahore: Book House, n.d.), 1: #193, 548, cited in Ali, "Forgiveness."

47. Robert McAfee Brown, in *The Sunflower*, 123.

48. Robert D. Enright, Suzanne Freedman, and Julio Rique, "The Psychology of Interpersonal Forgiveness," in *Exploring Forgiveness*, ed. Robert D. Enright and Joanna North (Madison: University of Wisconsin Press, 1998), 46–47.

49. Pumla Gobodo-Madikizela, *A Human Being Died That Night: A South African Woman Confronts the Legacy of Apartheid* (Boston: Houghton Mifflin, 2003), 117.

50. Gobodo-Madikizela, 112

51. Judith Herman, *Trauma and Recovery: The Aftermath of Violence—From Domestic Abuse to Political Terror* (New York: Basic Books, 1997), 169.

52. Tom Lodge, "The Bringing of Truth," *Mail & Guardian on line* (ZA), March 21, 2003.

53. It is therefore imperative to distinguish amnesty and forgiveness. Amnesty is a legal condition that affects the amenability of an individual to civil or criminal process. As such, it can be legally mandated even over the objections of victims or their representatives. Forgiveness is a personal decision that cannot be required by law.

54. Gabriel O'Malley, "Respecting Revenge: The Road to Revenge" *Law, Democracy and Development* 3 (2) (1999): 181, 188. O'Malley argues that "although a grant of forgiveness does release the victim from a cycle of fear and revenge that may be deleterious, a lack of institutional action against a perpetrator eviscerates the power of forgiveness over those who have wronged the victim. This is the only power the victim has over the perpetrator. To choose to exhibit compassion towards a wrongdoer may lift the victim from a state of pain to one of renewed hope."

55. Donald W. Shriver, Jr., *An Ethic for Enemies: Forgiveness in Politics* (New York: Oxford University Press, 1995), 7

56. Theodore M. Hesburgh, in *The Sunflower*, 169.

57. "Say: 'O My servants who have transgressed against their souls! do not despair of the Mercy of Allah: for Allah forgives all sins: for He is Oft-Forgiving, Most Merciful." The Qur'an, trans. Abdullah Yusuf Ali (New York: Tahrike Tarsile Qur'an, 2005) 39: 53.

58. The Dalai Lama, in *The Sunflower*, 130.

59. Update, June–July 2003, http://www.easttimor-reconciliation.org/cavr Update-JunJuly2003-en.pdf Appendix. See Carsten Stahn, "Accommodating Individual Criminal Responsibility and National Reconciliation: The UN Truth Commission for East Timor," *American Journal of International Law* 95 (4) (2001): 952–66.

60. Gobodo-Madikizela, *A Human Being Died*, 116.

61. William J. Long and Peter Brecke, *War and Reconciliation: Reason and Emotion in Conflict Resolution* (Cambridge, Mass.: MIT Press, 2003), 149.

62. In Islam, "forgiveness means closing an account of offense against God or any of His creation," according to Amir Ali. Other words used in the Qu'ran to signify forgiveness are "Safhu," meaning "to turn away from a sin or a misdeed"

(citing Qur'an 2:109, 15:85, and 43:89), and "Ghafara or maghfira" meaning "to cover," (citing Qu'ran 2:263, 42:37, and 43:43). www.iiie.net.

63. Long and Brecke, *War and Reconciliation*, 30, quoting Joanna North, "The Ideal of Forgiveness: A Philosopher's Exploration," in Enright and North, *Exploring Forgiveness*, 26.

64. Arendt, "A Daughter of Our People: A Response to Gershom Scholem," reprinted in *The Portable Arendt*, 396.

65. Desmond Tutu, in *The Sunflower*, 268.

66. Tutu, *No Future Without Forgiveness*, 273.

67. Gobodo-Madikizela, *A Human Being Died*, 122, 131.

68. Tutu, *No Future Without Forgiveness*, 273.

69. Roman David and Susanne Choi Yuk-ping, "'Victims on Transitional Justice: Lessons from the Reparation of Human Rights Abuses in the Czech Republic," *Human Rights Quarterly* 27 (2) (2005): 426.

70. Shriver, *An Ethic for Enemies*, 32.

71. Arendt, in *The Portable Arendt*, 151, emphasis hers, quoting Raymond Davies's reportage.

72. Moshe Bejski, in *The Sunflower*, 116. Barkan sees the failure of the denazification program as a "glaring example of how resistant Germany was to admit any guilt about its Nazi past," *The Guilt of Nations*, 13.

73. Tzvetan Todorov, in *The Sunflower*, 256.

74. Arendt, "Eichmann in Jerusalem," 373. She asks: "would any one of them have suffered a guilty conscience if they had won?"

75. Arendt, "Eichmann in Jerusalem," 356.

76. Marie Smyth, "Remembering in Northern Ireland: Victims, Perpetrators and Hierarchies of Pain and Responsibility," in *Past Imperfect: Dealing with the Past in Northern Ireland and Societies in Transition*, ed. Brandon Hamber (Derry: Incore/University of Ulster, 1998).

77. Nicholas Tavuchis, *Mea Culpa: A Sociology of Apology and Reconciliation* (Stanford, Calif.: Stanford University Press, 1991), 20.

78. Tavuchis, 20.

79. All, www.iiie.net.

80. Deborah E. Lipstadt, in *The Sunflower*, 194.

81. Gobodo-Madikizela, *A Human Being Died*, 97–98. She quotes Nyameka Goniwe, a widow of apartheid violence, who says that "Victims are looking for signs and when they see those signs, they are ready to forgive."

82. Tutu, *No Future Without Forgiveness*, 272.

83. Aaron Lazare, "Go Ahead, Say You're Sorry," *Psychology Today* 28 (1) (January–February 1995): 40, 42.

84. Rebecca Goldstein, in *The Sunflower*, 151.

85. Long and Brecke, *War and Reconciliation*, 67.

86. Aryeh Neier, "What Should Be Done About the Guilty?" *New York Review of Books*, February 1, 1990, 34.

87. See Richard Goldstone, "Exposing Human Rights Abuses – A Help or Hindrance to Reconciliation?" *Hastings Constitutional Law Quarterly* 22 (1995): 607, 615 (The "only hope of breaking cycles of violence is by public acknowledgment of such violence and the exposure of those responsible for it").

88. Tavuchis, *Mea Culpa*, 15.

89. This partially explains why governments and corporations are reluctant to apologize for past wrongs. If they admit responsibility without offering any countervailing or mitigating explanation, they subject themselves to legal liability.

90. Mike Afrani, "Truth and Reconciliation in Town," *New African* 399, September 2001.

91. Quoted in Elizabeth Knight, "Facing the Past: Retrospective Justice as a Means to Promote Democracy in Nigeria," *Connecticut Law Review* 35 (2003): 867.

92. Jeremy Sarkin, "Holding Multinational Corporations Accountable for Human Rights and Humanitarian Law Violations Committed During Colonialism and Apartheid: An Evaluation of the Prospects of Such Cases in Light of the Herero of Namibia's Genocide Case and South African Apartheid Cases Being Brought in the United States Under the Alien Torts Claims Act," in *Bedrijven en Mensenrechten*, ed. Eva Brems and Pieter van der Heede (Antwerp: Maklu, 2003), 174–204.

93. Ann L. Phillips, "The Politics of Reconciliation Revisited: Germany and East-Central Europe," *World Affairs* 163 (4) (Spring 2001).

94. Ivy Lee, "Probing the Issues of Reconciliation More Than Fifty Years After the Asia-Pacific War," *East Asia: An International Quarterly* 19 (4) (Winter 2001): 19.

95. Raymond Bonner and Norimitsu Onishi, "Japan's Chief Apologizes for War Misdeeds," *New York Times*, April 23, 2005; Raymond Bonner and Norimitsu Onishi, "China and Japan Leaders Pledge to Improve Relations," *New York Times*, April 24, 2005, 1: 20..

96. Vesna Peric Zimonjic, "After the War Crimes and Genocide, Old Balkan Foes Make Up," *The Independent*, September 11, 2003, http://news.independent.co.uk/.

97. Sarkin, "Holding Multinational Corporations Liable." See further Jeremy Sarkin, "Reparation for Past Wrongs: Using Domestic Courts Around the World, Especially the United States, to Pursue African Human Rights Claims," *International Journal of Legal Information* 32 (2) (2004): 339.

98. Thomas W. Donovan, "Jurisdictional Relationships Between Nations and Their Former Colonies," *Across Borders International Law Journal* 1 (2003): 5 n. 23, http://www.across-borders.com

99. BBC, "IRA 'Sorry' for Disappeared," October 25, 2003, http://news.bbc.co.uk/1/hi/nothern_ireland/3210967.stm

100. Organic Law No. 08/96 of Aug. 30, 1996 on the Organization of Prosecutions for Offences constituting the Crime of Genocide or Crimes Against Humanity committed since Oct. 1 1990, *Government of Rwanda Official Journal* (September 1, 1996), Article 6 (b).

101. Matthew Fox, in *The Sunflower*, 144.

102. "God Himself does not forgive a person who has sinned against a human being unless that human being has been forgiven by his victim, " Dennis Prager, in *The Sunflower*, 226.

103. Soyinka, *The Burden of Memory*, 81.

104. Thus Chilean President Aylwin's response to the TRC report was effective precisely because it was coupled with a commitment to improve the material lives of the victims; the same can be said for the Canadian government's response to the report on first peoples.

105. Tong Yu, "Reparations for Former Comfort Women of World War II," *Harvard International Law Journal* (Spring 1995): 528, 538.

106. The apology of the Canadian Church of Christ to the First Peoples of Canada for excessive zeal in prosletyzing was entirely verbal. Tavuchis, *Mea Culpa*, 110–11.

107. Long and Brecke, *War and Reconciliation*, 18: a "reconciliation event (and the reconciliation it symbolizes) is a costly (or potentially costly) signal that the

other party is likely to interpret as a genuine offer to improve relations and thus may break a deadlocked conflictual situation" (20).

108. Gerald R. Williams, "Negotiation as a Healing Process," *Journal of Dispute Resolution* (1996): 1 n. 124.

109. Sidney Shachnow, in *The Sunflower*, 242.

110. Long and Brecke, *War and Reconciliation*, 50.

111. In Hebrew, the term *teshuva* literally means to return, but signifies repentance. Lipstadt, in *The Sunflower*, 193. "Done properly, *teshuva* can result in the sinner returning to a repaired relationship with both God and with his/her fellow humans, even as God returns to the sinner." In Arabic, one term for forgiveness, *Safhu*, "means to turn away from a sin or a misdeed." Ali, www.iiie.net.

112. Long and Brecke, *War and Reconciliation*, 47.

113. Archbishop Tutu has said that "When people speak about justice, almost always they are thinking of retributive justice—the modern equivalent of, really, 'an eye for an eye.' Not quite, but they are saying when you have committed a crime there must be a commensurate punishment. And that is true." David Goodman, "Why Killers Should Go Free: Lessons from South Africa," *Washington Quarterly* 22 (2) (Spring 1999): 169 (quoting Archbishop Tutu).

114. Stephan Landsman, "Alternative Responses to Serious Human Rights Abuses: Of Prosecution and Truth Commissions," *Law and Contemporary Problems* 59 (1996): 81, 87.

115. Michael Humphrey, "From Victim to Victimhood: Truth Commissions and Trials as Rituals of Political Transition and Individual Healing," *Australian Journal of Anthropology* 14 (2) (August 2003), http://www.findarticles.com/p/articles/mi_m2472/is_2_14/ai_105657583/pg_2.

116. Barkan, *The Guilt of Nations*, 120.

117. Raquel Aldana-Pindell, "In Vindication of Justiciable Victims' Rights to Truth and Justice for State-Sponsored Crimes," *Vanderbilt Journal of Transnational Law* 35 (2002): 1399, 1494–95.

118. Aldana-Pindell, 1494–95.

119. Dilip Simeon, "A Finer Balance: An Essay on the Possibility of Reconciliation," in *Experiments with Truth: Transitional Justice and the Processes of Reconciliation*, ed. Okwui Enwezor, Carlos Basualdo, Ute Meta Bauer, Susanne Ghez, Sarat Maharaj, Mark Nash, and Octavio Zaya, Documenta 11_Platform 2 (Ostfildern-Ruit, Germany: Hatje-Cantz, 2002), 137.

120. Arendt, "Eichmann in Jerusalem," 339.

121. Barkan, *The Guilt of Nations*, 11 (noting that Germans "compared German suffering with the ultimate suffering endured by the Jews as the victims of the Nazi extermination camps.").

122. Barkan, 10.

123. Laurel E. Fletcher and Harvey M. Weinstein, "Violence and Social Repair: Rethinking the Contribution of Justice to Reconciliation," *Human Rights Quarterly* 24 (2002): 573–639, 580–81.

124. Simeon, "A Finer Balance," 147.

125. Barkan, *The Guilt of Nations*, xvii, citing Ian Buruma: "What is alarming is the extent to which so many minorities have come to define themselves above all as historical victims. . . . Not only does it reveal lack of historical perspective, but it also seems a very peculiar sources of pride."

126. This is true in Rwanda, where at least some perpetrators believe that they attacked because they feared being attacked themselves.

127. Robert Meister, "Forgiving and Forgetting: Lincoln and the Politics of

National Recovery," in *Human Rights in Political Transitions: Gettysburg to Bosnia,* ed. Carla Hesse and Robert Post (Cambridge, Mass.: MIT Press, 1999), 137.

128. Meister, 142.

129. Fletcher and Weinstein, "Violence and Social Repair," 578. See also Ruti Teitel, "Transitional Jurisprudence: The Role of Law in Political Transformation," *Yale Law Journal* 106 (1997): 2009.

130. Fletcher and Weinstein provide an excellent overview of this strand of transitional literature.

131. In South Africa, as elsewhere, the possibility of trials resulting in justice was further diminished by the cost of the trials. In a country struggling to pay its debts and to enhance the lives of its citizens, the government paid millions not only for the cost of the trials but for the *defense* of the perpetrators who had been civil servants. How many people could have had houses with that money? How many children could have had school books?

132. See Carlos Nino, "The Duty to Punish Past Abuses of Human Rights Put into Context: The Case of Argentina," *Yale Law Journal* 100 (1991): 2619.

133. Long and Brecke, *War and Reconciliation,* 45.

134. Gabor Halmai and Kim Lane Scheppele, "The Hungarian Approach to the Past: Living Well is the Best Revenge," in McAdams, *Transitional Justice,* 155, 168–70.

135. Tina Rosenberg, *The Haunted Land: Facing Europe's Ghosts After Communism* (New York: Random House, 1995), 401.

136. "The focus on individual crimes has been used by many to claim collective innocence." Fletcher and Weinstein, "Violence and Social Repair," 604.

137. "the focus on punishment of perpetrators may have the inadvertent consequence December 23, 2005 of transforming these wrongdoers into scapegoats or victims in order to perpetuate the political mythology of a particular social group." Fletcher and Weinstein, 592.

138. Fletcher and Weinstein, 602.

139. In Rwanda the disconnect between the ICTR and the population was even starker. For one thing, the defendants who were in ICTR custody were enjoying better living conditions than most Rwandans, 60 percent of whom live below the poverty line.

140. Fletcher and Weinstein, "Violence and Social Repair," 602.

141. Fletcher and Weinstein, 600–601.

142. Sumantra Bose, *Bosnia After Dayton: Nationalist Partition and International Intervention* (New York: Oxford University Press, 2000), 130.

143. Physicians for Human Rights, "Southern Iraq: Reports of Human Rights Abuses and Views on Justice, Reconstruction and Government," September 2003, http://www.phrusa.org/research/iraq/docs/iraqsurvey.pdf, 6. Under Qu'ranic law, revenge killing is permissible so long as it is not excessive.

144. Physicians for Human Rights, 6.

145. "Although conventional wisdom holds that criminal trials promote several goals, including uncovering the truth; avoiding collective accountability by individualizing guilt; breaking cycles of impunity; deterring future war crimes; providing closure for the victims and fostering democratic institutions, little is known about the role that judicial interventions have in rebuilding societies." Human Rights Center and International Human Rights Law Clinic, University of California, Berkeley, and Centre for Human Rights, University of Sarajevo, "Report: Justice, Accountability and Social Reconstruction: An Interview Study of Bosnian Judges and Prosecutors," *Berkeley Journal of International Law* 18 (2000): 102, 106.

146. "In comparison to the widespread firings of faculty in the former GDR in 1990, the absence of action in West Germany in the 1950s becomes glaring." "Among the German financial elite, few companies changed hands, and many individuals played their old roles under the new regime." Barkan, *The Guilt of Nations,* 20–21.

147. See Eric Stover, Hanny Megally, and Hania Mufti, "Bremer's 'Gordian Knot': Transitional Justice and the U.S. Occupation of Iraq," *Human Rights Quarterly* 27 (3) (2005): 830–57 (describing the deleterious consequences of the American debathification policy in the immediate wake of the fall of Saddam Hussein).

148. Truth and Reconciliation Commission of South Africa, *Truth and Reconciliation Commission of South Africa Report,* Foreword by Archbishop D. M. Tutu, 1998 (London: Macmillan Reference, 1999), 1: chap. 5.

149. Tutu, *No Future Without Forgiveness,* 31.

150. Tutu, 31.

151. South Africa Interim Constitution, "National Unity and Reconciliation" (1993), Postamble.

152. Barkan, *The Guilt of Nations,* 25, has also suggested that "partial reparation" helped promote a healthier relationship between Germany and Israel.

Chapter 7. Reconciliation Redirected

Epigraph: *Final Report of the Commission for Reception, Truth and Reconciliation in East Timor* (CAVR), Part 10, paras. 9, 11, http://etan.org/news/2006/cavr.htm

1. Pal Ahluwalia, "Towards (Re)Conciliation: The Postcolonial Economy of Giving," in *Relocating Postcolonialism,* ed. David Theo Goldberg and Ato Quayson (Oxford: Blackwell, 2002), 197.

2. Ivy Lee, "Probing the Issues of Reconciliation More Than Fifty Years After the Asia-Pacific War," *East Asia: An International Quarterly* 19 (1) (2001).

3. Kader Asmal, Louise Asmal, and Ronald Suresh Roberts, *Reconciliation Through Truth: A Reckoning of Apartheid's Criminal Governance* (Cape Town: David Philip, 1997), 46.

4. John Paul Lederach, "Beyond Violence: Building Sustainable Peace," in *The Handbook of Interethnic Coexistence,* ed. Eugene Weiner (New York: Continuum, 1998), 236, 245.

5. Charles Lerche, "Peace Building Through Reconciliation," *International Journal of Peace Studies* 5 (2) (2000): 66.

6. http://www.ventureline.com/glossary_R.asp.

7. Johan Galtung, *After Violence: 3R: Reconstruction, Reconciliation, Resolution: Coping with Visible and Invisible Effects of War and Violence,* http://www.transcend. org/(33), uses similar language when he writes: "Both trauma and guilt may be deposited in the world trauma and guilt banks. The traumatized has a violence credit, and the guilty a violence debit. Both carry interest over time, at the risk of inflation gnawing at the capital. Amortization is long term."

8. Jeremy Sarkin, "The Tension Between Justice and Reconciliation in Rwanda: Politics, Human Rights, Due Process and the Role of the Gacaca Courts in Dealing with the Genocide," *Journal of African Law* 45 (2001): 143. But see Pal Ahluwalia, "the very structures of colonialism continue to predominate within postcolonial Rwanda with the process of identity formation firmly locked into the representations and practices once ascribed by the colonial power. Hence, for a people inseparable in terms of culture, language, and religion, it is the colonial

identity card that above all becomes the signifier of difference." Ahluwalia, "Towards (Re)Conciliation," 192.

9. *Adarand Constructors v. Pena (Scalia J. Conc.)*, 515 U.S. 200, 239 (1995).

10. W. E. B. Du Bois, *The Souls of Black Folk* (1903), reprinted in *W. E. B. Du Bois: A Reader*, ed. David Levering Lewis (New York: Henry Holt, 1995), 29.

11. David Crocker notes that, in nonlethal coexistence, reconciliation occurs where former enemies no longer kill each other or routinely violate each other's basic rights. This thin sense of reconciliation, attained when ceasefires, peace accords, and negotiated settlements begin to take hold, can be a momentous achievement. "Punishment, Reconciliation, and Democratic Deliberation," *Buffalo Criminal Law Review* (2002): 528. Jonathan Tepperman suggests that mere "non lethal co-existence" all one can expect in societies where conflict has occurred. "Truth and Consequences," *Foreign Affairs* (March/April 2002): 142.

12. Andrzej S. Walicki, "Transitional Justice and the Political Struggles of Post-Communist Poland," in *Transitional Justice and the Rule of Law in New Democracies*, ed. James A. McAdams (South Bend, Ind.: University of Notre Dame Press, 1997), 212.

13. Maria Ericson, *Reconciliation and the Search for a Shared Moral Landscape: An Exploration Based upon a Study of Northern Ireland and South Africa* (New York: Peter Lang, 2001), 86–96. See also Mohammed Abu-Nimer, "Toward the Theory and Practice of Positive Approaches to Peacebuilding," in *Positive Approaches to Peacebuilding: A Resource for Innovators*, ed. Cynthia Sampson, Mohammed Abu-Nimer, Claudia Liebler, and Diana Whitney (Washington, D.C.: Pact Publications, 2003), 13–23.

14. Louis Kriesberg, quoted in Ronald J. Fisher, "Social-Psychological Processes in Interactive Conflict Analysis and Reconciliation," in *Conflict Resolution: Process, Dynamics and Structure*, ed. Jeong Ho-Won (Aldershot: Ashgate, 1999), 83.

15. Tone Bringa, "Reconciliation in Bosnia-Herzegovina," in *Roads to Reconciliation*, ed. Elin Skaar, Siri Gloppen, and Astri Suhrke (Lanham, Md.: Lexington Books, 2005), 194.

16. Fanie du Toit, ed., *Learning to Live Together: Practices of Social Reconciliation* (Cape Town: Institute for Justice and Reconciliation, 2003), 28, 33.

17. Donald W. Shriver, *An Ethic for Enemies: Forgiveness in Politics* (New York: Oxford University Press, 1995), 230.

18. Crocker, "Punishment, Reconciliation, and Democratic Deliberation," 528.

19. See, for example, cases in Haiti, Israel and Palestine, and the Balkans, where peacebuilding as a result of collaboration on projects peace building occurred. See Randi Garber, "Health as a Bridge for Peace: Theory, Practice and Prognosis, Reflections of a Practitioner," *Journal of Peacebuilding & Development* 1 (1) (2002).

20. See, for example, Alcinda Honwana, "The Collective Body: Challenging Western Concepts of Trauma and Healing," *Track Two* 8 (1) (1999); Kimberly A. Maynard, "Rebuilding Community: Psychosocial Healing, Reintegration and Reconciliation at the Grassroots Level," in *Rebuilding Societies After Civil War: Critical Roles for International Assistance*, ed. Krishna Kumar (Boulder, Colo.: Lynne Rienner, 1997), 203.

21. "We see a lot of balanda people changing their views and getting on well with Aboriginal people. That's reconciliation." Michael Gordon, *Reconciliation: A Journey* (Sydney: University of New South Wales Press, 2001), 69, quoting Raymatjja (last name not given).

22. Gordon, 67–68.

23. Manès Sperber, in *The Sunflower: On the Possibilities and Limits of Forgiveness,* ed. Henry James Cargas and Bonny V. Fetterman (New York: Schocken Books, 1997), 247.

24. See Martha Minow, "Between Vengeance and Forgiveness on the Value of Engaging in Constructive Community Enterprises," in Minow, *Between Vengeance and Forgiveness: Facing History After Genocide and Mass Violence* (Boston: Beacon Press, 1998).

25. Jonathan Tepperman, "Truth and Consequences," *Foreign Affairs* (March/April. 2002): 142; William J. Long and Peter Brecke, *War and Reconciliation: Reason and Emotion in Conflict Resolution* (Cambridge, Mass.: MIT Press, 2003), 65. See also Tom Winslow, "Reconciliation: The Road to Healing? Collective Good, Individual Harm?" *Track Two* 6 (3–4) (1997): 24, 35.

26. Canadian Charter of Rights and Freedoms (1982) s. 1.

27. http://www.ews.undp.ba/pdf/eng/2003/2003%20-%203%20Quarterly%20Report%20-%20English.pdfm

28. See Leon Festinger, *A Theory of Cognitive Dissonance* (Stanford, Calif.: Stanford University Press, 1957).

29. *Ex parte Harding,* 219 U.S. 363. See also *Minersville School Dist. v. Gobitis,* 310 U.S. 586, 594 (1940). "Our present task, then, as so often the case with courts, is to reconcile two rights in order to prevent either from destroying the other."

30. This occurred, for example, in Germany after the reunification of West and East Germany. See Jin Lee, "A Millennium Hope for Korea: Lessons from German Unification," *Michigan State University-DCL Journal of International Law* (2000): 453, 504.

31. Fletcher and Weinstein have suggested that reconciliation forms part of a broader objective of achieving social reconstruction in a transitional society. They understand social reconstruction as the construction of new societal structures and relationships to replace those that mass violence destroyed. Laurel E. Fletcher and Harvey M. Weinstein, "Violence and Social Repair: Rethinking the Contribution of Justice to Reconciliation," *Human Rights Quarterly* 24 (2002): 573, 623.

32. Thomas S. Kuhn, *The Structure of Scientific Revolutions,* 2nd ed. enlarged (Chicago: University of Chicago Press, 1986).

33. Kuhn, 47–48.

34. Truth and Reconciliation Commission of South Africa, *Truth and Reconciliation Commission of South Africa Report,* 1998 (London: Macmillan Reference, 1999), 49.

35. *Guatemala: Memory of Silence: Report of the Commission for Historical Clarification, Conclusions and Recommendations,* para 3. American Association for the Advancement of Science, http://shr.aaas.org/guatemala/ceh/report/english/toc.html.

36. *Guatemala: Memory of Silence,* paras. 6, 8.

37. Kuhn, *Structure of Scientific Revolutions,* 77. "The decision to reject one paradigm is always simultaneously the decision to accept another, and the judgment leading to that decision involves the comparison of both paradigms with nature *and* with each other."

38. See generally Stephen John Stedman, "Spoiler Problems in Peace Processes," *International Security* 22 (2) (1997): 5–53.

39. Kuhn, *Structure of Scientific Resolutions,* 76.

40. Kuhn, 83.

41. Kuhn, 85.

42. Kuhn, 85, quoting Herbert Butterfield, *The Origins of Modern Science, 1300–1800* (London: Bell, 1949), 1–7.

43. Michel Feher, "Terms of Reconciliation," in *Human Rights in Political Transitions: Gettysburg to Bosnia*, ed. Carla Hesse and Robert Post (Cambridge, Mass.: MIT Press, 1999), 328.

44. Feher, 331.

45. *Rapport final de l'Instance équité and réconciliation*, in Arabic and in French, http://www.ier.ma/_rapport_fr.php (translation in text by author).

46. Feher, "Terms of Reconciliation," 328.

47. Robert Meister, "Forgiving and Forgetting, Lincoln and the Politics of National Recovery," in Hesse and Post, *Human Rights in Political Transitions*, 137. Of course, calling all Americans "victims" and "survivors" hardly appreciates the distinctions among classes of survivors. This ideology is morally assailable insofar as it equates the victimhood of slaves with that of slaveowners and other white beneficiaries of the slave economy. But, characteristically, Lincoln was not focused on slaves at Gettysburg, and the divisions that he glossed over on that battlefield remain in force today.

48. Meister, 137.

49. Lincoln, Gettysburg Address, http://www.loc.gov/exhibits/gadd/gtran.html.

50. Meister, *Forgiving and Forgetting*, 140.

51. Paloma Aguilar, "Justice, Politics, and Memory in the Spanish Transition," in *The Politics of Memory: Transitional Justice in Democratizing Societies*, ed. Alexandra Barahona de Brito, Paloma Aguilar, and Carmen González-Enríquez (Oxford: Oxford University Press, 2001), 98.

52. See generally Ronald D. Chilcote, *Transitions from Dictatorship to Democracy: Comparative Studies of Spain, Portugal, and Greece* (New York: Taylor and Francis, 1990).

53. Aguilar, 92, 99.

54. Elazar Barkan, *The Guilt of Nations: Restitution and Negotiating Historical Injustices* (Baltimore: Johns Hopkins University Press, 2000), 118.

55. Gabor Halmai and Kim Lane Scheppele, "Living Well Is the Best Revenge: The Hungarian Approach to Judging the Past," in McAdams, *Transitional Justice*, 180.

56. Halmai and Scheppele, 162, quoting the Hungarian Constitutional Court, 11/1992 (III.5) ABh. English translation in Halmai and Scheppele, *Journal of Constitutional Law in Eastern and Central Europe* 1 (1994): 129–157, at 136

57. Halmai and Scheppele, 182.

58. Alfred Erich Senn, "Lithuania Awakening," *Mokslo ir enciklopedijå Leidybos Institutas* (Vilnius: Leidybos Institutas, 2002).

59. South African Interim Constitution (1993).

60. Kuhn, *Structure of Scientific Revolutions*, 180.

61. Barkan, *Guilt of Nations*, 277, notes that, with respect to the political upheavals involving the Maori in New Zealand, "A by-product of the negotiations over restitution was heightened stakes and strengthened Maori public discourse and culture."

62. Noel Pearson, quoted in Gordon, *Reconciliation*, 4.

63. Security Council, "4903rd Meeting Security Council Reaffirms 'Vital Importance' of United Nations' Role in Post-Conflict Reconciliation," http://www.un.org/News/Press/docs/2004/sc7990.doc.htm, by Henri Raubenheimer from South Africa.

64. Juan Linz and Alfred Stepan, *Problems of Democratic Transition and*

Consolidation: Southern Europe, South America, and Post-Communist Europe (Baltimore: Johns Hopkins University Press, 1996), 5.

Chapter 8. Politics and Money

Epigraph: J. Celliers Breytenbach, "Reconciliation: Shifts in Christian Soteriology," in *Reconciliation and Construction: Creative Options for a Rapidly Changing South Africa*, ed. W. S. Vorster (Pretoria: University of South Africa, 1986), 1, 16.

1. Rodolfo Stavenhagen, *Ethnic Conflicts and the Nation-State* (Basingstoke: Macmillan, 1996), 12.

2. Members of more than 200 ethnic groups, whose situations have been exacerbated by colonialism and underdevelopment, live in conditions of severe economic deprivation, resulting in years of conflict and extraordinary violence. Jeremy Sarkin, "Finding a Solution for the Problems Created by the Politics of Identity in the Democratic Republic of the Congo (DRC): Designing a Constitutional Framework for Peaceful Cooperation," in *The Politics of Identity and Exclusion in Africa: From Violent Confrontation to Peaceful Cooperation*, Seminar report / Konrad-Adenauer-Stiftung 11 (Johannesburg : Konrad-Adenauer-Stiftung, 2001), 67–80, 67.

3. As Nafziger, Stewart, and Väyrynen explain, "Economic, political and cultural sources [of complex humanitarian emergencies (CHE)] are intertwined; economic stagnation or collapse, especially when coupled with large disparities among groups (horizontal inequality) and individuals (vertical inequality), spur political discontent, which leaders use to mobilize people to support their struggles for power, thus deepening and exploiting perceived cultural differences." They go on to explain that "Group differences, based on differences in ethnicity, race, religion, caste or class, are reinforced, and sometimes created, by the conflict." E. Wayne Nafziger, Frances Stewart, and Raimo Väyrynen, eds,, *War, Hunger, and Displacement: The Origins of Humanitarian Emergencies* (New York: Oxford University Press, 2000), quoted in Kevin Clements, "Towards Conflict Transformation and a Just Peace," Berghof Research Center for Constructive Conflict Management, 2, 7, www.berghof-handbook.net/articles/clements_handbook.pdf

4. Clements.

5. *Rapport final de l'Instance èquité and réconciliation*, available in Arabic and in French, http://www.ier.ma/_rapport_fr.php (translation in text by author).

6. Jack Donnelly, *Universal Human Rights in Theory and Practice*, 2nd ed. (Ithaca, N.Y.: Cornell University Press, 2002), 51.

7. Many especially smaller nations that had opted for socialist approaches were often thwarted in their efforts until they reoriented themselves toward market economies and western-style democracies. See Roland Paris, *At War's End: Building Peace After Civil Conflict* (Cambridge: Cambridge University Press, 2004), describing the change of heart in Mozambique and Namibia.

8. OECD Development Assistance Committee, *Conflict, Peace and Development Cooperation on the Threshold of the 21st Century* (Paris: OECD Publications, 1998), quoted in Gunter Bachler, "Conflict Transformation Through State Reform," Berghof Research Center for Constructive Conflict Management 7, http://www.berghof-handbook.net/articles/baechler_handbook.pdf

9. K. J. Holsti, *The State, War and the State of War* (Cambridge: Cambridge University Press, 1986), 20–21, quoted in Clements, "Towards Conflict Transformation and a Just Peace," 7.

10. "When there are profound differences about the territorial boundaries of the political community's state and profound differences as to who has the right of citizenship in that state, there is what we call a 'stateness' problem." Juan Linz and Alfred Stepan, *Problems of Democratic Transition and Consolidation: Southern Europe, South America, and Post-Communist Europe* (Baltimore: Johns Hopkins University Press, 1996), 16.

11. Sumantra Bose, *Bosnia After Dayton: Nationalist Partition and International Intervention* (New York: Oxford University Press, 2000), 48.

12. Bose, 48, quoting Frederick Whelan, "Democratic Theory and the Boundary Problem," in *Liberal Democracy: NOMOS XXV*, ed. J. Roland Pennock and John William Chapman (New York: New York University Press, 1983), 13–47.

13. Bose shows that these polarized historical assumptions may also produce divergent views about the meaning of the war. If Yugoslavia was an artificial agglomeration of distinct peoples, then the war can be seen as a war of aggression in which the international community completely failed to protect the victimized Bosniaks from foreign aggression and foreign intervention now is morally appropriate. If, on the other hand, the war was an instance of internecine struggle, then the international presence during and after the war is unwarranted. Bose, 18–20.

14. Linz and Stepan, *Problems of Democratic Transition*, 27.

15. Edward Wong, "A Celebration of Kurds' Hopes for Their Region, Not the Country," *New York Times*, December 16, 2005, A26.

16. Linz and Stepan, *Problems of Democratic Transition*, 31.

17. Linz and Stepan, 26, quoting Robert Dahl.

18. "Memorandum of Understanding Between the Government of the Republic of Indonesia and the Free Aceh Movement," August 15, 2005, http://news.bbc.co.uk/-1/shared/bsp/hi/pdfs/15_08_05_aceh.pdf. The agreement also calls for more equitable distribution of natural resources, paras. 13.3, 13.4.

19. Michael Ignatieff, *Blood and Belonging: Journeys into the New Nationalism* (New York: Farrar, Strauss, Giroux, 1995), 10.

20. Belgian Constitution, Art. 4: "Belgium has four linguistic regions: the French-speaking region, the Dutch-speaking region, the bilingual region of Brussels Capital and the German-speaking region. Each «commune» (county borough) of the Kingdom is part of one of these linguistic regions." Spanish Constitution, art. 3: "1. Castilian is the official Spanish language of the State. All Spaniards have the duty to know it and the right to use it. 2. The other Spanish languages shall also be official in the respective Autonomous Communities in accordance with their Statutes. 3. The wealth of the different language variations of Spain is a cultural heritage which shall be the object of special respect and protection."

21. Linz and Stepan, *Problems of Democratic Transition*, 24 n. 20.

22. The term can be found in Bose, *Bosnia After Dayton*, 203.

23. Nicaragua, 1987 law granting autonomy to 2 regions. Ecuador, Guatemala, and Bolivia are also considering developing constitutions for indigenous groups.

24. Linz and Stepan, *Problems of Democratic Transition*, 34, argue for reevaluation of some of the rich experiments in *"non-territorial autonomy* that relate, for example, to the self-government of corporate ethnic or religious communities such as the Jewish Kabal in the Polish-Lithuanian Commonwealth, the millets in the Ottoman Empire, or the 'national curias' in the late Hapsburg Empire."

25. See Act LXXVII of 1993 on the Rights of the National and Ethnic Minorities 1993 (known as the "Minority Act").

26. Bosnia is divided vertically into municipalities, cantons, entities (the Federation of Bosnia and Herzegovina and the Republica Sprska) and the nation. In

many places, particularly in the Federation but less so in the RS, a majority at one level is a minority in the next.

27. James Madison, Federalist #45, in *The Federalist Papers*, ed. Clinton Rossiter, intro. Charles R. Kesler (New York: Signet Classics, 2003).

28. Quoted in Linda C. Reif, "Building Democratic Institutions: The Role of National Human Rights Institutions in Good Governance and Human Rights Protection," *Harvard Human Rights Journal* 13 (2001): 1, 16.

29. Jeremy Sarkin, "The Drafting of the Final South African Constitution from a Human Rights Perspective," *American Journal of Comparative Law* 47 (1) (1999): 67.

30. See Aileen Kavanagh,"The Role of a Bill of Rights in Reconstructing Northern Ireland," *Human Rights Quarterly* 26 (4) (2004): 956–82.

31. Heinz Klug, *Constituting Democracy: Law, Globalism and South Africa's Political Reconstruction* (Cambridge: Cambridge University Press, 2000), 12–13.

32. Organization of African Unity, Special Report of the International Panel of Eminent Personalities to Investigate the 1994 Genocide in Rwanda and the Surrounding Events ¶2.1 (2000); see also Erin Daly, "Between Punitive and Reconstructive Justice: The Gacaca Courts in Rwanda," *New York University Journal of International Law and Policy* 34 (2002): 355, 368.

33. Universal Declaration of Human Rights, G.A. Res. 217A, at 71, U.N. GAOR, 3d Sess., 1st plen. mtg., U.N. Doc A/810 (Dec. 12, 1948), preamble.

34. See I. William Zartman, ed., *Governance as Conflict Management: Politics and Violence in West Africa* (Washington, D.C.: Brookings Institution Press, 1997).

35. Madeleine Davis, "Is Spain Recovering Its Memory? Breaking the *Pacto del Olvido*," *Human Rights Quarterly* 27 (3) (2005): 858, 875, citing Ministerio de la Presidencia, Real Decreto 1891/2004, September 10, 2004, *Boletin Oficial del Estado* (*State Official Gazette*) 227 (September 20, 2004), www.boe.es/boe/dias/2004–09–20.

36. See, for example, Martin Ganzglass, "The Restoration of the Somali Justice System," in *Learning from Somalia: The Lessons of Armed Humanitarian Intervention*, ed. Walter Clarke and Jeffrey Herbst (Boulder, Colo.: Westview, 1997) and Hansjoerg Strohmeyer, "Building a New Judiciary for East Timor: Challenges of a Fledgling Nation," *Criminal Law Forum* 11 (2000): 259. See further Jeremy Sarkin, "National Human Rights Institutions in South Africa," in *Human Rights, the Citizen and the State*, ed. Jeremy Sarkin and William Binchy (Dublin: Round Hall, 2001): 13.

37. Fanie du Toit, ed., *Learning to Live Together: Practices of Social Reconciliation* (Cape Town: Institute for Justice and Reconciliation, 2003): 119.

38. Jeremy Sarkin, "Crime and Human Rights," in *Resolving the Tension Between Crime and Human Rights: European and South African Perspectives*, ed. Jeremy Sarkin, Johan vander Lanotte, and Yves Haeck (Antwerp: Maklu, 2001), 25.

39. Linz and Stepan, *Problems of Democratic Transition*, 97.

40. Linz and Stepan, 170.

41. Linz and Stepan, 92 "It was also essential to avoid a separate and open debate about the monarchy, which did not enjoy particularly strong legitimacy."

42. Dexter Filkins, "11 Million Go to Polls to Pick Parliament," *New York Times*, December 16, 2005, A1.

43. Bose, *Bosnia After Dayton*, 9.

44. Paris, *At War's End*, 104, noting that after 1996, international peacebuilders "apparently recognized that 'free and fair' elections could impede, rather than facilitate, the consolidation of a lasting peace in Bosnia" (105).

45. Paris, 103.

46. Bose, *Bosnia After Dayton*, 146. See also Ignatieff, *Blood and Belonging*, 24: "Ethnic hatred is the result of the terror that arises when legitimate authority disintegrates."

47. However, there are times when it is necessary to stand firm even in the face of increasing electoral violence, since delay can be seen as concession to the violent faction. In the runup to the 1994 elections in South Africa, violence escalated and the threat of major disruptions to the poll was only averted with less than a week to go.

48. Linz and Stepan, *Problems of Democratic Transition*, 97, describing Spain's decision to include all parties, even where this meant providing amnesty to previously outlawed groups.

49. Bose, *Bosnia After Dayton*, 205.

50. Bose, 216–17.

51. Bose, 90, citing Roland Paris. "The lesson is that the existence of at least some political parties of cross-ethnic base is very important to the juridical as well as the effective unity of a multiethnic democracy. This assumes, since it normally requires, a cross-ethnic orientation, which in turn entails for practical purposes a program that appeals across ethnic lines" (208).

52. Bose, 25–36.

53. Bose, 220–21.

54. Paris, *At War's End*, 87–89.

55. Bose, *Bosnia After Dayton*, 90, citing Roland Paris.

56. See Bose's study of Mostar (116–31) for an extended argument against premature elections..

57. Valerie Kerruish, "Reconciliation, Property and Rights," in *Lethe's Law: Justice, Law and Ethics in Reconciliation*, ed. Emilios Christodoulidis and Scott Veitch (Oxford: Hart, 2001), citing Kevin Gilbert, "What Are We To Reconcile Ourselves To?" in *Voices of Aboriginal Australia: Past, Present, Future*, ed. Irene Moores (Springwood, N.S.W.: Butterfly, 1994).

58. Dilip Simeon, "A Finer Balance: An Essay on the Possibility of Reconciliation," in *Experiments with Truth: Transitional Justice and the Processes of Reconciliation*, Documenta 11_Platform 2 (Ostfildern-Ruit, Germany: Hatje-Cantz, 2002), 136.

59. Noel Pearson, quoted in Michael Gordon, *Reconciliation: A Journey* (Sydney: University of New South Wales Press, 2001), 47.

60. William Schabas, "The Relationship Between Truth Commissions and International Courts: The Case of Sierra Leone," *Human Rights Quarterly* 25 (2003): 1046.

61. Schabas, 1035, 1039.

62. The TRC had recommended that reparations be paid in amounts five times greater than what has to date been paid. *See* Jeremy Sarkin, *Carrots and Sticks: The TRC and the South African Amnesty Process* (Antwerp: Intersentia, 2004), 100–104.

63. Pearson, quoted in Gordon, *Reconciliation*, 35.

64. Bose, *Bosnia After Dayton*, 67.

65. "Why do so many Brazilians feel ambivalent about democracy? One possible hypothesis is that, in a country with possibly the worst income distribution in the world, the poorest citizens feel that the combination of inefficacious government and prolonged politics of austerity has meant that democracy has made no positive impact on the economic quality of their life." Linz and Stepan, *Problems of Democratic Transition*, 174.

66. *New York Times*, "Week in Review," January 4, 2004, suggesting distributing

oil revenues to Iraqis through trust fund or in direct periodic payments in order to enhance the stake Iraqis have in the new government.

67. Linz and Stepan, *Problems of Democratic Transition*, 12, quoting Adam Smith, *The Wealth of Nations* (London: J.M. Dent, 1910), 2: 180–81, on the bare minima of state provisions: beyond defense from hostile external enemies, the state has "the duty of protecting . . . every member of the society from the injustice or oppression of every other member of it [through the establishment of an administration of justice] and . . . the duty of erecting and maintaining certain public works and certain public institutions."

68. Paris, *At War's End*, 167.

69. Branko Milanovic, *Income, Inequality and Poverty During the Transition from Planned to Market Economy* (Washington, D.C.: World Bank, 1998), showing that income inequality increased, sometimes sharply, in all but one of the 18 successor states of the Soviet bloc.

70. Paris argues that what is true of political transitions is also true of economic transitions: the transitional period itself needs to be taken seriously and countries need to be given time in which to build the institutions that will moderate the competitiveness of the political and economic reforms. See also Mac Darrow and Amparo Tomas, "Power, Capture, and Conflict: A Call for Human Rights Accountability in Development Cooperation," *Human Rights Quarterly* 27 (2) (2005): 470–538.

71. See generally Paris, *At War's End*.

72. Elazar Barkan, *The Guilt of Nations: Restitution and Negotiating Historical Injustices* (Baltimore: Johns Hopkins University Press, 2000), xix.

73. Barkan, 318.

74. Barkan, 112–56.

75. Barkan, 8.

76. Barkan, 24

77. Barkan, 9, mentioning the split within Jewish community on whether or not to push for or accept money from Germany after World War II. Some protestors believed "that accepting German 'blood money' was a betrayal of the concentration camp victims."

78. Universal Declaration of Human Rights, Art. 11.

79. John Kingsley Jarfo, testifying before the Ghana TRC, October 15, 2003, http://www.nrcghana.org/pressdetails.php?q=2003–10–15

80. Joseph Apeadu Siaw, testifying before the Ghana TRC, http://www.nrcghana.org/pressdetails.php?q=2003–10–16

81. Tim Kelsall, "Truth, Lies, Ritual: Preliminary Reflections on the Truth and Reconciliation Commission in Sierra Leone," *Human Rights Quarterly* 27 (2) (2005): 370.

82. Roman David and Susanne Choi Yuk-ping, ""Victims on Transitional Justice: Lessons from the Reparation of Human Rights Abuses in the Czech Republic," *Human Rights Quarterly* 27 (2) (2005): 424.

83. Wole Soyinka, *The Burden of Memory, the Muse of Forgiveness* (New York: Oxford University Press, 1999), 81.

84. Sarkin, *Carrots and Sticks*, 109–13.

85. Schabas, "The Relationship Between Truth Commissions and International Courts," 1035, 1039.

86. Linz and Stepan, *Problems of Democratic Transition*, 180.

87. Donald Shriver, *An Ethic for Enemies: Forgiveness in Politics* (New York, Oxford: Oxford University Press, 1995), 230.

Chapter 9. The Mechanics of Reconciliation

Epigraph: Kerry Arabena, quoted in Michael Gordon, *Reconciliation: A Journey* (Sydney: University of New South Wales Press, 2001), 37–38.

1. Derek Bloomfield, Teresa Barnes, and Luc Huyse, eds., *Reconciliation After Violent Conflict: A Handbook* (Stockholm: International Institute for Democracy and Electoral Assistance: 2003).

2. Monica Patterson, "Reconciliation as a Continuing and Differentiated Process," *Journal of the International Institute* 9 (2) (2002), http://www.umich.edu/~iinet/journal/- vol9no2/patterson_recon.html

3. Michelle Maiese, "Peacebuilding," http://www.intractableconflict.org/- m/peacebuilding.jsp

4. Derek Bloomfield, "The Context of Reconciliation," in Bloomfield, Barnes, and Huyse, *Reconciliation After Violent Conflict,* 40

5. Fanie du Toit, ed., *Learning to Live Together: Practices of Social Reconciliation* (Cape Town: Institute for Justice and Reconciliation, 2003), 141. See further Jeremy Sarkin, *Carrots and Sticks: The TRC and the South African Amnesty Process* (Antwerp: Intersentia 2004).

6. Anton Baaré, David Shearer, and Peter Uvin, "The Limits and Scope for the Use of Development Assistance Incentives and Disincentives for Influencing Conflict Situations: Case Study: Rwanda," in Development Assistance Committee Informal Task Force on Conflict, *Peace and Development Co-operation* (Paris: OECD, 1999), http://www.oecd.org/dataoecd/58/17.

7. For East Timor, Carsten Stahn,"Accommodating Individual Criminal Responsibility and National Reconciliation: The UN Truth Commission for East Timor," *American Journal of International Law* 95 (4) (2001): 952–66. For Sierra Leone, see Mark Malan, "The Challenge of Justice and Reconciliation," in Mark Malan, Sarah Meek, Thokozani Thusi, Jeremy Ginifer, and Patrick Coker, *Sierra Leone—Building the Road to Recovery,* ISS Monograph 80 (Pretoria: Institute for Security Studies, 2003), http://www.issafrica.org/Pubs/Monographs/No80/Content.html.

8. http://www.lr.undp.org/disarmament.html (March 3, 2004).

9. www.ews.undp.org (March 3, 2004).

10. Sumantra Bose, *Bosnia After Dayton: Nationalist Partition and International Intervention* (New York: Oxford University Press, 2000), 269.

11. Sarkin, *Carrots and Sticks,* 211.

12. The relevance of political structure to reconciliation has been discussed in the previous chapter.

13. Priscilla Hayner, "Fifteen Truth Commissions—1974–1984: A Comparative Study," *Human Rights Quarterly* 16 (4) (1994), reprinted in *Transitional Justice: How Emerging Democracies Reckon with Former Regimes,* vol. 1, *General Considerations,* ed. Neil J. Kritz (Washington, D.C.: U.S. Institute of Peace Press, 1995), 229.

14. "There's tourism in this place. There's cattle. There's timber works. Making traditional spears and stuff like that. That's what I want to see. Get my people off the streets. Having Bama (Aborigines) in the tourist industry, having them employed, that is one way of having reconciliation. Get tourists and take them through the bush, taking, breaking down barriers. That's what I'm looking at." Gordon, *Reconciliation,* 41, quoting Jay Burchill, an Aboriginal living in Cape Tribulation.

15. Tina Rosenberg, *The Haunted Land: Facing Europe's Ghosts After Communism* (New York: Random House, 1995): 386.

16. Sarkin, *Carrots and Sticks.*

17. Claudia Orange, *The Treaty of Waitangi* (Wellington: Bridget Williams Books, 2001). In fact, it could be argued that the British chose the word "sovereignty" deliberately to confuse the Maori chiefs.

18. In France, the strikes that paralyzed the country in the spring of 1968 are simply referred to as "les évennements"—"the events" of 1968.

19. The Center for the Prevention of Genocide, an American think- (and *activity*) tank uses an early warning system to identify regions where genocides might occur, www.genocideprevention.org (March 5, 2004). UNDP uses an "early warning system" to monitor post-conflict situations as well, such as in Bosnia, to prevent the *recurrence* of violence.

20. Patterson, "Reconciliation as a Continuing Process."

21. Elazar Barkan, "Symposium. Holocaust Restitution: Reconciling Moral Imperatives with Legal Initiatives and Diplomacy. Between Restitution and International Morality," *Fordham International Law Journal* 25 (2001): 46, 47.

22. Henk Botha, "Legal Meaning and the Other: Beyond a Mythology of Negation," *Myth & Symbol* 2 (1995). Botha does, however, state thereafter, "So much for a sympathetic appraisal of the 1993 Constitution. A less sympathetic assessment may call it an incoherent list of contradictory aims and principles; an attempt to please everybody which will, in the end, only satisfy the greed of lawyers, always ready to cash in on ambiguity and contradiction."

23. See Eric Stover, Hanny Megally, and Hania Mufti, "Bremer's 'Gordian Knot': Transitional Justice and the U.S. Occupation of Iraq," *Human Rights Quarterly* 27 (3) (2005): 830–57.

24. Yacob Haile-Mariam, "The Quest for Justice and Reconciliation: The International Criminal Tribunal for Rwanda and the Ethiopian High Court," *Hastings International and Comparative Law Review* 22 (1999): 736.

25. Max du Preez, "Too Many Truths to Tell," *Sunday Independent,* June 24 2001, 13, 15.

26. A regional example is the Afrobarometer, produced collaboratively by social scientists from 16 African countries and coordinated by the Institute for Democracy in South Africa (Idasa), the Centre for Democratic Development (CDD-Ghana), and Michigan State University. It produces reports that measure attitudes on issues in Africa. See, for example, Afrobarometer Briefing Paper 1, "Key Findings on Public Opinion in Africa," April 2002, www.afrobarometer.org

27. See Institute for Justice and Reconciliation website, www.ijr.org.za

Bibliography

Abu-Nimer, Mohammed, ed. *Reconciliation, Justice and Coexistence: Theory and Practice.* New York: Lexington, 2001.

Adebajo, Adekeye and Chandra Lekha Sriram, eds. *Managing Armed Conflicts in the 21st Century.* London: Frank Cass, 2001.

Aka, Philip C. "Nigeria: The Need for an Effective Policy of Ethnic Reconciliation in the New Century." *Temple International and Comparative Law Journal* 14 (2000): 327–61.

Alfredsson, Gudmunder. "Minority Rights and Peace: Available Standards, Procedures and Institutions." In *Minorities in Europe: Croatia, Estonia and Slovakia,* ed. Snezana Trifunovska. The Hague: T.M.C. Asser, 1999.

Alvarez, Alex. *Governments, Citizens, and Genocide: A Comparative and Interdisciplinary Approach.* Bloomington: Indiana University Press, 2001.

Ambos, Kai. "Impunity and International Criminal Law: A Case Study on Colombia, Peru, Bolivia, Chile, Argentina." *Human Rights Law Journal* 18 (1997): 1–15.

Andreopoulos, George J., ed. *Genocide: Conceptual and Historical Dimensions.* Philadelphia: University of Pennsylvania Press, 1994.

Andrews, Molly. "The Politics of Forgiveness." *International Journal of Politics, Culture & Society* 13, 1 (1999): 107–24.

Arendt, Hannah. *Eichmann in Jerusalem: A Report on the Banality of Evil.* New York: Viking Press, 1963.

Asmal, Kader, Louise Asmal, and Ronald Suresh Roberts. *Reconciliation Through Truth: A Reckoning of Apartheid's Criminal Governance.* Cape Town: David Philip, 1996.

Bandes, Susan. "When Victims Seek Closure: Forgiveness, Vengeance, and the Role of the Government." *Fordham Urban Law Journal* 27 (2000): 1599–1606.

Barkan, Elazar. "Between Restitution and International Morality." Symposium issue, "Holocaust Restitution: Reconciling Moral Imperatives with Legal Initiatives and Diplomacy." *Fordham International Law Journal* 25 (2001): 46–63.

———. *The Guilt of Nations.* Baltimore: Johns Hopkins University Press, 2000.

Barnes, Samuel H. "The Contribution of Democracy to Rebuilding Postconflict Societies." *American Journal of International Law* 95 (2001): 86–101.

———. "The Mobilization of Political Identity in New Democracies." In *The Postcommunist Citizen,* ed. Samuel H. Barnes and Janos Simon. Budapest: Erasmus Foundation and Institute for Political Science of the Hungarian Academy of Sciences, 1998.

Bar-On, Dan, ed. *Bridging the Gap: Storytelling as a Way to Work Through Political and Collective Hostilities.* Hamburg: Korber-Stiftung, 2000.

Bass, Gary Jonathan. *Stay the Hand of Vengeance: The Politics of War Crimes Tribunals.* Princeton, N.J.: Princeton University Press, 2000.

Baum, Gregory. "The Role of the Churches in Polish-German Reconciliation." In *The Reconciliation of Peoples: Challenge to the Churches,* ed. Gregory Baum and Harold Wells. Geneva: Orbis, 1997.

Baumeister, Roy F., Arlene Stillwell, and Sara R. Wotman. "Victim and Perpetrator Accounts of Interpersonal Conflict: Autobiographical Narratives About Anger." *Journal of Personality and Social Psychology* 59 (1990): 994–1005.

Baumeister, Roy, Arlene M. Stillwell and Todd F. Heatherton. "Guilt: An Interpersonal Approach." *Psychological Bulletin* 115, 2 (1994): 243–67.

Becker, David, Elizabeth Lira, Maria Isabel Castillo, Elena Gomez, and Jauna Kovalskys. "Therapy with Victims of Political Repression in Chile: The Challenge of Social Reparation," *Journal of Social Issues* 46, 3 (1990): 133.

Bell-Fialoff, Andrew. *Ethnic Cleansing.* New York: St. Martin's Press, 1996.

Bennet, Mark and Deborah Earwaker. "Victims' Responses to Apologies: The Effects of Offender Responsibility and Offense Severity." *Journal of Social Psychology* 134, 4 (1993): 457–64.

Biggar, Nigel, ed. *Burying the Past: Making Peace and Doing Justice After Civil Conflict.* Washington, D.C.: Georgetown University Press, 2001.

Bloomfield, David. "The Process of Reconciliation." In *Reconciliation After Violent Conflict: A Handbook,* ed. David Bloomfield, Teresa Barnes, and Luc Huyse. Stockholm: International Institute for Democracy and Electoral Assistance, 2003.

Borneman, John. "Reconciliation After Ethnic Cleansing: Listening, Retribution, Affiliation." *Public Culture* 14, 2 (2002): 281–302.

Borris, Eileen R. and Paul F. Diehl. "Forgiveness, Reconciliation, and the Contribution of International Peacekeeping." In *The Psychology of Peacekeeping,* ed. Harvey J. Langholtz. New York: Praeger, 1998.

Braithwaite, John. *Crime, Shame and Reintegration.* Cambridge: Cambridge University Press, 1989.

Bronkhorst, D. *Truth and Reconciliation: Obstacles and Opportunities for Human Rights.* Amsterdam: Amnesty International Dutch Section, 1995.

Brooks, Roy L., ed. *When Sorry Isn't Enough: The Controversy over Apologies and Reparations for Human Injustice.* New York: New York University Press, 1999.

Brown, Jerome ed. *Social Pathology in Comparative Perspective: The Nature and Psychology of Civil Society.* Westport, Conn.: Praeger, 1995.

Brubaker, Roger. *Nationalism Reframed: Nationhood and the National Question in the New Europe.* Cambridge: Cambridge University Press, 1996.

Byrne, Sean and Cynthia L. Irvin, eds. *Reconcilable Differences: Turning Points in Ethnopolitical Conflict.* West Hartford, Conn.: Kumarian Press, 2000.

Canovan, Margaret. *Nationhood and Political Theory.* Cheltenham: Edward Elgar, 1996.

Campbell, Colm, Fionnuala Ní Aoláin, and Colin Harvey. "The Frontiers of Legal Analysis: Reframing the Transition in Northern Ireland." *Modern Law Review* 66 (2003): 317–45.

Choudree, R. B. G. "Traditions of Conflict Resolution in South Africa." *African Journal on Conflict Resolution* 1 (1999) 9–27.

Christodoulidis, Emilios and Scott Veitch. *Lethe's Law: Justice, Law and Ethics in Reconciliation.* Oxford: Hart, 2001.

Cohen, Stanley. *Denial and Acknowledgment: The Impact of Information About Human Rights Violations.* Jerusalem: Center for Human Rights, the Hebrew University, 1995.

———. "Human-Rights and Crimes of the State: The Culture of Denial." *Australian and New Zealand Journal of Criminology* 26, 2 (1993): 97–115.

———. "State Crimes of Previous Regimes: Knowledge, Accountability and the Policing of the Past." *Law and Social Inquiry* 20, 1 (Winter 1995): 1–273.

Consedine, Jim. *Restorative Justice: Healing the Effects of Crime.* Lyttleton: Ploughshares Press, 1999.

Cousens, Elisabeth and Chetan Kumar eds. *Peacebuilding as Politics: Cultivating Peace in Fragile Societies.* Boulder: Lynne Rienner, 2001.

Crocker, David. "Punishment, Reconciliation, and Democratic Deliberation." *Buffalo Criminal Law Review* 5, 2 (2002): 509–49.

Daly, Erin. "Between Punitive and Reconstructive Justice: The Gacaca Courts in Rwanda" *New York University Journal of International Law and Policy* 34 (2002): 355–96.

———. "Reparations in South Africa: A Cautionary Tale." *University of Memphis Law Review* 33 (2003): 367.

———. "Transformative Justice: Charting a Path to Reconciliation." *International Legal Perspectives* 12 (2002): 73.

Davis, Madeleine. "Is Spain Recovering Its Memory? Breaking the *Pacto del Olvido.*" *Human Rights Quarterly* 27, 3 (2005): 858–80.

de Brito, Alexandra Barahona, Carmen González-Enríques, and Paloma Aguilar, eds. *The Politics of Memory: Transitional Justice in Democratising Societies.* Oxford: Oxford University Press, 2001.

De Waal, Victor. *The Politics of Reconciliation: Zimbabwe's First Decade.* London: Hurst, 1990.

Donovan, Robert J. and Susan Leivers. "Using Paid Advertising to Modify Racial Stereotype Beliefs." *Public Opinion Quarterly* 57, 1 (1993): 205–18.

Dreifuss, Gustav. "Psychotherapy of Nazi Victims." *Journal of Psychology and Judaism* 15, 2 (1991): 113.

Drumbl, Mark A. "Punishment, Postgenocide: From Guilt to Shame to *Civis* in Rwanda." *New York University Law Review* 75 (2000): 1221–1326.

du Toit, Fanie, ed. *Learning to Live Together: Practices of Social Reconciliation.* Cape Town: Institute for Justice and Reconciliation, 2003.

Ericson, Maria. *Reconciliation and the Search for a Shared Moral Landscape: An Exploration Based upon a Study of Northern Ireland and South Africa.* Frankfurt am Main: Peter Lang, 2001.

Fatic, Aleksandar. *Reconciliation via the War Crimes Tribunal?* Aldershot: Ashgate, 2000.

Fearon, James D. and David D. Laitin. "Explaining Interethnic Cooperation." *American Political Science Review* 90 (1996): 715.

Fisher, Ronald J. "Social-Psychological Processes in Interactive Conflict Analysis and Reconciliation." In *Conflict Resolution: Process, Dynamics and Structure,* ed. Ho-Won Jeong. Aldershot: Ashgate, 1999.

Fletcher, Laural and Harvey Weinstein. "Violence and Social Repair: Rethinking the Contribution of Justice to Reconciliation." *Human Rights Quarterly* 24 (2002): 573–639.

Frost, Brian. *Struggling to Forgive: Nelson Mandela and South Africa's Search for Reconciliation.* New York: HarperCollins, 1998.

Galtung, Johan. *Conflict Transformation by Peaceful Means.* Geneva: United Nations, 1998.

Gardner Feldman, Lily. "The Principle and Practice of 'Reconciliation' in German Foreign Policy: Relations with France, Israel, Poland and the Czech Republic." *International Affairs* 75, 2 (1999): 333–56.

Gerson, Allan. "Peace Building: The Private Sector's Role." *American Journal of international Law* 95 (2001): 102–19.

Gibbs, Sara. "Postwar Social Reconstruction in Mozambique: Reframing Children's Experiences on Trauma and Healing." In *Rebuilding Societies After Civil War: Critical Role for International Assistance*, ed. Krishma Kumar. London: Lynne Reinner, 1997.

Gibson, James L. "The Paradoxes of Political Tolerance in Processes of Democratisation." *Politikon* 23, 2 (1996): 5–21.

Gibson, James L. and Amanda Gouws. "Political Intolerance and Ethnicity: Investigating Social Identity." *Indicator South Africa* 15, 3 (1998): 15–20.

Gibson, James L. and Helen MacDonald. *Truth—Yes, Reconciliation—Maybe: South Africans Judge the Truth and Reconciliation Process*. Rondebosch: Institute for Justice and Reconciliation South Africa, 2001.

Gilbert, Paul, J. Pehl, and S. Allan. "The Phenomenology of Shame and Guilt: An Empirical Investigation." *British Journal of Medical Psychology* 67, 1 (1994): 23–36.

Goldstone, Richard. "Exposing Human Rights Abuses: A Help or Hindrance to Reconciliation?" *Hastings Constitutional Law Quarterly* 22 (1995): 607–21.

Govier, Trudy and Wilhelm Verwoerd. "The Promise and Pitfalls of Apology." *Journal of Social Philosophy* 33, 1 (2002): 67–82.

————. "Trust and the Problem of National Reconciliation." *Philosophy of the Social Sciences* 32, 2 (2002): 178–205.

Grunebaum-Ralph, Heidi. "Re-Placing Pasts, Forgetting Presents: Narrative, Place, and Memory in the Time of the Truth and Reconciliation Commission." *Research in African Literatures* 32, 3 (2001): 198–212.

Gurr, Ted Robert. "Transforming Ethno-Political Conflicts: Exit, Autonomy, or Access." In *Conflict Transformation*, ed. Kumar Rupesinghe, New York: St. Martin's Press, 1995.

Hamber, Brandon. "'Ere Their Story Die: Truth, Justice and Reconciliation in South Africa." *Race and Class* 44, 1 (2002): 61.

Harrison, Graham. "Conflict Resolution in a 'Non-Conflict Situation': Tension and Reconciliation in Mecufi, Northern Mozambique." *Review of African Political Economy* 26, 81 (1999): 407.

Hay, Mark. "Grappling with the Past: The Truth and Reconciliation Commission of South Africa." *African Journal of Conflict Resolution* 1, 1 (1999): 29–51.

————. *Ukubuyisana: Reconciliation in South Africa*. Pietermaritzburg: Cluster Publications, 1998.

Hayner, Priscilla. *Unspeakable Truths: Confronting State Terror and Atrocities*. New York: Routledge, 2001

Henderson, Michael. *The Forgiveness Factor: Stories of Hope in a World of Conflict*. Salem, Ore.: Grosvenor Books, 1996.

Howitt, Richard. "Recognition, Respect and Reconciliation: Steps Towards Decolonisation?" *Australian Aboriginal Studies* (Spring 1998): 28.

Humphrey, Michael. "From Terror to Trauma: Commissioning Truth for National Reconciliation." *Social Identities* 6, 1 (March 2000): 7.

Huyse, Luc. "Justice After Transition: On the Choices Successor Elites Make in Dealing with the Past." *Law and Social Inquiry* 20, 1 (1995): 51–78.

————. "The Process of Reconciliation." In *Reconciliation After Violent Conflict: A*

Handbook, ed. ed. David Bloomfield, Teresa Barnes, and Luc Huyse. Stockholm: International Institute for Democracy and Electoral Assistance, 2003.

Ignatieff, Michael. *Blood and Belonging: Journeys into the New Nationalism.* New York: Farrar, Straus, Giroux, 1994.

———. *Human Rights as Politics and Idolatry.* Princeton, N.J.: Princeton University Press, 2001.

———. *The Warrior's Honor: Ethnic War and the Modern Conscience.* New York: Metropolitan Books, 1997.

Irwin-Zarecka, Iwona and Peter N. Stearns. "Frames of Remembrance: The Dynamics of Collective Memory." *Journal of Interdisciplinary History* 27, 1 (1996): 102.

Kaufmann, Chaim. "Possible and Impossible Solutions to Ethnic Civil Wars." *International Security* 20 (1996): 136.

Kegley, Charles W. and Gregory A. Raymond. *How Nations Make Peace.* New York: St. Martin's/Worth, 1999.

Kim, Sung Hee and Richard H. Smith. "Revenge and Conflict Escalation." *Negotiation Journal* 9, 1 (1993): 37–43.

Klug, Heinz. *Constituting Democracy: Law, Globalism and South Africa's Political Reconstruction.* Cambridge: Cambridge University Press, 2000.

Knight, Elizabeth. "Facing the Past: Retrospective Justice as a Means to Promote Democracy in Nigeria." *Connecticut Law Review* 35 (2003): 867–914.

Kriger, Norma J. "The Politics of Creating National Heroes: The Search for Political Legitimacy and National Identity." In *Soldiers in Zimbabwe's Liberation War,* ed. Nawabi Bhebe and Terrence Ranger. Harare: University of Zimbabwe Publications, 1995.

Kritz, Neil J., ed. *Transitional Justice: How Emerging Democracies Reckon with Former Regimes.* Washington, D.C.: U.S. Institute of Peace Press, 1995.

Krog, Antjie. *Country of My Skull: Guilt, Sorrow, and the Limits of Forgiveness in the New South Africa.* New York: Random House, 1998.

Kumar, Krishna. *Promoting Social Reconciliation in Post Conflict Societies: Selected Lessons from USAID's Experience.* USAID Program and Operations Assessment Report 24. Center for Development Information and Evaluation, U.S. Agency for International Development, 1999. http://www.dec.org/pdf_docs/pnaca923.pdf

Lake, David A. and Donald Rothchild. "Containing Fear: The Origins and Management of Ethnic Conflict." *International Security* 21, 2 (1996): 41–75.

Lampen, John, ed. *No Alternative? Nonviolent Responses to Repressive Regimes.* York,: Ebor Press, 2000.

Lapidoth, Ruth. *Autonomy: Flexible Solutions to Ethnic Conflicts.* Washington, D.C.: U.S. Institute of Peace Press, 1996.

Lederach, John Paul. *Building Peace: Sustainable Reconciliation in Divided Societies.* Washington, D.C.: U.S. Institute of Peace Press, 1997.

———. *Preparing for Peace: Conflict Transformation Across Cultures.* Syracuse, N.Y.: Syracuse University Press, 1995.

Levinson, Sanford. "They Whisper: Reflections on Flags, Monuments, and State Holidays, and the Construction of Social Meaning in a Multicultural Society." *Chicago-Kent Law Review* 70 (1995): 107–19.

Levi, Deborah L. "The Role of Apology in Mediation." *New York University Law Review* 72 (1997): 1165–1210.

Mamdani, Mahmood. *Imperialism and Fascism in Uganda.* Nairobi: Heinemann Educational Books, 1983.

———. "Reconciliation Without Justice." *South African Review of Books* (November/December 1996): 3.

Mani, Rama. *Beyond Retribution: Seeking Justice in the Shadows of War.* Cambridge: Polity Press, 2002.

Markakis, John, ed. *Conflict and the Decline of Pastoralism in the Horn of Africa.* London: Macmillan Press, 1993

Michnik, Adam and Vaclav Havel. "Justice or Revenge?" *Journal of Democracy* 4, 1 (1993): 20–27.

Minow, Martha. *Between Vengeance and Forgiveness: Facing History After Genocide and Mass Violence.* Boston: Beacon Press, 1998.

Murphy, Jeffrie G. "Forgiveness, Reconciliation and Responding to Evil: A Philosophical Overview." *Fordham Urban Law Review* (2000): 1353–66.

Murphy, Jeffrie G. and Jean Hampton, eds. *Forgiveness and Mercy.* New York: Cambridge University Press, 1998.

Naimark, Norman. *Fires of Hatred: Ethnic Cleansing in Twentieth-Century Europe.* Cambridge, Mass.: Harvard University Press, 2001.

Neier, Aryeh. *War Crimes: Brutality, Genocide, Terror, and the Struggle for Justice.* New York: Times Books, 1998.

Neuffer, Elizabeth. *The Key to My Neighbor's House: Seeking Justice in Bosnia and Rwanda.* New York: Picador, 2002.

Norval, Aletta J. "Truth and Reconciliation: The Birth of the Present and the Reworking of History." *Journal of Southern African Studies* 25, 3 (1999): 499–519.

Orange, Claudia. *The Treaty of Waitangi.* Wellington: Bridget Williams Books, 2001.

Osiel, Mark. *Mass Atrocity, Collective Memory, and the Law.* New Brunswick, N.J.: Transaction Publishers, 1997.

Patterson, Monica. "Reconciliation as a Continuing and Differentiated Process." *Journal of the International Institute* 9, 2 (Winter 2002).

Phillips, Ann L. "The Politics of Reconciliation Revisited: Germany and East-Central Europe." *World Affairs* 163, 4 (Spring 2001): 171.

Pines, Malcolm. "The Universality of Shame: A Psychoanalytic Approach." *British Journal of Psychotherapy* 11, 3 (1995): 346–57.

Pommersheim, Frank. "Looking Forward and Looking Back: The Promise and Potential of a Sioux Nation Judicial Support Center and Sioux Nation Supreme Court." *Arizona State Law Journal* 34 (2002): 269–98.

Popkin, Margaret and Naomi Roht-Arriaza. "Truth as Justice: Investigatory Commissions in Latin America." *Law & Social Inquiry* 20 (1995): 79–116.

Rabi, Muhammad. *Conflict Resolution and Ethnicity.* London: Praeger, 1994.

Ramphele, Mamphela "Political Widowhood in South Africa: The Embodiment of Ambiguity." *Daedalus* 125, 1 (1996): 99.

Ramsbotham, Oliver, Rom Woodhouse, and Hugh Miall. *Contemporary Conflict Resolution.* 2nd ed. Cambridge: Polity Press, 2005.

Ratner, Steven R. and Jason S. Abrams. *Accountability for Human Rights Atrocities in International Law: Beyond the Nuremberg Legacy.* 2nd ed. Oxford: Oxford University Press, 2001.

Rock, Stephen R. *Why Peace Breaks Out: Great Power Rapprochement in Historical Perspective.* Chapel Hill: University of North Carolina Press, 1993.

Roht-Arriaza, Naomi, ed. *Impunity and Human Rights in International Law and Practice.* New York: Oxford University Press, 1995.

———. "Truth Commissions and Amnesties in Latin America: The Second Generation." *Contemporary International Law Issues* 92 (1999): 313.

Rolph-Trouillot, Michel. "Abortive Rituals: Historical Apologies in the Global Era." *Interventions: The International Journal of Postcolonial Studies* 2, 2 (2000): 171–86.

Rosenberg, Tina. *The Haunted Land: Facing Europe's Ghosts After Communism.* New York: Random House, 1995.

Rotberg, Robert I. and Dennis Thompson, eds. *Truth v. Justice: The Morality of Truth Commissions.* Princeton, N.J.: Princeton University Press, 2000.

Samba, Josiah O. "Peace Building and Transformation from Below: Indigenous Approaches to Conflict Resolution and Reconciliation Among the Pastoral Societies in the Borderlands of Eastern Africa." *African Journal on Conflict Resolution* 2, 1 (2001), http://www.accord.org.za/ajcr/2001-1/accordr_v2_n1_a6.html (accessed April 10, 2004)

Sambanis, Nicholas. "Partition as a Solution to Ethnic War: An Empirical Critique of the Theoretical Literature." *World Politics* 52 (2000): 437.

Sarkin, Jeremy. *Carrots and Sticks: The TRC and the South African Amnesty Process.* Antwerp: Intersentia, 2004.

———. "Comparing and Contrasting Democracy and Human Rights Provisions in Two Draft Burmese Constitutions from an International Perspective." *Legal Issues on Burma Journal* 4 (1999): 56.

———. "Dealing With Past Human Rights Abuses: Promoting Reconciliation in a Future Democratic Burma." *Legal Issues on Burma Journal* 7 (2000): 1.

———. "Democratizacao e justice no periodo de transicao em Angola." In *Conferencia Internacional Angola: Direito, Democracia, Paz E Desenvolvimento.* Luanda: Faculdade de Direito, Universidade Agostinho Neto, 2001.

———. "The Development of a Human Rights Culture in South Africa." *Human Rights Quarterly* 20 (1998): 628–665.

———. "The Drafting of the Final South African Constitution from a Human Rights Perspective." *American Journal of Comparative Law* 47, 1 (1999): 67–87.

———. "L'écriture de la Constitution Sud-Africaine de 1996: Approche Formelle et Matérielle." *Revue Française: Droit Constitutionnel* 44 (2000): 746–67.

———. "The Effect of Constitutional Borrowings on the Drafting of South Africa's Bill of Rights and Interpretation of Human Rights Provisions." *University of Pennsylvania Journal of Constitutional Law* 1, 2 (1998): 176–204.

———. "Ensuring Free and Fair Elections in a Democratic Burma: Establishing an Electoral System and Election Processes." *Legal Issues on Burma Journal* 8 (2001): 25–36.

———. "Examining the Competing Constitutional Processes In Burma/ Myanmar from a Comparative and International Democratic and Human Rights Perspective." *Asia-Pacific Journal of Human Rights and the Law* 2, 2 (2001): 42–68.

———. "Finding a Solution for the Problems Created by the Politics of Identity in the Democratic Republic of the Congo (DRC): Designing A Constitutional Framework for Peaceful Co-Operation." In *Politics of Identity and Exclusion in Africa: From Violent Confrontation to Peaceful Cooperation.* Johannesburg: Konrad-Adenauer-Stiftung, 2001.

———. "Holding Multinational Corporations Accountable for Human Rights and Humanitarian Law Violations Committed During Colonialism and Apartheid: An Evaluation of the Prospects of Such Cases in Light of the Herero of Namibia's Genocide Case and South African Apartheid Cases Being Brought in the United States Under the Alien Torts Claims Act." In *Bedrijven En Mensenrechten,* ed. Eva Brems and Pieter Vanden Heede. Antwerp: Maklu, 2003.

———. "Human Rights in South Africa: Constitutional and Pan-African Concept." In *The Principle of Equality: A South African and Belgian Perspective,* ed. Johan Vande Lanotte, Yves Haeck and Jeremy Sarkin. Antwerp: Maklu, 2001.

————. "Innovations in the Interim and 1996 South African Constitutions." *The Review* (June 1998): 57.

————. "The Natal Violence." *The Review* 46 (1990): 14.

————. "National Human Rights Institutions in South Africa." In *Human Rights, the Citizen and the State: South African and Irish Approaches,* ed. Jeremy Sarkin and William Binchy. Blackrock: Round Hall, 2001.

————.The Necessity and Challenges of a Truth and Reconciliation Commission in Rwanda." *Human Rights Quarterly* (August 1999): 667–823.

————. "Promoting Justice, Truth and Reconciliation in Transitional Societies: Evaluating Rwanda's Approach in the New Millennium of Using Community Based Gacaca Tribunals to Deal with the Past." *International Law Forum* 2 (2000): 112.

————. "Reviewing and Reformulating Appointment Processes to Constitutional (Chapter Nine) Structures." *South African Journal on Human Rights* 15 (1999): 587.

————. "The South African Constitution as Memory and Promise." In *Transcending a Century of Injustice,* ed. Charles Villa-Vicencio. Rondebosch: Institute for Justice and Reconciliation, 2000.

————. "The Tension Between Justice and Reconciliation in Rwanda: Politics, Human Rights, Due Process and the Role of the Gacaca Courts in Dealing with the Genocide." *Journal of African Law* 45 (2001): 143–73.

————. "Transitional Justice and the Prosecution Model: The Experience of Ethiopia." *Law Democracy and Development* 2 (1999): 253–66.

————. "The Trials and Tribulations of South Africa's Truth and Reconciliation Commission." *South African Journal on Human Rights* 12 (1996): 617.

————. "Using Gacaca Community Courts in Rwanda to Prosecute Genocide Suspects: Are Issues of Expediency and Efficiency More Important Than Those of Due Process, Fairness and Reconciliation?" In *Rwanda and South Africa in Dialogue: Addressing the Legacies of Genocide and a Crime Against Humanity,* ed. Charles Villa-Vicencio and Tyrone Savage. Rondebosch: Institute for Justice and Reconciliation, 2000.

Sarkin, Jeremy and Marek Pietschmann. "Legitimate Humanitarian Intervention Under International Law in the Context of the Current Human Rights and Humanitarian Crisis in Burma/Myanmar." *Hong Kong Law Journal* 33 (2003): 371.

Sarkin, Jeremy and Howard Varney. "Traditional Weapons, Cultural Expediency and the Political Conflict in South Africa: A Culture of Weapons and a Culture of Violence." *South African Journal of Criminal Justice* 6 (1993): 2.

Schabacker, Emily. "Reconciliation or Justice and Ashes: Amnesty Commissions and the Duty to Punish Human Rights Offenses." *New York International Law Review* 12 (1999): 1, 21.

Schuman, Howard and Amy D. Corning. "A Collective Knowledge of Public Events: The Soviet Era from the Great Purge to Glasnost." *American Journal of Sociology* 105, 4 (2000): 913–56.

Schuman, Howard and Jacqueline Scott. "Generations and Collective Memories." *American Sociological Review* 54, 3 (1989): 359–81.

Shriver, Donald W. *An Ethic for Enemies: Forgiveness in Politics.* New York: Oxford University Press, 1995.

Skaar, Elin, Siri Gloppen, and Astri Suhrke, eds. *Roads to Reconciliation.* Lanham, Md.: Lexington, 2005.

Sisk, Timothy D. *Power Sharing and International Mediation in Ethnic Conflicts.* Washington, D.C.: U.S. Institute of Peace, 1996.

Smyth, Marie. "Putting the Past in Its Place: Issues of Victimhood and Reconciliation in Northern Irelands Peace Process." In *Burying the Past: Making Peace and Doing Justice After Civil Conflict*, ed. Nigel Biggar. Washington, D.C.: Georgetown University Press, 2001.

Soyinka, Wole. *The Burden of Memory, the Muse of Forgiveness*. New York: Oxford University Press, 1999.

Soza, Raul. "The Church: A Witness to the Truth on the Way to Freedom." In *Impunity: An Ethical Perspective: Six Case Studies from Latin America*, ed. Charles Harper. Geneva: WCC Publications, 1996.

Stahn, Carsten. "Accommodating Individual Criminal Responsibility and National Reconciliation: The UN Truth Commission for East Timor." *American Journal of International Law* 95, 4 (2001): 952–66.

Stalsett, Gunnar et al. *Reconciliation in Practice: The Role of Churches and Church-Related Agencies in Areas of Conflict*. Oslo: Norwegian Church Aid, Dan Church Aid, Church of Sweden Aid, 1997.

Stavenhagen, Rodolfo. *Ethnic Conflicts and the Nation-State*. Basingstoke: Macmillan, 1996.

Sturm, Douglas. "Moving Toward Political Reconciliation: The Role of Christian Churches." *Journal of Law and Religion* 13, 1 (1996): 239–47.

Summerfield, Derek. "The Psychological Legacy of War and Atrocity: The Question of Long-Term and Trans-Generational Effects and the Need for a Broad View." *Journal of Nervous and Mental Disease* 184, 6 (1996): 375–76.

Suny, Ronald G. "Living with the Other: Conflict and Cooperation Among the Transcaucasian Peoples." *Caucasian Regional Studies* 2, 1 (1997).

Sveaas, Nora and Nils Johan Lavik. "Psychological Aspects of Human Rights Violations: The Importance of Justice and Reconciliation." *Nordic Journal of International Law* 69, 1 (2000): 35–52.

Tavuchis, Nicholas. *Mea Culpa: A Sociology of Apology and Reconciliation*. Stanford, Calif.: Stanford University Press, 1991.

Terris, Robert and Vera Inoue-Terris. "A Case Study of Third World Jurisprudence: Palestine, Conflict Resolution and Customary Law in a Neopatrimonial Society." *Berkeley Journal of International Law* 20, 2 (2002): 462–95.

Teitel, Ruti G. *Transitional Justice*. Oxford: Oxford University Press, 2000.

Torpey, John. *Politics and The Past: On Repairing Historical Injustices*. Lanham, Md.: Rowman & Littlefield, 2003.

Truth and Reconciliation Commission of South Africa Report. New York: Macmillan Reference, 1998.

Tutu, Desmond. *No Future Without Forgiveness*. New York: Doubleday 1999.

Uvin, Peter. "The Influence of Aid in Situations of Violent Conflict: A Synthesis and a Commentary on the Lessons Learned from Case Studies on the Limits and Scope for the Use of Development Assistance Incentives and Disincentives for Influencing Conflict Situations." Paris: Informal Task Force on Conflict, Peace and Development, Co-operation, OECD Development Assistance Committee, 1999.

Van DerAuweraert, Peter and Jeremy Sarkin, eds. *Social, Economic, and Cultural Rights: An Appraisal of Current International and European Developments*. Antwerp: Maklu, 2002.

Van Ness, Daniel and Pat Nolan. "Legislating for Restorative Justice." *Regent University Law Review* 10 (1998): 53.

Varney, Howard and Jeremy Sarkin. "Failing to Pierce the Hit Squad Veil: An Analysis of the Malan Trial." *South African Journal of Criminal Justice* 10 (1997): 141.

Villa-Vicencio, Charles, ed. *Transcending a Century of Injustice*. Rondebosch, South Africa: Institute of Justice and Reconciliation, 2000.

Wacks, Jamie. "A Proposal for Community-Based Racial Reconciliation in the United States Through Personal Stories." *Virginia Journal of Social Policy and the Law* 7 (2000): 195, 207.

Wagatsuma, Hiroshi and Arthur Rosett. "The Implications of Apology." *Law & Society Review* 20, 4 (1986): 461–98.

Wallis, Jim. *The Soul of Politics: A Practical and Prophetic Vision for Change*. New York: Harcourt Brace, 1995.

Wiesenthal, Simon, Henry James Cargas, and Bonny V. Fetterman, eds. *The Sunflower: On the Possibilities and Limits of Forgiveness*, 2nd ed. New York: Schocken Books, 1997.

Yancey, George. "An Examination of the Effects of Residential and Church Integration on Racial Attitudes of Whites." *Sociological Perspectives* 42, 2 (1999): 279.

Index

As societies emerge from oppression, war, or genocide, their most important task is to create a civil society strong and stable enough to support democratic governance. More and more conflict-torn countries throughout the world are promoting reconciliation as central to their new social order as they move toward peace and stability.

Since the South African transition, countries as diverse as Timor Leste, Sierra Leone, Fiji, Morocco, and Peru, among others, have placed reconciliation at the center of their reconstruction and development programs. Other efforts to promote reconciliation—including trials and governmental programs—are also becoming more prominent in transitional times. But until now there has been no real effort to understand exactly what reconciliation means in these different situations. What does true reconciliation entail? Does it require enemies to become friends? The payment of reparations? The punishment of perpetrators? How can governments promote reconciliation? And how should their efforts be assessed? This book digs beneath the surface to answer these questions. It explains what the concepts of truth, justice, forgiveness, and reconciliation really mean in societies that are recovering from internecine strife.

Looking to the future as much as to the past, Erin Daly and Jeremy Sarkin maintain that reconciliation requires fundamental political and economic reform along with personal healing if it is to be effective in establishing lasting peace and stability. Reconciliation, they argue, is best thought of as a means for transformation. It is the engine that helps divided societies become communities where people work together, raise children, and live productive, hopeful lives.

9805